A
MEDIEVAL
MISCELLANY

A MEDIEVAL MISCELLANY

SELECTED AND EDITED BY
JUDITH HERRIN

MANUSCRIPT SELECTION AND BOOK DESIGN BY
LINDA & MICHAEL FALTER

WITH AN INTRODUCTION BY
EMMANUEL LE ROY LADURIE

VIKING STUDIO
FACSIMILE EDITIONS

Contents

Introduction

Before introducing these dazzling texts, selected with great skill by Judith Herrin, perhaps I may outline the possible content of this type of medieval miscellany. I take as my starting point Georges Dumézil's general theory of the three functions, also favoured by the great French scholars Georges Duby and Jacques Le Goff. This theory allows me to give you an overview of the basic medieval landscape, as it is illustrated by this rich study of the Middle Ages.

The three functions: priests, soldiers and peasants (*oratores, bellatores, aratores*), or, broadly speaking the fields of church and state (sovereignty); of battle and nobility; and the field, both in the literal and metaphorical sense, of fertility. Though the word is

7

redolent of the pastoral and agricultural, it extends to all that is fecund, including the leading role of woman in giving birth to children ⁄ and more generally in reproducing society. The offices of those who pray, those who fight and those who produce and reproduce: were these (as a simplistic reading of Dumézil might suggest) the legacy of our Indo⁄European 'ancestors'? Or did they spring from the tripartite mentality of the Celts and the Germans, who are, in their turn, distant cousins of the Anglo⁄Saxons; or ⁄ in the final analysis (what a surprise!) ⁄ would they be a legacy of biblical tradition? In the Book of Genesis, an *angel*, armed with a *sword*, expels from the *verdant* paradise the *fecund* Eve; is this not trifunctional? Duby and Le Goff mention occasionally these ultimately muddled hypotheses, but are more interested in the development of the famous 'triplet' during the Middle Ages.

The stories, people and events recounted here are peppered with elements that would be relished by those great medieval scholars. In that distant age, priests prayed long and hard, and this activity gave them a status comparable to that of monks, and enabled them to ask God for favours which would benefit society. The soldiers of the Middle Ages (especially from the twelfth century onwards) were mounted knights who carried the heavy swords of battle, very different from the ancient Gallo⁄Roman nobility, who had worn belts of office which assimilated them into the imperial bureaucracy of Emperor Constantine. The third element of the triplet, the medieval peasants, were the object of ill⁄deserved contempt, though a stratum of *laboratores* ⁄ skilled labourers, and rich farmers ⁄ raised themselves above the common herd. They were more like the craftsmen and merchants who lived in towns.

The *King* had the quasi⁄magical sovereignty of a crowned priest or of an independent bishop. But as Le Goff says, the King's main function, above all, was to bind the three functions together. In effect, he was finally responsible for anything that went wrong, and a useful scapegoat who might lose his head for the 'common good' (something which Louis XIV and Charles I discovered after the end of what we call the Middle Ages).

A few words about the rural base, the ground floor of this great medieval edifice, which features prominently in the *Miscellany*. For the most part, the country inhabitants who had been valued in the ancient world disappeared ⁄ culturally speaking, at least ⁄ from the Merovingian period onwards. Or more precisely they sank into a state which we may characterise as the Pejorative. The peasant of the fifth century became synonymous with *paganus* (pagan) in the terms of the late Roman Empire; or what the ancient Hebrews called a *goy,* and the Greeks *ethnikos*: in other words, an uneducated farmer. He was thought of as the type who prevents the destruction of pagan temples, which nonetheless are destined sooner or later to be replaced, of course, by churches of the true Christian faith. To writers of the post⁄classical period, the peasant was no more than a brute, barely human, a monster with a human face: the sinner, the lecher, the drunk, the pauper, the rustic; in short, a Caliban who had not yet found his Shakespeare. Thus it is all the more interesting to note the appearance of the word *labourer* (*kulak* in the good sense of the term) with most positive and favourable connotations

8

after the year 926. The beginning of a new era, which valued the management of fertility, such as the science of husbandry and agriculture, which is often demonstrated in the texts selected with such learning by Judith Herrin.

It took a lot longer for the sexual productivity ⁄ that is, fertility ⁄ of women to be perceived as 'good' (and not only of those women who worked in the fields). As early as the third century, Clement of Alexandria had linked the sexual act to original sin, and St Augustine in turn nailed the problem between 395 and 430, asserting that lust was indeed the carrier of original sin, which thus became by definition sexually transmitted ⁄ a sort of metaphysical AIDS. The theory was not foolish; most civilisations have displayed a good dose of puritanism about what goes on 'down there'. Nonetheless, the consequences of St Augustine's writings were extensive and sometimes painful.

The second function concerns the weaponry ⁄ sharp and blunt ⁄ at the disposal of the 'aristos' and nobles, the trappings of a feudal system not to be confused with the tired image of feudalism handed down by post⁄'68 Marxist⁄Althusserians. The best medieval scholars view things as anthropologists or, better, as entomologists, observing the habits of red ants. They are interested above all in the gestures and the objects used in feudal acts of homage. Here is a world of allegory and parable; of image and figure: it defines a very particular symbolic system which is revealed in many features of this book. For example, the ceding of a fief (from lord to vassal), is symbolised by transference of simple objects: a stave of wood or a holly branch, a knife, a baton, an incense spoon; on another level, by a handshake, the contact of right thumbs or a kiss.

The third floor of our building houses religion ⁄ always closely allied to the political and power ⁄ and is well furnished. The primeval forest might be evoked in the pages that follow, but no longer as a sylvan link to labourers and peasants. To the intellectuals of the twelfth century, the woods were a place of renunciation, where monks and hermits withdrew from the world: the verdant equivalent of the sandy desert where the first anchorites of Sinai lived, or of that other 'desert' where the Camisards, persecuted Protestants of the eighteenth⁄century Cevennes, found a retreat, one well known to their English counterparts across the Channel. It also has an echo in the American Far West, where the 'horse whisperer' might seek refuge, far from the cor⁄ruption of New York.

We thus firmly retie the triple braid of society, the finely interwoven strands of the trio of major functions; but we must also recognise other shared values ⁄ those represented, for example, by the serpent and the dragon in folk⁄tales which, despite the best efforts of the church, were still an integral part of urban life. Nor should we forget political history, often too quickly dismissed by historians of the *Annales* school when it is excessively narrative, but which they do not hesitate to use when assessing the ideological symbolism of the classic objects of power: the ring, the sceptre, the crown, the sword, the hand of justice and the red robes of the Chancellor of France...

II

Not surprisingly, religion takes pride of place in Judith Herrin's collection. In this realm of the sacred, pre-eminent in the Middle Ages, we learn first (and certainly not in alphabetical order) of Christ, of Augustinian theology and love of God; of the near-hysterical devotion of Catherine of Siena and of Margery Kempe; of the hereafter and of the Christian conversion of the Normans and Danes.

Miracles abound: those that tell of Christ's burial shroud, of abandoned children saved, of scholarly success, of the soul of a sinner imprisoned in a block of ice, or the supernatural lights of the Holy Sepulchre; even, the incredible severed head of St Genesius. Many document the cult of relics, which link mankind to heaven; tales of the 'music of the spheres', the fascination with famous sanctuaries and sacred cities, even when they are muddy; with processions and pilgrimages, which provided an outing for the Wife of Bath, and with the major feast days, beginning with Christmas. We should also mention other ways of going beyond the 'classic' devotion to religion: whether it involves total renunciation, individual combat with diabolical forces (the serpent Satan), or investigating other non-Christian elements of the miraculous, such as astrology.

The survey of political sovereignty (royal or imperial), inseparable from the realm of the supernatural but markedly Christian, is well documented here. It may reflect the 'model of models' - which is none other than a version of the Roman *imperium* with its magnetic qualities. Later King David appears (the model of Christian kingship); the spectacular *Basileus* in Byzantium; and Charlemagne, of course, swimming champion before Mao Tse-tung; then the Caliph of Baghdad and every western king, each with his long, long arm. Conflicts between kingdoms, and diplomatic links between England and Byzantium fall into the same category of the 'sacred ruler', which Jean Bodin would not have scorned. Similarly, the imperial court of Constantinople and the park of the Great Palace; the breaking of a seal as a symbol of the death of the one who held power while his successor waits to be enthroned; the inheritance of power by male heirs only (Salic Law before the letter); the game of chess as a political allegory *par excellence*. Also invoked are concepts such as Justice (by ordeal), Reason and its opponent Madness, Fortuna, Roman Liberty, the indispensable Education, even the sometimes smelly ruses employed by political leaders.

III

Herrin's collection contains fewer texts on the military and the nobility, but those there are, are excellent ('excellent fat' as Rabelais would have it). Here we assist at two falls of Constantinople, one in 1204, from inside the barricades, the other in 1453 when the Turkish artillery played its customary role in the final fall of Byzantium. The same for the capture of Antioch in 1098 and the conquest of England in 1066. Nor are strategies neglected: Pope

Urban II has much advice on this score, as does a Byzantine military commander, both sounding like the superannuated generals of today sagely making their idiotic comments. War, of course, is a beautiful daughter who becomes repellent, even when the Hungarians are defeated.

The warrior instincts of the nobility are treated, not directly but through aristocratic pastimes, in which they appear more or less explicitly. Hunting boar and big game, horse racing, and races between horses and warriors on foot (who often won); and carnival battles between Christian knights and others disguised as Moors.

IV

After the sacred and the violent, the third of our great functions is devoted to production and reproduction. The mention of agriculture means a discussion of the weather. At the turn of the millennium, this seems to have been warmer and milder than was later the case (in the 'little ice age' of the seventeenth century) and relations between medieval Europe and a temperate Greenland were 'alive and well'. But memories of harsh winters before the millennium feature in Herrin's pages, as well as blistering summers and grasshoppers! Autumn has a thousand glories heaped upon it by a Jewish author. Other articles are dedicated to the production of honey, to harvesting ⁄ the harvesters were struck by sunstroke ⁄ to threshing and more specifically to the Mediterranean style of 'dépiquage', very different from the threshing with rods practised in northern lands. Against this, there are few allusions to husbandry itself, apart from an article on shepherds. Wild beasts are represented by a bear, or rather by a bear⁄keeper of the seventh century.

The rural labourers I spoke of earlier find their incarnation in the figure (particularly puny, as it turns out) of Piers Plowman. There is a servant in our splendid string of texts but she is not a country girl but a laundress, a slave living in an urban environment. However, the singing of the *Magnificat* reminds us that whatever social differences divide us, we are all equal in the sight of God, in principle.

From agriculture and social concerns in general we pass to the world of commerce: fairs ⁄ English and Byzantine ⁄ negotiations with China, the crisis in the Mediterranean silk trade in 1118, importation of luxuries from Russia, Byzantium, Arabia and France.

But there are many other ways to make money, for the most part, illicit: piracy is the most important, especially on the Asian and Arab coasts; theft and minor rural delinquencies; racketeering by ferrymen and Basque brigands, and finally more 'innocent' ways through betting on games of dice. Material life (food and lodging) are treated in the case of a starving Norwegian and the shack of a poor woman set in the rich land of Flanders.

For human reproduction, Saint Artemios is the Asclepius of testicles and at the other end of the body, Saint Foy de Conques takes care of baldness. Birth can be dramatic as Guibert de Nogent recalls, and childhood seems to be more appreciated ⁄ even fondly remembered by some adults ⁄ than Philippe Ariès believed. As life progresses through youth and adolescence, love takes the lion's share and not only thanks to the poems of troubadours: love also dominates poetry of the Jews or Byzantines, the dress of young ladies, the elegy of a bird likened to a lover, dancing and the erotic function of games and wine (the latter presented in a more negative fashion).

Love should lead to marriage, but some girls prefer a convent life. Conjugal love between people of different social classes is frowned upon, but a wedding feast can be a princely affair, unsurpassed. Once married, don't forget to take your marriage certificate if you travel across frontiers. And we must not overlook the impediments to sexual life and good marriages: adultery, rape and prostitution. If all goes well and the marriage follows its allotted course, children are born ⁄ unfortunately into gross inequality. The sons of King Alfred each inherited £500, his daughters received only £100. And then, as they say, one dies; rarely in that distant epoch did one live to grow old and senile, a terrible situation both for the carers and those they look after.

In conclusion, one must render a final homage to this armful of wonderful texts, by noting that neither the mysteries of the year zero (the birth of Christ!), nor those of the Black Death of 1348, that great rupture of the medieval centuries, have escaped the shrewd eyes of our compiler. Judith Herrin knows how to focus on events, when necessary. But this is a way of saying that she defies categorisation, avoiding historical trends and fashions of all sorts, more American than British in fact. And we can forget the 'postmodern', which does not seem to be her cup of tea. Instead, we have a wonderful *Miscellany*, what our Belgian friends would call with their comic turn of invention, a *Mischpopott*; or as we would say, in the best and most tasteful sense, a *pot-pourri*.

EMMANUEL LE ROY LADURIE
Paris, October 1999

Scenes from medieval life often appear familiar, intensely human and recognisable, yet also distant. They depict the everyday concerns of people who loved, worried, feasted, starved and prayed across a vast area from Scandinavia to Constantinople, from Ireland to Sicily, and from Spain to Jerusalem, for nearly a thousand years. Many recorded their fears, jokes and anxieties, especially with their health and pains, as well as their delights. In this miscellany I have tried wherever possible to select their own words from poems, chronicles, wills, romances, epitaphs, letters and legal regulations, all translated into modern English, rather than

opinions put into their mouths by others. Drawn from history but in no way a history, *A Medieval Miscellany* is a mosaic, necessarily incomplete, whose colourful stones have been gathered from every corner and period of the medieval world. I have pressed them into a rough seasonal pattern which is accompanied by the marvellous reproductions of medieval images selected by Linda and Michael Falter. We hope the combination will allow the reader to enjoy the presence and experience something of this way of life that is so remote from ours, despite many similarities.

The chronological range of this material, from the sixth to the fifteenth century, reflects a long, slow process of change, from the period still dominated by inherited patterns of Roman rule, to the humanistic world of the Renaissance city inhabited by Boccaccio and Petrarch. Despite this dramatic transformation, all the sources represent something distinctly medieval, a word that derives from the idea of the Middle Ages, *medium aevum*, a period between the ancient and the modern worlds.

Inevitably, the selection of texts from different points in such a long 'Middle Age' means there are some contradictions - for instance, the canon of 692 proscribing public entertainments throughout the week after Easter Sunday, and reports of fairs and fiestas later associated with Easter. Yet in both responses we can appreciate the centrality of the Church in the medieval world and the significance of its major feasts, which established the basic calendar for people who lived in the Middle Ages. Even if people had difficulty calculating the date (see 'The Calendar', page 33), their year was marked as much by the cycle of Christian festivals as by the changing seasons.

The medievals were aware of the existence of non-Christians, Jews, pagans, even of those in the remote world of the Great Khan of China, as well as heretics excluded from the Church for wrong belief and practice. But the vast majority knew no alternative to the Christian creed. The underlying framework of Christian belief formed their daily lives and they lived by its dogmas to the best of their ability. This also means that they were critical of its clerics and enjoyed jokes at their

expense. Nor did the church authorities uproot a deep tradition of secular humour, which flourished in the form of tales told around the fire at night: epics of ancient combat, romances peopled with superhuman figures, tales set in fabulous foreign lands, fables of talking beasts and stories of proverbial wisdom, strength and vengeance. War, pilgrimage, exploration and trade took medieval people to distant places with non-Christian traditions, which produced their share of fascinating reports. These surface not only in the great epics and romances of the Middle Ages, but also in accounts by modest pilgrims and travellers.

It was Anthony Cheetham's idea to produce *A Medieval Miscellany* and I would like to thank him and his colleagues at Weidenfeld and Nicolson for persuading me to select the texts to accompany the exquisite manuscript illustrations. Preparing this book was a delight. Many individuals helped with suggestions, not all of which could be incorporated. I particularly thank the following for their assistance: Teofilo Ruíz, Katherine Holman, George Baloglou, Charlotte Roueché and Peter Ricketts for their previously unpublished translations of foreign works. Thanks also go to: John Gillingham, Janet Nelson, Michael Richter, Bibi Sawyer, Linda Falter, William North, Joan Burchardt, Georgina Capel, Tamara Barnett-Herrin and Anthony Barnett.

JUDITH HERRIN

When in April 1998 Anthony Cheetham invited us to share his vision for a new book, we had little idea of the roller-coaster journey on which we were about to embark. We had met Anthony some years earlier and he had been captivated by the facsimiles of medieval illuminated manuscripts we had published.

Originally inspired by a Sunday-afternoon visit to the King's Library in the British Museum and a three-generation-long tradition of printing in the family, we founded

Facsimile Editions in order to recreate the aura of illuminated manuscripts. We spared no effort in reproducing the feel and appearance of parchment, burnished gold, delicate miniature painting and hand-binding, and sucessfully produced what were inevitably expensive limited editions accessible only to collectors and great libraries throughout the world.

Anthony, an historian and fellow lover of manuscripts, wanted to make this largely unknown and often mysterious world of manuscripts accessible to a wider public; and how better to achieve this than to combine medieval texts and art in order to depict for modern book-buyers the skill and inner life of medieval artists and scribes.

In over twenty years of work we have examined many of the world's greatest collections and have published facsimiles of some of their finest manuscripts. Our knowledge of these collections and our own substantial library of images enabled us to select beautiful manuscripts to illustrate the texts. We hope our captions will add to the appeal of the images and explain what they may have meant to their patrons.

There are many people we wish to thank for their help and inspiration, but our gratitude must go first to Anthony Cheetham for entrusting us with his vision, to Michael Dover for helping us execute it and to Judith Herrin for her fascinating text selections. We would also like to thank David Bussey, Amos Davis, Michel Garel, Raphael Loewe, Mauricio Hatchwell Toledano, Judith McLaren, Michael Pächt, Chris Rawlings, Brian Rich, Ruth Rosenthal, Michael Salem, Jeremy Schonfield and Nice Ugolotti Serventi for their help and support.

Bernadette Byrne at Clinton Smith worked all hours to help complete this book; and we could not have achieved the precision of detail without the dedicated teamwork of our colleagues at Graphicolor and Grafiche Milani in Italy.

None of this, needless to say, would have been possible without the scribes and illuminators themselves, many of them anonymous, whose work has been 'borrowed' for this book. We can only hope they would have approved of the way we have ensured that they will now be able to speak to a wider public.

And lastly, we must thank our wonderful sons, Gideon and Joseph, who in the midst of examinations have put up gracefully with the turmoil and excitement of this Medieval Miscellany.

LINDA AND MICHAEL FALTER

Spring

A late thirteenth-century spring song by the poet Nahum, a Jew from Spain.

Winter is gone, gone is my sorrow. The fruit-tree is in flower, and my heart flowers with joy.

The spikenards, as one, give forth their scent; the orchard of rare fruits is in full blossom. The hearts of friends are filled with merriment. O hunted gazelle who escaped far from my hut, come back, come drink my mulled wine and my milk!

Sorrows fled the day the flower-beds revived, fenced in by myrtles, braided with embroideries. Swiftly, then, all cares took flight. I am surrounded by coffers full of perfumes, dripping liquid myrrh. The boughs of the nut-tree trail low along my couch.

Trees of delight sway among the shadows: assia on the left, aloes on the right. With an emerald-coloured cup, ringed [with gold], and garnet-coloured wine, mixed with dew, I shall forget the misery and grief hidden deep in my heart.

What made my beloved, who used to graze between my fawn [-like breasts], leave me and take to the woods? Come to the arms of your dearest, who sings of her longing for you. O, my fair love, light the western lamp for me. In you, towering cherub, my flame will burn anew.

Top: The opening page of the Book of Job. In the Talmud, it states that 'God gave to Job a foretaste of the bliss of paradise'.

19

Love

This definition of love occurs in the
Romance of Akrites, *a Byzantine epic probably
written down in the eleventh century.*

Love produces kissing and kissing desire;
desire causes cares, worries and reflection
and threats and danger and separation from parents;
it fights against the sea, it recks nothing of fire;
and one in a state of desire loses his reason for love,
he thinks nothing at all of cliffs and rivers;
he thinks vigils are rest and passes plains.
And all of you who are tormented for the love of a maid
have heard in writing of those famous Hellenes;
of how many torments they too endured for the sake of desire.
Consider, readers, those heroes
the Hellenes, those wonderful and famous soldiers,
and all that came to pass for the sake of that Helen,
when they defeated all Asia
and were all made glorious by their exceeding valour,
and yet in their case too, when it came to matters of
love none could resist.

I Opposite: Troilus and Criseyde from a
French prose translation of Boccaccio's
Filostrato, written and illuminated *c.* 1480.

Love Personified

The Greek Anthology *contains a collection of amorous epigrams by Meleager put together in the sixth century. These two are devoted to Zenophilia.*

Already the white violet is in flower and narcissus that loves the rain, and the lilies that haunt the hillside, and already she is in bloom, Zenophilia, lover's darling, the sweet rose of Persuasion, flower of the flowers of spring. Why laugh ye joyously, ye meadows, vainglorious for your bright tresses? More to be preferred than all sweet-smelling posies is she.

The noise of Love is ever in my ears, and my eyes in silence bring their tribute of sweet tears to Desire. Nor night nor daylight lays love to rest, and

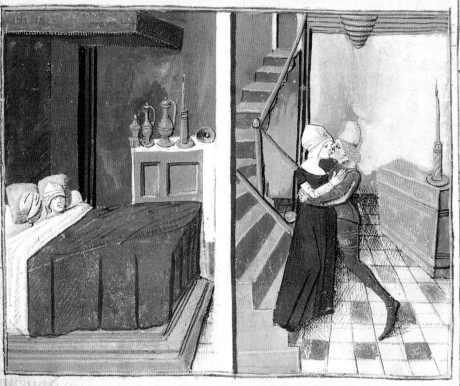

already the spell has set its well-known stamp on my heart. O winged Loves, is it that you are able to fly to us, but have no strength at all to fly away?

Mutual Love

This comes from an early twelfth-century correspondence between a man and woman, both unnamed, in the region of Troyes, northern France.

The more I drink my fill of your sweetness, the more I thirst. All my wealth has gathered in you alone, all I have power to do has its source in you. So, that we may devote ourselves to each other, you are I and I am you.

Love's Radiance

A Hebrew poem, 'The Laundress', by Judah Halevi (1075–1141).

My love washes her clothes in the water of my tears and spreads them out in the sun of her beauty. She has no need of spring-water - she has my two eyes; nor of the sun - she has her own radiance.

1 Tacuinum of Paris ⁄ *Coitus*: Is the union of two in order to introduce the sperm. *Optimum*: That which lasts until all the sperm has been emitted. *Uses*: It preserves the species. *Dangers*: Harmful to those who have cold and dry breathing. *Neutralization of the Dangers*: With sperm producing foods.

Fortune-telling

Predicting the future was a common activity, but one regularly condemned by the Church. In this regulation the Eastern bishops, gathered in council in 692, provide details of the many varied forms of ancient prophesy and condemn them all.

Those who have recourse to diviners, or to so-called 'centurians', or to any such persons, in order to learn from them whatever it is they want to discover, shall be subject to the canonical penalty of six years, in accordance with the decrees made by the Fathers not long ago in such matters. The same penalty ought to be inflicted on those who keep bears in tow and other

such animals in order to deceive and cause mischief to the more simple-minded, haranguing the throng with fortune and fate and genealogy and other such words used in the trumpery of imposture, as well as the so-called cloud-chasers, sorcerers, purveyors of amulets and diviners.

I A fortune-telling tract from the thirteenth century made at the Abbey of St Albans by the monk Matthew Paris. Socrates, with Plato at his shoulder is writing predictions. During the Middle Ages, both philosophers were regarded as diviners.

II The idols made by the immigrants to Israel. A fiery idol extends its hand towards a naked boy while Nibhaz, a dog idol, protects Tartak shown as a naked couple (entwined, a symbol of fornication).

Whitsun

The Romance of Horn *describes the celebration of Whitsun in late twelfth-century Norman England. The young hero, Horn, is chosen as cup bearer to the king.*

They assembled at Pentecost for the great annual feast which was handsomely celebrated. Many mighty lords came from many regions, and their wives with them. Magnificent ladies, thus conferring more honour on the king's great court. Herland the seneschal was in charge of the court... Horn accompanied him, his face admired by all: no lady seeing him was not deeply affected and troubled by the pains of love. His well-cut tunic was of fine cloth, his hose close-fitting, his legs straight and slender. A short mantle hung from his shoulders, its strings untied to allow him to do whatever he was ordered...

Horn served the king well with the cup that day. He carefully scanned the rows and made many a round for he wanted no one discontented with his service. Thus he willingly had them all well served. Lord! How they praised his bearing and complexion now! No lady seeing him did not love him and want to hold him softly to her under an ermine coverlet, unknown to her lord, for he was the paragon of the whole court.

Love Condemned

In his compendium of advice, Matfre Ermengaud, the late thirteenth-century Provençal poet denounces certain aspects of love.

And they want to joust all day, be in tournaments, dance with ladies; and know for sure that the Devil leads their dance, and Satan so enflames their folly and so fires their passion that, through an excess of love, he makes them worship their ladies; for, since they should love the Creator with true love, with all their heart, their soul and all their understanding, so they love their ladies sinfully, and because of this they make him their deity. And know that, in worshipping them, they are in truth worshipping Satan and make their god the treacherous devil, Satan, Belial.

Love of Christ

Margery Kempe, an English visionary and mystic (c. 1373–c. 1440), caused great disturbance throughout Christendom because of her intense feelings of love for Christ and the Virgin. She went on pilgrimages to Compostela and Jerusalem, as the following passage indicates.

When she [Margery] knew that she was going to cry, she held it in as long as she could, and did all that she could to withstand it or else to suppress it, until she turned the colour of lead... And when the body might no longer endure the spiritual effort, but was overcome with the unspeakable love that worked so fervently in her soul, then she fell down and cried astonishingly loud...

And thus she did on the Mount of Calvary: she had as true contemplation in the sight of her soul as if Christ had hung before her bodily eye in his manhood. And when through dispensation of the high mercy of our sovereign saviour, Christ Jesus, it was granted to her to behold so truly his precious tender body, all rent and torn with scourges, more full of wounds than a dove-cote ever was of holes, hanging upon the cross with the crown of thorns upon his head, his blessed hands, his tender feet nailed to the hard wood, the rivers of blood flowing out plenteously from every limb, the grisly and grievous wound in his precious side shedding out blood and water for her love and her salvation, then she fell down and cried with a loud voice, twisting and turning her body amazingly on every side, spreading her arms out wide as if she would have died, and could not keep herself from crying and these physical movements, because of the fire of love that burned so fervently in her soul with pure pity and compassion.

Love of God

Catherine of Siena wrote to Cardinal Iacopo Orsini in 1374.

Dearest and very loved father in Christ Jesus, I Caterina, servant and slave of the servants of Jesus Christ, am writing to you in his precious blood. I long to see you by the same blazing

divine clarity that moved God to draw us from within himself, from his infinite wisdom, so that we might share in and enjoy his supreme eternal good...

For God was so engrafted into humanity that one who was both God and human ran like one in love to the shameful death of the cross. This incarnate Word wanted to be engrafted onto that tree. And it was not the cross or the nails that held him there; these were not strong enough to hold the God-Man. No, it was love that held him there...

Love is so powerful that it makes one heart and one will of lover and beloved. Whatever the one loves, so does the other; if it were otherwise, it would not be perfect love. I have often noticed that when we love something - either because it would be useful to us or because it would give us some gratification or pleasure - we don't care what sort of abuse or injury or pain we might have to endure to get it; the effort means nothing to us; we are concerned only with satisfying our desire for the thing we love.

Oh dearest father, let us not disgrace ourselves before the children of darkness! What a shame that would be for the children of light - I mean God's servants chosen and taken from the world, and especially those who have been set as flowers and pillars in the garden of holy Church! You ought to be a fragrant flower, not a stinking weed. You should be clothed in purity's white, fragrant with patience and blazing with love, magnanimous and generous, not stingy...

There is only one thing to do then, and that is to invest our affection, our desire, our love in something stronger than ourselves – I mean in God, the source of all strength. He is our God who loved us without being loved. And once we have discovered and experienced such a gentle love, strong beyond all other strength, we cannot cling to or desire any other love but him. Apart from him there is nothing at all we seek or want...

I San Raphaele in an Italian Book of Hours   II Santa Catherina. Italian Book of Hours, fifteenth century.

Astrology

Anna Komnene (1083–1153/4) wrote a history of her father, the Byzantine Emperor Alexios I Komnenos, in which she displays her wide learning and intellectual interests.

...the following are the facts about astrological prophecies. The discovery is fairly recent, and the science of it was not known to the ancients. For this method of divination did not exist in the time of Eudoxus, the greatest of all astronomers, neither did Plato have any knowledge of it... Now these [astrologers] observe the hour of the birth of the persons about whom they intend to prophesy, and fix the cardinal points and carefully note the disposition of all the stars, in short they do everything that the inventor of this science bequeathed to posterity and which those who trouble about such trifles understand. We, also, at one time dabbled a little in this science, not in order to cast horoscopes

I Above: Astrologer with an astrolabe.

II Below: Ezekiel's vision of four creatures holding the seven planetary spheres.

(God forbid!), but by gaining a more accurate idea of this vain study to be able to pass judgment upon its devotees.

There was no dearth of astrologers at that time... a famous Egyptian, Alexandreus, was consulted by many and used to give most accurate forecasts in many cases, not even using the astrolabe, but [he] made his prophecies by a certain casting of the dice. There was nothing magical about that either... When the Emperor [Alexios I] saw how the young people flocked to him and regarded

the man as a species of prophet, he himself consulted him twice and each time Alexandreus gave very correct answers. But the Emperor was afraid that harm might come to many from it and that all would be led away to the vain pursuit of astrology, so he banished him from the capital...

Later again, a man called Catanances from Athens came to the capital... and when questioned by some about the date of the Emperor's death, he foretold it as he thought, but was proved wrong in his prognostication. It happened, however, that the lion which was kept in the palace died that day, after four days' fever, so the vulgar considered that the prophecy of Catanances had been accomplished.

Misfortune

The Spanish poet, Abraham Ibn Ezra (1092–1169), wrote this short poem on misfortune in Hebrew.

Out of Luck
However I struggle, I cannot succeed, for my stars have ruined me:
If I were a dealer in shrouds, no one would die as long as I lived.

I Above: Vexed at being ignored by their Prince, a group of astrologers in a certain kingdom decided to rouse the people to overthrow him. Hearing of this, the King's concubine warned the King, forestalling the plot. The astrologers, however, were unaware of the developments and are seen here reading signs for an auspicious date on which to launch the insurrection against the Prince.

II Right: Balaam, according to legend, was one of three seers who prophesied that Moses would destroy Egypt.

Fortune

In The Book of Chivalry, *Geoffroi de Charny, a French knight who died on the battlefield of Poitiers in 1356, warns against fickle fortune.*

Do not put too much faith in people who have risen above others by good fortune, not merit, for this will not last: they can fall as quickly as they rise...

One should not put trust in the benefits of fortune which are not earned for fortune is fickle and is destined to come to an end... But those who are reputed to be wise and are not, and those who are reputed to have won honour through deeds of arms and are unworthy of this renown, and those who have been raised up to noble rank and great wealth and high estate, when people of that kind are elevated to such a good fortune... the foundation on which their height of fortune is based is so weak that it must crumble and collapse... They therefore suffer more from the descent through having mounted so high. Hence the proverb of the ancients is true: 'He that climbs higher than he should, falls lower than he would.'

I Joseph is led away in chains at the hands of the Moors.

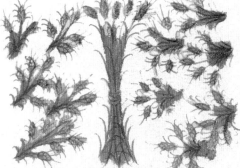

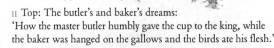

II Top: The butler's and baker's dreams: 'How the master butler humbly gave the cup to the king, while the baker was hanged on the gallows and the birds ate his flesh.'

III Above: Joseph's dream: the eleven sheaves of his brothers' corn bow down before Joseph's, prophesying his supremacy over them.

IV Opposite top: Elementary education. The teacher sits with a whip at the ready, while an hourglass marks the time. The child writes down part of *The Golden Rule,* a text by Hillel the Older intended to show the profound importance of education in Jewish life. German, fourteenth century.

V Opposite: Five teachers and their students, Barcelona *c.* 1340.

A Teacher's Warning

A collection of letters, written by an unidentified scholar based in Constantinople in the tenth century, reveal typical problems with students. The Metropolitan is probably the patron of some young clerics who are failing to study seriously.

Letter 69: to Alexander, Metropolitan of Nicaea... I hesitated whether to write to you or not, but decided that I ought to. Children naturally prefer play to study: fathers naturally train them to follow good courses, using persuasion or force. Your children, like their companions, neglected their work and were in need of correction. I resolved to punish them, and to inform their father. They returned to work and studied diligently for some time. But they are now occupied with birds once again, and neglecting their studies. Their father, passing through the city, commented acidly on their conduct. Instead of coming to me, or to their uncles, they have run away to you or to Olympus. If they are with you, treat them mercifully as suppliants. Even if they have gone elsewhere, help them to return to the fold. You will have my gratitude.

Children

During the entrance of King Henry IV of Castile to the city of Jaén in 1464, the children were allowed a major role.

Close to half a league from the city, all the canons of the cathedral, the municipal officials came to meet the king... Five hundred knights very well dressed and some dressed in the Moorish fashion, with false beards and heavy wooden lances (*cannas*) came [to meet the king] and engaged in mock battle. Further along the road, thirty other men came dressed as Moorish women playing tambourines and bells and giving great cries [in the Moorish fashion]... And further along the road four thousand children came out of the city riding on wicker horses and playing music, plus another one thousand children armed with wicker crossbows and also engaged in mock battle.

The Miracle of the Blind Boy

The miraculous cure of a small boy, abandoned by his parents, is recorded in the Book of Miracles of Sainte Foy, compiled in the eleventh century.

[The fugitive parents] left behind at home a son almost five years old... When the dead man's kindred saw the little boy and understood that his father... had fled... they were impelled by the same Furies who drove Orestes to slay his mother! They seized the little boy and, disdaining to kill such an insignificant person, they pierced the pupils of his eyes with sharp, pointed sticks and left him half dead.

But omnipotent God, to Whom is left the care of the wretched, was present for this boy abandoned by his parents, and He did not deprive the boy of His usual mercy. For the men of that village lifted him from the ground and carried him down to the church door, and they instructed him that with the others who were sick or injured he should beg alms from the people coming to pray. For several months he sought contributions there. Then one day when the sun was hastening to the west the inhabitants of Conques led him by the hand up to the holy virgin's altar. They eagerly requested of the highly renowned virgin that she deign to provide her customary mercy by granting a miracle for him. But I'll not waste time in long digressions. Just as a tiny little spark of fire set to a dead coal will cause it to brighten slowly until it glows with red heat, light sent down from heaven began to burn through the boy's clouded vision little by little, clearing the eyes that had been extinguished for so long. He reached out to touch the forms of things opposite him as if by the dim light of a dark moon, then he began to cry out with boyish glee that he could see a little... For with scarcely any delay the light continued to increase and he saw everything so clearly that he both recognized by sight and named whatever was shown to him. Everyone was filled with indescribable joy by this; the air rang mightily with their exuberant shouts; with their voices rivalling one another they made the whole basilica reverberate with declarations of praise. What more is there to say?...
The boy was reciting the Psalmist's words, 'My father and my mother have left me, but the Lord has taken me up,' as the brothers carried him to the blessed virgin's holiest place. They nourished him with monastic support for the rest of his life, until death claimed what was owed and his soul flew up to the heavenly kingdoms.

The Calendar

Only from the sixth century onward was the system of calculating the date of the birth of Christ developed, but as the following text shows it was difficult to establish the AD method accurately.

5,954 years have passed from the beginning of the world to the era 792 [the equivalent of AD 754], which has now begun, the tenth year of the emperor Constantine, the fourth of Abd Allah, the *Amir Almuminim*, the seventh of Yusuf in the land of Spain, and the one hundred and thirty-sixth of the Arabs. If you wish, you may subtract four of these years in accordance with certain historians who diligently affirm this, computing the fifty-sixth year of the reign of Octavian to have expired in the 5,210th year of the world, and asserting that Christ was born in the forty-second year of the emperor Octavian. So it is in the sixth chapter of the first book of the *Ecclesiastical History* of lord Bishop Eusebius of Caesarea, as well as the *Chronicle* of

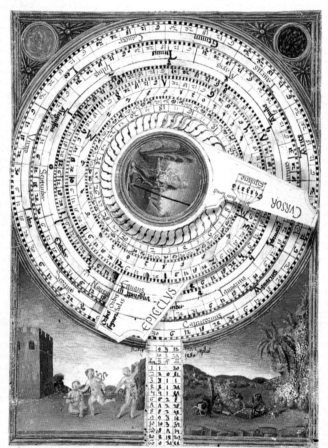
Jupiter, from a treatise on the signs of the zodiac

master Isidore and all the scriptures... When the fifth year of Julius Caesar was completed, 5,154 years of the world had passed. Adding the forty-two of Octavian, 5,196 years had passed from Adam to the nativity of Christ, which, as we said above, is four years less than 5,200... But because the years of the world have not been calculated sufficiently clearly by our predecessors so as to be numbered equally according to the same system or reckoned alike by all historians within a single sequence... we have added those four years in accordance with the many who contend that Christ was born in the year 5,200, lest we stray too far from the path about which so many distinguished men agree.

The White Cat

'The Student and his White Cat' *was a poem written in the margin of a manuscript of* St Paul's Epistles *by an Irish student in a monastery of Carinthia, in Austria, probably in the ninth century. 'Bán' means white.*

I and Pangur Bán, my cat
'Tis a like task we are at;
Hunting mice is his delight,
Hunting words I sit all night.

Better far than praise of men
'Tis to sit with book and pen;
Pangur bears me no ill-will,
He, too, plies his simple skill.

'Tis a merry thing to see
At our tasks how glad are we,
When at home we sit and find
Entertainment to our mind.

Oftentimes a mouse will stray
In the path of Pangur's way;
Oftentimes my keen thought set
Takes a meaning in its net.

'Gainst the wall
he sets his eye
Full and fierce and sharp and sly;
'Gainst the wall of knowledge I
All my little wisdom try.

When a mouse darts from its den,
O! how glad is Pangur then;
O! what gladness do I prove
When I solve the doubts I love.

So in peace our task we ply,
Pangur Bán, my cat, and I;
In our arts we find our bliss,
I have mine and he has his.

Practice every day has made
Pangur perfect in his trade;
I get wisdom day and night,
Turning darkness into light.

I Above: Rats were a constant scourge in the Middle Ages. A certain preacher in Italy would not take up his position until he was assured that he would be provided with a cat to stop vermin eating his food and books.

II Opposite top: In around 1460, it was customary for Jewish infants to be swaddled in a shawl that restricted movement.

III Opposite: The naked figure is probably Nebuchadnezzar, who is shown riding a lion while forcing his jaws apart.

An Arranged Marriage

In the mid-tenth century, Bishop Paul of Monembasia in southern Greece collected stories, which he qualified as 'spiritually beneficial'. This one was recorded by a monk returning from Rome, who discovered a naked woman on an Aegean island. She told him her life history.

I am of the Helladôn country most worthy father, from the city of Larissa, the daughter of poor parents. When they died and left me an orphan, one of the ruling class took pity on me and received me into his house. He nourished me and raised me with care as though I were his own daughter. When I came of age that Christ-loving man married me to his only son as his wife, paying no attention to my poverty and lowly birth. When this was done, my husband's kin-folk and friends reviled him daily, saying: 'What is this your father has done to you; a woman of your own social standing was never found for you; and he has given you this penniless and low-born wife?' The son would answer: 'I am pleased with whatever my holy father has done for me. Since he raised her and knew her to be [a woman] of great value and beauty, his first considerations were not riches and noble birth, but virtue which is attractive to God; and that is what he gave me.' But even though my husband answered his kinsfolk like this, they did not stop reviling him. When I saw him one day after being reproached like this by his friends and relatives, I said to him: 'For the love of God, my husband, let me go into a monastery and you take a distinguished and illustrious wife of your own rank.' He said: 'I set no account whatever on their foolish talk. I am pleased with what my holy father did for me.' Yet... they still went on making their foolish and contemptuous remarks to him.

Seeing him being persecuted by them like this, I decided to run away, and that is what I did. Unknown to anyone, I got up during the night and fled, all alone, taking nothing with me but the clothes I stood in. I came to the shore and I found a boat in which I embarked. With God's guidance I came to this island - without having realised that I was pregnant. I have strange and wonderful things to tell you, man of God: how from the time of my arrival here (suffering from fatigue and hunger) I gathered plants as food for this miserable body. In that way I just managed to stay alive and to nourish the child in my womb. But who can narrate the mighty and remarkable wonders of God? When the nine months had passed by I gave birth to a male child. I cut up the clothes I was wearing to make swaddling clothes for him and I raised him, by the unspeakable mercies of God who makes and directs all things according to his will and desire. [The child] is now just thirty years old and naked, as am I. Every day, together with me, he offers hymns to God with his thoughts turned to heaven, himself a reflection of divine beauty. Every day I have implored God to... send a priest to illuminate my son by holy baptism. And behold, the Lord has not refused my prayer but has sent you, his servant, to fulfil my desire.

Advice to an Officer

In the eleventh century, a retired Byzantine general, Kekaumenos, addressed a collection of moral stories and anecdotes full of advice to his sons.

When you are at leisure, and not busy with military duties, read military handbooks and histories, and the books of the church. Don't say: 'What benefit is there for a soldier from dogmas and church books?'; for you will benefit a great deal. And, if you pay careful attention, you will gather from them not merely dogmas, and edifying stories, but also maxims of intelligence, of morality and of strategy; for nearly all the Old Testament is stories of strategy.

A diligent reader will also gather maxims of intelligence, as well as many from the New Testament. I want you to be such a man that everyone may marvel at your courage, and your good planning, and your knowledge and eloquence; and if you adopt and observe these rules you will be happy. I drew these things up for you ‚ which are not in any other military manual nor in any other book ‚ I drew them up from my own reflections, and from real experience; for they will benefit you a great deal. Follow up the stratagems of the ancients as well; you won't find these things there; but you'll find other, better things, marvellous and full of wisdom.

1 Above and above, right: Gospels. In the entombment scenes, the physical act of burial is turned into a lamentation for the dead Christ. Constantinople, 1050–1100.

Dress

In 692 the assembled bishops of Eastern Christendom met in council in Constantinople and regulated the style of dress appropriate for young girls and women taking monastic vows.

... Those who are to be promoted to the holy monastic habit are first dressed by those presenting them in silk and all manner of other raiment, as well as ornaments embellished with gold and jewels; and then, as they approach the altar, are divested of this rich attire and straightway are given the blessing to wear the monastic habit and are clothed in the black garment; we decree that henceforth this should not be done. For it is iniquitous that one who through her own choice has renounced every worldly joy and has espoused the life according to God... should again be reminded by this worthless and transitory adornment of those things which she has already consigned to oblivion... For if, as is natural, one little tear should escape, those who watched might not suppose that it came from her attitude toward the ascetic combat, but on account of quitting the world and worldly things.

i Above: The richness of worldly dress that nuns renounce. 'A woman of valour who can find? For her price is far above rubies.' The Book of Proverbs, final chapter.

The Gift of a Book

Petrarch gives a much-loved copy of The Confessions of St Augustine *to a younger friend.*

To Father Luigi Marsili, from Arquà,
7 January 1374

... You ask me for a certain little book. I send it to you gladly as a gift. I should do so the more gladly if it were in the same condition as it was when given me by that Dionysius of your order, eminent student of sacred literature, a man of distinction in all things, and a most kind father to me. But as in my restless youth I was a wanderer by nature, I carried the book through most of Italy and through France and Germany because I was delighted with its substance, with its author, and with its easy portable size. Thus by constant use hand and book became so inseparable that they seemed to grow together. I omit various tumbles on land and in rivers; but once at Nice we were plunged into the sea together. We should certainly have perished, had not Christ rescued us both from imminent peril. Thus travelling with me it has grown old with me, and in its decrepitude it cannot be read by an old man without great difficulty. Now, long after leaving its Augustinian quarters, it returns home again; and again, I suspect, it will make its journeys with you. Accept it then as it is and enjoy it.

Farewell, be happy, and pray to Christ for me whenever you approach his table.

I An elderly Italian Jew studies books with velvet bindings, leather thongs and metal clasps.

II Opposite page: A magnificent historiated letter from an English fourteenth-century Psalter. The knight in the margin is holding the shield of the baronial family who commissioned the manuscript.

A New Fair

Medieval fairs were often held on holy days, when crowds would congregate at shrines, on the feasts of Easter, All Saints (1 November) or Epiphany (6 January). Matthew Paris describes how a new date was fixed on 13 October in 1248, to mark the feast of St Edward.

And the lord king ordered it to be officially announced and proclaimed throughout the whole city of London and elsewhere by public crier that he had instituted a new fair to be held at Westminster to continue for a full fortnight, and, in order that the Westminster fair should more copiously abound with people and merchandise, he absolutely forbade on penalty of weighty forfeiture and fine all markets usually held in England for such a period of time, for instance the fairs at Ely and elsewhere, as well as all trade normally carried on in London both in and out of doors. As a result, a vast crowd of people flocked there as if to the most famous fair, and so the translation of the blessed Edward and the blood of Christ was amazingly venerated by the people assembled there. But all those who exhibited their goods for sale there suffered great inconvenience because of the lack of roofs apart from canvas awnings; for the variable gusts of wind, usual at that time of year, battered the merchants so that they were

cold, wet, hungry and thirsty. Their feet were dirtied by the mud and their merchandise spoilt by rain. When they sat down there at table, those who normally took their meals at home by the

family fireside could not stand this discomfort. The bishop of Ely, because of the loss of his fair at Ely, which the royal edict had suspended, made a very serious complaint about this to the king for introducing such novelties to the detriment of his subjects. But he gained nothing except empty words and comforting promises of future consolation.

Rag Day

Students have contributed their own songs to the secular repertoire. This anonymous one is preserved in a twelfth-century collection.

Hooray! Today's a holiday:
a happy day ، a jolly day:
a day to strum guitars and play
the good old songs the good old way:
to love your neighbour and display
the side of you that's bright and gay:
and students most of all, for they
excel at parties anyway!

So throw your books and slates away ،
there's food for which you needn't pay
forget the works of Ovid, eh? ،
and tell his friends to go and play.
Never mind what people say
youth needs its recreations:
since the world is making hay
let's join the celebrations!

1 Left: A miniature of the Tower of London, with London Bridge and the City in the background. Manuscript of the poems of Charles d'Orleans, *c.* 1480–3.

41

Dress Sense

Writing in the fourteenth century, Geoffroi de Charny describes the dangers of fine clothing and counsels humility among those seeking to dress fashionably.

If anyone is thus elegantly dressed and in good fashion, as befits a young man, it should not be done through pride nor should Our Lord be forgotten; but be careful not to spruce yourself up so much that you do not remember God, for, if you do not remember God, God will not remember you. But one should dress well when in company with other young people and to fit in with them; and it is a fine and good thing to spend one's youth in honest fashion, and those who spend it thus should praise God all their lives.

As for the youth of noble ladies, damsels and other women of high rank, it can indeed be said that... it is fitting to wear fine circlets, coronetals, pearls, precious stones, rings, embroidery, to be beautifully dressed, their heads and bodies well adorned according to what is right and fitting for each person to do; it is much more suitable for them to wear fine adornments than for men, for young damsels sometimes achieve better marriages when they are seen in rich apparel which suits them.

These rich ornaments should be left to them [noble ladies and damsels]. For those who have the will to rise to great achievement, how can they better adorn themselves than by being equipped for it by all the good qualities? They can do so by being men of worth, wise, loyal, without arrogance, joyful, generous, courteous, expert, bold and active...

Opposite: Dancing in the Garden of Love . Guillaume de Loris and Jean de Meun from *Le Roman de la Rose,* Flanders, 1490–1500.

A Scarlet Dress

One of the Canterbury Pilgrims, the Wife of Bath, described her life and her five husbands in the Prologue to her tale, c. 1386.

My fifth and last ⁄ God keep his soul in health!
The one I took for love and not for wealth,
Had been at Oxford not so long before
But had left school and gone to lodge next door,
Yes, it was to my godmother's he'd gone
God bless her soul! Her name was Alison.
She knew my heart and more of what I thought
Than did the parish priest, and so she ought!
She was my confidante, I told her all.
For had my husband pissed against a wall

I Above: Revellers in an orchard. Lutenists and Singers by the Masters of the Prayer Books. From *Le Roman de la Rose*, Flanders 1490⁄1500.

Or done some crime that would have cost his life,
To her and to another worthy wife
And to my niece, because I loved her well,
I'd have told everything there was to tell.
And so I often did, and Heaven knows
It used to set him blushing like a rose
For shame, and he would blame his lack of sense
In telling me secrets of such consequence.

And so one time it happened that in Lent,
As I so often did, I rose and went
To see her, ever wanting to be gay
And go a-strolling, March, April and May,
From house to house for chat and village malice.

Johnny (the boy from Oxford) and Dame Alice
And I myself, into the fields we went.
My husband was in London all that Lent;
All the more fun for me ⁄ I only mean
The fun of seeing people and being seen

By cocky lads; for how was I to know
Where or what graces Fortune might bestow?
And so I made a round of visitations,
Went to processions, festivals, orations,
Preachments and pilgrimages, watched the carriages
They used for plays and pageants, went to marriages,
And always wore my gayest scarlet dress.

These worms, these moths, these mites, I must confess
Got little chance to eat it, by the way,
Why not? Because I wore it every day.

I Above: Chaucer is shown here as a portly man with fair hair and a forked beard.

II Left: Opening page of Chaucer's *The Canterbury Tales*.

A Wedding Feast

The reception of the Infanta Doña Blanca on arrival in Castile to marry the Infante Don Enrique, in 1440.

The princess Doña Blanca, her mother the Queen, her brother the prince Don Carlos... and a retinue of ecclesiastical dignitaries and knights from the kingdoms of Aragon and Navarre also arrived... [They] continued on the way to Briviesca, where festivities were prepared for them and where all [the inhabitants] of the town welcomed them with much solemnity. Each of the guilds came out with their banners and theatrical skits, in the best possible fashion; and with great dances, great enjoyment and happiness. Following them came the Jews with the Torah and the Moors with the Koran [dancing] in the manner usually reserved for [the entry of] kings who come to rule a foreign country. There were also many trumpets, tambourines, drums and flute players which made such a great noise that it seemed as if a very large host was coming. On arriving in the town all together, they accompanied the Queen and the princess to the Count's palace. There the important people dismounted and repaired to a place where a collation was prepared, supplied with such a diversity of poultry, meats, fish, delicacies and fruits that it was a marvellous thing to see; the table and servers were set in a fashion becoming such great ladies. And they were served by knights and gentlemen and by richly dressed pages from the Count's household.

A tent was set, covered with an elegant tapestry and there were there also tables and servers for Don Alonso, bishop of Burgos, the prelates and foreign clergymen... The others were also fed abundantly in other tents. The feast lasted four days... In a chamber on the fourth floor [of the count's palace] there was a silver fountain pouring out wine, and people took as much of it as they wanted.

1 Belshazzar's Feast. The divine curse is revealed to Belshazzar.

Warships

In the late ninth century, southern England suffered repeated attacks by the Danes established in East Anglia, which the Anglo-Saxon king countered by constructing special new ships.

Then King Alfred ordered 'long-ships' to be built with which to oppose the Viking warships. They were almost twice as long as the others. Some had sixty oars, some more. They were both swifter and more stable, and also higher, than the others. They were built neither on the Frisian nor on the Danish pattern, but as it seemed to Alfred himself that they would be most useful.

Then on a certain occasion in the same year six Viking ships came to the Isle of Wight and did considerable damage there, both in Devon and all along the sea-coast. Then the king ordered his men to set out with nine of the new ships, and they blocked them off in the estuary from the seaward end. Then the Vikings went out with three ships against them; and three were beached further up the estuary on dry land: the men had gone off inland. Then the English captured two of the three ships at the mouth of the estuary and killed the men. The other one escaped: the men on that one were also killed, except five, these got away because the English ships ran aground on that side of the channel where the Danish ships were beached, and all the others on the other side so that none of them could get to the others. But when the water had ebbed many furlongs from the ships, the Danes from the three beached ships then went to the other three English ships which were stranded on their side, and there they then fought... and of all the Frisians and English, sixty-two were killed, and of the Danes, 120. Then, however, the flood-tide came first to the Danish ships before the Christians could push theirs off, and so they rowed out and away. They were wounded by then to such an extent that they were unable to row past Sussex, but there the sea cast two of the ships on to the land, and then they were taken to Winchester to the king, and he ordered them to be hanged there. And the men who were in the one remaining ship made it back to East Anglia, severely wounded.

47

Warfare

In 1453 Sultan Mehmed brought up his cannon to end the siege of Constantinople. Emperor Constantine XI rallied the defenders against the Ottomans. On 29 May the final assault began.

The hour was already advanced, the day was declining and near evening and the sun was at the Ottomans' backs but shining in the faces of their enemies. This was just as the Sultan had wished; accordingly he

 gave the order first for the trumpets to sound the battle-signal, and the other instruments, the pipes and flutes and cymbals too, as loud as they could... a great and fearsome sound. Everything shook and quivered at the noise. After that the standards were displayed.

To begin, the archers and slingers and those in charge of cannon and the muskets, in accord with the commands given them, advanced against the wall slowly and gradually. When they got within bowshot, they halted to fight. And first they exchanged fire with the heavier weapons, with arrows from the archers, stones from the slingers, and then leaden balls from the cannon and muskets. Then, they closed with battleaxes and javelins and spears, hurling them at each other and being hurled at pitilessly in rage and fierce anger... This kept up till sunset...

Sultan Mehmed saw that the attacking divisions were very much worn out by the battle and had not made any progress worth mentioning... Immediately he brought up the divisions which he had been reserving for later on, men who were extremely well armed, daring and brave, and far in advance of the rest in experience and valour. They were the elite of the army: heavy infantry, bowmen, and lancers, and his own bodyguard, and along with them those of the division called Janissaries.

Calling on them and urging them to prove themselves now as heroes, he led the attack against the wall, himself at the head... With a loud and terrifying war-cry and with fierce impetuosity and wrath they advanced as if mad. Being young and strong and full of daring, and especially because they were fighting in the Sultan's presence, their valour exceeded every expectation. They attacked the palisade and fought bravely without any hesitation... and forced the defenders back inside...

The Emperor Constantine... took his stand in front of the palisade and fought bravely. Sultan Mehmed who happened to be fighting quite near by, saw that the palisade and the other part of the wall that had been destroyed were now empty of men and deserted by the defenders. Realising that the wall was deserted, he shouted out: 'Friends, we have the City, we have it!'... So saying he led them himself...

Now there was a great struggle and great slaughter among those stationed there. There the Emperor Constantine, with all who were with him, fell in gallant combat... After this the Sultan entered the City and looked about to see its great size, its situation, its grandeur and beauty, its teeming population, its loveliness, and the costliness of its churches and public buildings and of the private houses... When he saw what a large number had been killed, and the ruin of the buildings, and the wholesale ruin and destruction of the City, he was filled with compassion and repented not a little... Tears fell from his eyes as he groaned deeply and passionately: 'What a city we have given over to plunder and destruction!'

1 Opposite: The conquest of the city of Crator. From a manuscript by Jean de Bueil, Brittany.

Building

Abbot Suger of St Denis was very active in rebuilding the ancient abbey of St Denis in which the kings of France were buried. In the mid-twelfth century, he planned the extension to the main church described here.

Thus, when, with wise counsel and under the dictation of the Holy Ghost... that which we proposed to carry out had been designed with perspicuous order, we brought together an assembly of illustrious men, both bishops and abbots, and also requested the presence of our Lord, the Most Serene King of the Franks, Louis. On Sunday, the day before the Ides of July, we arranged a procession beautiful by its ornaments and notable by its personages. Carrying before ourselves, in the hands of the bishops and the abbots, the insignia of Our Lord's Passion, viz. the Nail and the Crown of the Lord, also the arm of the aged St Simeon and the tutelage of other holy relics, we descended with humble devotion to the excavations made ready for the foundations. Then, when the consolation of the Comforter, the Holy Spirit, had been invoked so that He might crown the good beginning of the house of God with a good end, the bishops... laid the first stones, singing a hymn to God and solemnly chanting the *Fundamenta ejus* to the end of the Psalm. The Most Serene King himself stepped down [into the excavations] and with his own hands laid his [stone]. Also we and many others, both abbots and monks, laid their stones. Certain persons also [deposited] gems out of love and reverence for Jesus Christ, chanting: *All thy walls are precious stones*. We, however,... anxious for what was still to be done and fearful of the changes of time, the diminution of persons and my own passing away, ordained in a common council of the brethren... an annual revenue for completing this work; namely one hundred and fifty pounds from the treasury... one hundred [derived from the offerings] at the fair, and fifty [from the offerings] at the feast of Saint Denis. In addition, fifty from the possession called Villaine... And we decreed that these two hundred pounds... be applied to the continuation of these works until, without any question, these edifices... will be entirely and honourably completed throughout, including their towers.

Travel Documents

A thirteenth-century note, probably inserted into a letter by the unknown author, reveals the difficulty of travelling from Ceuta in Morocco to Bijaya (Bougie) in Algeria with insufficient evidence of identification.

Furthermore, I inform you that I long and yearn for you, I also inform you that someone arrived here and told us that your son Nissim travelled from Ceuta to Bijaya, where the governor of the town found that a woman was in his company. He asked him: How is this woman related to you? He answered: She is my wife. However, when he was asked for her marriage certificate, he replied that she had none. Upon this the governor took all his goods and put him into prison. Nothing remained in his possession. By God, do not tarry. Take note of this. Greetings. *And Peace.*

I Opposite: The Tower of Babel under construction in Mozarabic style. Spain, fifteenth century.

II Above: A procession of travellers drawn in Spain in 1340.

III Left: In this medieval ship, the artist fills in the hull with a brick like pattern, the crow's nest has spears in it and a red dragon forms the figurehead.

51

A Shepherd's Duty

An anonymous French text on estate management, dating from the thirteenth century, defines the duties and responsibilities of farm employees.

Each shepherd... ought to cover, enclose, and repair the folds, repair and do hedging, fences, and hurdles, and he and his watchdog ought to lie in the fold with the sheep.

He ought to pasture and feed his sheep well and watch over them well so that they are not killed

or tormented by dogs, stolen, lost, or exchanged and they do not pasture in forbidden moors, ditches, and bogs thereby contracting illness and rot through lack of supervision.

No shepherd ought to leave his sheep to go to fairs, markets and wrestling matches or to spend the evenings with friends or go to the tavern without asking for leave and putting a good keeper in his place to look after the sheep, so that no harm or loss occurs through his fault. All the sheep of the lord ought to be marked with the same mark, and no ewe

ought to be milked after the feast of the Nativity of Our Lady (8 September) because they are then slow to mate in the following year and the lambs will be worth less.

ɪ This page: 'Image of the shepherd burning incense and sacrificing on the wood which is upon the altar'. Ibn Sahula, Fables of the Ancients, part of the Rothschild Miscellany, Italy 1479.

ɪɪ Opposite page: The King of Navarre's bed catching fire. Froissart's, *Chroniques de France, c.*1480.

Magic

In the first half of the thirteenth century, Gregory collected stories connected with the monuments of Rome, many of which had ancient and unknown origins, hence their classification as Mirabilia *[Marvels].*

Here begins the account of the wonders of the city of Rome, which have been fashioned either by magic craft or by human labour... Among all the strange works which were once in Rome, the multitude of statues known as the 'Salvation of the Citizens' is to be much admired. By magic art statues were dedicated to all those peoples who were subject to Roman rule, and indeed there was no race or region under Roman authority which did not have its statue in this particular hall. A large portion of its walls still stand, and the vaults seem stark and inaccessible.

In this hall these statues stood in a row, each one having written on its breast the name of the race which it represented, and each wearing around its neck a bell made of silver, because silver is more resonant than other metals. And there were priests who watched over them, ever vigilant both by day and by night. If any nation dared to rise in rebellion against Roman rule, its statue would immediately move, causing the bell to ring, and at once a priest would write down its name and convey this to the government. Above this hall of statues there was a bronze soldier on horseback who would move in conjunction with the statue, aiming his lance at the race whose image had stirred. Warned in this unequivocal manner, without delay the Romans would dispatch an army to suppress that nation's rebellion, and they would often forestall their enemies before they could prepare their weapons and supplies, thus subjugating them easily and without bloodshed.

The Miracle of the Testicles

In the mid-seventh century, Stephen, a deacon of St Sophia, the Great Church of Constantinople, related how he was miraculously cured by St Artemios, whose shrine in the region of Oxeia was famous for the treatment of male genital disorders.

'In my testicles,' he said 'I suffered a rupture, whether from shouting acclamations or from a heavy weight, I can not really say. This happened to me a short time before Herakleios of blessed memory died (641) and out of shame I concealed myself for a considerable time, watching carefully for a chance to bathe alone in the small hours. At long last I disclosed the misfortune to my parents and after many treatments (how many!) had been performed on me, finally after taking counsel with them, I entrusted myself for surgery to the surgeons in the hospital of Sampson and I reclined in the hospital room near the entrance to the area devoted to eyes. After I had been treated all over for three nights and days with cold cauteries, surgery was performed on the fourth day. I will omit what horrible things I experienced while on my back.

To sum up everything, I state that I actually despaired of life itself at the hands of the physicians. After God, entreated by the tears of my parents, restored my life to me, and after the scar from the incision and the cautery had healed, and just as I was believing that I was healthy, a short time later the same condition recurred and so I reverted to my former state...

I had a plan to approach the holy martyr, as I had heard of his many great miracles. Still I was unwilling to wait in the venerable church, feeling ashamed before friends and acquaintances to be seen by them in such a condition. But I

ELMODO DETAIARLA ROTVRA

1 Above: An operation for a scrotal hernia. Italy.

frequently used to pass by (for at that time, he said, I was staying in the Oxeia) and so I descended to the holy tomb of his precious relics and I cast some of his holy blessing *i.e. oil* on my testicles, hoping to procure a cure in this manner. And frequently I entreated him to deliver me from the troublesome condition...

After descending to the holy tomb, I found the doors in front open and I was astounded that they were open at such an hour. This was the doing of the martyr in his desire to pity me. Stretching out face down on the holy coffin, I straddled it and thus contrived to rub the corner of the same holy tomb on the spot where I was ailing. And with tears I spoke again to the martyr: "St Artemios, by God Who has given you the gift of cures, no doctor on earth will ever touch me again. So if you please, cure me. But if not, to your everlasting shame I will live thus without a cure." And after some days I went to the bath in the quarter of Anthemios, the one called Livanon, to bathe by myself at dawn in order not to be seen by anyone. And entering the hot chamber, I noticed that I still had the injury. But upon exiting, I had no injury, and recognizing the act of kindness on the part of God and the martyr which had befallen me... in thanksgiving... I do now glorify them proclaiming their deeds of greatness throughout my whole life.'

11 Top: The excision of haemorrhoids, removal of cataracts and the extirpation of nasal polyps. It was thought that cataracts were a whitish liquid that ran down from the brain. England, twelfth century.

Trading in India

Marco Polo recorded numerous details of the crops and products he noticed on his travels (1260–1295). Here he describes those from Gujarat in India.

There is pepper here in profusion and also ginger and indigo. There is also plenty of cotton, for the cotton trees grow here to a great height ⁄ as much as six paces after twenty years' growth. But when they reach this age they no longer produce cotton fit for spinning, but only for use in wadding or padded quilts. The growth of these trees is such that for up to twelve years they produce cotton for spinning, but from twelve to twenty an inferior fibre only.

1 Above: 'La cité de Polombe'. The black and white pepper harvest in India. France, *Livre des Merveilles c.* 1405.

The manufactures of this kingdom include great quantities of leather goods, that is, the tanned hides of goat and buffalo, wild ox and unicorn and many other beasts. Enough is manufactured to load several ships a year. They are exported to Arabia and many other countries... They also manufacture handsome mats of scarlet leather, embossed with birds and beasts and stitched with gold and silver of very fine workmanship... You must understand that these leather mats of which I speak are such as the Saracens sleep on, and very good they are for the purpose. They also make cushions stitched with gold, so splendid that they are worth fully six marks of silver... some are of such a quality that they are worth ten marks of silver.

II Above: 'Pygmies on the banks of the Ganges who find nourishment in the odours of the fruits.'

III Centre: The Book of Ezekiel, Alba Bible, Maqueda, Spain, 1422–30. The text describes how 'By the river upon the bank thereof... shall grow all trees for meat... and the leaf thereof for medicine'.

After Dinner Entertainment

During his first trip to Byzantium in 949, Liutprand, Bishop of Cremona, was greatly impressed by one after-dinner entertainment. His Latin text was sprinkled with Greek phrases, which are rendered in French in the following translation.

As for the various entertainments I saw there... one... was so remarkable that it will not be out of place to insert an account of it here. A man came in carrying on his head, without using his hands, a wooden pole twenty-four feet or more long, which a foot and a half from the top had a cross-piece three feet wide. Then two boys appeared, naked except for loin cloths round their middle, who went up the pole, did various tricks on it, and then came down head first, keeping the pole all the time as steady as though it were rooted in the earth. When one had come down, the other remained on the pole and performed by himself, which filled me with even greater astonishment and admiration. While they were both performing, their feats seemed barely possible; for, wonderful as it was, the evenness of their

weights kept the pole up which they climbed balanced. But when one remained at the top and kept his balance so accurately that he could both do his tricks and come down again without mishap, I was so bewildered that the emperor himself noticed my astonishment. He therefore called an interpreter, and asked me which seemed the more wonderful, the boy who had moved so carefully that the pole remained firm, or the man who had so deftly balanced it on his head that neither the boys' weight nor their performance had disturbed it in the least. I said that I did not know which I thought *plus merveilleux* that is, more wonderful; and he burst into a loud laugh and said he was in the same case, he did not know either.

1 Humay at the Chinese Court. By Junayd *Khamsa* of Khvaju Kirman. Jalayirid style. Baghdad 1396.

On the Need for Discretion

In July 1347 Petrarch wrote to Cola di Rienzo from Avignon, where he was employed in the papal court of the Roman pontiffs, who were exiled there from 1313.

To Cola di Rienzo, Tribune of the Roman people

I do not know whether you are aware of, or suspect, or are entirely ignorant of, a certain fact. Do not suppose for a moment that the letters that you write from Rome remain long in the possession of those to whom they are addressed. On the contrary, everyone rushes to make a copy of them with as much earnestness, and circulates them around the pontiff's court with as much zeal, as if they were sent not by a man of our own race but by an inhabitant of another world or of the antipodes. All press round to interpret your epistles; and never was an oracle of the Delphic Apollo turned and twisted into so many different meanings. I therefore praise the caution that you have displayed up to now. Until now you have exerted great care in moderating your tone and have succeeded beyond reproach. I urge you and beg you to display greater and greater care in the future...

1 Above: Reading, writing, copying and debating. Early fifteenth-century Hebrew manuscript written in Darmstadt.

I have witnessed several persons struck with amazement as they read, when they saw your self-assurance struggling with your modesty so as to leave only a doubtful victory; astonished when they saw that neither debasing fear nor swelling pride found admittance to that contest. I have seen others perplexed as to whether they should more deeply admire your deeds or your words...

Persevere, therefore, as you have begun. Always write as if everyone were to read, and not merely read, but as if they were about to set out from every shore and bear your message to every land. You have laid the strongest of foundations: truth, peace, justice, and liberty. Build on these. Whatever structure you erect will remain firm; and whoever hurls himself against it will be dashed to pieces. He who wars against truth will declare himself a liar; against peace, a restless spirit; against justice, a dishonest man; and if against liberty, an arrogant and shameless wretch.

War Personified

The Spanish poet, Samuel Hanagid (993–1056), observed:

War is at first like a beautiful girl with whom all men long to play, but in the end like a repulsive hag whose suitors all weep and ache.

1 'How the Tartars troubled the Sultan of Turkey and all his Court.' Mangu Khan, in his boat under attack before the walls of Hou-Tchou. From a fifteenth-century French travel book containing the description of Marco Polo's voyages entitled *Livre des Merveilles*.

61

I The destruction of Sodom. Talmudic sources attribute this to the angel Gabriel. In the dawn sky an angel is seen hurling fiery rocks onto the richly turreted city; flames are erupting from the windows and doors, human life has vanished and all is silence.

Summer Storms

An account by the anonymous chronicler attached to the monastery of Fulda, dated 870.

At Mainz the sky shone red like blood for many nights, and other portents were seen in the heavens. One night a cloud climbed up from the north and another from the south and east, and they exchanged bolts of lightning continuously. In the end they met overhead and as it were fought a great battle. All who saw this were amazed and afraid and prayed that these monstrous things might be turned to good. The lands around that same city were struck by two earthquakes. Several men gathering in the harvest in the district of Worms were found dead because of the heat of the sun, which was fiercer than usual. Many were also drowned in the Rhine.

II The destruction of Jericho. The Israelites, led by Joshua, encircle the town that tumbles down in the centre of the picture. Some blow trumpets, while others carry the Ark of the Covenant with the cherubim. Still others pray with their hands joined and the remaining men in armour advance, each with a spear in his right hand.

Ugly Feet

From the medieval Norse epic, The Saga of St Olav.

There was a man called Toraren Nevjolvson. He was an Icelander... not of great family, but he was wise and clever of speech, and bold in talk with princes. He was a great traveller and was abroad for long stretches of time. Toraren was an ugly man, and especially so because he was ill-shaped in the limbs. He had great ugly hands, but his feet were very much uglier...

King Olav had Toraren as a guest for some days and talked much with him. Toraren slept in the king's room. Early one morning the king lay awake, but the other men in the room were asleep; the sun had just risen, and there was much light within. The king saw that Toraren had stretched one foot forth from the bedclothes. He looked at the foot for a time; then they woke up in the room. The king said to Toraren: 'I have

1 The Lindisfarne Gospels. Miniature of St Matthew from the famous Latin manuscript of the four Gospels made about AD 698 in the Northumbrian island monastery of Lindisfarne. Eadfrith, its scribe and illuminator, later became Bishop of Lindisfarne.

been awake some time and I have seen a sight which seems of great worth; it is a man's foot, so ugly that I believe there will not be one uglier in the whole town,' and he bade the others look and see whether it seemed the same to them. And all who saw said truly that it was so. Toraren understood then what they were talking about and answered: 'There are few things so odd that you cannot expect to find the like to them, and it is most likely that it is so now.' The king said: 'I will not hold with it that you can find so ugly a foot, even if I should bet on it.' Then Toraren answered: 'I am ready to bet you that here in this house I can find an uglier foot.' The king said: 'Then shall the one of us who is right crave a boon of the other.' 'So shall it be,' said Toraren; he stuck forth from the bedclothes the other foot, and it was no whit fairer and the big toe was off too. Then said Toraren: 'Look here, O king, at another foot which is so much uglier as there is a toe off. I have won the bet.'

63

Summer Love

One of the famous twelfth-century lais [tales] *of Marie de France, 'The Nightingale' concerns two knights of Saint-Malo who lived in adjacent and strongly fortified houses.*

One had married a wife who was well-behaved, courteous and elegant... The other young man was a bachelor knight, unmarried, well-known among his peers for his bold exploits...

He fell in love with his neighbour's wife. He begged so hard and pleaded with her, and he was so excellent a man, that she came to love him more than anything in the world... They loved each other prudently and discreetly. They took care to conceal their behaviour and to guard against being perceived, disturbed, or suspected.

1 Pygmalion and Galatea. *Le Roman de la Rose.* France *c.* 1405.

They succeeded in this since they lived near each other... There was no barrier, nothing to separate them except a high wall of darkened stone. From the chambers where the lady slept she was able, when she stood at the window, to converse with her friend on the other side, and he with her. They were able to exchange their love tokens by tossing or throwing them. There was nothing to mar their happiness even though they could not come together to fulfil their desires...

For a long time they were in love, until summer came, when woods and fields grow green again and orchards bloom. Small birds sing sweetly from the flowering treetops. It's not surprising that whoever longs for love can think of this and nothing else...

At night when the moon shone and her husband lay sleeping, she would often steal from his side; with her cloak wrapped about her she would go to the window, for she knew her friend would be at his. This is how they lived, gazing at each other for most of the night. They derived pleasure from seeing each other, denied as they were a greater bliss. She stayed so often at the window and would get up out of bed so often at night, that her husband lost his temper, and more than once demanded to know the reason why she rose in this way and where she went. 'My husband,' replied the lady, 'anyone who hasn't heard the nightingale sing has not experienced joy in the world. That is why I go to stand at the window. I hear its sweet voice in the night... so intensely do I long to hear it, that I cannot close my eyes to sleep.'

When her husband heard what she said, he laughed with angry contempt. An idea occurred to him to trap the nightingale. He ordered the household servants to work on traps, nets and snares and to set them in the orchard. There wasn't a hazel or a chestnut tree anywhere that was not hung with nets or smeared with lime. Eventually they captured the nightingale. They took it alive to the lord, who was overjoyed when he saw it. He went to the lady's chambers. 'Madam, where are you? Come now, let us talk, I've used birdlime to catch this nightingale, the cause of your nightlong vigils. Now you'll be able to slumber in peace, as it will never bother you again.'

... In a fit of perversity he killed it. He villainously broke its neck with his two hands. He threw the dead bird at his wife so that the front of her gown was bloodied over her breast. Then he went out of the room...

The lady took the little corpse and softly wept over it. She cursed those who had treacherously caught the nightingale... for they had killed a great joy... In a length of satin embroidered and inscribed in letters of gold thread she wrapped the body of the tiny bird. She called one of her servants and entrusted him with a message to her friend. He arrived at the knight's house on his lady's behalf... and offered him the nightingale. When the knight had listened carefully... he had a little coffer made, fashioned not of iron or steel but of pure gold ornamented with precious stones. It had a closely fitting lid. In it he placed the nightingale. Then he had the chest sealed. He carried it with him always.

65

Heat

In 1386 John of Gaunt, Duke of Lancaster, and the King of Portugal, led an expedition to Galicia, north-western Spain, against the King of Castile, who was supported by the French. The English troops were accompanied by noble ladies of the Duke's household.

So these two great lords and their armies were in Galicia. They stripped the country of food. The days grew hotter and hotter, until no one dared to go out riding after nine o'clock unless he wanted to be scorched by the sun... No grass could grow, nor any other eatable thing, so hard and dry and sunbaked was the earth...

The knights and squires saw how dangerous the situation might become and the shortage of foodstuffs, and the increasing strength of the sun. They began to grumble and their complaints ran through the army: 'This campaign is shaping badly... Two things tell against us particularly. We are taking women with us and they always want to sit about... This Spanish land is not a pleasant one, agreeable to campaign across as France is with all those big villages, that rich country, those cool rivers, lakes and pools, mild and palatable wines to give new strength to fighting men, and temperate climate. Everything is different here.'

The summer wore on and the sun rose higher in the sky and the days became marvellously hot. It was around mid-summer when the sun is in his strength and pride, especially in those countries of Spain and Granada and the kingdoms far from the regions of the north. Since

66   I Top: Infant death. Spain, fifteenth-century.   II Above: Moses before the burning bush.

the beginning of April no moisture had descended on the earth, neither rain nor dew, and the grass was burnt brown. The English ate quantities of grapes when they could get them, because they were refreshing and juicy, and then they drank those strong wines of Lisbon and Portugal to quench their thirst. But the more they drank the hotter they became, for the wines burnt their livers and lungs and all the entrails of their stomachs being quite foreign to their natural diet. The English live on mild-flavoured food and good, heavy ales, which keep their bodies humid. Now they had dry, sharp wines and drank copiously to forget their sorrows. The nights there are hot, after the heat of the previous day, but near dawn the air suddenly grows cold. This caught them unawares, for at night they could not bear to have a blanket over them and slept naked because heated by the wine. Then came the morning chill which struck through their whole bodies, giving them sickness and fever and afflicting them with dysentery, of which they inevitably died. It was the same with barons, knights and squires as with humble people.

These are the fortunes of war. It must be said that the Duke of Lancaster in Castile would never have lost so many good men in battle as died of illness in that campaign. He himself nearly died of the epidemic... out of fifteen hundred men-at-arms and a full four thousand archers whom the Duke of Lancaster had led out from England not more than half returned or even fewer.

⊥ Top: A plague of boils.

Harvest

The Farmer's Law, a series of regulations governing rural life, was issued in the Byzantine Empire, probably in the seventh century.

60. Let those who come into another man's furrow at harvest-time and cut bundles or ears of corn or pulse be whipped and stripped of their shirts.

61. Where people enter another man's vineyard or figyard, if they come to eat, let them go unpunished; if they are there to steal, let them be beaten and stripped of their shirts.

78. If a man harvests his plot before the plots next door to his have been harvested and he brings in his beasts and they damage his neighbours' land, let him receive thirty lashes and make good the damage to the party injured.

79. If a man gathers in the fruits of his vineyard and brings in his beasts while the fruits of some plots are still ungathered, let him receive thirty lashes and make good the damage to the party injured.

1 Reaping. Queen Mary Psalter. England, early fourteenth century.

Hunger

In the fourteenth-century poem, Piers Plowman
reflects on the hunger that prevailed annually until the
first crops ripened in mid-August. (Lammas-Day is 1 August.)

'I haven't a penny left,' said Piers, 'so I can't buy you pullets or geese or
pigs. All I've got is a couple of fresh cheeses, a little curds and cream, an oat cake, and
two loaves of beans and bran which I baked for my children. Upon my soul, I haven't
a scrap of bacon, and I haven't a cook to fry you steak and onions. But I've some
parsley and shallots and plenty of cabbages, and a cow and a calf, and a mare to cart
my dung, till the drought is over. And with these few things we must live till Lammas
time, when I hope to reap a harvest in my fields. Then I can spread you a feast, as
I'd really like to.'

1 Harvesting apples. Petrus de Crescentiis, *Des profits ruraux des champs.* France, late fifteenth century.

Monks Reaping

The Spiritual Meadow *from which this comes preserves a collection of moral stories put together by John Moschos, a Greek author who flourished in the late sixth and early seventh centuries.*

There was an elder [monk] at Skete called David and once he went out with some other monks to reap. The Sketiotes have this custom that they go out to the estates and reap. The elder offered himself for hire on a day-to-day basis and a farmer hired him. About the sixth hour it was very hot, so the elder entered a shack and sat down. When the farmer saw him sitting there he said to him angrily: 'Elder, why are you not reaping? Don't you realise that I'm paying you?' He said: 'Yes, but the heat is so intense that the grains of wheat are falling out of the husks. I am waiting a little for the heat to abate so that you suffer no loss.' The farmer said to him: 'Get up and work, even if everything bursts into flames'... The elder stood up and suddenly the whole field began to burn. Then in fear the farmer came to the other part of the field with the elder for him to pray that the fire might cease... He offered a prayer and immediately the fire in the field was extinguished. The rest of the crop was saved. Everybody was amazed and glorified God.

I Top: Reaper. *Book of Hours*. Paris, mid-fifteenth-century.

II Above: A man sowing. *Luttrell Psalter*, English, fourteenth century.

Hiring Reapers

An anonymous thirteenth-century French treatise on husbandry includes clear advice on practical matters, such as the hiring of seasonal labour for the harvest.

And you ought to know that five men can easily reap and bind two acres of any kind of corn in a day, sometimes more and other times less... You should engage the reapers as a team, that is to say five men or women, whichever you wish, and whom you term 'men', make one team and twenty-five 'men' make five teams. And twenty-five men can reap and bind ten acres a day, working full time, and in ten days one hundred acres and in twenty days two hundred acres... Ascertain how many acres there are altogether which ought to be reaped and see whether they agree with the number of working days (put down) and then allow them if correct. And if they charge you with more working days than is correct according to this calculation it should not be allowed them, because it is their fault that the proper amount has not been reaped and that they have not done the work as well as they ought to have done.

1 'The villein who could only recite one half of the Hail Mary' is shown here with his plough and oxen. He was saved by the Virgin just as he was about to be snatched up by Satan. From *The Miracles of Our Lady*, France, early thirteenth-century. The manuscript was seized at Poitiers in 1356 by the English and was brought back by Charles V who gave it to his brother, Jean de Berry.

71

Prayer Before an Ordeal

A prayer to bless the instruments of the ordeal.

Then the priest says this prayer:

O Lord, our God, the omnipotent Father, the unfailing Light, hear us, for you are the maker of all lights. Bless O God, the fire which we have sanctified and blessed in your name, you who have illumined the whole world, that we may receive from it the light of your glory. As you did illumine Moses with the fire, so illumine our hearts and minds that we may win eternal life...

O God, the just judge, who are the author of peace and judgest with equity, we humbly beseech you so to bless this iron, which is to be used for the trial of this case, that if this

man is innocent of the charge he may take the iron in his hand, or walk upon it, without receiving harm or injury; and if he is guilty this may be made manifest upon him by your righteous power; that iniquity may not prevail over justice, nor falsehood over truth.

O Lord, the holy Father, we beseech you by the invocation of your most holy name,

1 Abraham praying. His face is framed by long hair and a grey beard indicating his wisdom.

Prayer

The fourteenth-century mystic St Symeon of Thessaloniki on the Jesus Prayer, which is documented since the sixth century and still very widely used.

This holy prayer, the invocation of our Saviour: 'Lord Jesus Christ, Son of God, have mercy upon me,' is prayer and blessing, confession of faith and purveyor of the Holy Spirit, bringer of divine gifts and purifier of the heart, expeller of demons, indwelling of Jesus Christ, source of spiritual thoughts and godly intentions, ransomer from sin, healer of souls and bodies, conveyor of divine illumination, spring of God's mercy and crown of revelations, and gold mysteries in humility. In short, it is the only thing saving of itself, since it contains the saving name of our God, Jesus Christ, the Son of God, which is the only name we invoke, 'there is no salvation for us in any other,' as Paul says.

by the advent of your Son our Lord Jesus Christ, and by the gift of the Holy Spirit, the comforter, to bless these pieces of iron to the manifestation of your righteous judgment, that they may be so sanctified and dedicated that your truth may be made known to your faithful subjects in this trial. In the name of our Lord Jesus Christ...

II Centre: The Harleian Golden Gospels. One of the greatest Carolingian manuscripts, written entirely in gold, *c.* 800.

73

Natur. C.et.s.mi.mettus ex eo qp est in fano. Juuamentum. monorficat laxat et phyket coruptione carnu et altox humetat nocumietum situm efficat et sititur. Remotio nocumeti. Cum po mie curus.

Ht

Health

Bartolomeo Sacchi (1421–81) wrote a treatise under the name Platina, entitled On Right Pleasure and Good Health, *in which he describes the quality of certain foodstuffs.*

On Honey

A great care and concern of bees is making honey and wax, but even greater is storing it, whence Virgil rightly calls them frugal. They do not feast like flies but are considered very clean, for no bee lights in filthy places or those which smell bad. The natural food for the bee is the rose, thyme, bee-balm, poppy, bean-blossom, the lentil, the pea, basil, and clover, for from these they gather their morning dew, from which they make honey, and flower, from which they make wax.

The best honey making is what is made from thyme, and on this account Sicilian and Attic honey bear the palm because of the abundance and sweetness of thyme. Certain authors write about Pontic and Spanish honey in which there is the force of poison, but it is pointless to discuss this when we are seeking what creates pleasure. Honey is the only substance which spits its dregs out on top; the heavier it is the better. Honey is praised differently from wine; the latter is valued because it is old and moist, the former because it is fresh and warm.

Cooked honey is considered better than raw, for it does not bloat one so much or increase pains in the midriff or bile. Summer honey is better than autumn, for it agrees with bodies which are cold and damp, heals many ills, does not allow bodies to decay, is considered best in preserving apples, gourds, citron, and nuts, and creates mouth-watering appeal in many foods.

1 Top: Caption reads: Honey
Nature: Warm and dry. *Optimum:* When it is still in the honeycomb.
Uses: It purifies, is a laxative, preserves meats, and has humidifying properties.
Dangers: Causes thirst and undergoes changes. *Neutralization of the Dangers:* With sour apples. Liege, fourteenth century.

Threshing

A seventh-century description of threshing in Anatolia from 'The Life of St Theodore of Sykeon'.

In the village of Sandos in the district of Protomeria, a certain householder, Eutolmios by name, wanted to enlarge his threshing floor because of the rich abundance of crops that had been given him and because the floor could not take a double yoke of oxen; it was close to a hillock in which there were many demons. Now as he dug and was levelling the ground in a circle round his floor he happened to dig into the neighbouring hillock and remove a stone out of it. And unclean spirits came forth and entered into the animals in the village and made them savage, and later began to work their mischief upon the villagers also... When the villagers saw the distress of their own people and thought that Eutolmios had dug in order to get money out of the hill... they grew mad against the householder and rushed to burn down him and his household... But those who held the highest positions in the village sent to the monastery begging the saint and servant of Christ, Theodore, to come and free them from the evils which had befallen them. The saint came back with them... On the morrow he made arrangements for a procession and in company with them he led the procession with prayer round the village ⁄ and the persons who were being tormented followed too ⁄ and came to the hillock which had been dug open. As he bent his head and prayed, all the spirits which had come out of it and worked mischief among the beasts and

in various places were quickly collected to that spot. The saint then turned to the afflicted and rebuked the unclean spirits that were in them. And by invocation to his master, Christ, he cast them out, and shut them all up there. After putting back the stone which had been thrown out and filling up the trench with earth, he placed above it a model of the Holy Cross, and stayed there sleepless the whole night, singing and praying to God.

I Top: Virgo, from a treatise on the signs of the zodiac.

II Above: 'Image of the lion and his ministers rejoicing, eating, drinking and celebrating.' *The Fables of the Ancients.*

Warfare

During a campaign in 882 against the Vikings, in which the Emperor Charles the Bald besieged the Norse Kings Sigifrid and Godafrid for twelve days, he succeeded in converting one of their leaders.

One day a thing remarkable for both besiegers and besieged occurred. For on July 21 in the afternoon a sudden darkness covered the whole of the sun and with thunder and lightning there was such a hailstorm that no mortal could claim to have seen anything like it before. The hailstones were not as they usually are, smooth and equal in size, but jagged and unequal and with rough edges, so that they offered to all who beheld them an unusual and extraordinary spectacle. It is remarkable and incredible to relate that they could scarcely or not at all be spanned with one's thumb and middle finger. The horses were so startled that they uprooted their tethering-posts and tore their bridles and ran around wildly and in fright both inside and outside the camps. A great part of the city which they were besieging also collapsed under the storm, so that a column in formation could have ridden in if the wall which surrounded it had not held them back. Because the siege had gone on for so many days in summer, the great army began to fall ill and be nauseated by the putrefaction of the many corpses. Those who were trapped inside were no less oppressed. There were negotiations between the two sides and it was agreed that we should give hostages, and that Sigifrid, who was stronger, should come outside the fortifications for a distance of six miles to the king. First he swore on oath that from that hour onwards as long as the Emperor Charles should live he would never again come into his kingdom to plunder it as an enemy. Then he accepted Christianity, and the emperor himself stood godfather at his baptism. They spent two days there together in joy and then our hostages were sent back from the fortification, and he contrariwise returned home with great gifts.

1 Ezekiel's vision: the siege of Jerusalem

Disguise

During civil unrest in Flanders in 1381–2, the Count of Flanders fled in disguise, having exchanged clothes with his servant, and found himself alone in the hostile city of Bruges being hunted by mercenaries.

For some time at this late hour – it was about midnight or a little after – the Count of Flanders wandered desperately through streets and alleys, until he felt forced to go into some house or other... So he entered a poor woman's house. It was no lordly manor, with halls and chambers and courtyards, but a poor grimy hovel, blackened by the smoke of the peat fire. The house consisted simply of one miserable room on the street, with an old sheet of smoke-stained cloth in it to shield the fire, and overhead a cramped little loft which was reached by a ladder with seven rungs. In the loft was a wretched bed in which the poor woman's children were sleeping.

Distraught and trembling, the Count went in and said to the woman, who was terrified at his appearance: 'Woman, save me. I am your lord the Count of Flanders. But now I must hide, my enemies are after me. If you help me, I shall reward you well.'

The poor woman recognized him, for she had often been to his door for alms... She made up her mind quickly, which was a good thing for the Count, because if she had hesitated for a moment he would have been caught talking to her by the fire. 'Sir,' she said, 'go up to the loft and get under the bed where my children are sleeping.' He did as she told him, while she stayed looking after the fire and seeing to another small child which lay in a cradle...

Then the mercenaries of Ghent arrived at the house, some of them saying that they had seen a man going in. They found the poor woman nursing her baby by the fire. 'Woman,' they asked her, 'where is the man we just saw coming in and shutting the door behind him?' 'Bless your hearts,' she replied, 'I've seen no man come in here tonight. I went out myself a few minutes ago to throw out some water, and then shut the door again. Where could I hide him? You can see all I've got here. There is my bed and my children are upstairs in another.'

One of them took a candle and went up the ladder. He poked his head into the loft and saw nothing but the little bed with the children in it. He looked round carefully and said to his comrades: 'Come on, we're wasting our time here. The woman's telling the truth. There's no one here but her and the kids.'

With this they left the house and continued their search elsewhere... The Count of Flanders had heard the whole conversation as he lay huddled in the little bed. The state of fear he was in can be imagined. What thoughts must he have had who in the morning could say, 'I am one of the great princes of Christendom,' and that same night was reduced to such littleness? Well could he say that the chances of this world are precarious.

1 A woman wrapped in a blue-violet cloak wearing a green dress. She holds a suckling babe dressed in red. The three colours are those of the Virgin (blue, also a symbol of Christ's humanity), of love (red, for Christ's love for mankind), and of hope (green, for hope in the coming of the Messiah).

Fiesta

During the Carnival in 1464 the Constable, Don Miguel Lucas de Iranzo, organized a special fiesta in Jaén, with mummers, dances and jousts.

Then came the gardeners of the city with shields and armour and carrying great pumpkins in their hands and in the street a great tournament of pumpkins [took place], the gardeners hitting each other until there was not one pumpkin whole.

[Later in the same year] the Constable ordered a castle on wheels to be built, which was brought onto the street of Magdalen, surrounded by gardeners dressed for battle, and other men with trumpets and weapons. And a great battle ensued.

When the mobile castle reached the tower where the Constable was with his men, a great combat began [which they fought] with hard-boiled eggs against the gardeners and against each other, and between 3,000 and 4,000 eggs were used and the battle lasted for one or two hours.

1 'A watcher will blow the trumpet to alert the people if he sees the sword approaching.' The text goes on to explain how people must guard themselves from sin, like those on an enemy frontier who post a man with a trumpet in a watch-tower to alert its citizens to defend themselves against the enemy. In the same way, rabbis and priests would stand in a wooden pulpit and preach often to mixed groups of Jews and Christians on the merits of following God's path, thus saving their souls.

The Trial of Joan of Arc

After her capture by the English in 1429 Joan was passed to the French authorities, who were determined to put her on trial. When they found her declarations of Christian faith to be sound, further charges were brought against her to demonstrate that she should be burnt as a witch.

Being asked whether she would take a woman's dress so that she might receive her Saviour [in communion] at Easter,
She answered that she would not leave off her dress either to receive her Saviour or for any other reason. She added that to receive her Saviour neither man's nor woman's dress made any difference; and It ought not to be refused her on account of this dress...

She admitted that at Arras and Beaurevoir she had been repeatedly asked to wear a woman's dress; which she had refused and still refuses,
And as for womanly duties,
She said there were enough other women to do them.

1 Top: Joan of Arc, in the only known contemporary likeness, sketched by the Notary of the *Paris Parlement* in the margin of the official history of the siege of Orleans.

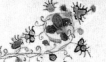

Ceremony of Marriage

The epic poem, The Ruodlieb, dating from the mid-eleventh century, is written in medieval Latin although it describes courtly society in the Germanic lands, with dramatic accounts of adventures both abroad and at home. Here, the hero Ruodlieb presides over a marriage ceremony.

Then Ruodlieb... said that it was agreed by all relations and friends that this youth and this girl were burning with love for one another. They all asked him if he wished to take her as his wife, and with a smile on his face he replied, 'I do.' Then they asked her if she for her part wished willingly to take him as her lord; she too smiled a little, and then said, 'Should I not want a slave vanquished in a game, whom I beat at dice with this agreement as our stake, that whether he won or whether he lost he should marry only me? I want him to serve me with all his might both night and day, and the better he does this, the dearer he shall be to me.' Then there was a tremendous roar of laughter from everyone, because she had spoken so brazenly and yet in such a friendly way. When they saw that her mother did not oppose these things and that the families of both were well-matched in status and wealth, they took counsel and decided that they were well suited to one another, and that she should be betrothed to him in a lawful bond.

The bridegroom drew his sword and scraped it along the stonework. A gold ring was fixed onto its hilt, and the bridegroom offered it to his bride, saying to her, 'As this ring encircles the whole of your finger all around, so I bind my faith to you firmly and forever, and you must observe it towards me, or lose your head.' She very wittily gave him the apt reply, 'It is fitting for both to suffer the same judgment: why must I keep better faith towards you than you towards me?... When you went off wenching, would you have liked me to be a whore for you? May it not be that I should be joined to you on this condition; be off with you, farewell, you may go wenching as much as you wish, but not with me. There are plenty in the world whom I can wed as well as you.' So saying, she left him his sword and his ring. The young man said to her, 'Let it be done as you wish, darling. If I ever do this, let me lose the goods I gave you, and let you have the right to cut off this head of mine.' A smile passed over her lips as she turned back to him and said, 'Let us be joined now on those terms, with no deceit.' Her suitor said 'Amen' to this and kissed her. When they were thus united the people gave a roar of approval and praising God, they sang a wedding hymn.

Jews of Babylonia

Benjamin of Tudela set out from Saragossa, Spain, in 1160 to visit Jewish communities throughout the Near East and Persia, including Baghdad.

Bagdad contains about one thousand Jews, who enjoy peace, comfort and much honour under the government of the great king... The principal of all these... is Daniel, the son of Chisdei, who bears the titles of Prince of the Captivity and Lord, and who possesses a pedigree which proves his descent from King David. The Jews call him 'Lord, Prince of the Captivity', and the Mahometans entitle him Saidna Ben Daoud, noble descendent of David... The Emir-al-Mumenin, the lord of the Mahometans, has... confirmed his power by granting him a seal of office... All the Jewish congregations receive authority from the prince of the captivity to elect rabbis and ministers, all of whom appear before him in order to receive consecration and the permission to officiate... The prince of the captivity possesses hostelries, gardens, and orchards in Babylonia, and extensive landed property inherited from his forefathers, of which nobody can deprive him... He is very rich, an excellent scholar, and so hospitable that numerous Israelites dine at his table.

Many of the Jews of Bagdad are good scholars and very rich. The city contains twenty-eight synagogues, situated partly in Bagdad and partly in Al-Khorkh, on the other side of the river Tigris, which runs through and divides the city. The metropolitan synagogue of the prince of the captivity is ornamented with pillars of richly coloured marble, plated with gold and silver; on the pillars are inscribed verses of the Psalms in letters of gold. The ascent to the holy ark is composed of ten marble steps, on the uppermost of which are the stalls set apart for the prince of the captivity and the other princes of the house of David.

I Jewish wedding scenes. Northern Italy, after 1450.

II The scroll of the Law, draped in red and gold damask, is removed by a Jew from the Ark for a Festival or Sabbath morning ceremony. Italy, c. 1479.

Difficult Choices

*In this anonymous twelfth-century Provençal poem,
two young girls ask Lady Carenza for her advice on
marriage and are recommended to devote themselves to
Coronat de Scienza, the Crown of Knowledge, i.e. God.*

Na Carenzat al bel cors avinen

Alais: Lady Carenza, you of the graceful and lovely body,
  give counsel to us two sisters.
And since you know best how to sift over the best,
  counsel me according to your own wisdom.
Shall I take a husband from among our
  acquaintance?
or remain a virgin? That would please me,
since I don't think much of having babies,
and being married seems too depressing to me.

Iselda: Lady Carenza, having a husband would agree with me,
  but I think having babies is a great penance.
Your breasts hang right down to the ground
and your belly is burdensome and annoying.

Carenza: Lady Alais and Lady Iselda, you have a good education,
  reputation and beauty, youth and fresh colour,
you have understanding, courtesy, and merit ⁄
above all the other ladies of my acquaintance.
For this reason I counsel you, in order to get good seed,
  take Coronat de Scienza for your husband,
From him you'll have the fruit of glorious children.
Those who marry him remain virgins...

1 The birth of Alexander. *Livre des fais d 'Alexandre le grant.* Bruges, *c.* 1475.

An Artist's Vision

In eleventh-century London, a painter by the name of Teodwin was scourged because he dared to work on the holy day of Bishop Erkenwald.

During the period when the body of the holy prelate was still being kept in its coffin in the crypt, the vault of the crypt had to be painted. Now Erkenwald's festival took place while this was going on, but on this particular day mass was not being celebrated there... on account of the erection of the scaffolding the painter needed for his work.

However, a great crowd of people of both sexes, who wished to pray, assembled at the oratory bearing offerings and candles. But they were denied entrance. For the painter had barred the door and carried on painting the curve of the vault with his paint and dyes.

While he was painting away, with great industry, however, he was all at once bereft of his strength and, gripped by a sudden pain, he fell to the ground as if his life had left him. When he suffered this for a long time, sleep enveloped him and lo, the aforesaid prelate, garbed in his episcopal regalia, came to him and beat him hard with his pastoral staff, reminding him how disrespectful he had been to persist in working on that day and to lock people out...

After he had recovered from his illness, he made known to many people this vision and chastisement.

I Opposite page: Medieval congregation and organist from the Prayer Book of King Alphonso V of Aragon, 1442.

II Right: The preparation of parchment was an art. Parchment was extremely expensive and only the most important works were executed on 'fresh' parchment. Others were written on palimpsests where the original writing was erased so that the parchment could be reused. This parchment maker's shop is from Floriano da Villola's Chronicle, Italy.

85

Artistic Techniques

In the first half of the twelfth century, 'Theophilus' produced a very detailed treatise on the techniques used in artistic production of the time. He was probably Roger of Helmarshausen, a skilled metalworker and Benedictine monk, and he addresses his readers thus:

Wherefore, dearest son ⸝ be eager and anxious to look at this little work... You will find in it whatever kinds and blends of various colours Greece possesses; whatever Russia knows of workmanship in enamels or variety of niello: whatever Arabia adorns with repoussé or cast work, or engravings in relief: whatever gold embellishments Italy applies to various vessels or to the carving of gems and ivories: whatever France esteems in her precious variety of windows: whatever skilled Germany praises in subtle work in gold, silver, copper, iron, wood and stone...

There are many kinds of gold, of which the best derives from the land of Havilah... When men, skilled in this art, find veins of it in the ground, they dig them up and, when it has been refined in the fire and proved in the furnace, make use of it for their own purposes. There is also a very precious Arabian gold, which is of an exceptional red colour. It is frequently found used in antique vases. Modern workmen counterfeit its appearance by adding a fifth part of red copper to pale gold, and they deceive many unwary people. This can be guarded against in this way. The gold is put in the fire and, if it is pure, it does not lose its brightness. If, however, it is adulterated, it completely changes colour.

There is also gold, called Spanish gold, which is prepared from red copper, powder of basilisk and human blood and vinegar... There is another gold, called sand gold, which is found on the banks of the Rhine in this way. The sand is dug up in those places where one expects to find it, and is placed on wooden boards. Then water is repeatedly and carefully poured over it. The sand flows away, and very fine gold remains, which is put in a vessel by itself. When the vessel is half full, quicksilver is added, and is vigorously worked with the hand until the contents are completely mixed together. This is placed in a fine cloth, the quicksilver is squeezed out and what remains is placed in a crucible and melted.

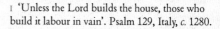

I 'Unless the Lord builds the house, those who build it labour in vain'. Psalm 129, Italy, *c.* 1280.

II Opposite page: Alchemists from Thomas Norton's *Ordinal of Alchemy*. England, *c.* 1490.

The Elephant

In the anonymous fourteenth-century Byzantine story,
Entertaining Tales of Quadrupeds, *King Lion summons all*
the beasts in 1364 to introduce their merits. Each makes fun
of the others until at the end they give up peaceful debate
and a battle royal breaks up the gathering.

The elephant then came to centre stage,
and he addressed the whole assembly thus:
'Just like a tower, safe and fortified,
a fort impregnable, firm to the end,
thus too stand I, robust beyond compare.
Thus bastions are built on me, made of boards,
and solid towers, also, out of wood,
soundly fortified. Soldiers in those towers
stand resolute, fiercely combat their foes,
and overpower and defeat them all.

90

1 Previous Pages: The battle between the
Great Khan's marshal and the King of Mien.

Also my tusks are put to many uses:
in royal beds, and seats of patriarchs,
and thrones of emperors, and queens as well,
and in carved staffs, with jewel settings lathed,
for metropolitans to hold, and bishops,
and for head abbots with their beards so long.
The noblemen and merchants use them, too,
for games they own: lathed chess-pieces and chessboards,
backgammon boards, and all things of the sort.
They make knife-handles, too, for fine, long knives,
as well as the exquisite smaller ones;
and very pretty combs, all bound in gold,
and wrought with silver and with emeralds,
which noblemen possess, both young and old.
The young lads use these combs to comb their hair;
they comb that long blond hair they often have.
Blonde ladies of the court and noble dames
will also comb their hair and their blond tresses;
and ladies of the court adjust their partings.
Young girls, it must be said, will part their hair,
as do blonde damsels, to look fair and decent.
They even use my tusks to frame those glasses,
or mirrors, as they're known, in which young lasses
gaze on their image. Such, then, are the merits
and the advantages that I enjoy.'

II Top left:
A dragon coiled
around an elephant
from the *Aberdeen
Bestiary*. English,
twelfth-century.

III Kublai Khan
leaves to hunt for
gyrfalcons. *Livre des
Merveilles*, written
at the beginning
of the fifteenth
century, recounting
the story of Marco
Polo's travels.

The Cock and the Wolf

In the late eighth and early ninth century, the Anglo-Saxon scholar, Alcuin, was in residence at the court of Charlemagne and reworked the familiar fable of 'The Cock and the Wolf'.

There is a bird called by the special surname, 'cock'. This bird announces daybreak, dispels shadows from the earth, marks the times of the day, and is girded in his loins. The flock of chickens is ruled subject to his authority...

Oh what a sorrow! A barrier of roads once constrained him as he was hastening a long way off, testing for food with his beak. Therefore, as he seeks food by himself and ranges over the crossroads, alas! Boasting, too bold and very proud, he is snatched by the lurking wolf.

Oppressed by this burden, the cock at once finds for himself this scheme for escaping: 'Often your fame, O wolf of exceeding strength, has come to my ears and has told me in a strange rumour that your great voice can produce a deep sound with bright harmonies. I do not grieve so much to be devoured by a hated mouth as to be cheated of being allowed to learn from you what was possible to believe about your voice.'

The beast put credence in what was said, and the wolf, swollen with love of the praise that had been offered, opens his hellish throat, spreads wide his gluttonous jaws, and unlocks the innermost chamber of the vast cavern.

But swiftly the bird, harbinger of daybreak, is rescued, and in a bound flies and quickly clings to a tree branch. As soon as he has gained sudden freedom, the bird sitting on high brings forth songs with these words: 'Whoever grows proud without reason is deservedly deceived, and whoever is taken in by false praise will go without food, so long as he tries to spread about empty words before eating.'

1 Top: 'Image of the cock speaking and composing fables against the hawk.' *The Fable of the Ancients*, a book of moral tales full of witticisms and double entendres, written in verse in 1281 by Isaac Ibn Sahula.

Prayer

St Francis of Assisi, the founder of the Franciscan order, who died in 1226, was particularly famous for his inspiring preaching and vernacular hymns.

Where there is love and wisdom,
there is neither fear nor ignorance.
Where there is patience and humility,
there is neither anger nor annoyance.
Where there is poverty and joy,
there is neither cupidity nor avarice.
Where there is peace and contemplation,
    there is neither care nor restlessness.
        Where fear of the Lord guards the house,
            there no enemy can enter.
                    Where there is
                    mercy and prudence,
                    there is neither excess
                    nor harshness.

I Ad Vesperas. Scene from the Life of Mary.

A Miraculous Statue

Little is known about Master Gregory, author of this piece. He may have been English and appears to have visited Rome in the thirteenth century.

There was in Rome an incredible wonder, an iron statue of Bellerophon and his horse, positioned in mid air, neither suspended from above by any chain nor supported by any post beneath. You see, the vault had an arc of magnetic stones on each side, which attracted the statue proportionately from different directions, and thus it remained balanced. Its weight was thought to be about 15,000 pounds of iron.

II The Horse and the naked figure of Hercules as if in flight, carrying a club and a lion's skin. Both from a manuscript *Hyginus, De astronomia*, written and illuminated in Padua, fifteenth-century.

93

Pilgrimage

The twelfth century Pilgrim's Guide *to the route to Compostela describes the four common routes and the sights and dangers encountered along the way.*

On leaving that country [of Gascony], to be sure on the road of St James, there are two rivers that flow near the village of Saint-Jean-de-Sorde, one to the right and one to the left, and of which one is called brook and the other river. There is no way of crossing them without a raft. May their ferrymen be damned! Though each of the streams is indeed quite narrow, they have the habit of demanding one coin from each man, whether poor or rich, whom they ferry over, and for a horse they ignominiously extort by force four. Now, their boat is small, made of a single tree, hardly capable of holding horses. Also, when boarding it one must be most careful not to fall by chance into the water. You will do well in pulling your horse by the reins behind yourself in the water, outside the boat, and to embark but with few passengers, for if it is overloaded it will soon become endangered...

Then, already near the pass of Cize, one reaches the Basque country, on the seashore of which, towards the north, lies the city of Bayonne. This land, whose language is barbarous, is wooded, mountainous, devoid of bread, wine, and all sorts of food for the body, except that, in compensation, it abounds in apples, cider, and milk.

In this land, that is to say near Port-de-Cize in the town called Ostabat and in those of Saint-Jean and Saint-Michel-Pied-de-Port, there are evil toll-gatherers who will certainly be damned through and through. In point of fact, they actually advance towards the pilgrims with two or three sticks, extorting by force an unjust tribute. And if some traveller refuses to hand over the money at their request, they beat him with the sticks and snatch away the toll-money while cursing him and searching even through his breeches. These are ferocious people... and their barbarous speech scares the wits out of those who see them.

Travel

Benjamin of Tudela set out from Saragossa, Spain, in 1160 and travelled throughout the Near East and Persia to the frontiers of China, visiting Baghdad.

Bagdad [sic] is the large metropolis of the Calif Emir-al Mumenin al Abassi, of the family of their prophet, who is the chief of the Mahometan religion. All Mahometan kings acknowledge him, and he holds the same dignity over them which the Pope enjoys over the Christians... This great Abbaside is extremely friendly towards the Jews, many of his officers being of that nation; he understands all languages, is well versed in the Mosaic law, and reads and writes the Hebrew tongue... The calif leaves his palace but once every year, namely, at the time of the feast called Ramadan; on which occasion many visitors assemble from distant parts, in order to have an opportunity of beholding his countenance. He then bestrides the royal mule, dressed in kingly robes, which are composed of gold and silver cloth. On his head he wears a turban, ornamented with precious stones of inestimable value; but over this turban is thrown a black veil, as a sign of humility, and as much as to say: 'See all this worldly honour will be converted into darkness on the day of death.'

He is accompanied by a numerous retinue of Mahometan nobles, arrayed in rich dresses and riding upon horses, princes of Arabia, of Media, or Persia, and even of Tibet, a country distant three months' journey from Arabia... All who walk in procession, both men and women, are dressed in silk and purple... The procession moves on into the court of the mosque, where the calif mounts a wooden pulpit and expounds their law unto them. The learned Mahometans rise, pray for him, and praise his great kindness and piety; upon which the whole assembly answers, 'Amen!' The calif then pronounces his blessing, and kills a camel, which is led thither for that purpose, and this is their offering...

The city of Bagdad is three miles in circumference; the country in which it is situated is rich in palm-trees, gardens, and orchards, so that nothing equals it in Mesopotamia. Merchants of all countries resort thither for purposes of trade, and it contains many wise philosophers, well skilled in sciences, and magicians proficient in all sorts of enchantment.

1 Sultan Sanjar and the old woman from a Persian manuscript written in Baghdad in 1396

The Swan

In his catalogue of birds, Hugh of Fouilloy, who died in 1172/3, often quotes from ancient authorities. Here he prefaces his entry on the swan by a quotation from Isidore of Seville, whose seventh-century Etymologies *was considered an encyclopaedia of accurate information.*

'The swan is named surely for its singing, because with melodious notes it gives forth a sweet song. Moreover, it [is said] to sing so sweetly because it has a long and curving neck, and it is inevitable that a voice forcing its way through a long and flexible passage will produce various melodies. It is reported that many swans fly to the singing lyricists in the northern regions, and join properly in the mode.'

The swan has snowy plumage, but black skin. Allegorically the snowy colour of plumage denotes the effect of the pretence by which the black flesh is hidden, because a sin of the flesh is

veiled by pretence. While the swan swims in the river it carries its neck erect, because a proud man who is enticed by worldly possessions also at the same time prides himself in possession of transitory things.

'It is reported that many swans fly to the singing lyricists in the northern regions, and join properly in the mode,' because those who covet pleasures with all their hearts harmonize with pleasure seekers as if flying to them. But at the last, when the swan is dying, it is said to sing exceedingly sweetly as it dies. Likewise, when the proud man departs this life, he delights still in the sweetness of this world, and dying, he remembers the things which he did wrong.

I 'Image of the cock showing his broken wing to the partridge and to all members of the party.' *Fables of the Ancients*, a moralistic book written in 1281 by Isaac Ibn Sahula and copied here in the fifteenth-century in Italy.

II Top: The swan from one of the most dramatic of all bestiaries. Latin, 1230-40.

But when the swan is deprived of its snowy plumage, set on a spit, it is roasted at a fire. Likewise, when at death the wealthy, proud man is stripped of his worldly glory, descending to the flames of hell, he will be punished with torments, and he who was accustomed to seek nourishment in the lowest quarters, descending into the abyss, becomes food for the fire.

III The 'swan' constellation, from the *Phaenomena* of Aratus. Carolingian, ninth-century.

97

Ambassadors

Liutprand of Cremona was twice ambassador to Byzantium and left a detailed account of his first trip in 949 when he represented Berengar, ruler of Italy, to Constantine VII (913–59).

On the first of August [949] I left Pavia and sailing down the Po arrived in three days at Venice. There I met a Greek envoy, the eunuch Salemo, chamberlain of the palace, who had just returned from Spain and Saxony. He was anxious to sail for Constantinople and was taking there with him [another envoy]... a rich merchant of Maintz called Liutefred... who was the bearer of costly presents. Finally, we left Venice on the twenty-fifth of August and reached Constantinople on the seventeenth of September. It will be a pleasant task to describe the marvellous and unheard of manner of our reception.

Next to the imperial residence at Constantinople there is a palace of remarkable size and beauty which the Greeks called Magnavra... the name being equivalent to 'Fresh Breeze'. In order to receive some Spanish envoys, who had recently arrived, as well as myself and Liutefred, Constantine [the emperor] gave orders that this palace should be got ready and the following preparations made.

Before the emperor's seat stood a tree, made of bronze gilded over, whose branches were filled with birds, also made of gilded bronze, which uttered different cries, each according to its species. The throne itself was so marvellously fashioned that at one moment it seemed a low structure, and at another it rose high into the air. It was of immense size and was guarded by lions made either of bronze or of wood covered over with gold, who beat the ground with their tails and gave a dreadful roar with open mouth and quivering tongue. Leaning upon the shoulders of two eunuchs I was brought into the emperor's presence. At my approach the lions began to roar and the birds to cry out... but I was neither terrified nor surprised, for I had previously made enquiry about all these things from people who were well acquainted with them. So after I had three times made obeisance to the emperor with my face upon the ground, I lifted my head, and behold! The man whom just before I had seen sitting on a moderately elevated seat had now changed his raiment and was sitting on the level of the ceiling. How it was done I could not imagine, unless perhaps he was lifted up by some such sort of device as we use for raising the timbers of a wine press...

1 Opposite page: Solomon's throne. The text of the Ten Commandments in Castilian is written on the steps of the throne.

Prayer for a Soul in Purgatory

Jacobus de Voragine included in his collection of saints' lives,
The Golden Legend, *several stories used as examples (*exempla*).*
In this one he demonstrates how prayers said by the living can aid
the dead who languish in Purgatory.

Souls can reveal to the living their misery and obtain from them
offerings that will shorten their penalty. Thus we read that the

fishers of Saint-Theobald, while fishing in the autumn, caught in their nets a huge block of ice instead of fish, which pleased them more than if they had caught fishes because their bishop was suffering from pains in his feet and by applying this ice to them they would offer him a refreshing relief. But at a certain moment the bishop heard a voice coming from the ice. And when he begged the voice to identify itself, it said, 'I am a soul, imprisoned in this ice for my sins; I may be delivered if you say thirty masses for me on thirty successive days without interruption.'

The bishop had said half of this series of masses and prepared himself for the next mass when at the instigation of the devil a violent quarrel broke out in the city, which involved nearly all the inhabitants. So the bishop was called to put down the disorder; he took off his sacred vestments and could not say the mass that day. So he had to begin again from the beginning and had already accomplished two-thirds of the series when a vast army appeared to besiege the city. He was obliged to interrupt the series of masses. He began again; he had said all the masses except the last one when the palace and the bishop's property seemed about to burn down. His servants told him to interrupt the mass but he refused saying, 'Even if the whole property has to burn down, I would finish saying this mass.' The celebration was thus achieved, the ice melted immediately, and the fire which all thought they had seen straightway disappeared like a ghost, without causing the slightest damage...

I Michael wins victory over Satan with Gabriel at his side. A group of men cover their eyes while Daniel, their leader, points with his forefinger. A hand stretches out towards them from a cloud, symbolising divine intervention. The scene represents the end of iniquity and the advent of eternal justice.

101

The Feast of St Demetrios

A twelfth-century Byzantine text, called Timarion *after its hero, preserves an account of a visit to Thessaloniki at the time of the festival of St Demetrios (8 October).*

After we had visited the most sacred and holy places, where we paid the appropriate respects, we spent some time at the fair that was set up outside the city gates... The fair is the most important held in Macedonia. Not only does the native and indigenous throng pour in but also men of every conceivable race and country...

I myself, being just a Cappadocian tourist from abroad... wanted to see everything there was to see at the same time, to make sure I didn't miss a thing. So I climbed up a hill overlooking the fair where I could sit down and observe everything at leisure. And this is what there was. There were merchants' booths facing each other, set up in parallel rows. These rows extended for a long way and were far enough apart to form a walkway in the middle that was wide enough to allow space to move for the teeming crowd. Looking at the closeness of the booths and the evenness of their positioning, you could compare them to lines drawn over a long distance from two opposite points. At various points at an angle to the rows, other booths were set up. They were in rows as well, not long ones, but like the tiny feet that grow alongside reptiles' coils... I couldn't help but compare it to the centipede with a very long body showing innumerable little feet under its belly.

And... there were all kinds of men's and women's clothes both woven and spun, everything that comes from Boeotia and the Peloponnese, and all the things that merchant ships bring from Italy and Greece. Phoenicia also supplies many goods, as do Egypt, Spain, and the Pillars of Hercules, where the finest altar cloths are made. These items the merchants export directly from their respective countries to old Macedonia and Thessalonica. The Black Sea also contributes to the fair by sending across its own products to Constantinople, from where they are conveyed by large numbers of horses and mules...

When I had had a good long look at all of this... I went back into the city very keen to see other things, above all the sacred gathering.

I Opposite page: The fortified town in the centre of the illustration is probably Constantinople while it was still in Christian hands. The Golden Horn and the Bosphorus appear in the miniature, while in the foreground, palm trees mix incongruously with bulrushes.

II Above: An icon of St Demetrios holding a lance and shield. The cross was added at a later date. The tall, slender figure of the young warrior, painted around 1500, is in the tradition of the thin, elongated warrior saints of the fourteenth and fifteenth centuries.

A Cunning Escape

Anna Komnene, daughter of Emperor Alexios I, mistrusted the Norman leader Bohemund (c. 1050/8—1111), who participated in the First Crusade. As an instance of his trickery, she reported the way he escaped from Antioch by feigning his own death.

When Bohemund had neither an army on land nor a fleet at sea; and danger menaced him from both sides... he devised a plan which was exceedingly sordid, and yet exceedingly ingenious. [He] had a report spread about himself, which said that Bohemund had died, and when he found that it had taken good hold, a wooden coffin was soon prepared and a bireme, in which the coffin was placed, and also he, the living corpse, sailed away from... Antioch, to Rome. Thus Bohemund was carried across the sea as a corpse, for to all appearance he was a corpse to judge by the coffin and the demeanour of his companions (for wherever they stopped the barbarians plucked out their hair and mourned him ostentatiously), and inside he was lying stretched out dead for the time being, but for the rest inhaling and exhaling air through unseen holes. This took place at the sea-ports; but when the boat was out at sea, they gave him food and attention; and then afterwards the same lamentations and trickeries were repeated. And to make the corpse appear stale and odoriferous, they strangled or killed a cock and placed it with the corpse. And when a cock has been dead for four or five days its smell is most disagreeable for those who have a sense of smell. And this smell seemed to those who are deceived by outward appearance to be that of Bohemund's body; and that villain Bohemund enjoyed this fictitious evil all the more.

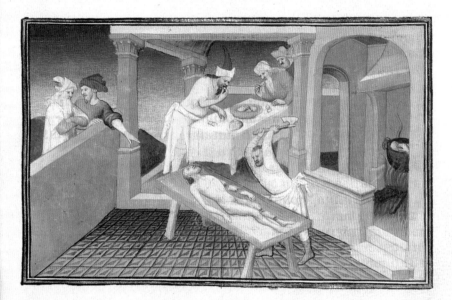

When he reached Corfu... and was now safe, he arose from the dead and left the corpse-bearing coffin there and basked in more sunlight and breathed purer air and wandered about the town of Corfu. And the inhabitants seeing him in his foreign and barbaric garb asked his lineage and his fortune, and who he was, whence he came and to whom he was going. However, he treated them all with contempt...

I Above: Cannibals on the Andaman Islands

II A section of the Mappa Mundi by Abraham Cresques of Majorca, 1375. One of the best complete maps of the period, inspired in part by Marco Polo's travel journal, it gave a physical, economic, political, historical and mythological description of his time.

105

Fiesta

An old German proverb.

No play without fools!

The Autumn of Life

From the Carmina Burana, *a collection of songs made in the twelfth century.*

While life's April blossom blew,
What I willed I then might do,
Lust and law seemed comrades true.
    As I listed, unresisted,
Hither, thither, could I play,
And my wanton flesh obey.

When life's autumn days decline,
Thus to live, a libertine,
Fancy-free as thoughts incline,
    Manhood's older age and colder
Now forbids; removes, destroys
All those ways of wonted joys.

Age with admonition wise
Thus doth counsel and advise,
While her voice within me cries:
    For repenting and relenting
There is room; forgiveness falls
On all contrite prodigals.

I will seek a better mind;
Change, correct, and leave behind
What I did with purpose blind:
    From vice sever, with endeavour
Yield my soul to serious things,
Seek the joy that virtue brings.

I Opposite page: Sobriety; Gluttony; A Frugal Meal; Dives and Lazarus. Frère Laurent, La Somme le roi. France, *c.* 1294.

II Above: 'Image of the astrologers, two and two they came and were hid in prison houses.' *Fables of the Ancients*, a book of Hebrew morality copied here in a fifteenth-century miscellany.

III Top right: 'Image of the fool behaving strangely'

IV Above: 'Image of the Interlocutor and the author, speaking to each other.'

Autumn

An anonymous Hebrew poem on the coming of autumn, written in Spain between the ninth and eleventh centuries.

The days of summer are gone. The rainy season is here. Its showers will gather, then pour themselves, more and more, upon the earth. Grain, wine, and oil will flourish quickly. The clouds will send down rain, and urge the earth to bring forth grass. Seeds and buds will grow in beauty. Voices of thunder will herald: 'Those who sow in tears shall reap with songs of joy!'

I Above: The text contains a warning that autumn may be harmful to people with a tendency towards melancholy.

II Opposite page: Preparation of linen which is said to moderate the heat of the body and can be used to dry up ulcerations.

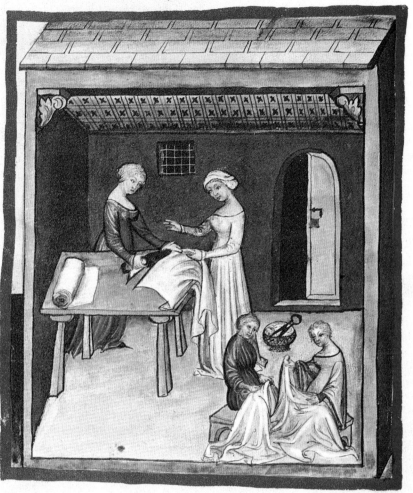

The Miracle of the Bloody Shirt

In 862 the anonymous chronicler associated with the monastery of St Bertin recorded this event, which persuaded the bishop to establish the Feast of the Virgin's Assumption in Thérouanne.

Meanwhile a miracle occurred at Thérouanne. On the morning of the day of Mary's Assumption [15 August], the slave-woman of a certain citizen of that town began to iron a linen garment, the sort called in the vulgar tongue a shirt, so that it would be all ready for her master to wear when he went to mass. The first time she put the iron down on it and pushed it across it, the shirt became stained with blood. And so it went on: whenever the slave put the iron across, blood followed it, until the whole garment was quite dyed in the blood pressed on to it. Hunfrid, the venerable bishop of that town, had the shirt brought to him and kept in the church as witness to the miracle. Because the feast of Mary's Assumption had not previously been celebrated by the inhabitants of his diocese, he gave orders that this solemn occasion should be celebrated by all and kept as a feast with due reverence.

1 This map compresses a great deal of information into a small area ⁃ it is less than 10 centimetres across ⁃ and is related to the large Ebstorf and Hereford maps. Like them, it has Jerusalem at the centre, while depicted along the right-hand edge are a series of monstrous races.

Jerusalem Fair

In the late seventh century, Adamnan, Abbot of the monastery of Iona in western Scotland, wrote down an account by Bishop Arculf of his pilgrimage to the Holy Land.

On the twelfth day of the month of September... there is an annual custom whereby a huge concourse of people from various nations everywhere is wont to come together in Jerusalem to do business by mutual buying and selling. Consequently it happens inevitably that crowds of different peoples are lodged in this hospitable city for some days. Owing to the very great number of their camels, horses, asses, and oxen, all carriers of divers merchandise, filth from their discharges spreads everywhere throughout the city streets, the stench proving no little annoyance to the citizens, and walking being impeded. Wonderful to relate, on the night of the day on which the said bands depart with their various beasts of burden, there is released from the clouds an immense downpour of rain, which descends on the city, and renders it clean of dirt by purging away all the abominable filth from the streets... The flood of heavenly waters, then, pouring through the eastern gates, and bearing all the filth and nuisance with it, enters the valley of Josaphat, swells the torrent of Cedron, and after such a baptism of Jerusalem straightway the copious flood ceases. Thus one should carefully note the magnitude and character of the honour which this chosen and famous city has in the sight of the eternal father, who does not suffer it to remain soiled for long, but quickly cleanses it out of reverence for his only begotten son, who has the honoured places of his holy cross and resurrection within the compass of its walls.

111

Pagans

Liutprand, appointed Bishop of Cremona in 962, chronicled the violent attacks of the pagan Hungarians who threatened central, eastern and western Europe.

King Henry [of Saxony] was laid up with a serious illness when he was informed of the Hungarians' near approach. He scarcely waited for the report to end but sent off messengers at once through Saxony, bidding every man who could come to him in five days under pain of death. Before the time had expired a strong army had assembled; for it is the laudable and praiseworthy custom of the Saxons to allow no male above the age of thirteen to shirk military service... A flying messenger rushed in with news that the Hungarians were at Merseburg, a castle on the borders of the Saxons, Thuringians and Slavonians. He added that they had taken a huge company of women and children prisoners and had killed an immense number of men; for they had declared, in order to strike terror into the Saxons, that they would leave no one over ten years of age alive. The king's firm courage, however, was not dismayed, but he urged his men all the more vehemently to battle, telling them it was their bounden duty to fight for their country and meet a glorious end...

The battle began immediately. From the Christians' ranks on all sides was heard the holy, and wonderous cry, 'Kyrie eleison' 'Lord have mercy upon us': from the heathen came the foul and diabolical shout 'Hui Hui'.

Before the beginning of the engagement Henry had given his men this sagacious and practical advice: 'When you are hastening forward to the first skirmish, let no one of you try to get ahead of his comrades just because he has a swifter horse. Cover yourselves on one side with your bucklers, and catch the first flight of arrows on your shields: then rush at them at full speed as furiously as you can, so that before they have time to fire a second volley they may feel the blows of our swords upon their heads.' The Saxons accordingly... advanced in level line. No one used his horse's speed to get in front of his slower neighbour, but covering themselves on one side with their shields... they caught the enemies' arrows on them and rendered them harmless. Then... they rushed at full speed upon the foe, who groaned and gave up the ghost before they could shoot again. So, by the kindness of God's grace, the Hungarians found flight preferable to battle. Their swiftest horses then seemed sluggish to them: their gorgeous trappings and bright shields appeared a burden rather than a protection. They threw aside their bows, flung away their arrows, tore off their horses' trappings, that nothing might check their speed, and thought of nothing but precipitate flight. But Almighty God, who had stripped them of courage for the fray, denied them any chance of escape. The Hungarians accordingly were cut to pieces and put to flight, the great throng of their prisoners was released, and the voice of lamentation changed to songs of joy.

I Above right: Joshua slays the kings vanquished by the Israelites.

II Opposite page: The defence of Jerusalem's walls while they are under reconstruction. The defenders of Jerusalem, with a weapon in one hand and a rod in the other, illustrate the fact that the builders had to keep one hand free at all times to defend themselves.

The Effects of Wine

Verses on the perils of drinking wine from Juan Ruiz's The Book of Good Love.

Excessive drinking shortens life and makes
the vision faint;
It takes the vital force away if drunk
without restraint;
It makes the members tremble and it gives the
mind a taint;
Indeed, with every bottle comes another new complaint.

But worst of all it fouls the breath by causing halitosis,
And science yet has found no cure for such a diagnosis,
Besides, it burns the gut and wastes the liver with cirrhosis
So, if you will succeed in love, take wine in smaller doses.

I A youth takes a ripe grape from a bunch he has just picked from the vine.

II A husband and wife sit together at a festive table. He drinks his fill while his young bride looks on.

III Opposite page: The four wives of the Great Khan and their sons, *Livre des Merveilles*, early fifteenth century, France.

A Warning Against Wine

From a question-and-answer dialogue attributed to Bede come these words of wisdom.

Better to study for one hour with the wise than to drink
wine with the foolish!

An Auspicious Birth

This is Gerald of Wales' account of the birth of a male heir to the French throne in 1165. The child, Philip Augustus, would rule from 1180 to 1223.

I think I should not pass over a thing which befell the writer of these words. When in the years of his youth he was devoting himself most zealously to the study of the liberal arts at Paris, it came to pass that at the beginning of autumn, about the first sleep when the night was yet young, the said Philip was by the grace of God born of his mother's womb. And when the fame thereof was heard in the city and received with joy inexpressible by human speech through the whole of that great city there was such a sound and clanging of bells and such a multitude of tapers were kindled through all the open places of the town, that not knowing what such a sound and unwonted tumult might mean together with such a blaze of light by night, men deemed that the city was threatened by a great conflagration. Wherefore the author of this work, a stripling living in the city and then near the completion of his twentieth year, was awakened from the bed on which he had just fallen asleep and looking forth beheld in the place without, two women old and very poor, but none the less carrying tapers in their hands and showing great joy in their faces and in every movement of their bodies running with hasty steps to meet each other as though they would dash one against the other. And when he asked them for the cause of such commotion and rejoicing, one of them looked back at him and thus made answer: 'We have a King now given us by God, an heir to the Kingdom, who by God's grace shall be a man of great might, through whom loss and dishonour, punishment and great shame, full of confusion and woe, shall befall your King'...

A Portent Of Death

In 1239 George Akropolites was a young courtier in attendance at the Byzantine palace in Nicaea, the city in Asia Minor from which the exiled Byzantine Emperor, John Doukas, planned the reconquest of Constantinople. His wife, Empress Irene, was a very educated person, interested in philosophy and science, two subjects that George had studied a little.

And when there was an eclipse, the sun travelling through the sign of Cancer at around midday, she [Empress Irene] asked me the cause of the eclipse. Now I couldn't give her a very precise answer because I had only just begun to cling to the secrets of philosophy as a young student of the wise teacher Blemmydes, but I had learned just enough so that it was reasonable for me to tell her the following:

I said that the cause of the darkening was due to the moon passing in front of the sun so that the sun appeared to lose its light; but it was not really a removal of the sun's heat and light but rather the effect of the moon when all of it enters into the shadow of the earth, for the moon takes its light from the sun.

I People praying below a sun figure. *Jacobus Omne Bonum*. English, 1360-80.

II Signalling St Cuthbert's death to Lindisfarne. From the *Life of St Cuthbert*, English 1100-99.

116

As the discussion went on for a very long time, and the doctor Nikolaos denied what I had said ، he was a man who knew absolutely nothing of philosophy though he excelled in his own discipline and most especially in practical matters. He was also a great favourite of the empress and held the honour of court physi، cian ، now when he contradicted me and I was chattering away with many words, in the middle of this exchange, the empress called me a fool.

Then as if she had caused something inap، propriate, she called to the emperor: 'I have done something un، seemly when I called this boy a fool.' The emperor replied, 'It's not important, for he's only a lad.' For I was 21 years old so the term was not unsuitable. But the empress said in response: 'It's not right for anyone who brings forth philosophical words in this way to be addressed thus by us.' I have spoken of this exchange in order to show how greatly the empress loved learning and honoured those who were knowledgeable. Then she died... and I believe that the eclipse of the sun prefigured her death.

I The battle of Gog and Magog that took place near Jerusalem. Gog is identified with the Antichrist in the
commentary written in the margins of the Alba Bible, Maqueda, Spain 1422-30.

Crusading in the West

Pope Urban II's letter to the Counts of Besalú, Empurias, Roussillon and Cerdaña, written between January 1096 and July 1099, points out that it is as worthy to fight against the Muslims in Spain as to go off to the East.

You know what a great defence it would be for Christ's people and what a terrible blow it would be to the Saracens if, by the goodness of God, the position of that famous city [of Tarragona in Spain] were restored. If the knights of other provinces have decided with one mind to go to the aid of the Asian Church and to liberate their brothers from the tyranny of the Saracens, so ought you with one mind and with our encouragement to work with greater endurance to help a church so near you to resist the invasions of the Saracens. No one must doubt that if he dies on this expedition for the love of God and his brothers his sins will surely be forgiven and he will gain a share of eternal life through the most compassionate mercy of our God. So if any of you has made up his mind to go to Asia, it is here instead that he try to fulfil his vow, because it is no virtue to rescue Christians from the Saracens in one place, only to expose them to the tyranny and oppression of the Saracens in another.

11 The Surrender of Antioch to the Saracens, the Greeks hand over the keys of the city in 632.
Livre des Merveilles, France, *c.* 1405.

Crusading in the East

Part of a letter written from Antioch in October 1098 by Bruno, a citizen of Lucca who went on the First Crusade. It is addressed to all faithful Christians.

When we who were voyaging by sea had come to Antioch, the army, which had gathered together from everywhere by land, had already surrounded the city in siege, though not very well... Our princes decided to erect a fortress at the western gate of the city. This fortress, a very short ballista-shot away [from the city], is now called by the name of the Blessed Mary. There, on that same day, in an attack of the Turks, in which they killed 2,055 of our men, we killed 800 of the enemy. From the third day, moreover, when the fortress had been erected, until the

I The War of Gath. Alba Bible, Maqueda, Spain, 1422-30.

third day before the Nones of June, our men endured many hardships, and, weakened by hunger and the sword, they toiled there at great cost. However, on this day the city was captured in the following manner: Four brothers, noble men of Antioch, on the second day of June promise to surrender the city to Bohemund, Robert Curthose, and Robert, Count of Flanders. These, however, with the common assent of all our princes, at nightfall conduct the whole army to the wall of the city, without the knowledge of the Turks. And in the morning, when the citizens of Antioch open the gates to receive the three named princes alone, according to promise, all of our men suddenly rush in together. There is the greatest clamour: our men obtain all the fortified places, except the very high citadel; the Turks, ⟋ these they kill, those they hurl to destruction over the precipice.

Hunting

In his poem on the sparrowhawk, 'The Tale of the Alerion', Guillaume de Machaut makes a brilliant comparison between a hunting bird and a lady. Here, having trapped a particularly beautiful bird, he begins to train it to hunt.

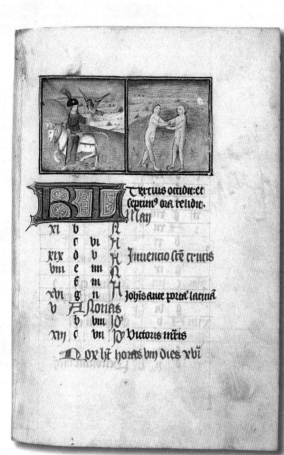

1 The sign of Gemini and a hunting scene from a fifteenth-century astrological manuscript written in Italy.

In any case, I heard a click
and knew that she was in the trap –
the noble, worthy Sparrowhawk.
Then I got up and went towards her,
and thus addressed the sparrowhawk:
'Dear friend, for you I've laboured long.
Though I've remained awake and toiled
already many nights for you,
henceforth I'll spend more sleepless nights,
for from this day my pain begins,
but that is pain that brings me joy
to my enjoyment and delight:
thus I can bear the pain with ease.'
　... Then I took apart the structure
that was put together there,
and in the trap I carried off
the sparrowhawk, which gave me joy
until I came to my retreat
rejoicing, and, when I was there
began to train her joyously.
First I set to work to make
the hawk accustomed to my touch.
When I'd done this without a hitch,
and I could hold her on my fist,
I could see by her behaviour,
by her plumage and her manner,
she would be easy to instruct,
for she learned all things easily.

Then I took thought of how I should
provide for all that she would need,
so that at once I then arranged
that she should be provided for,
Then quickly I procured for her
lunes and creances of leather.
Then I abandoned every trace
of melancholy for her sake:
no other creature mattered now,

or any other enterprise,
not past or present, or to come...
    So I possessed entirely
the sparrowhawk I cherished so:
I valued her that much and more.
Valued? Why? It was quite right
for from the loving point of view,
it's clear from what I've told of her
that she was good in every way.
Above all, she was noble, true,
and possessed of every grace
expected of a sparrowhawk
that holds to its nobility,
in plumage elegant and sleek,
in manner gay and beautiful;
I've never seen a sparrowhawk
more noble or more well behaved,
more joyful or less difficult,
or one with less presumptuousness:
but always all the courtesy
one might find in a sparrowhawk –
all these things one could find in her,
so that I kept her joyfully.
    Now I have adorned this well
when to the lady I've compared
the sparrowhawk, which always did
unfailingly what pleased me best.
My pleasure, I may well believe,
was nurtured by sufficiency,
for she was never once inclined
to do what might have displeased me:
at least, it so appeared to me,
she carried off my heart so well.
And she was then the more inclined
to let me hold and carry her.
Indeed such gracious services
were an easy burden for me.

II 'And he seized the knife to slaughter it and the bird opened
its beak and sang.'

III 'Image of the hawk hanging.' Copied from *Fables of the
Ancients*, a fifteenth-century book of moralistic tales.

123

Disruption of Trade

A letter from Isaac Nisaburi, a Jewish trader in Alexandria, to a colleague in Fustat reports on bad sailing conditions, which brought the silk trade to a standstill in September 1118.

At the arrival of the Spanish ship, all business stopped, no one sold and no one bought. After some days, small quantities were sold at the price of 21–2 (dinars) per ten (pounds).

When, however, all the ships tarried in coming, the merchants

were eager to buy, but those who had silk kept it. Today it is thirty-three days that only one ship has arrived and only one ship has sailed. Now there is much confusion and worry about the ships. For today it is twenty-three days from the Feast of the Cross and not a single ship has arrived from the Maghreb, nor has any news come from there. The winds are adverse, neither east nor west. On this very day they paid for coarse silk 23 dinars. No one sold or will sell until it is known what it will be. So please, do not move with the silk except in the event that trustworthy unravellers are available to whom you might give a small reel to unravel, good only for the countryside...

Kindest regards to you and all the friends.
And may your well-being wax indefinitely.

1 Top: Two spice merchants riding on laden camels next to the sea. Ships in the distance transport spices to the East. Pliny the Elder, *Historia Naturalis.*

The Old Nun

In the ninth century, Theodora, a wealthy young widow entered a convent in Thessaloniki. She became a most devout nun and took care of the elderly mother superior in her final illness.

When the blessed Theodora was in her fifty-sixth year... the mother superior [Anna], while walking in the courtyard without anyone to guide her, slipped and fell; and the head of her thighbone was dislocated from the right socket located at the sacral bone beneath her lower back. And from that time on she was unable to move and was confined to bed. After she had been bedridden for four years, her mind also became confused because of her extreme old age...

Then one could see the blessed Theodora ministering almost alone to Anna's every need, carrying her and frequently shifting her position, bringing her food with her own hands and taking her to the bath, and in general taking total care of her, even though Anna reviled and hit her...

When the blessed Theodora was in her sixty-eighth year, the great confessor Anna, who from childhood had donned the holy monastic habit and by the grace of God had lived a blameless life, found repose in the death that is owed to the righteous. The entire span of her life was reputedly 120 years.

II Top:'Image of the Man of God speaking in the manner for which he is praised. And the author listens because he has inclined his ear to him.' From *Fables of the Ancients,* a book of Hebrew morality tales copied here from a fifteenth-century miscellany.

III Below: A biblical illustration of the story of Jephthah's daughter, depicted in the garb of a medieval nun.

125

herre gepoten hat durch die
hant moyses zu den kindern
israhels in den veldungen
moab ouf dem iordan gegē
nericho · etetera · Die hat das
buch das do genant ist das
buch der zal ein ende · Dor
nach hebt sich an das buch
Deutronomius · das do ist
also gesprochen das buch
der anderweidunge der · e ·

virzigisten iare in dem eilsten
manden an dem ersten tage
des menedis · Moyses redte
zu den kindern israhels aller
das im unser herre hette gepo
ten ſo das her in das sagte ·
Dornach do her geslug den k
kuning seon der amorren der
do wonte zu esebon · Und og
den kuning basan der do won
te zu aseroth und zu edrai in
der erden moab · Und moyses
hub an zu berichten die · e ·
und zu sprechen · Unser her
re got hat zu uns geredt zu
oreb sprechende · Genugen
sol euch · das ir ouf dem per
ge seit gewesen · kumet und
widerkeret zu den pergen
der amorren und zu andn
steten des veldis · die in na
hen sint · Und zu den midern
steten gegen mittem tage
Und bei dem uber des meres
die erden der chananeer und
des libanischen pergis untz
bis zu dem grosen wasser eu
fraten · Secht sprach her euch
hab ich sie gegeben · Czihet
ein und besitzet die erde uber
die gesworn hat unser herre
ewern vetern abraham ysa
ac und iacob · so das her in
die gebe und irem samen noch
in · Und ich sagte euch in den
selben czeiten · Ich mag nicht

as sint die wort die do geredt
hat moyses zu allem israel
uber den iordan in den velden
der wustenunge gegen dē
roten mer · tzwischen und
tophel und laban und ase
roth · do etwas vil goldes ist
eilf tag reise von oreb durch
den wek des pergis seir untz
bis zu cades barne in dem

A Miraculous Cure of Depression

The gold statue reliquary of St Foy at Conques in France attracted pilgrims from far and wide. This story is dated by the mention of Abbot Girbert to c. 1000.

In Auvergne there was a brave warrior named Bernard... After he returned from a journey to Rome, Bernard suffered a serious physical illness. Then, when he was just beginning to regain his strength, he was denuded of every lock of hair from his head, just as the leafy-tressed forests are deprived of all the beauty of their foliage by the Ides of September. He was so ashamed of his baldness, which seemed ugly to him, that he abandoned all his martial activities and stopped going to the places frequented by the noblemen who were his peers... he began to be troubled by so much depression, which we call weakness of mind, that he thought death more desirable than life.

One night while Bernard was resting quietly beneath his bedcovers and turning over many things silently in his mind, a deep sleep crept in and dissolved all his cares. While he was in this deep sleep... behold! the glorious martyr Foy came to him, and... she immediately burst forth with these commands: 'Do not delay to go confidently to the monastery at Conques. When you have arrived, make known to Abbot Girbert in my name that in my memory he should celebrate the divine mystery before the shrine of my body, while you stand on his left side until the reading of the holy Gospel has been completed. After the offertory, when the abbot has washed his hands, collect that water. He should moisten your head, and after that you must go over to the right side of the altar.'

Bernard awakened at daybreak, leapt up from his bed, and informed his mother about the night's vision in some detail... When she had gathered provisions for the journey, she and her son travelled to the monastery. There they told Abbot Girbert about the vision point by point, but he, as is usually the case with spiritually advanced persons, immediately protested that he was not worthy of being involved in such a business. His resistance was finally overcome by their urgent pleas and he devoutly carried out everything he had been directed to do. The following night while Bernard was keeping vigil in holy prayers before the sacred virgin's mortal remains, his scalp seemed to swell with little hairs, like the head of a newborn boy. And as he was returning to his home in the morning, his head began to grow so rosy red in colour that people thought the whole top of his head was stained with fresh blood. After he got home, Bernard shaved off all that hair with a razor. New hair appeared, thicker than before; he was clothed in tresses, and through the holy martyr's intercession he was found worthy of recovering the lost glory of his hair after being bald so long.

1 Bath maids washing hair from the Wenceslas Bible. Bohemian, 1390-1400.

Pleasure Gardens

The sixth-century historian, Procopius, recorded the achievements of the Emperor Justinian (527–65), including his monuments and public building works. Here he describes the pleasure gardens outside the Byzantine capital.

As one sails from the Propontis up toward the eastern side of the city, there is on the left a public bath. This is called Arcadianae, and it is an ornament to Constantinople, large as the city is. There this Emperor [Justinian] built a court which lies outside the city, and it is always open to those who tarry there for promenades and to those who anchor there as they are sailing by. This is flooded with light when the sun rises, and when it passes on toward the west it is pleasantly shaded. And the unruffled sea flows quietly about this court, encircling it with its stream, coming from the Pontus like a river, so that those who are promenading can actually converse with those who are sailing by. For the sea preserves its depth even though it reaches up to the very foundations of the court and so is navigable there for ships, and by reason of the deep calm which prevails it brings together those on land and those on the sea so that they can converse with each other. Such, then, is the side of the court which borders on the sea, adorned by the view over it, and breathed upon by the gentle breezes which come from it. Columns and marbles of surpassing beauty cover the whole of it, both the pavement and the parts above. And from these gleams an intensely brilliant white light as the rays of the sun are flashed back almost undimmed. Nay more, it is adorned with great numbers of statues, some of bronze, some of polished stone, a sight worthy of a long description. There also the Empress Theodora [wife of Justinian] stands upon a column, which the city in gratitude for the court dedicated to her. The statue is indeed beautiful, but still inferior to the beauty of the empress; for to express her loveliness in words or to portray it in a statue would be, for a mere human being, altogether impossible. The column is purple, and it clearly declares even before one sees the statue that it bears an Empress.

I Psalm 106 from the Anglo-Saxon copy of the Utrecht Psalter, early eleventh-century

II Opposite page: The first bible of Charles the Bald known as the Vivian Bible.
The scene shows a number of monks led by Vivian presenting the bible to the Emperor. Tours, France, c. 846.

Relics

In his account of Bishop Arculf's pilgrimage to the Holy Land in the seventh century, Adamnan, Abbot of Iona, preserved the story of how Caliph Muawiya (661–80) adjudicated rival claims on the shroud, now known as the Turin Shroud.

The king of the Saracens... said: 'Give into my hand the sacred cloth that you have.' They obeyed... took it forth from its reliquary, and laid it in his lap. The king took it with great reverence, and bade a pyre be prepared in the court before all the people. When it was burning with great intensity, he got up, went right up to the pyre, and said in a loud voice to the dissident parties: 'Now let Christ the saviour of the world... judge by the flame of the fire between you who contend for this cloth, that we may know on which of these two contending bands he will deign to bestow such a gift.' And so saying he cast the Lord's sacred shroud into the flames. But the fire was completely unable to touch it. Whole and unimpaired it rose from the pyre, and began to flutter on high like a bird with outstretched wings gazing down from above on the two factions of the people... For a space of some minutes it fluttered about in the empty air, then gradually coming down it swerved by God's guidance towards the Christian party, who meantime kept beseeching Christ the judge, and it settled in their midst. Lifting their hands to heaven they give thanks to God with great rejoicing, and falling on their knees they receive with great honour this venerable gift sent down to them from heaven. They render hymns of praise to Christ its donor, and wrapping it in another cloth deposit it in a reliquary in the church. One day our brother Arculf saw it raised up from its reliquary, and in the crowded church kissed it himself amongst the multitude of people who were kissing it. It measures about eight feet in length.

I Personifications of Night and Dawn flank the prophet Isaiah. Constantinople, mid tenth-century.

II St John. Soissons Gospels, Court School of Charlemagne. Early ninth-century.

Relics of the Saints

On the route to Compostela, pilgrims were recommended by a twelfth-century guide book to visit the tombs of the saints at Arles.

First of all, those who go to Santiago by way of Saint-Gilles must visit in Arles the remains of the Blessed Trophimus the confessor... His feast is celebrated on December 29.

In like manner, one must visit too the remains of the Blessed Caesarius, bishop and martyr, who established in the same city the monastic rule and whose feast is celebrated on November 1.

In like manner, in the cemetery of the said city, the assistance of the Blessed Honoratus, bishop, should be invoked, whose solemn feast is celebrated on January 16, and in whose venerable and magnificent basilica the remains of the most illustrious martyr, the Blessed Genesius, are resting. There is... a village next to Arles called Trinquetaille where there is a certain magnificent and very high marble column... It is to this column, as it is told, that the perfidious populace tied the Blessed Genesius before beheading him. Even today it appears reddish from his rosy blood. No sooner had he been beheaded, than the saint himself, taking the head into his hands, cast it into the Rhone. As to his body, it was carried by the river as far as the basilica of the Blessed Honoratus where it honourably rests. The head, on the other hand, floating down the Rhone to the sea, led by an angel, reached Cartagena, a Spanish city, where now it splendidly rests and performs many a miracle. His feast is celebrated on August 25.

Subsequently, one should visit the cemetery next to the city of Arles, in a place called Alyscamps, and intercede there, as is customary, for the deceased with prayers, psalms, and alms. Its length and width are one mile each. In no cemetery anywhere, except in this one, can one find so many and so large marble tombs set upon the ground. They are of various workmanship and bear antique engravings...

1 A monk takes a cart bearing St Edmund's relics across the bridge to the Monastery of Bury St Edmunds. From *The Life of St Edmund, c. 1130.*

Old Age

After many years of living separately and chastely, Margery Kempe was summoned to look after her elderly husband. This English text written in about 1443 graphically illustrates many familiar problems of old age.

It happened one time that the husband of the said creature [Margery] ⁄ a man of great age, over sixty years old ⁄ would have come down from his chamber bare⁄foot and bare⁄legged, and he slithered, or else missed his footing, and fell to the ground from the stairs, with his head twisted underneath him, seriously broken and bruised, so much that he had five lined plugs in the wounds in his head for many days while his head was healing...

And, as God willed, it was known to some of his neighbours how he had fallen down the stairs, perhaps through the din and the rushing of his falling. And so they came in to him and found him lying with his head twisted under himself, half alive, all streaked with blood, and never likely to have spoken with priest nor clerk, except through high grace and miracle.

Then... his wife [Margery] was sent for, and so she came to him. Then he was taken up and his head was sewn, and was ill for a long time after, so that people thought he would die... She took her husband home with her and looked after him for years afterwards, as long as he lived. She had very much trouble with him, for in his last days he turned childish and lacked reason, so that he could not go to a stool to relieve himself, or else he would not, but like a child discharged his excrement into his lined clothes as he sat there by the fire or at the table, wherever it was, he would spare no place. And therefore her labour was all the greater, in washing and wringing, and so were her expenses for keeping a fire going. All this hindered her a very great deal from her contemplation, so that many times she would have disliked her work, except that she thought to herself how she in her young days had had very many delectable thoughts, physical lust, and inordinate love for his body. And therefore she was glad to be punished by means of the same body, and took it much the more easily, and served him and helped him, she thought, as she would have done Christ himself.

I 'Image of the miser trapped in his denial and his wife gives him balm to drink as his soul leaves him.'

II Right: The Caladrius bird was known for its power to foretell whether a sick person would live or die. If it turned away, the person was doomed but if it inclined its face towards him, he would recover.

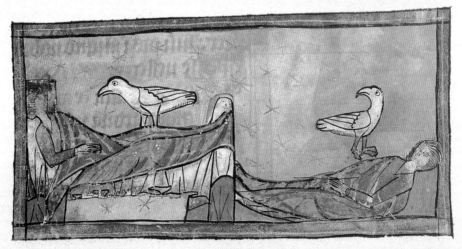

Inquisition

In central France in the thirteenth century, the inquisitor, Stephen of Bourbon, discovered practices connected with the cult of St Guinefort, the Holy Greyhound, which he considered most reprehensible.

I should speak of offensive superstitions, some of which are offensive to God, others to our fellow men. Offensive to God are those which honour demons or other creatures as if they were divine; it is what idolatry does, and it is what the wretched women who cast lots do, who seek salvation by worshipping elder trees or making offerings to them scorning churches and holy relics, they take their children to these elder trees, or to ant hills, or to other things in order that a cure may be effected.

This recently happened in the diocese of Lyons where, when I preached against the reading of oracles, and was hearing confession, numerous women confessed that they had taken their children to Saint Guinefort. As I thought that this was some holy person, I continued with my enquiry and finally learned that this was actually a greyhound...

Above all, it was women with sick or weak children who took them to this place [where the greyhound had been buried]... We went to this place, we called together all the people on the estate, and we preached against everything that had been said. We had the dog disinterred, and the sacred wood cut down and burnt, along with the remains of the dog. And I had an edict passed by the lords of the estate, warning that anyone going henceforth to that place for any such reason would be liable to have his possessions seized and then sold.

I Top: The beaver was hunted mercilessly for its testicles which were said to contain medicinal properties. Accustomed to their fate, they would bite off their own testicles, leaving them for their hunters so that their lives at least might be spared.

II 'Seen by me, Luigi of the Order of San Domenico, 1599'. The censor's comments on a Hebrew manuscript. Barcelona, *c.* 1348.

The Black Death

The Black Death provided Boccaccio with the setting for his Decameron - *one hundred stories told by seven ladies and three young men, who in 1348 sought refuge from the plague outside Florence.*

Thus, for the countless multitude of men and women who fell sick, there remained no support except the charity of their friends (and these were few) or the greed of servants, who worked for inflated salaries without regard to the service they performed and who, in spite of this, were few and far between... Out of sheer necessity, there arose among those who remained alive customs which were contrary to the established practices of the time.

With the fury of the pestilence increasing... there were many who passed away without having even a single witness present, and very few were granted the piteous laments and bitter tears of their relatives... Very few were the dead whose bodies were accompanied to the church by more than ten or twelve of their neighbours, and these dead bodies were not even carried on the shoulders of honoured and reputable citizens but rather by gravediggers from the lower classes that were called *becchini*. Working for pay, they would pick up the bier and hurry it off, not to the church the dead

I In the city of Jerusalem, men carry coffins and prepare others.

man had chosen before his death but, in most cases, to the church closest by, accompanied by four or six churchmen with just a few candles, and often none at all. With the help of these *becchini*, the churchmen would place the body as fast as they could in whatever unoccupied grave they could find without going to the trouble of saying long or solemn burial services.

The city was full of corpses... things had reached such a point that the people who died were cared for as we care for goats today... So many corpses would arrive in front of a church every day and at every hour that the amount of holy ground for burials was certainly insufficient for the ancient custom of giving each body its individual place; when all the graves were full, huge trenches were dug in all of the cemeteries of the churches and into them the new arrivals were dumped by the hundreds; and they were packed in there with dirt, one on top of another, like a ship's cargo, until the trench was filled...

More than one hundred thousand human beings are believed to have lost their lives for certain inside the walls of the city of Florence, whereas before the deadly plague, one would not even have estimated there were actually that many people dwelling in the city.

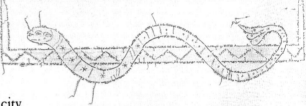

II Top: The valley of dry bones. The image reflects Ezekiel's vision of the resurrection of the dead after the coming of the Messiah.

III Saul consults the witch at En-dor. Alba Bible, Maqueda, 1422-30.

137

Coping with Plague

The Black Death, which ravaged Europe in the years 1347–51, caused a major demographic disaster, reducing the population by perhaps as much as a quarter. Among those who survived it, Tommaso del Garbo developed hygienic practice that remained standard for centuries.

Notaries, confessors, relations and doctors who visit the plague victims on entering their houses should open the windows so that the air is renewed [i.e. the corrupt air], and wash their hands with vinegar and rose water and also their faces, especially around their mouth and nostrils. It is also a good idea before entering the room to place in your mouth several cloves and eat two slices of bread soaked in the best wine and then drink the rest of the wine. Then when leaving the room you should douse yourself and your pulses with vinegar and rose water and touch your nose frequently with a sponge soaked in vinegar. Take care not to stay too close to the patient.

The Epitaph of Harald

In the second half of the tenth century, this rune epitaph was carved on the Jelling stone, which was erected at Jutland, Denmark.

King Harald ordered this monument to be made in memory of Gorm, his father, and in memory of Thyre, his mother. This was the Harald who conquered the whole of Denmark and Norway, and made the Danes Christian.

I Top left: Monks with plague being blessed by a priest. Jacobus Omne Bonum, English, 1360-80.

II Left: The death of a king. Latin Bestiary, 1260-80.

III Top: A Viking warship. Anglo-Saxon view of the Viking raids, 1025-50.

IV A regal burial. Alba Bible, Maqueda, Spain, 1422-30.

A Miraculous Icon

In the late thirteenth century, Manuel Philes wrote a series of epigrams associated with the shrine of the Virgin of the Source in Constantinople. The female patron who commissioned this one is otherwise unknown.

On behalf of Kasiane Raoulaina to an icon of the Mother of God

O you who delivered Eve from her intense suffering
 And do sympathetically watch over my birth pangs
(For God [was born] of you without the natural pain of childbirth)
 Accept this thank-offering, holy Virgin,
 You, through whom my infant child who all but died
Lives and breathes beyond [all] hope.
 For you are life and the source of miracles,
  Washing away the mud of sin.
 Maria Kasiane, the daughter of Raoul,
of the lineage of the Komnenoi,
 Has spoken these words to you in gratitude.

Birth

In his Memoirs, *Guibert of Nogent (c.1064–c.1125) describes his own birth.*

As she approached the end of her pregnancy my mother had been in the most intense pain throughout the season of Lent. How often she reproached me in later years for those pangs of childbirth when she saw me straying and following the slippery downhill path! Finally Holy Saturday, the solemn vigil of Easter, dawned. My mother was wracked with continuous pain. As the hour of delivery approached, the pains increased, but they were presumed to lead to a natural delivery. Then I turned around in her womb, with my head upward. My father, his friends, members of the family, all feared for both our lives. The child, they thought, was hastening the mother's death; and the offspring's exit from the world at the very moment he was being denied an entrance into it added to their sense of pity... The family held an urgent meeting. They rushed to the altar of the Mother of God, to the one who was, and ever will be, the only Virgin to give birth, they made the following vow and left it as an offering at our lady's altar: if the child were male, it would be consecrated a cleric in God's service and hers; if the child were of the lesser sex, it would be given over to a corresponding religious vocation.

At that moment a frail little thing came forth, looking almost like an aborted foetus, except that it was born at term. It looked like a most miserable being, and the only reason for rejoicing was that the mother had been saved. This tiny human being that had just seen the light was so lamentably frail that it looked like the corpse of a stillborn baby... On the same day, as I was brought to the baptismal font... a woman kept rolling me over from one hand to the other and saying: 'Do you think this little creature's going to live? I guess Mother Nature never quite finished this one. She gave him an outline more than a body.'

... If it is obvious and irrefutable that one's merits cannot precede the day of one's birth, they can, nevertheless, precede the day of one's death; but if one's life is spent without doing good, then I think it makes no difference whether the day of one's birth, or death, was glorious or not.

I Right: Eve gives birth to Cain, her hand raised to her head in an expression of pain that denotes how he was born tainted with original sin. The tree of knowledge is seen here with two types of leaves. The serpent points his red tongue of blame at Eve. Adam in the earlier scenes has blond hair but later it becomes red to signify his sin. The scenes are linked by the River of Paradise.

II Opposite page: The legendary Dame Trotula of Salerno was attributed authorship of the best known work on obstetrics in the Middle Ages. She was hailed as 'an empress among midwives' and is seen here holding an orb.

141

Cohitus

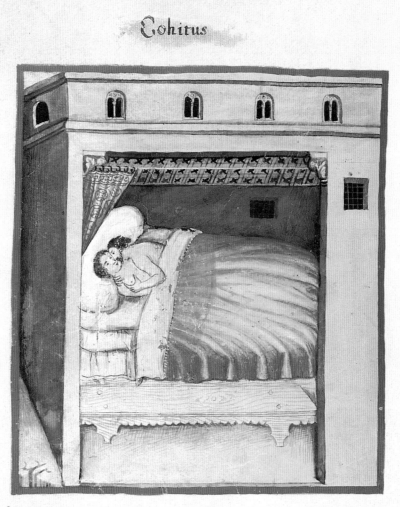

Restriction of Prostitution

In this regulation of 1393, the City of London tried to restrict the activity of female prostitutes, identified by their hoods of striped cloth.

... and whereas many and divers affrays, broils, and dissensions, have arisen in times past, and many men have been slain and murdered, by reason of the frequent resort of, and consorting with, common harlots, at taverns, brewhouses of hucksters [peddlers] and other places of ill-fame, within the said city, and the suburbs thereof; and more especially through Flemish women, who profess and follow such shameful and dolorous life: ∕ we do by our command forbid, on behalf of our Lord the King, and the Mayor and Alderman [sic] of the City of London, that any such women shall go about or lodge in the said city, or in the suburbs thereof, by night or by day; but they are to keep themselves to the places thereunto assigned, that is to say, the Stews [bathhouses] on the other side of the Thames, and Cokkeslane; on pain of losing and forfeiting the upper garments that she shall be wearing, together with her hood, every time any one of them shall be found doing to the contrary of this proclamation.

I The Marriage Bed. *Theatrum Sanitatis*. Italian, *c.* 1400.

II Opposite page: The Bath House. Valerius Maximus, *Des faits des Romains*, French, fifteenth-century.

Reform of Prostitution

The Byzantine Emperor, Michael IV (1031–41), was a great philanthropist. His contemporary, the historian Michael Psellus, describes how 'he devised a plan for the salvation of lost souls'.

Scattered all over the city was a vast multitude of harlots, and without attempting to turn them away from their trade by argument ‚ that class of woman is deaf anyway to all advice that would save them ‚ without even trying to curb their activities by force, lest he earn the reputation of violence, he built in the Queen of Cities a place of refuge to house them, an edifice of enormous size and very great beauty. Then, in the stentorian notes of the public herald he issued a proclamation: all women who trafficked in their beauty, provided they were willing to renounce their trade and live in luxury, were to find sanctuary in their building: they were to change their own clothes for the habit of nuns, and all fear of poverty would be banished from their lives for ever... Thereupon a great swarm of prostitutes descended upon this refuge, relying on the emperor's edict, and changed both their garments and their manner of life, a youthful band enrolled in the service of God, as soldiers of virtue.

Ballade

Dante (1265–1321)
began his lyrical work,
New Life, *aged twenty-seven,*
two years after the death
of Beatrice, who inspired it.

Ballade, I want you to seek out Love,
and with him go before my lady...
With sweet melody, when you are with him,
begin these words,
after you have asked for mercy:
'My lady, he who sends me to you,
when it pleases you, desires
that if he had an excuse you may hear it from me...
Tell her: 'My lady, his heart has attended
with such steadfast faith
that in your service he has been moulded by every thought:
from the first he has been yours, and never has he strayed.'
... Through the grace of my sweet melody
remain here with her,
and of your servant speak what you will;
and if through your prayer she forgives him,
have her fair countenance announce to him peace.
My gentle ballade, when it pleases you,
go forth at that moment when you may receive honour.

I Top: 'Sing to the Lord.' Below the staves are the
words, 'There is none like thee among the gods' written
in Hebrew. From a thirteenth-century book of Psalms.

II Opposite page: Emily making a garland. Giovanni
Boccaccio, French, *c.* 1470.

145

An Accusation of Rape

Froissart records a case of alleged rape, which occurred in 1386 when Sir Jean de Carrouges left his wife in charge of their castle and a local squire, Jacques Le Gris, took advantage of his absence. The account opens with a description of the squire.

[He] was a man of humble birth who had risen in the world, favoured by fortune as many people are. But when they are right on top and think themselves secure, fortune flings them back into the mire and they end up lower than they began...

It happened that Sir Jean de Carrouges made plans to go on an expedition overseas ⁄ a thing he had always been fond of doing ⁄ to help him in his advancement. He bid his wife who was young, beautiful, good, sensible and modest in her behaviour a loving goodbye, as knights do when they leave for distant lands...

It then happened ⁄ and this was the whole point at issue ⁄ that, through a strange, perverse temptation, the devil entered the body of Jacques Le Gris... His thoughts became fixed upon Sir Jean de Carrouges' wife, who he knew was living almost alone with her servants in the castle of Argenteuil. So he left Alençon one day on a good horse and spurred swiftly forward until he reached the castle. The servants welcomed him in, because he and their master both served the same lord and were companions⁄in⁄arms. In the same way, the lady, not suspecting anything wrong, gave him a friendly reception, led him to her room and showed him a number of her things. Bent on his evil design, Jacques asked the lady to take him to see the keep, saying that that was partly the object of his visit. The lady agreed without question and the two of them went to it alone...

No sooner had they entered the keep than Jacques le Gris shut the door behind him. The lady paid little attention to it, thinking that the wind had blown it shut... And when they were alone there together, Jacques Le Gris, ensnared by the wiles of the Enemy, put his arms round her and said: 'Lady, I swear to you that I love you better than my life, but I must have my will of you.'

The lady was astounded and tried to cry out, but the squire stuffed a little glove which he carried into her mouth to silence her, gripped her tight for he was a strong man and pushed her down to the floor. He raped her, having his desire of her against her will. When this was done, he said: 'Lady, if you ever mention what has happened, you will be dishonoured. Say nothing and I will keep quiet too for your honour's sake.' The lady, weeping bitterly, replied: 'Ah, you wicked, treacherous man, I will keep quiet but not for as long as you will need me to.'

She then opened the door of the room in the keep and came down, followed by the squire...

The young wife shut herself in her room and there gave way to bitter lamentations... She revealed nothing to any of her servants, feeling sure that if she did so she was more likely to incur blame than credit. But she fixed firmly in her memory the day and the time when Jacques Le Gris had come to the castle.

I Above: 'The Little Nun Who Left Her Convent and Walked Off Into the Century.' The young nun escapes from her convent but takes the veil again thirty years later after seeing the Virgin in a dream. By the renowned and prolific early fourteenth-century artist, Jean Pucelle.

II Opposite page: 'The Lover Contemplates his Lady.' From *Le Remède de Fortune c.* 1350, one of the outstanding works of the fourteenth-century.

Trial by Combat

When Sir Jean de Carrouges was told by his wife that she had been raped by the squire Jacques Le Gris, he believed her innocence and tried to obtain justice on her behalf, while Le Gris denied everything. The fourteenth-century chronicler, Froissart, records the outcome of their dispute.

The legal proceedings went on for more than a year and a half... After much deliberation and argument the court pronounced that, since the lady of Carrouges could not prove anything against Jacques Le Gris, the matter should be settled by a duel to the death...

The day of the combat arrived at about the beginning of the year counted as 1387 according to the custom of Rome. The lists were prepared in St Catherine's Square, behind the Temple. The King of France was there with his uncles and vast crowds of people came to watch... Before the knight entered the lists, he went over to his wife, who was sitting clothed in black in a carriage draped entirely in black also, and said to her: 'Lady, on your evidence I am about to hazard my life in combat with Jacques le Gris. You know if my cause is just and true.' 'My lord,' said the lady, 'it is so. You can fight confidently. The cause is just.' 'In God's hand be it then,' said the knight. He kissed his wife, pressed her hand, then made the sign of the cross and entered the lists...

When the two champions had taken the oath, as is usual before such combats, they were placed opposite each other and told to say why they had come together. They then mounted their

I A mock joust between children riding deer. The lances are rendered inoffensive by two small white pinwheels.

148

horses and sat them very prettily, for both were skilled in arms. The first part of the combat was a joust, in which neither of them was injured. They then dismounted and continued on foot, both fighting very courageously. The first to suffer was Sir Jean de Carrouges, who was wounded in the thigh, to the great alarm of his supporters, but he fought on so stoutly that he felled his opponent, and, thrusting his sword into his body, killed him on the spot. He turned and asked whether he had done his duty and was told that he had. Jacques Le Gris' body was delivered to the executioner of Paris, who dragged it to Mountfaucon and hanged it there.

Then Sir Jean de Carrouges went up to the King and kneeled before him. The King made him rise and presented him with a thousand francs, making him also a member of his chamber with a pension of two hundred francs a year for life. After thanking the King and the great nobles, the knight went to his wife and kissed her, then they went together to the Cathedral of Notre-Dame to make their thank-offerings before returning to their house.

Swimming

In the ninth century, the Frankish court poet and historian, Einhard, wrote a biography of the Emperor Charlemagne. He captures much of the ruler's character through descriptions of his activities.

The Emperor was strong and well built... He spent much of his time on horseback and out hunting, which came naturally to him, for it would be difficult to find another race on earth who could equal the Franks in this activity. He took delight in steam-baths at the thermal springs, and loved to exercise himself in the water whenever he could. He was an extremely strong swimmer and in this sport no one could surpass him. It was for this reason that he built his palace at Aachen and remained continuously in residence there during the last years of his life and indeed until the moment of his death. He would invite not only his sons to bathe with him, but his nobles and friends as well, and occasionally even a crowd of his attendants and bodyguards, so that sometimes a hundred men or more would be in the water together.

1 Pharoah in a suit of golden armour seen crossing the Red Sea in pursuit of the Israelites.
The illuminator follows the biblical text: 'You split the sea before them; they passed through
the sea on dry land, but You threw their pursuers into the depths, like a stone into the raging waters.'

11 Scenes from a fourteenth-century treatise on bathing and the taking of thermal baths.

Rape

In 1405, Christine de Pizan wrote her most famous prose work, The Book of the City of Ladies, *in which Reason, Justice and Rectitude help her to construct a city peopled by distinguished women. Here she consults Rectitude about the argument made by men that many women want to be raped, even when they protest verbally.*

[Rectitude] answered, 'Rest assured, dear friend, chaste ladies who live honestly take absolutely no pleasure in being raped. Indeed, rape is the greatest possible sorrow for them...

The story of the noble queen of the Galatians, the wife of King Orgiagon, is appropriate to this subject. When the Romans were making their great conquests in foreign lands, they captured this king of the Galatians in battle, and his wife along with him. While they were in the Roman camp, the noble queen, who was quite beautiful, simple, chaste and virtuous, greatly pleased one of the officers of the Roman army, who was holding the king and queen prisoner. He entreated her and coaxed her with fine presents, but after he saw that pleading would not work, he violently raped her. The lady suffered terrible sorrow over this outrage and could not stop thinking of a way to avenge herself, biding her time until she saw her chance. When the ransom was brought to deliver her husband and herself, the lady said that the money should be turned over in her presence to the officer who was holding them. She told him to weigh the gold to have a better count, so that he would not be deceived. When she saw that he intended to weigh the ransom and that none of his men would be there, the lady, who had a knife, stabbed him in the neck and killed him. She took his head and without difficulty brought it to her husband and told him the entire story and how she had taken vengeance...

It was the same when a city in Lombardy was once captured by its enemies who killed the lord. The beautiful daughters of this lord, thinking that their enemies were going to rape them, found a strange remedy, for which they deserve much praise: they took raw chicken meat and placed it between their breasts. This meat quickly rotted because of the heat so that when the enemies approached them and smelled the odour, they immediately left, saying, 'God, how these Lombards stink!' But this stink made them quite fragrant indeed.

I Opposite page: Jael kills Sisera by driving a stake into his blood-stained temple.

II A woman on the ramparts shows Sheba's head to Joab who is leading his soldiers, in order to stop him from destroying her town.

Winter

From the chronicle written in the early ninth century by Theophanes, a Byzantine monk.

In the same year [762], starting in early October, there was very bitter cold, not only in our land, but even more so to the east, the north, and the west, so that on the north coast of the Pontos to a distance of 100 miles the [Black] sea froze from the cold to a depth of thirty cubits... All this ice was snowed upon and grew by another twenty cubits, so that the sea became indistinguishable from land: upon this ice wild men and tame animals could walk from the direction of Chazaria, Bulgaria and other adjoining countries. In the month of February of the same second indiction this ice was, by God's command, split up into many different mountain-like sections, which were carried down... the Straits... and reached the City and filled the whole coast... Of this I was myself an eyewitness for I climbed on one of those icebergs and played on it together with some thirty boys of the same age... One of the icebergs struck the jetty of the Acropolis and crushed it. Another huge one struck the wall and shook it greatly so that the houses on the inside partook of the quake. It then broke into three pieces and ringed the City from the Mangana to the Bosphoros, rising in height above the walls.

I Above: A fishing scene from an eleventh-century Greek manuscript.

II Opposite page: Foetal positions. Physicians had puzzled over how to depict the foetus in the womb for several centuries, in particular over the question of twins emerging simultaneously. English, fifteenth-century manuscript.

An Orphaned Child

This tenth-century account records the capture of three Greek monks and a boy living in southern Italy by Arab pirates from Africa, and their successful ransom.

In the district of Calabria there is a monastery inhabited by pious and virtuous monks, one of whom found a child for sale. He purchased the child and raised him with care. He also taught him how to read and write in the hope of tonsuring him and clothing him with the monastic habit. One day, three of the monks decided to go down to the sea to fish and as they went along, they took the child with them. When they came to the sea, some Saracens from Africa were there with their ship and seized them. When the abbot and fathers of the monastery learned of this, they suffered no small grief, especially the monk who was master to the boy. [He then offered to go and ransom the captives.]

As he was walking through the market place [in Africa], his child came face-to-face with him. Taking and embracing him, the monk asked him with tears in his eyes: 'Oh child! What has become of you?' The child replied: 'Worthy father, a man who is an enemy of God purchased me. He abuses me every day, coercing me to become a Muslim. But my trust is in God and in your holy prayers that I will not do that, even if I have to die.'

... [The monk works various miracles and is summoned to the African ruler.] The Prince of Believers said: 'Since it has been made known to us that you are a servant of God, we will surrender the three monks and the youth to you free of charge. This we do so that you will remember us too in your prayers to God.'

155

Piracy

The journeys of the Polo brothers to the Great Khan of China between 1260 and 1295 involved Marco's return through India.

You must know that from Malabar, and from the neighbouring province called Gujarat, more than 100 ships cruise out every year as corsairs, seizing other ships and robbing the merchants. For they are pirates on a big scale. I assure you that they bring their wives and little children with them. They spend the whole summer on a cruise and work havoc among the merchants...

Gujarat likewise is a great kingdom. The people are idolaters and have a king and a language of their own and pay tribute to none. The country lies towards the west. Here the Pole Star is still more clearly visible, with an apparent altitude of six cubits. In this kingdom are the most arrant corsairs in the world. Let me tell you one of their nasty tricks. You must know that, when they capture merchants, they make them drink tamarind and sea-water, so that they pass or vomit up all the contents of their stomachs. Then the corsairs collect all that they have cast up and rummage through it to see if it contains any pearls or precious stones. For the corsairs say that when the merchants are captured they swallow their pearls and other gems to prevent their discovery. That is why they do not scruple to treat them to this drink.

I Opposite top: The island of Sumatra.

II Opposite bottom: How the soldiers of the Great Khan were unable to land in Java. *Livre des Merveilles* an anthology of Marco Polo's travels between 1271 and 1295, written around 1405 and presented to Jean, Duc de Berry in 1413.

Dangerous Games

The Book of Chivalry, *written by a French knight in the mid-fourteenth century, set standards for all forms of courtly behaviour.*

All young men who desire to attain... an honourable status... should not concern themselves too much with nor devote too much attention to any game where greed might overcome them, such as the game of dice, for it is no longer a game when it is engaged in through greed for gain. And what usually happens is that when one thinks one will win another's money, one loses one's own, and there are many who lose three hundred, five hundred, a thousand *livres*, and more of their money...

There is also a game called real tennis at which many people lose and have lost some of their chattels and their inheritance; and while playing such games, one would not want to see nor meet any men of good standing for whom it would be necessary to leave the game and speak to them and keep them company. One should leave playing dice for money to rakes, bawds, and tavern rogues...

The situation is the same for real tennis; women have greatly suffered over this, for ball games used to be women's pastime and pleasure. Yet it should be apparent that the finest games and pastimes that people who seek such honour should never tire of engaging in would be in the pastimes of jousting, conversation, dancing, and singing in the company of ladies and

damsels as honourably as is possible and fitting, while maintaining in word and deed and in all places their honour and status.

I Top: The valiant knight saves the damsel in distress from the jaws of the green dragon.

II Left: Scipio and Laelius play chess while Scaevola plays pelota.

Music

In the twelfth-century Anglo-Norman epic, The Romance of Horn, *musical expertise is highly praised.*

In those days everyone knew how to play the harp well: the higher the rank, the greater the knowledge of the art. It was now Gudmod's turn to entertain them with it... He did not want to refuse them... Then he took the harp, for he wanted to tune it. Lord, whoever then watched his knowledgeable handling of it, how he touched the strings and made them vibrate sometimes causing them to sing and at other times join in harmonies, would have been reminded of the harmony of heaven! Of all the men there, this one caused most wonder. When he had played his notes, he began to raise the pitch and to make the strings give out completely different notes. Everyone was astonished at his skilful handling of it. And when he had done this, he began to sing the lay of Baltof... loud and clearly, just like the Bretons, who are versed in such performances. Next he made the harp strings play exactly the same melody as he had just sung. He performed the whole lay for them and did not want to omit any of it. And Lord, how his audience then had occasion to love him!

I Above: A scene from the Barcelona Haggadah. Written before 1248, the manuscript is an important early source for musicologists as it contains twenty-eight different musical instruments.

Courtship

When Horn, disguised as the less high-born Gudmod, arrived at court, he attracted the attention of not only the king's sons, who took him hunting, but also their sister Lenburc. The Romance of Horn *records their courtship over a game of chess.*

One day as they returned from their sport in the forest, the king's sons had the idea that they would like to go and divert themselves in Lenburc's rooms: they would drink good wine, spiced and unspiced, with her, play chess and listen to the harp because those were the things they enjoyed most... The two brothers went to their sister's chambers. The elder brother took his chess-player with him who played very well ⁄ that was his entire occupation ⁄ and his strong knight, the best he had, and the younger took Gudmod, who was no boaster...

She called to a boy to fetch the chessmen and sat down with the expert player at the chessboard... The knight who was outplayed was very vexed...

Then on all sides they begged Gudmod to play and Lenburc greatly desired it above all the rest, so much did she long for them to be close enough together that he could be touched on hand or foot... They sat down and set out their chessmen and she who had checkmated the other man moved first.

Now they played the game in such a way that not a word was spoken suggesting discourtesy, but whatever was said expressed good manners. They played four games skilfully, one after the other, without her winning a fig's worth in any of the them. Nevertheless it seemed as if it did not grieve her, because she loved him so much she did not envy him. But if anyone else had done it, she would have been very cross, even had it been the king, who had so tenderly brought her up. Then Gudmod rose and Lenburc begged him to play one more game, for the love of his sweetheart. And Gudmod, laughing, gently admonished her not to entreat or say another word about it to him.

160   1 A lover presenting his songs to his lady from the Manasse Codex.

A Game of Chess

In The Ruodlieb, *an eleventh-century epic romance, the eponymous hero reports on his mission to a foreign kingdom, where the ruler negotiated over a game of chess.*

The king, asking for a table, ordered that a chair be brought for him and ordered me to sit down on the bench opposite him to play with him. I declined firmly, saying, 'It is fearful and lamentable to play against a king.' But when I saw that I dared not withstand him, I determined to play, hoping to be beaten by him. I said: 'Poor me! How can being beaten by the king hurt me? But, my Lord, I am afraid that you will soon be angry with me, if fortune is pleased to give the victory to me.' The king smiled and said as if in jest: 'My dear fellow, there is no need for you to have any fears in this matter. I shall not be roused to anger if I never win, but I want you to play with me as intently as you can; you see, I want to learn the moves you make of which I am ignorant.' At once the king and I began to play eagerly, and, may thanks be to her [Fortune], the victory fell to me three times; many of his nobles were utterly astounded at this. He laid a wager against me, but wanted me to wager

nothing against him, and he gave me what he had put down, because he didn't have a pea left... I said: 'I am not in the habit of winning anything by playing games.' They (the nobles) replied: 'While you live amongst us, you live as we do! When you get back home, then you can live as you like.' I refused what they held out to me for a time, and then took them. Fortune gave me presents as well as praise...

1 Chessplayers. Shirvan, 1468.

Normans

In September 1066 William of Normandy invaded England and defeated the Anglo-Saxon King Harold. The Anglo-Saxon Chronicle *preserves several accounts, including this one which reveals a particularly English point of view.*

Then Count William came from Normandy to Pevensey on Michaelmas eve, and as soon as they were able to move on they built a castle at Hastings. King Harold was informed of this and he assembled a large army and came against him at the hoary apple-tree. And William came against him by surprise before his army was drawn up in battle array... There King Harold was killed... and the French remained masters of the field... Count William went back to Hastings, and waited there to see whether submission would be made to him. But when he understood that no one meant to come to him, he went inland with all his army that was left to him and that came to him afterwards from overseas, and ravaged all the region that he overran until he reached Berkhamsted. There he was met by Archbishop Aldred and Edgar and Edwin and Morcar, and all the chief men from London. And they submitted out of necessity after most damage had been done... And they gave hostages and swore oaths to him. And he promised them that he would be a gracious liege lord, and yet in the meantime they ravaged all that they overran. Then on Christmas Day, Archbishop Aldred consecrated him king at Westminster. And he promised Aldred on Christ's book and swore moreover... that he would rule all this people as well as the best of the kings before him if they would be loyal to him. All the same he laid taxes on people very severely, and then went in spring overseas to Normandy, and took with him Archbishop Stigand, Edgar and Edwin and Morcar and many other good men from England. And Bishop Odo and Earl William stayed behind and built castles far and wide throughout this country, and distressed the wretched folk and always after that it grew much worse. May the end be good when God wills!

A Race

In The Saga of Sigurd the Crusader, *King Sigurd's son Magnus makes a bet with Harald Gille, who claimed that 'men may be found in Ireland, that no horse in Norway can run past them'.*

Magnus answered: 'I will not go to Ireland; we two shall bet here, and not there.' Harald then went to sleep and would have no more talk with him. This happened in Oslo. Next morning after Mass, Magnus rode up in the street; he sent word to Harald to come there. And when he came he was clad in this way; he had on a shirt and breeches with straps, a short cape, an Irish hat on his head, and a spear shaft in his hand. Magnus set up a mark for the race. Harald said: 'You make the run too long.' Magnus straightway made it much longer and said that this was even then all too short. Many men were present. They then began the race and Harald always kept pace with the horse. And when they came to the end, Magnus said: 'You held to the saddle strap and the horse pulled you.' Magnus had a very fast horse from Gautland. They now ran the race again and Harald ran all the time in front of the horse. And when they came to the end of the race, Harald asked: 'Did I hold on to the saddle strap then?' Magnus said: 'You were first off.'

Then Magnus let his horse breathe a while, and when he was ready, he smote the horse with his spurs and straightway came at a gallop. Harald then stood still and Magnus looked round and shouted: 'Run now,' he said. Then Harald ran and at once came forth past the horse and much farther in front and so to the end of the race; he was so much to the fore that he lay down and sprang up and greeted Magnus when he came.

1 Horses were regarded as being completely loyal beasts
and are depicted here fighting alongside their masters.
Bestiary Latin, *c.* 1255.

A Boar Hunt

Before keeping his appointment with the Green Knight, Sir Gawain stayed at an unknown castle and spent Christmas with an unidentified castellan. He was encouraged to sleep late while his host, who was in fact the Green Knight, went out hunting.

The cock having crowed and called only thrice,
The lord leaped from bed, and his liegemen too,
So that mass and a meal were meetly dealt with,
And by first light the folk to the forest were bound
For the chase. Proudly the hunt with horns
Soon drove through a desert place;
Uncoupled through the thorns,
The great hounds pressed apace.
By a quagmire they quickly scented quarry and gave tongue,
And the chief huntsman urged on the first hounds up,
Spurring them on with a splendid spate of words.
The hounds, hearing it, hurried there at once,
Fell on the trail furiously, forty together,
And made such echoing uproar, all howling at once,
That the rocky banks round about rang with the din.

Hunters inspirited them with
  sounds of speech and horn.
Then together in a group, across
  the ground they surged
At speed between a pool and a
  spiteful crag.
On a stony knoll by a steep cliff
  at the side of a bog,
Where rugged rocks had roughly
  tumbled down,
They careered on the quest, the
  cry following,
Then surrounded the crag and
  the rocky knoll as well,
Certain their prey skulked inside
  their ring,
For the baying of the bloodhounds
  meant the beast was there.
Then they beat upon the bushes
  and bade him come out,
And he swung out savagely
  aslant the line of men,
A baneful boar of unbelievable size,
A solitary long since sundered
  from the herd,
Being old and brawny, the biggest of them all,
And grim and ghastly when he grunted: great was the grief
When he thrust through the hounds, hurling three to earth,
And sped on scot-free, swift and unscathed.
They hallooed, yelled, 'Look out!' cried, 'Hey, we have him!'
And blew horns boldly, to bring the bloodhounds together...
Then men shoved forward, shaped to shoot at him,
Loosed arrows at him, hitting him often,
But the points, for all their power, could not pierce his flanks,
Nor would the barbs bite on his bristling brow...
But when the boar was battered by blows unceasing,
Goaded and driven demented, he dashed at the men,
Striking them savagely as he assailed them in rushes,

I Above: The temptation of Sir
Gawain by the wife of his opponent
from *Sir Gawain and the Green Knight*,
c. 1400, possibly the earliest illustrated
work of literature in English.

II Opposite page: November.
A hunting scene from a German
manuscript calendar. The enraged
boar is trapped in a snare in a winter
landscape.

165

So that some lacking stomach stood back in fear.
But the lord on a lithe horse lunged after him,
Blew on his bugle like a bold knight in battle,
Rallied the hounds as he rode through the rank thickets,
Pursuing this savage boar till the sun set...
The castellan coursed across the country time and again,
Hunted his hapless boar as it hurtled over the hills...
But in time he became so tired he could tear away no more,
And with the speed he still possessed, he spurted to a hole
On a rise by a rock with a running stream beside.
He got the bank at his back, and began to abrade
    the ground,
The froth was foaming foully at his mouth,
And he whetted his white tusks; a weary time it was
For the bold men about, who were bound to harass him
From a distance, for none dared to draw near him...
Till the castellan came himself, encouraging his horse,
And saw the boar at bay with his band of men around.
He alighted in lively fashion, left his courser,
Drew and brandished his bright sword and boldly
    strode forward,
Striding at speed through the stream to where the savage
    beast was.

The wild thing was aware of the weapon and its wielder,
And so bridled with its bristles in a burst of fierce snorts
That all were anxious for the lord, lest he have the worst of it.
Straight away the savage brute sprang at the man,
And baron and boar were both in a heap
In the swirling water: the worst went to the beast,
For the man had marked him well at the moment of impact,
Had put the point precisely at the pit of his chest,
And drove it in to the hilt, so that the heart was shattered,
And the spent beast sank snarling and was swept downstream,
Teeth bare.
A hundred hounds and more
Attack and seize and tear;
Men tug him to the shore
And the dogs destroy him there.

III Top: Bestiary Latin, c. 1255.

Teaching

The following story records a situation well known to both teachers and pupils. It was written by Arcoid, canon of St Paul's, London, in the mid-twelfth century.

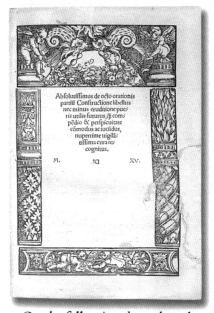

In the catholic community of St Paul's in London there was a certain scholar, Elwin by name, a man noted for his morality and learning...

One day he had expounded to one of his pupils, in the usual grammar-school fashion, a passage that the boy was to recite the following day, and he threatened him repeatedly with a severe flogging if he should not be able to recite it...

The boy, on the other hand, who was at that tender, undisciplined age, was seduced by his peers into playing games, and forgot both his teacher's warning and his own lessons. On the following day, when the time for the recitation was at hand... the boy could not think of any way of saving the situation... After much fretting and anguishing it occurred to [him] that he might avoid and escape punishment by fleeing or by praying to a special person... He quickly got up and fled away and came to the church in which rested the body of St Erkenwald, and there he prostrated himself at St Erkenwald's side. It has not been revealed to human understanding what the boy said as he prayed... we must believe, however, that his contrite, humbled heart was pleasing to God...

Well, the master... went into the school as usual and when he did not find the boy there, realizing that he had run away, he acted on intuition and came straight to the place where the boy was lying in humble prayer to the saint... The teacher dragged him out of the church and made him stand in the school to suffer his angry judgement... It pleased the schoolmaster... to hear the boy recite to him; he intended that as often as he found him making an error in his lesson he would give him two stripes with the rod...

But by the prayers and merits of Erkenwald, himself a wonderful teacher, wisdom was suddenly with the boy... not only did he repeat, without stumbling and without assistance, what the master had assigned, but also, to the latter's amazement, he recited at length and completely from memory what the teacher had been about to give him for the next assignment! Then indeed the teacher came to his senses... and forgave the boy.

I Above: A medieval hand ball game.

II Top: An elementary grammar for use in St Paul's School, London, published in 1515.

Dance

In the fifteenth century, Guglielmo Ebreo of Pesaro wrote a treatise on The Art of Dancing.

Whoever wishes diligently to pursue the science and art of dancing with a joyful spirit and a sincere and well-disposed mind must first understand, with resolute heart, reflecting mind, and with consideration, what dance is in general and its true definition; which is none other than an outward act which accords with the measured melody of any voice or instrument. This act is composed of and bound to six rules or principal elements which are the following: Measure, Memory, Partitioning the Ground, Air, Manner, and Body Movement. These six elements must be minutely and perfectly grasped and kept well in mind, for if one of these is lacking in any way, the art [of the dance] would not be truly perfect... They are the foundation, the means, and the true introduction to the complete and perfect art of the dance.

Rules for women

It behoves the young and virtuous woman... to behave and conduct herself with far more discretion and modesty than the man. She therefore should fully understand and observe perfectly the aforesaid elements, rules, and exercises... The movement of her body should be humble and meek, and her carriage dignified and stately; her step should be light and her gestures shapely. Nor should her gaze be haughty or roaming (peering here and there as many do), but she should for the most part keep her eyes modestly on the ground; not, however, as some do who sink their head on their breast. Rather, she should carry it upright, aligned with the body, as nature itself - as it were - teaches us. And when she moves she should be nimble, light, and restrained... Then at the end of the dance, when released by the man, she should, turning her sweet gaze on him alone, make a courteous and tender bow in answer to his...

On Dancing In Long Attire

Note that someone dancing in a long garment should dance with solemnity and in a different fashion... All his gestures and movements should be grave and as refined as his attire requires, and of an apt fashion, because the *turca* or long robe that he is wearing would not work with too much moving here and there... since a short garment requires dancing a little more vigorously...

On Dancing With A Cape

Note further that another sort of dancing is required when wearing a short cape as opposed to a *turca* or even a [short?] garment. And the reason is, the cape catches the wind, so that as you do a jump or a turn, the cape swings about. And with certain gestures and movements, and with certain rhythms, you need to hold your cape by an edge, and with [other] rhythms you have to hold both edges, which is a lordly thing to see when done in time. And if this is not done when the rhythms require it, it is a sign of little skill.

Opposite page: King Solomon and the Queen of Sheba. From The Song of Songs, Winchester Bible.

Dance Song

An anonymous Provençal dance song of the twelfth century about a loveless marriage: Coindeta sui, si cum n'ai greu cossire.

I'll tell you why I'm someone else's lover:
(I'm lovely but miserable)
I'm fresh and young, I've a dainty body,
(I'm lovely but miserable)
and I ought to have a husband who can make me glad,
someone I can play and laugh with.
(I'm lovely but miserable
because of a husband I don't want or desire).

God knows I'm not the least in love
with him.
(I'm lovely but miserable)
I've little wish to make love with him.
(I'm lovely but miserable)
I'm filled with shame to look at him.
I wish that death would do him in.
(I'm lovely but miserable
because of a husband I don't want
or desire).

1 Male and female bathers exchange glances in a historiated letter which forms the first word of a chapter on bathing. From *Li livres dou santé,* by Aldobrandino da Siena.

But let me say one thing:
(I'm lovely but miserable)
this friend of mine makes it up to me in love,
(I'm lovely but miserable)
I indulge in fondest, sweetest hopes;
I cry and sigh when I don't see or gaze at him.
(I'm lovely but miserable
because of a husband I don't want or desire).

And let me say another thing:
(I'm lovely but miserable)
since my friend has loved me a long time,
(I'm lovely but miserable)
I'll indulge in love
and fondest hopes for the one I crave.

(I'm lovely but miserable
because of a husband I don't want or desire).

I've made a pretty dance song to this tune,
(I'm lovely but miserable)
and I ask everyone to sing it, far and wide.
(I'm lovely but miserable)
And let all learned ladies sing it too,
about my friend whom I love and long for.
(I'm lovely but miserable
because of a husband I don't want or desire).

II Above left: Psalm 33 from a thirteenth century Psalter: 'Praise the Lord with the lyre…Sing to him a new song, play skilfully on the strings…'

III Above right: From a fourteenth century thunder-chart, illustrated for the benefit of semi-literate people. In this instance the image suggests there should be 'Concord among the people.'

Entertainments

During the marriage feast of the Infanta Doña Blanca and the Infante Don Enrique in 1440, elaborate constructions were built in order that the guests could overlook the jousting as well as a pond and a copse during the four-day fiesta.

The knights and gentlemen danced at the palace; there were also mummers, running of bulls, and jousts... On the fourth day, the Count had an immense room built in a large fenced meadow behind his palace. In this artificial hall, a very high stage was built, requiring twenty steps to ascend to the top. It was covered with grass to look like a natural mound. There sat the Queen, the princess and the countess of Haro on rich scarlet brocade, as befitted such great ladies.

On the side of the meadow, there was a list for a joust with twenty knights and gentlemen. On the other side there was a pond which had been specially stocked for the feast with large trout and barbel. As the fish were caught, they were brought to the princess. In another part of the meadow, there was a beautiful copse of trees, which the Count had ordered to be stocked with bears, boars, and deer. The wood was surrounded by almost fifty huntsmen with 'gentle' mastiffs, grey-hounds and hounds in such a manner that no animal was able to escape. Unleashing the dogs, the huntsmen pursued and killed the beasts and brought them to the princess. And it seemed a very strange thing that in a house so many different sports could be carried out at the same time...

After the joust, the hunt and the fishing had been concluded, the dance began lasting almost all day... The Count generously distributed money to the trumpeters and minstrels from two large bags of coins...

That way the feast ended and all went to sleep the few hours of the night that were left.

1 Opposite page: The opening page of Book IV of Virgil's *Aeneid*. Naples *c.* 1470-1500.

The Pleasures of Music

In his fifteenth-century treatise on dancing, Guglielmo Ebreo of Pesaro reflects on the 'sublime and lofty art of music', which he reckons to be not the least important of the seven liberal arts.

In some ways Music suits and befits human nature more than any other [art] inasmuch as, through the four principal and concordant voices of which it is formed and composed (corresponding to our four principal humours), it offers, as we listen, singular comfort to all our senses, as if it were our souls' most natural food. Nor does it seem that there is anyone in the world so uncouth and barbarous as not to be moved to utmost pleasure by the sweet song and the pleasant sound of a well-tuned instrument. Thus is it truly written of renowned Orpheus that he played his sweet-sounding *cithara* with such grace as to soothe not only the spirits of men, but wild Pluto and the infernal deities, as well as brutish animals, ferocious lions, and other savage beasts. The great sweetness [of music] also transmuted the very nature of rocks and hills into a more kindly one; as in the tale of Amphion of yore who, according to the poets, with the fair sound of his *cithara*, made the stones descend from the high hills and arrange themselves miraculously into the building of the high walls of the city of Thebes. And I could similarly describe many others who, through the sweetness and virtue of this delightful and most pleasurable science, wrought extraordinary changes and marvellous motions in the world.

I Three young, richly clothed couples move elegantly to the music played by two lutenists.

174   II Opposite page: Torch-dance at a feast; bowling hoops. From a Flemish calendar of the early sixteenth century.

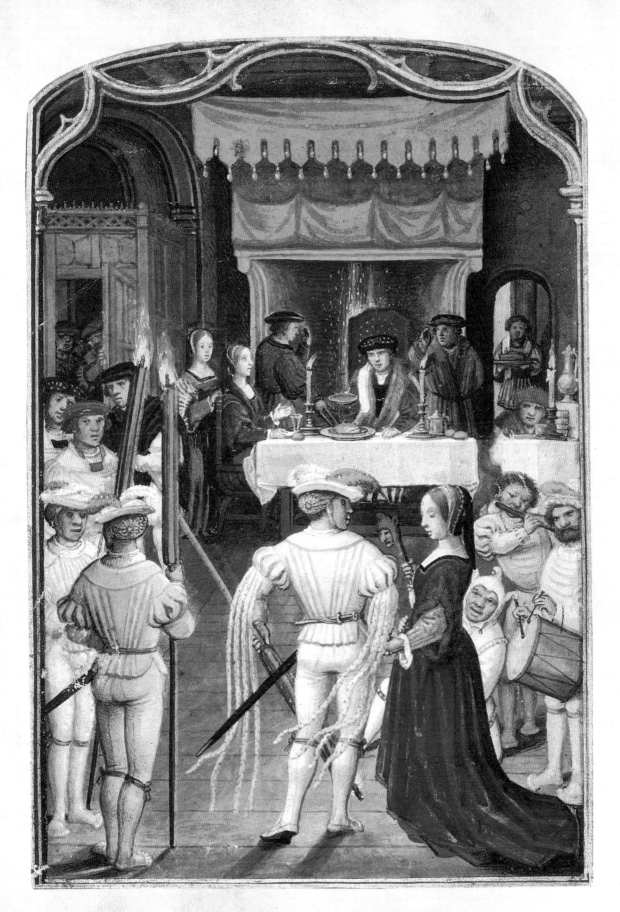

Prayer to the Virgin

St Anselm (1033–1109) served as Abbot of Bec and Archbishop of Canterbury in the period of Gregorian reform. He also wrote numerous works, including prayers.

Mary, holy Mary,
among the holy ones the most holy after God.
Mother with virginity to be wondered at,
Virgin with fertility to be cherished,
you bore the Son of the most High,
and brought forth the Saviour of the
lost human race.
Lady, shining before all others with
such sanctity,
pre-eminent with such dignity,
it is very sure that you are not least in
power and in honour.
Life-bearer, mother of salvation,
shrine of goodness and mercy,
I long to come before you in
my misery,
sick with the sickness of vice,
in pain from the wounds of crimes,
putrid with the ulcers of sin,
However near I am to death, I reach
out to you,
and I long to ask that by your
powerful merits
and your loving prayers,
you will deign to heal me.

Good Lady,
a huge dullness is between you and me,
so that I am scarcely aware of the extent of my sickness.
I am so filthy and stinking
that I am afraid you will turn your merciful face from me.
So I look to you to convert me,
but I am held back by despair,
and even my lips are shut against prayer...

I Above: Christ Enthroned. From a magnificent thirteenth-century choir book, Florence.

II Opposite page: The Genealogy of Christ.

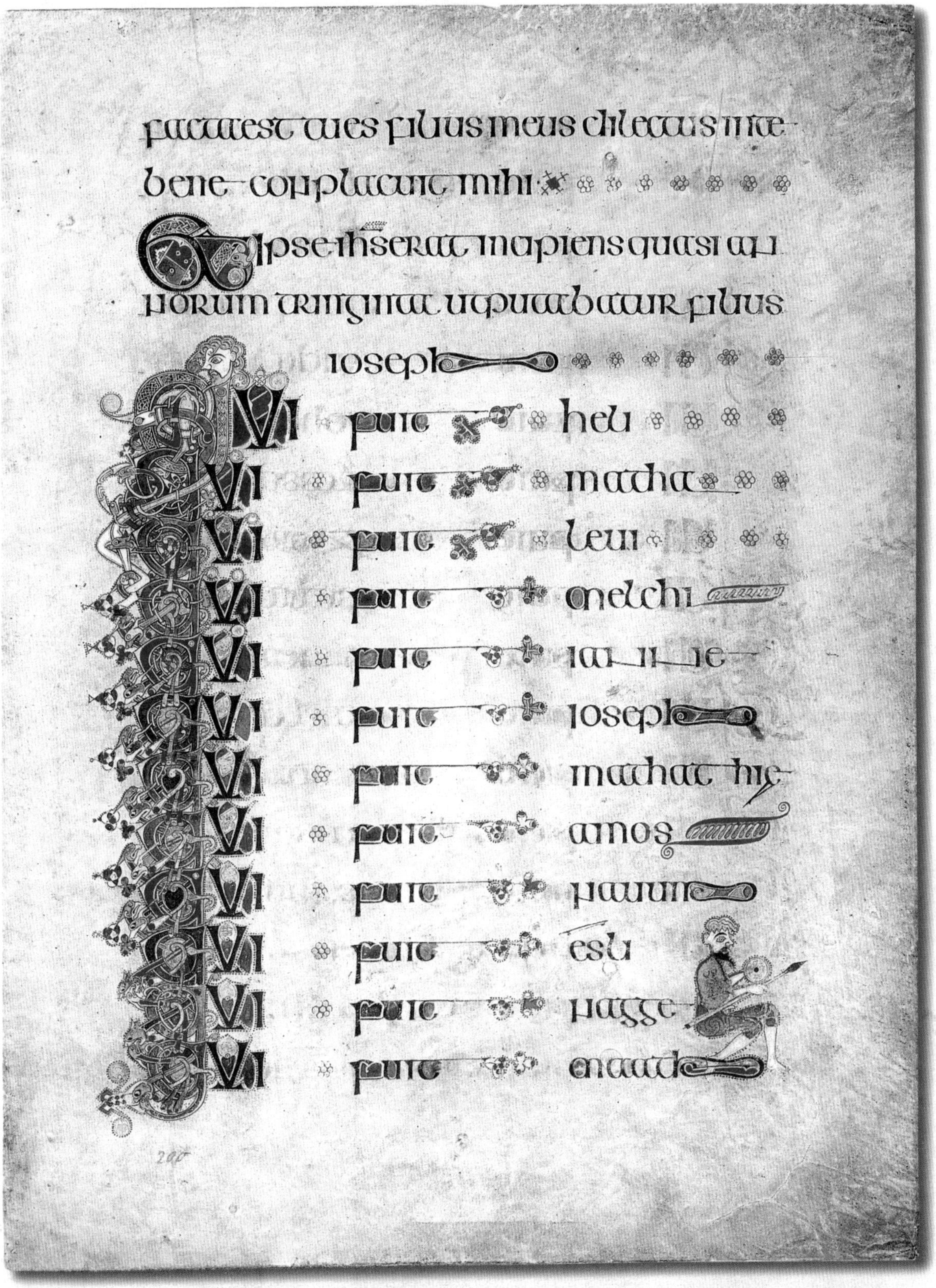

Christmas

A fourteenth-century description of King Arthur's celebration of Christmas.

This king lay at Camelot one Christmastide
With many mighty lords, manly liegemen,
Members rightly reckoned of the Round Table,
In splendid celebration, seemly and carefree.
There tussling in tournament time and again
Jousted in jollity these gentle knights,
Then in court carnival sang catches and danced;
For fifteen days the feasting there was full in like measure
With all the meat and merry-making men could devise,
Gladly ringing glee, glorious to hear,
A noble din by day, dancing at night!
All was happiness in the height in halls
    and chambers
For lords and their ladies, delectable joy...

Mass sung and service ended, straight
    from the chapel
The King and his company came
    into hall.
Called on with cries from clergy
    and laity,
Noël was newly announced, named
    time and again.
Then lords and ladies leaped forth,
    largesse distributing,
Offered New Year gifts in high voices,
    handed them out,
Bustling and bantering about these offerings...
And all this merriment they made until meal time.
Then in progress to their places they passed after washing,
In authorised order, the high-ranking first;
With glorious Guinevere, gay in the midst,
On the princely platform with its precious hangings
Of splendid silk at the sides, a state over her
Of rich tapestry of Toulouse and Turkestan
Brilliantly embroidered with the best gems
Of warranted worth that wealth at any time
Could buy.

I Above: Wedding Celebration. *Histoire de Regnault de Montauban*. French, second half of the fifteenth century.

II Opposite page: Scenes from the Life of Christ. The De Lisle Psalter, English, fourteenth-century.

179

Snow

A harsh winter in 874 attracted the attention of the anonymous chronicler of the monastery of Fulda.

The winter was very hard and longer than usual; there were also great falls of snow from November 1 to the vernal equinox [March 21] without intermission, and these caused great difficulty to men wanting to go to the woods to collect fuel. Hence it came about that not only animals but also many men died of cold. The Rhine and the Main were frozen by the intense cold and for a long time would bear the weight of those who set foot on them.

I Opposite page: Hail beating the trees. Emilia, Italy, 1470-71.

II Above: It was said that the deeper a stallion placed his muzzle in water when he drank, the more virile he was likely to be. However, his virility would be impaired if his mane was cut. Bestiary in Latin, 1230-40.

The Virgin's Complaint

The Jewish poet, Immanuel of Rome (1261–1332), depicts the problems of a young girl with older sisters, who may never be able to raise the money for a dowry, and thus would never get married.

My breasts are firm and my hair is long, yet I still sit in nakedness and shame. My poverty has frightened away all the suitors, and I sit [as if] at the head of the table in a house of mourning.

How can my heart ever rejoice when all my silver is gone and I have no gold or bronze? How will I ever find a husband, when all I have are three older [impoverished] sisters and a groaning heart?

How can I tell, suitors, if my bones will be scorched [by desire] or if I will be able to strike a bargain with treacherous Time? My years are flying away, spreading their wings like locusts!

And what is more, the wise men sit and scheme together against me: 'She that dies a virgin is cut off; she will have no share in the world to come!'

Poverty

In the first half of the fourteenth century, this message was carved in runes on a wooden stick excavated in Bergen, Hordaland, Norway. It is a communication between two trading partners, Thorir and Havgrim, who rent business premises from a landlord in Bergen. Thorir here gives instructions to look after Sigrid and to conceal the bad news of his poverty, particularly from a man called Thorstein Long – for what reason we do not know.

Thorir the Fair sends God's and his own greetings, true fellowship and friendship to Havgrim, his partner. There is much I lack, partner. There is no beer, nor is there any fish. I want you to know this, and don't ask anything from me. Tell the landlord to come south to see how things are with us. Encourage him to do this, but demand nothing for my sake; and don't let Thorstein Long know about any of this. Send me some gloves. If Sigrid needs anything, then get it for her. Promise me that you will not rebuke me for my poor state.

1 Top: David and Bathsheba. David leans down from a flat roof and watches Bathsheba bathing, her long hair falling over her naked breasts.

11 Astronomers at the top of Mount Athos. From the travels of Sir John Mandeville, Bohemia, fifteenth century.

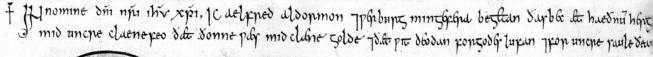

+ In nomine dni nri ihu xpi, Ic ælfred aldormon ⁊ wærburg min gefera begetan ðas bec æt hæðnum herge mid uncre claene feo ðæt ðonne wæs mid clæne golde ⁊ ðæt wit deodan for godes lufan ⁊ for uncre saule ðear

XP AUTEM
GENERATIO
SIC ERAT CUM ESSET DIS
PONSATA MATER EIVS
MARIA IOSEB ANTEQ͡VA
CONVENIRENT INUENTA
EST IN UTERO HABENS

Ond wordon ðæm woldan ðæt ðas bec noldan ... æt hæðnum beoc lonce ⁊ nu wille hæððissre punadci, ⁊ nu willað heo ᵹᵹellan in to ...
... godes lufan ⁊ for uldne ⁊ for sonde ⁊ þis dropunce to donenne, ⁊ ðæm ᵹodcundan ᵹeðic ...
de in myrcþ cyrcan ... godhlor nþud, to ðæm þeade ðæt heomon arede æᵹhwelce monaðe for ælfred
⁊ for wærburᵹe ⁊ for alhðryðe heora saulum to ecum lace dome, ða hwile ðe ᵹod ᵹehᵹen hæbbe ðæt fulþiht æt ...
ðosse stowe beon mote. Ec swelce ic ælfred dux ⁊ wærburᵹ biddað ⁊ halsiað on ᵹodes almaehtiges noman ⁊ on allra
his haliᵹna ðæt nænigmon ... ᵹeo to donᵹedyrstiᵹ ðætte ðas bec hæᵹen bloc aselle oðde aðiode fromcryrch cypean ðahwile

The Will of Alfred

Before his death in 899, the Anglo-Saxon King Alfred revised his will and destroyed all copies of the previous one he had made.

... I, Alfred, king of the West Saxons, by the grace of God and with this witness, declare what I desire concerning my inheritance after my lifetime. First, I grant to Edward my elder son the land at Stratton... and Hartland... and I entreat the community at Cheddar to choose him on the terms which we have previously agreed...

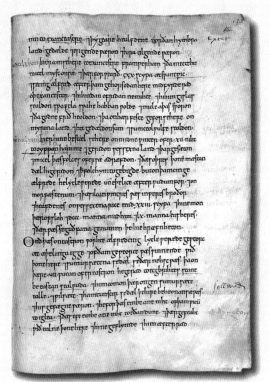

And to my two sons 1,000 pounds, 500 pounds each; to my eldest daughter, to the middle one, to the youngest and to Ealhswith... 100 pounds each. And to each of my ealdormen 100 mancuses [a money of account worth 30 pennies], and to Æthelhelm, Æthelwold, and Osferth likewise. And to Ealdorman Æthelred a sword worth 100 mancuses. And to the men who serve me, to whom I have just now given money at Eastertide, 200 pounds are to be given and divided between them... And to the archbishop 100 mancuses, and to Bishop Esne and to Bishop Werferth and to the bishop of Sherbourne. Likewise, 200 pounds is to be distributed for my sake, for my father and the friends for whom he used to intercede and I intercede, fifty to the mass-priests throughout all my kingdom, fifty to the poor servants of God, fifty to the poor and destitute, fifty to the church in which I shall rest. I do not know for certain whether there is so much money, nor do I know whether there is more, though I suspect so. If there is more, it is to be shared among all those to whom I have bequeathed money...

My grandfather had bequeathed his land on the spear side and not on the spindle side. If, then, I have given to any one on the female side what he acquired, my kinsmen are to pay for it... because they are receiving my property, which I may give on the female side as well as on the male side, whichever I please.

And I pray in the name of God and of his saints that none of my kinsmen or heirs oppress any of the dependants among those whom I have supported; and the councilors of the West Saxons

I Above: *The Anglo-Saxon Chronicle* was the first history of England written in the vernacular and was commissioned by King Alfred during his reign, 871-99.

II Previous page: The portraits of the Evangelists, St Matthew and St John probably produced at Canterbury in the mid-eighth century. The script and ornament unite in a composition of astonishing virtuosity.

pronounced it right for me that I could leave them free or servile, whichever I should choose. But I desire for the love of God and for the needs of my soul that they be entitled to their freedom and their free choice. And in the name of the living God I command that no man should oppress them either with claims for money or with anything, in such a way that they cannot choose whatever lord they desire.

The Death of Guillaume Champlitte

The fourteenth-century Chronicle of Morea *records the conquest and occupation of southern Greece by western crusaders after 1204. Guillaume Champlitte, grandson of the first Prince of Morea, died in 1278.*

He drew up his will with great care... He commanded and ordered that after he had died, and not before a full year had passed, his bones alone were to be placed in a coffin in the church of St Jacob of Morea in Andravida, in this church which he had built and which he had given to the Temple, in the tomb he had built and in which lay his father; his brother to lie to the right of him, he to be on the left, and his father in between. He instructed and endowed four chaplains, whom all the Romans call *heireis* [priests], to continue without cease unto eons of eons to chant and celebrate masses everlastingly for their souls...

And when he arranged all these things... he surrendered his soul, and the angels took it and bore it to where all the righteous are found; commemorate him, all of you; he was a good prince. Behold the evil that befell, for which the small and great of Morea must grieve, for he did not leave a male, son of his body, to inherit the land which his father had won with such travail. But, on the contrary, he produced daughters and his labours went wasted; for it is never found established that a female child may inherit a lord's inheritance, for at the very beginning a curse was laid upon woman; and never in his life should a lord who had produced daughters as heirs rejoice...

I Above: St Alban's Psalter. The Entombment, *c.* 1119-23

II Right: Four scenes from the Gospels. Constantinople, eleventh century.

I Above: Distribution of wheat and alms by the Great Khan in times of famine. 'Livre des Merveilles', a magnificent manuscript about Marco Polo's travels. France, c. 1405.

II Top: The annual birthday celebration of the Great Khan.

Riches

Sir John Mandeville's account of his travels to the Far East, probably written in 1355, proved immensely popular, despite the fact that it was mainly a pastiche of information from other accounts.

The land of Cathay is a great country, beautiful, rich, fertile, full of good merchandise. Every year merchants come there to get spices and other sorts of merchandise - they go there more frequently than they do elsewhere. You should understand that the merchants who come from Venice or Genoa or other places in Lombardy or the Greek Empire travel by land and sea for eleven or twelve months before they get to Cathay, the chief realm of the Great Khan...

The Emperor can spend as much as he wishes to, for he coins no money except from leather, or paper, or the bark of trees. When this money gets old, and the printing on it is defaced by heavy use, it is brought to the king's treasury and his treasurer gives new for old. This money is printed on both sides, like money is in other countries, and it is current throughout the Great Khan's lands. They make no money there of gold and silver, when it is brought thither by different nationalities from other lands, but the Emperor has his palace adorned with it and makes useful things of it as he pleases. In his chamber on a pillar of gold is a ruby and a carbuncle, each a foot long; and this carbuncle lights all the chamber at night. He also has many precious stones and rubies in his chamber; but those two are the greatest and most precious of all.

III Top: 'Image of the diligent loyal one, with a great crown of gold and with a garment of fine linen and purple.'

IV Above: 'Image of the eagle and his guests eating.' *Fables of the Ancients*, from the Rothschild Miscellany, Italy, 1470-80.

Travel

In the years 1399–1402 Emperor Manuel II Palaiologos made a long tour of European capitals in search of military aid for the Byzantine Empire against the Turks. From London early in 1401, he wrote to his teacher and friend, Manuel Chrysoloras.

Now what is the reason for the present letter?... Most important is the ruler with whom we are now staying, the king of *Bretania* the Great [Henry IV, 1399–1413], of a second civilized world, you might say, who abounds in so many good qualities and is adorned with all sorts of virtues...

This ruler, then, is most illustrious because of his position, most illustrious too because of his intelligence; his might amazed everyone, and his understanding wins him friends; he extends his hand to all and in every way he places himself at the service of those who need help. And now, in accord with his nature, he had made himself a virtual haven for us in the midst of a twofold tempest, that of the season and that of fortune, and we have found refuge in the man himself and in his character. His conversation is quite charming he pleases us in every way; he honours us to the greatest extent and loves us no less. Although he has gone to

extremes in all he had done for us, he seems almost to blush in the belief ⁄ in this he is alone ⁄ that he might have fallen considerably short of what he should have done. This is how magnanimous the man is... In the end he has given greater proof of his nobility by adding a crowning touch to our negotiations, worthy of his character and of the negotiations, themselves. For he is providing us with military assistance, with soldiers, archers, money and ships to transport the army where it is needed.

[Sadly, Manuel was to be disappointed in the amount of help forthcoming, but the Mongol defeat of the Turks in 1402 brought Byzantium some relief.]

I Above: 'Image of the judge and the eloquent ministers consulting and taking counsel'.

II Right: An encounter between an old king and a young black woman. From *Fables of the Ancients*, by Isaac Ibn Sahula, 1281, part of the Rothschild Miscellany, Italy 1479.

A Byzantine Emperor Abroad

Manuel II's visit to London in 1401 was commented on by many observers, including the chronicler, Adam of Usk.

This Emperor always walked with his men, dressed alike and in one colour, namely white, in long robes cut like tabards; he finding fault with the many fashions and distinctions in dress of the English, which he said indicated fickleness and changeable temper. No razor touched head or beard of his chaplains. These Greeks were most devout in their church services, which were joined in as well by soldiers as by priests, for they chanted them without distinction in their native tongue... I thought within myself, what a grievous thing it was that this great Christian prince from the farther east should perforce be driven by unbelievers to visit the distant lands of the west, to seek aid against them.

1 How the Great Khan sent his brothers with messages for the Pope. *Livre des Merveilles,* early fifteenth century.

Death

In the mid-eleventh century, the Byzantine historian, Michael Psellus, lost his daughter in an outbreak of smallpox. This is part of the oration he wrote for her funeral.

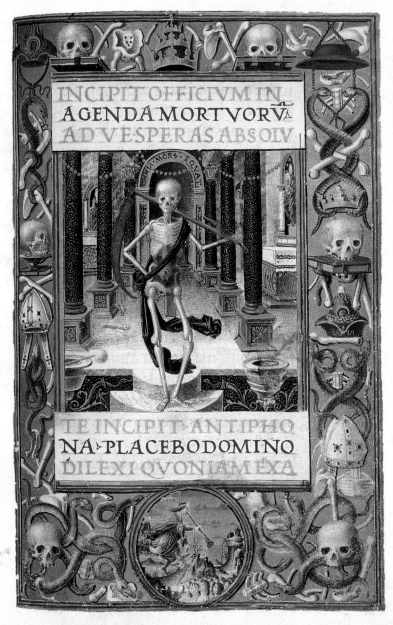

God let this maiden, so good, so modest and so beloved, be encircled by pestilential disease... It began by altering the entire structure of the body, and in the beginning filled it with fever. Then blisters appeared and spread like grapes all over the surface of the skin and having destroyed the harmony of her body left it horrible to see...

So she lay there crushed by innumerable, festering sores (in number and kinds one could hardly imagine). They were around the openings of her ears, around her nostrils, in her throat and even on the palate of her mouth, causing pain and difficulty in the ailing girl. But as the twentieth day dawned we had better hopes: for the sores dried up and began to fall from her body like flakes. But then suddenly what happened to her, who seemed like a wrecked ship that had just been towed to port? Violent fever came on, we know not from where or how, and it consumed the remaining flesh while she lay there as if embalmed. Yet she endured the unbelievable flames without complaint... She displayed fortitude like a diamond...

Above: Death, the 'Grim Reaper.' *Mirandola Hours.* Written in Padua or Venice, *c.* 1499.

When the maiden sensed that the end was near, as she was unable to speak or cry out, she motioned to her mother with senseless, inarticulate sounds. Then raising her hands a little, hands that had been destroyed by sores and were without skin or bones, she joined these to her mother's and gave what I thought was the last embrace. This gesture burned and tore the mother's heart and brought streams of tears to the eyes of all those present. For they were parents too and shared our woe...

But then the moment of death passed and the thirtieth day came and she lay there, voiceless and in a hurry to leave this world. The crowd of people around her were crying and striking their breasts in lamentation, and wished that they too could die along with the expiring girl. Then she gave up her spirit to the glowing angels standing by her side.

O my child, formerly so beautiful and now a frightful sight to see!... Go then on that good, eternal journey, and rest in those heavenly places. Shine in spirit among the Prudent Virgins. And reveal yourself in our dreams as you were prior to your illness, bringing solace to our hearts... You will thus bring joy to your parents; and they may recover a little from this heavy sorrow.

It has been shown that nothing is stronger than Nature; nor is there anything more calamitous than the loss of a child.

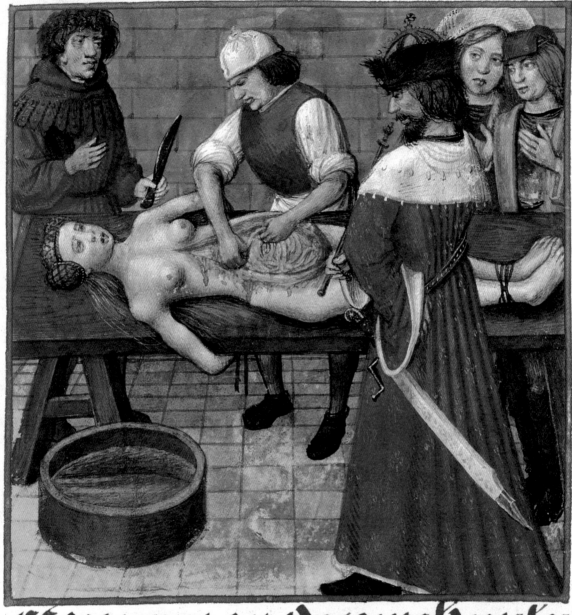

Et pour ce que veoir il vouloit
Le lieu ouquel conceu lauoit

1 Nero watches while his mother is dissected.
From the *Roman de la Rose*, Flemish, c. 1500.

Burial

The ceremony of burial of William of Trumpington, Abbot of St Alban's monastery on 27 February 1235.

The body was stripped and washed and, if he had not shaved the day before, his tonsure and beard would certainly have to be shaved. Then some, but by no means all, of the more senior and prudent monks and a single secular servant, namely the sacrist's assistant, who was to undertake the task of anatomist, were admitted, and the body was opened with an incision from the trachea to the lower part. Everything found in it was placed, sprinkled with salt, in a cask, which was reverently interred in the cemetery with blessings and psalms... The body was washed

and soaked inside with vinegar, a great deal of salt was sprinkled into it, and it was sewn up. This was done with care and prudence lest the body, which had to be kept for three or more days, should give off an offensive smell and occasion some unpleasantness to those handling it when it was buried. By this time, not without the admiration of many, the body was so clean and spruce, and the face so rubicund and unblemished, that to many it seemed pleasant and desirable to touch it with their hands and carry it on their shoulders like some saint. And so you would see some of the brothers grieving, wringing their hands, weeping, lamenting, and gently and tenderly kissing his vivid face while embracing him with both hands; for he looked as if he was asleep, rather than dead...

The body was carried into the church, while a bell was solemnly peeled, and the convent followed it singing the customary psalms. There, in the sight of the entire convent and anyone else who was present, the abbot's seal was broken with a hammer on a stone step in front of the high altar, so that all the embossing, that is the image and the lettering, was effaced. From then on there was no lack of solemn and assiduous psalmody, by night and by day; and solemn mass [was celebrated] daily at the high altar as is the custom for a deceased brother, in albs at prime and in copes for those in the choir, with numerous candles lit. This continued till the day of his reverent obsequies... Meanwhile, a lengthy distribution of alms to the poor was made, while everyone groaned over the loss of such a great and good shepherd of souls and bodies.

A Byzantine View of Crusaders

In 1204 the historian Niketas Choniates was inside the city of Constantinople when the western crusaders broke through the triple walls and thoroughly sacked the Byzantine capital. He gives here an eye-witness account of his family's escape.

There was a certain acquaintance of mine who shared my hearth with me, a Venetian by birth, who was deemed worthy of protection, and with him, his household and wife were preserved from physical harm. He proved to be helpful to us in those troubled times. Putting on his armour and transforming himself from merchant to soldier, he pretended to be a companion in arms and, speaking to them in their own barbaric tongue, claimed that he had occupied the dwelling first. Thus he beat off the despoilers to a man. But they continued to pour in in large numbers, and he despaired of opposing them, especially the French, who were not like the others in temperament or physique and boasted that the only thing they feared was heaven. As it was impossible for him to fall upon them, he enjoined us to depart...

1 Becket takes leave of Pope Alexander III fortified by his support. English, *c.* 1230-40 .

We left a short time later, dragged away by the hand as though we had been allotted to him as captives of his spear, and downcast and ill-clad we were sent on our way... When our servants dispersed in all directions, inhumanly abandoning us, we were compelled to carry on our shoulders the children who could not yet walk and to hold in our arms a male infant at breast, and thus to make our way through the streets.

Having remained in the City for five days after her fall, we departed [17 April 1204]. The day was Saturday, and what had taken place was not, I believe, an event without meaning, a fortuitous circumstance or a coincidence, but the will of God. It was a stormy and wintry day... As we came to the Church of the Noble Martyr Mokios, a lecherous and unholy barbarian, like a wolf pursuing a lamb, snatched from our midst a fair-tressed maiden, the young daughter of a judge. Before this most piteous spectacle our entire company shouted out in alarm. The girl's father, afflicted by old age and sickness, stumbled, fell into a mud-hole, and lay on his side wailing and wallowing in the mire; turning to me in utter helplessness... he entreated that I do everything possible to free his daughter. I immediately turned back and set out after the abductor, following his tracks; in tears I cried out against the abduction, and with gestures of supplication I prevailed upon those passing troops who were not wholly ignorant of our language to come to my aid, and I even held on to some with my hand...

When we arrived at the lodgings of this lover of women, he sent the girl inside and stood at the gateway to repulse his opponents. Pointing my finger at him, I said, 'This is he to whose wrong-doing the light of day bears witness, and who disregards the commands of your wellborn chiefs... This man has flouted your injunctions before many witnesses and was not afraid to bray like a salacious ass at the sight of chaste maidens. Defend, therefore, those who are protected by your laws and who have been put in our charge'...

With such arguments, I aroused the sympathies of these men, and they insisted on the girl's release. At first, the barbarian showed contempt, as he was held captive by the two most tyrannical of passions, lust and wrath. When he saw, however, that the men were bristling with anger and proposed to hang him from a stake as an unjust and shame-less man... he yielded reluctantly and surrendered the girl. The father rejoiced at the sight of his daughter, shedding tears as libations to God for having saved her from this union without marriage crowns and bridal songs. Then he rose to his feet and continued on the way with us.

II Top: The fate of the adulterers. Maqueda, Spain 1422-30.

III Right: Phinehas the priest slays the fornicators by throwing a lance that penetrates their genitals. Alba Bible, Maqueda, Spain 1422-30.

Easter Regulations

As the holiest festival of the ecclesiastical calendar, the celebration of the Resurrection, which brought to an end the period of fasting associated with Lent, was also a feast. But churchmen were anxious that Christians should not enjoy too many additional pleasures, as the canon passed in 692 makes clear.

From the holy day of the Resurrection of Christ until New Sunday, the faithful are to frequent the holy Churches without ceasing during the entire week, with psalms and hymns and spiritual songs. Rejoicing in Christ and celebrating, listening to the reading of holy Scripture and delighting in the holy Mysteries; for thus shall we arise and be exalted together with Christ. In no wise, then, ought horse-races or public spectacles to be performed during the aforesaid days.

Calculating the Date of Easter

Conflicting methods of calculating the date of Easter were resolved at the Synod of Whitby, on the north-east coast of England in 664. Here the great historian and polymath, Bede (673–735), describes the consequences of adopting the Roman system.

Not long afterwards, those monks of Irish extraction who lived in Iona, together with the monasteries under their rule, were brought by the Lord's guidance to canonical usages in the matter of Easter... The monks of Iona accepted the catholic ways of life under the teaching of Egbert... In the year of our Lord 729, when Easter fell on 24 April, after he had celebrated a solemn mass in memory of the Lord's resurrection, he departed to be with the Lord on the same day. So he began the joyful celebration of the greatest of all festivals with the brothers whom he had converted to the grace of unity, and completed it, or rather continues the endless celebration of it, with the Lord and His apostles and the other citizens of heaven. It was a wonderful dispensation of the divine providence that the venerable man not only passed from this world to the Father on Easter Day, but also when Easter was being celebrated on a date on which it had never before been kept in those places.

Opposite page: The symbols for the Evangelists.
The Book of Kells, eighth to ninth century.

Easter in Jerusalem

Many pilgrims recorded their emotions at celebrating Easter in the shrine of the Holy Sepulchre in Jerusalem, which all Christians considered not only the holiest site but also the very centre (omphalos) of the entire world. Here is the account by a twelfth-century pilgrim, Theoderich.

It is customary in the church of the Holy Sepulchre, both in the church itself and in all the other churches in the city, at daybreak on the morning of Easter Eve, to put out the earthly lights, and to await the coming of light from heaven for the reception of which light one of the silver lamps, seven of which hang there, is prepared. Then all the clergy and people stand there waiting with great and anxious expectation, until God shall send his hand down from on high. Among other prayers, they often shout loudly and with tears, 'God help us!' and 'Holy Sepulchre!'

Meanwhile, the patriarch or some of the other bishops who have assembled to receive the holy fire, and also the rest of the clergy, bearing a cross in which a large piece of our Lord's cross is inserted, and with other relics of the saints, frequently visit the Holy Sepulchre to pray there; watching also whether God has sent his gracious light into the vessel prepared to receive it. The fire has the habit of appearing at certain hours and in certain places; for sometimes it appears about the first hour, sometimes about the third, the sixth, or the ninth, or even so late as the time of compline. Moreover, it comes sometimes to the sepulchre itself, sometimes to the Temple of the Lord, and sometimes to the Church of St John. However, on the day when our humble selves, with the other pilgrims, were awaiting the sacred fire, immediately after the ninth hour that sacred fire came, upon which, behold, with ringing of church bells, the

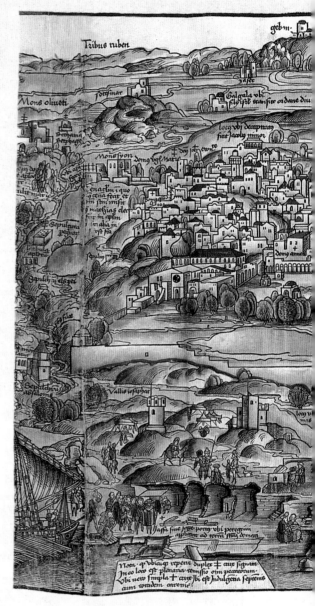

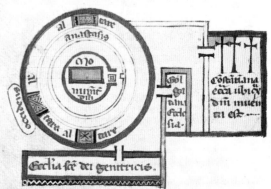

©2013 Project Management Institute. *A Guide to the Project Management Body of Knowledge (PMBOK® Guide) – Fifth Edition*

LIST OF TABLES AND FIGURES

©2013 Project Management Institute. *A Guide to the Project Management Body of Knowledge (PMBOK® Guide) – Fifth Edition*

©2013 Project Management Institute. *A Guide to the Project Management Body of Knowledge (PMBOK® Guide) – Fifth Edition*

1

INTRODUCTION

A Guide to the Project Management Body of Knowledge (PMBOK® Guide) – Fifth Edition provides guidelines for managing individual projects and defines project management related concepts. It also describes the project management life cycle and its related processes, as well as the project life cycle.

The *PMBOK® Guide* contains the globally recognized standard and guide for the project management profession (found in Annex A1). A standard is a formal document that describes established norms, methods, processes, and practices. As with other professions, the knowledge contained in this standard has evolved from the recognized good practices of project management practitioners who have contributed to the development of this standard.

The first two sections of the *PMBOK® Guide* provide an introduction to key concepts in the project management field. Section 3 summarizes the Process Groups and provides an overview of process interactions among the ten Knowledge Areas and five Process Groups. Sections 4 through 13 are the guide to the project management body of knowledge. These sections expand on the information in the standard by describing the inputs and outputs, as well as tools and techniques used in managing projects. Annex A1 is the standard for project management and presents the processes, inputs, and outputs that are considered to be good practice on most projects most of the time.

This section defines several key terms and the relationship among portfolio management, program management, project management and organizational project management. An overview of the *PMBOK® Guide* is found within the following sections:

1.1 Purpose of the *PMBOK® Guide*

1.2 What is a Project?

1.3 What is Project Management?

1.4 Relationships Among Portfolio Management, Program Management, Project Management, and Organizational Project Management

1.5 Relationship Between Project Management, Operations Management, and Organizational Strategy

1.6 Business Value

1.7 Role of the Project Manager

1.8 Project Management Body of Knowledge

1.1 Purpose of the *PMBOK® Guide*

The acceptance of project management as a profession indicates that the application of knowledge, processes, skills, tools, and techniques can have a significant impact on project success. The *PMBOK® Guide* identifies that subset of the project management body of knowledge that is generally recognized as good practice. "Generally recognized" means the knowledge and practices described are applicable to most projects most of the time, and there is consensus about their value and usefulness. "Good practice" means there is general agreement that the application of the knowledge, skills, tools, and techniques can enhance the chances of success over many projects. "Good practice" does not mean that the knowledge described should always be applied uniformly to all projects; the organization and/or project management team is responsible for determining what is appropriate for any given project.

The *PMBOK® Guide* also provides and promotes a common vocabulary within the project management profession for using and applying project management concepts. A common vocabulary is an essential element of a professional discipline. The *PMI Lexicon of Project Management Terms* [1][1] provides the foundational professional vocabulary that can be consistently used by project, program, and portfolio managers and other stakeholders.

Annex A1 is a foundational reference for PMI's project management professional development programs. Annex A1 continues to evolve along with the profession, and is therefore not all-inclusive; this standard is a guide rather than a specific methodology. One can use different methodologies and tools (e.g., agile, waterfall, PRINCE2) to implement the project management framework.

In addition to the standards that establish guidelines for project management processes, the *Project Management Institute Code of Ethics and Professional Conduct* [2] guides practitioners of the profession and describes the expectations that practitioners should hold for themselves and others. The *Project Management Institute Code of Ethics and Professional Conduct* is specific about the basic obligation of responsibility, respect, fairness, and honesty. It requires that practitioners demonstrate a commitment to ethical and professional conduct. It carries the obligation to comply with laws, regulations, and organizational and professional policies. Practitioners come from diverse backgrounds and cultures, and the *Project Management Institute Code of Ethics and Professional Conduct* applies globally. When interacting with any stakeholder, practitioners should be committed to honest, responsible, fair practices and respectful dealings. Acceptance of the code is essential for project managers, and is a requirement for the following PMI® exams:

- Certified Associate in Project Management (CAPM)®
- Project Management Professional (PMP)®
- Program Management Professional (PgMP)®
- PMI Agile Certified Practitioner (PMI-ACP)^{SM}
- PMI Risk Management Professional (PMI-RMP)®
- PMI Scheduling Professional (PMI-SP)®

[1]The numbers in brackets refer to the list of references at the end of this standard.

1.2 What is a Project?

A project is a temporary endeavor undertaken to create a unique product, service, or result. The temporary nature of projects indicates that a project has a definite beginning and end. The end is reached when the project's objectives have been achieved or when the project is terminated because its objectives will not or cannot be met, or when the need for the project no longer exists. A project may also be terminated if the client (customer, sponsor, or champion) wishes to terminate the project. Temporary does not necessarily mean the duration of the project is short. It refers to the project's engagement and its longevity. Temporary does not typically apply to the product, service, or result created by the project; most projects are undertaken to create a lasting outcome. For example, a project to build a national monument will create a result expected to last for centuries. Projects can also have social, economic, and environmental impacts that far outlive the projects themselves.

Every project creates a unique product, service, or result. The outcome of the project may be tangible or intangible. Although repetitive elements may be present in some project deliverables and activities, this repetition does not change the fundamental, unique characteristics of the project work. For example, office buildings can be constructed with the same or similar materials and by the same or different teams. However, each building project remains unique with a different location, different design, different circumstances and situations, different stakeholders, and so on.

An ongoing work effort is generally a repetitive process that follows an organization's existing procedures. In contrast, because of the unique nature of projects, there may be uncertainties or differences in the products, services, or results that the project creates. Project activities can be new to members of a project team, which may necessitate more dedicated planning than other routine work. In addition, projects are undertaken at all organizational levels. A project can involve a single individual or multiple individuals, a single organizational unit, or multiple organizational units from multiple organizations.

A project can create:

- A product that can be either a component of another item, an enhancement of an item, or an end item in itself;

- A service or a capability to perform a service (e.g., a business function that supports production or distribution);

- An improvement in the existing product or service lines (e.g., A Six Sigma project undertaken to reduce defects); or

- A result, such as an outcome or document (e.g., a research project that develops knowledge that can be used to determine whether a trend exists or a new process will benefit society).

Examples of projects include, but are not limited to:

- Developing a new product, service, or result;

- Effecting a change in the structure, processes, staffing, or style of an organization;

- Developing or acquiring a new or modified information system (hardware or software);

- Conducting a research effort whose outcome will be aptly recorded;

- Constructing a building, industrial plant, or infrastructure; or

- Implementing, improving, or enhancing existing business processes and procedures.

1.2.1. The Relationships Among Portfolios, Programs, and Projects

The relationship among portfolios, programs, and projects is such that a portfolio refers to a collection of projects, programs, subportfolios, and operations managed as a group to achieve strategic objectives. Programs are grouped within a portfolio and are comprised of subprograms, projects, or other work that are managed in a coordinated fashion in support of the portfolio. Individual projects that are either within or outside of a program are still considered part of a portfolio. Although the projects or programs within the portfolio may not necessarily be interdependent or directly related, they are linked to the organization's strategic plan by means of the organization's portfolio.

As Figure 1-1 illustrates, organizational strategies and priorities are linked and have relationships between portfolios and programs, and between programs and individual projects. Organizational planning impacts the projects by means of project prioritization based on risk, funding, and other considerations relevant to the organization's strategic plan. Organizational planning can direct the management of resources, and support for the component projects on the basis of risk categories, specific lines of business, or general types of projects, such as infrastructure and process improvement.

 ©2013 Project Management Institute. *A Guide to the Project Management Body of Knowledge (PMBOK® Guide) – Fifth Edition*

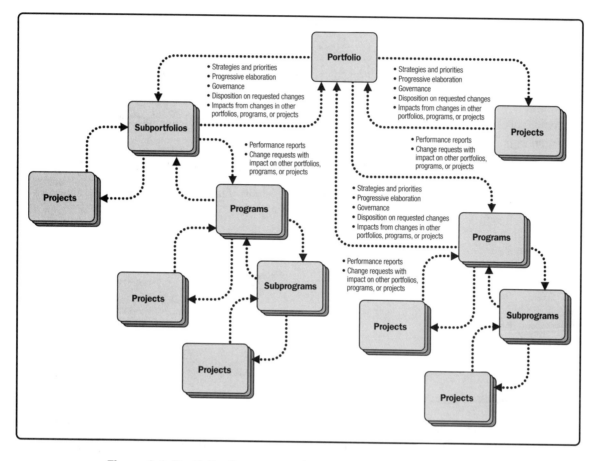

Figure 1-1. Portfolio, Program, and Project Management Interactions

1.3 What is Project Management?

Project management is the application of knowledge, skills, tools, and techniques to project activities to meet the project requirements. Project management is accomplished through the appropriate application and integration of the 47 logically grouped project management processes, which are categorized into five Process Groups. These five Process Groups are:

- Initiating,

- Planning,

- Executing,

- Monitoring and Controlling, and

- Closing.

Managing a project typically includes, but is not limited to:

- Identifying requirements;
- Addressing the various needs, concerns, and expectations of the stakeholders in planning and executing the project;
- Setting up, maintaining, and carrying out communications among stakeholders that are active, effective, and collaborative in nature;
- Managing stakeholders towards meeting project requirements and creating project deliverables;
- Balancing the competing project constraints, which include, but are not limited to:
  - Scope,
  - Quality,
  - Schedule,
  - Budget,
  - Resources, and
  - Risks.

The specific project characteristics and circumstances can influence the constraints on which the project management team needs to focus.

The relationship among these factors is such that if any one factor changes, at least one other factor is likely to be affected. For example, if the schedule is shortened, often the budget needs to be increased to add additional resources to complete the same amount of work in less time. If a budget increase is not possible, the scope or targeted quality may be reduced to deliver the project's end result in less time within the same budget amount. Project stakeholders may have differing ideas as to which factors are the most important, creating an even greater challenge. Changing the project requirements or objectives may create additional risks. The project team needs to be able to assess the situation, balance the demands, and maintain proactive communication with stakeholders in order to deliver a successful project.

Due to the potential for change, the development of the project management plan is an iterative activity and is progressively elaborated throughout the project's life cycle. Progressive elaboration involves continuously improving and detailing a plan as more detailed and specific information and more accurate estimates become available. Progressive elaboration allows a project management team to define work and manage it to a greater level of detail as the project evolves.

1.4 Relationships Among Portfolio Management, Program Management, Project Management, and Organizational Project Management

In order to understand portfolio, program, and project management, it is important to recognize the similarities and differences among these disciplines. It is also helpful to understand how they relate to organizational project management (OPM). OPM is a strategy execution framework utilizing project, program, and portfolio management as well as organizational enabling practices to consistently and predictably deliver organizational strategy producing better performance, better results, and a sustainable competitive advantage.

Portfolio, program, and project management are aligned with or driven by organizational strategies. Conversely, portfolio, program, and project management differ in the way each contributes to the achievement of strategic goals. Portfolio management aligns with organizational strategies by selecting the right programs or projects, prioritizing the work, and providing the needed resources, whereas program management harmonizes its projects and program components and controls interdependencies in order to realize specified benefits. Project management develops and implements plans to achieve a specific scope that is driven by the objectives of the program or portfolio it is subjected to and, ultimately, to organizational strategies. OPM advances organizational capability by linking project, program, and portfolio management principles and practices with organizational enablers (e.g. structural, cultural, technological, and human resource practices) to support strategic goals. An organization measures its capabilities, then plans and implements improvements towards the systematic achievement of best practices.

Table 1-1 shows the comparison of project, program, and portfolio views across several dimensions within the organization.

Table 1-1. Comparative Overview of Project, Program, and Portfolio Management

Organizational Project Management			
	Projects	**Programs**	**Portfolios**
Scope	Projects have defined objectives. Scope is progressively elaborated throughout the project life cycle.	Programs have a larger scope and provide more significant benefits.	Portfolios have an organizational scope that changes with the strategic objectives of the organization.
Change	Project managers expect change and implement processes to keep change managed and controlled.	Program managers expect change from both inside and outside the program and are prepared to manage it.	Portfolio managers continuously monitor changes in the broader internal and external environment.
Planning	Project managers progressively elaborate high-level information into detailed plans throughout the project life cycle.	Program managers develop the overall program plan and create high-level plans to guide detailed planning at the component level.	Portfolio managers create and maintain necessary processes and communication relative to the aggregate portfolio.
Management	Project managers manage the project team to meet the project objectives.	Program managers manage the program staff and the project managers; they provide vision and overall leadership.	Portfolio managers may manage or coordinate portfolio management staff, or program and project staff that may have reporting responsibilities into the aggregate portfolio.
Success	Success is measured by product and project quality, timeliness, budget compliance, and degree of customer satisfaction.	Success is measured by the degree to which the program satisfies the needs and benefits for which it was undertaken.	Success is measured in terms of the aggregate investment performance and benefit realization of the portfolio.
Monitoring	Project managers monitor and control the work of producing the products, services, or results that the project was undertaken to produce.	Program managers monitor the progress of program components to ensure the overall goals, schedules, budget, and benefits of the program will be met.	Portfolio managers monitor strategic changes and aggregate resource allocation, performance results, and risk of the portfolio.

1.4.1 Program Management

A program is defined as a group of related projects, subprograms, and program activities managed in a coordinated way to obtain benefits not available from managing them individually. Programs may include elements of related work outside the scope of the discrete projects in the program. A project may or may not be part of a program but a program will always have projects.

Program management is the application of knowledge, skills, tools, and techniques to a program in order to meet the program requirements and to obtain benefits and control not available by managing projects individually.

Projects within a program are related through the common outcome or collective capability. If the relationship between projects is only that of a shared client, seller, technology, or resource, the effort should be managed as a portfolio of projects rather than as a program.

Program management focuses on the project interdependencies and helps to determine the optimal approach for managing them. Actions related to these interdependencies may include:

- Resolving resource constraints and/or conflicts that affect multiple projects within the program,
- Aligning organizational/strategic direction that affects project and program goals and objectives, and
- Resolving issues and change management within a shared governance structure.

An example of a program is a new communications satellite system with projects for design of the satellite and the ground stations, the construction of each, the integration of the system, and the launch of the satellite.

1.4.2 Portfolio Management

A portfolio refers to projects, programs, subportfolios, and operations managed as a group to achieve strategic objectives. The projects or programs of the portfolio may not necessarily be interdependent or directly related. For example, an infrastructure firm that has the strategic objective of "maximizing the return on its investments" may put together a portfolio that includes a mix of projects in oil and gas, power, water, roads, rail, and airports. From this mix, the firm may choose to manage related projects as one program. All of the power projects may be grouped together as a power program. Similarly, all of the water projects may be grouped together as a water program. Thus, the power program and the water program become integral components of the enterprise portfolio of the infrastructure firm.

Portfolio management refers to the centralized management of one or more portfolios to achieve strategic objectives. Portfolio management focuses on ensuring that projects and programs are reviewed to prioritize resource allocation, and that the management of the portfolio is consistent with and aligned to organizational strategies.

1.4.3 Projects and Strategic Planning

Projects are often utilized as a means of directly or indirectly achieving objectives within an organization's strategic plan. Projects are typically authorized as a result of one or more of the following strategic considerations:

- Market demand (e.g., a car company authorizing a project to build more fuel-efficient cars in response to gasoline shortages);

- Strategic opportunity/business need (e.g., a training company authorizing a project to create a new course to increase its revenues);

- Social need (e.g., a nongovernmental organization in a developing country authorizing a project to provide potable water systems, latrines, and sanitation education to communities suffering from high rates of infectious diseases);

- Environmental consideration (e.g., a public company authorizing a project to create a new service for electric car sharing to reduce pollution);

- Customer request (e.g., an electric utility authorizing a project to build a new substation to serve a new industrial park);

- Technological advance (e.g., an electronics firm authorizing a new project to develop a faster, cheaper, and smaller laptop based on advances in computer memory and electronics technology); and

- Legal requirement (e.g., a chemical manufacturer authorizing a project to establish guidelines for proper handling of a new toxic material).

1.4.4 Project Management Office

A project management office (PMO) is a management structure that standardizes the project-related governance processes and facilitates the sharing of resources, methodologies, tools, and techniques. The responsibilities of a PMO can range from providing project management support functions to actually being responsible for the direct management of one or more projects.

There are several types of PMO structures in organizations, each varying in the degree of control and influence they have on projects within the organization, such as:

1

- **Supportive.** Supportive PMOs provide a consultative role to projects by supplying templates, best practices, training, access to information and lessons learned from other projects. This type of PMO serves as a project repository. The degree of control provided by the PMO is low.

- **Controlling.** Controlling PMOs provide support and require compliance through various means. Compliance may involve adopting project management frameworks or methodologies, using specific templates, forms and tools, or conformance to governance. The degree of control provided by the PMO is moderate.

- **Directive.** Directive PMOs take control of the projects by directly managing the projects. The degree of control provided by the PMO is high.

The PMO integrates data and information from corporate strategic projects and evaluates how higher level strategic objectives are being fulfilled. The PMO is the natural liaison between the organization's portfolios, programs, projects, and the corporate measurement systems (e.g. balanced scorecard).

The projects supported or administered by the PMO may not be related, other than by being managed together. The specific form, function, and structure of a PMO are dependent upon the needs of the organization that it supports.

A PMO may have the authority to act as an integral stakeholder and a key decision maker throughout the life of each project, to make recommendations, or to terminate projects or take other actions, as required, to remain aligned with the business objectives. In addition, the PMO may be involved in the selection, management, and deployment of shared or dedicated project resources.

A primary function of a PMO is to support project managers in a variety of ways which may include, but are not limited to:

- Managing shared resources across all projects administered by the PMO;

- Identifying and developing project management methodology, best practices, and standards;

- Coaching, mentoring, training, and oversight;

- Monitoring compliance with project management standards, policies, procedures, and templates by means of project audits;

- Developing and managing project policies, procedures, templates, and other shared documentation (organizational process assets); and

- Coordinating communication across projects.

Project managers and PMOs pursue different objectives and, as such, are driven by different requirements. All of these efforts are aligned with the strategic needs of the organization. Differences between the role of project managers and a PMO may include the following:

- The project manager focuses on the specified project objectives, while the PMO manages major program scope changes, which may be seen as potential opportunities to better achieve business objectives.

- The project manager controls the assigned project resources to best meet project objectives, while the PMO optimizes the use of shared organizational resources across all projects.

- The project manager manages the constraints (scope, schedule, cost, quality, etc.) of the individual projects, while the PMO manages the methodologies, standards, overall risks/opportunities, metrics, and interdependencies among projects at the enterprise level.

1.5 Relationship Between Project Management, Operations Management, and Organizational Strategy

Operations management is responsible for overseeing, directing, and controlling business operations. Operations evolve to support the day-to-day business, and are necessary to achieve strategic and tactical goals of the business. Examples include: production operations, manufacturing operations, accounting operations, software support, and maintenance.

Though temporary in nature, projects can help achieve the organizational goals when they are aligned with the organization's strategy. Organizations sometimes change their operations, products, or systems by creating strategic business initiatives that are developed and implemented through projects. Projects require project management activities and skill sets, while operations require business process management, operations management activities, and skill sets.

1.5.1 Operations and Project Management

Changes in business operations may be the focus of a dedicated project—especially if there are substantial changes to business operations as a result of a new product or service delivery. Ongoing operations are outside of the scope of a project; however, there are intersecting points where the two areas cross.

Projects can intersect with operations at various points during the product life cycle, such as:

1

- At each closeout phase;
- When developing a new product, upgrading a product, or expanding outputs;
- While improving operations or the product development process; or
- Until the end of the product life cycle.

At each point, deliverables and knowledge are transferred between the project and operations for implementation of the delivered work. This implementation occurs through a transfer of project resources to operations toward the end of the project, or through a transfer of operational resources to the project at the start.

Operations are ongoing endeavors that produce repetitive outputs, with resources assigned to do basically the same set of tasks according to the standards institutionalized in a product life cycle. Unlike the ongoing nature of operations, projects are temporary endeavors.

1.5.1.1 Operations Management

Operations management is a subject area that is outside the scope of formal project management as described in this standard.

Operations management is an area of management concerned with ongoing production of goods and/or services. It involves ensuring that business operations continue efficiently by using the optimum resources needed and meeting customer demands. It is concerned with managing processes that transform inputs (e.g., materials, components, energy, and labor) into outputs (e.g., products, goods, and/or services).

1.5.1.2 Operational Stakeholders in Project Management

While operations management is different from project management (see 1.5.1.1), the needs of stakeholders who perform and conduct business operations are important considerations in projects that will affect their future work and endeavors. Project managers who consider and appropriately include operational stakeholders in all phases of projects, gain insight and avoid unnecessary issues that often arise when their input is overlooked.

Operational stakeholders should be engaged and their needs identified as part of the stakeholder register, and their influence (positive or negative) should be addressed as part of the risk management plan.

The following list includes examples of operational stakeholders (depending upon the business):

- Plant operators,
- Manufacturing line supervisors,
- Help desk staff,
- Production system support analysts,
- Customer service representative,
- Salespersons,
- Maintenance workers,
- Telephone sales personnel,
- Call center personnel,
- Retail workers,
- Line managers, and
- Training officers.

1.5.2 Organizations and Project Management

Organizations use governance to establish strategic direction and performance parameters. The strategic direction provides the purpose, expectations, goals, and actions necessary to guide business pursuit and is aligned with business objectives. Project management activities should be aligned with top-level business direction, and if there is a change, then project objectives need to be realigned. In a project environment, changes to project objectives affect project efficiency and success. When the business alignment for a project is constant, the chance for project success greatly increases because the project remains aligned with the strategic direction of the organization. Should something change, projects should change accordingly.

1.5.2.1 Project-Based Organizations

Project-based organizations (PBOs) refer to various organizational forms that create temporary systems for carrying out their work. PBOs can be created by different types of organizations (i.e., functional, matrix, or projectized (see 2.1.3)). The use of PBOs may diminish the hierarchy and bureaucracy inside the organizations as the success of the work is measured by the final result rather than by position or politics.

PBOs conduct the majority of their work as projects and/or provide project rather than functional approaches. PBOs can refer to either entire firms (as in telecommunications, oil and gas, construction, consultancy, and professional services) multi-firm consortia, or networks; it is also possible that some large project-based organizations have functional support areas or that the PBO is nested within subsidiaries or divisions of larger corporations.

1.5.2.2 The Link Between Project Management and Organizational Governance

Projects (and programs) are undertaken to achieve strategic business outcomes, for which many organizations now adopt formal organizational governance processes and procedures. Organizational governance criteria can impose constraints on projects—particularly if the project delivers a service which will be subject to strict organizational governance.

Because project success may be judged on the basis of how well the resultant product or service supports organizational governance, it is important for the project manager to be knowledgeable about corporate/ organizational governance policies and procedures pertaining to the subject matter of the product or service (e.g., if an organization has adopted policies in support of sustainability practices and the project involves construction of a new office building, the project manager should be aware of sustainability requirements related to building construction.)

1.5.2.3 The Relationship Between Project Management and Organizational Strategy

Organizational strategy should provide guidance and direction to project management—especially when one considers that projects exist to support organizational strategies. Often it is the project sponsor or the portfolio or program manager who identifies alignment or potential conflicts between organizational strategies and project goals and then communicates these to the project manager. If the goals of a project are in conflict with an established organizational strategy, it is incumbent upon the project manager to document and identify such conflicts as early as possible in the project. At times, the development of an organizational strategy could be the goal of a project rather than a guiding principle. In such a case, it is important for the project to specifically define what constitutes an appropriate organizational strategy that will sustain the organization.

1.6 Business Value

Business value is a concept that is unique to each organization. Business value is defined as the entire value of the business; the total sum of all tangible and intangible elements. Examples of tangible elements include monetary assets, fixtures, stockholder equity, and utility. Examples of intangible elements include good will, brand recognition, public benefit, and trademarks. Depending on the organization, business value scope can be short-, medium-, or long-term. Value may be created through the effective management of ongoing operations. However, through the effective use of portfolio, program, and project management, organizations will possess the ability to employ reliable, established processes to meet strategic objectives and obtain greater business value from their project investments. While not all organizations are business driven, all organizations conduct business-related activities. Whether an organization is a government agency or a nonprofit organization, all organizations focus on attaining business value for their activities.

Successful business value realization begins with comprehensive strategic planning and management. Organizational strategy can be expressed through the organization's mission and vision, including orientation to markets, competition, and other environmental factors. Effective organizational strategy provides defined directions for development and growth, in addition to performance metrics for success. In order to bridge the gap between organizational strategy and successful business value realization, the use of portfolio, program, and project management techniques is essential.

Portfolio management aligns components (projects, programs, or operations) to the organizational strategy, organized into portfolios or subportfolios to optimize project or program objectives, dependencies, costs, timelines, benefits, resources, and risks. This allows organizations to have an overall view of how the strategic goals are reflected in the portfolio, institute appropriate governance management, and authorize human, financial, or material resources to be allocated based on expected performance and benefits.

Using program management, organizations have the ability to align multiple projects for optimized or integrated costs, schedule, effort, and benefits. Program management focuses on project interdependencies and helps to determine the optimal approach for managing and realizing the desired benefits.

With project management, organizations have the ability to apply knowledge, processes, skills, and tools and techniques that enhance the likelihood of success over a wide range of projects. Project management focuses on the successful delivery of products, services, or results. Within programs and portfolios, projects are a means of achieving organizational strategy and objectives.

Organizations can further facilitate the alignment of these portfolio, program, and project management activities by strengthening organizational enablers such as structural, cultural, technological, and human resource practices. By continuously conducting portfolio strategic alignment and optimization, performing business impact analyses, and developing robust organizational enablers, organizations can achieve successful transitions within the portfolio, program, and project domains and attain effective investment management and business value realization.

1.7 Role of the Project Manager

The project manager is the person assigned by the performing organization to lead the team that is responsible for achieving the project objectives. The role of a project manager is distinct from a functional manager or operations manager. Typically the functional manager is focused on providing management oversight for a functional or a business unit, and operations managers are responsible for ensuring that business operations are efficient.

Depending on the organizational structure, a project manager may report to a functional manager. In other cases, a project manager may be one of several project managers who report to a program or portfolio manager who is ultimately responsible for enterprise-wide projects. In this type of structure, the project manager works closely with the program or portfolio manager to achieve the project objectives and to ensure the project management plan aligns with the overarching program plan. The project manager also works closely and in collaboration with other roles, such as a business analyst, quality assurance manager, and subject matter experts.

1.7.1 Responsibilities and Competencies of the Project Manager

In general, project managers have the responsibility to satisfy the needs: task needs, team needs, and individual needs. As project management is a critical strategic discipline, the project manager becomes the link between the strategy and the team. Projects are essential to the growth and survival of organizations. Projects create value in the form of improved business processes, are indispensable in the development of new products and services, and make it easier for companies to respond to changes in the environment, competition, and the marketplace. The project manager's role therefore becomes increasingly strategic. However, understanding and applying the knowledge, tools, and techniques that are recognized as good practice are not sufficient for effective project management. In addition to any area-specific skills and general management proficiencies required for the project, effective project management requires that the project manager possess the following competencies:

- **Knowledge**—Refers to what the project manager knows about project management.
- **Performance**—Refers to what the project manager is able to do or accomplish while applying his or her project management knowledge.
- **Personal**—Refers to how the project manager behaves when performing the project or related activity. Personal effectiveness encompasses attitudes, core personality characteristics, and leadership, which provides the ability to guide the project team while achieving project objectives and balancing the project constraints.

1.7.2 Interpersonal Skills of a Project Manager

Project managers accomplish work through the project team and other stakeholders. Effective project managers require a balance of ethical, interpersonal, and conceptual skills that help them analyze situations and interact appropriately. Appendix X3 on Interpersonal Skills describes important interpersonal skills, such as:

- Leadership,
- Team building,
- Motivation,
- Communication,
- Influencing,
- Decision making,
- Political and cultural awareness,
- Negotiation,
- Trust building,
- Conflict management, and
- Coaching.

1.8 Project Management Body of Knowledge

The *PMBOK® Guide* contains the standard for managing most projects most of the time across many types of industries. The standard, included in Annex A1, describes the project management processes used to manage a project toward a more successful outcome.

This standard is unique to the project management field and has interrelationships to other project management disciplines such as program management and portfolio management.

Project management standards do not address all details of every topic. This standard is limited to individual projects and the project management processes that are generally recognized as good practice. Other standards may be consulted for additional information on the broader context in which projects are accomplished, such as:

- *The Standard for Program Management* [3] addresses the management of programs,
- *The Standard for Portfolio Management* [4] addresses the management of portfolios,
- *Organizational Project Management Maturity Model (OPM3®)* [5] examines an enterprise's project management process capabilities.

ORGANIZATIONAL INFLUENCES AND PROJECT LIFE CYCLE

Projects and project management take place in an environment that is broader than that of the project itself. Understanding this broader context helps ensure that work is carried out in alignment with the organization's goals and managed in accordance with the organization's established practices. This section describes how organizational influences affect the methods used for staffing, managing, and executing the project. It discusses the influence of stakeholders on the project and its governance, the project team's structure and membership, and different approaches to the phasing and relationship of activities within the project's life cycle. The following major sections are addressed:

2.1 Organizational Influences on Project Management

2.2 Project Stakeholders and Governance

2.3 Project Team

2.4 Project Life Cycle

2.1 Organizational Influences on Project Management

An organization's culture, style, and structure influence how its projects are performed. The organization's level of project management maturity and its project management systems can also influence the project. When a project involves external entities such as those that are part of a joint venture or partnering agreement, the project will be influenced by more than one organization. The following sections describe organizational characteristics, factors, and assets within an enterprise that are likely to influence the project.

2.1.1 Organizational Cultures and Styles

Organizations are systematic arrangements of entities (persons and/or departments) aimed at accomplishing a purpose, which may involve undertaking projects. An organization's culture and style affect how it conducts projects. Cultures and styles are group phenomena known as cultural norms, which develop over time. The norms include established approaches to initiating and planning projects, the means considered acceptable for getting the work done, and recognized authorities who make or influence decisions.

Organizational culture is shaped by the common experiences of members of the organization and most organizations have developed unique cultures over time by practice and common usage. Common experiences include, but are not limited to:

- Shared visions, mission, values, beliefs, and expectations;
- Regulations, policies, methods, and procedures;
- Motivation and reward systems;
- Risk tolerance;
- View of leadership, hierarchy, and authority relationships;
- Code of conduct, work ethic, and work hours; and
- Operating environments.

The organization's culture is an enterprise environmental factor, as described in Section 2.1.5. Cultures and styles are learned and shared and may have a strong influence on a project's ability to meet its objectives. A project manager should therefore understand the different organizational styles and cultures that may affect a project. The project manager needs to know which individuals in the organization are the decision makers or influencers and work with them to increase the probability of project success.

In light of globalization, understanding the impact of cultural influences is critical in projects involving diverse organizations and locations around the world. Culture becomes a critical factor in defining project success, and multi-cultural competence becomes critical for the project manager.

2.1.2 Organizational Communications

Project management success in an organization is highly dependent on an effective organizational communication style, especially in the face of globalization of the project management profession. Organizational communications capabilities have great influence on how projects are conducted. As a consequence, project managers in distant locations are able to more effectively communicate with all relevant stakeholders within the organizational structure to facilitate decision making. Stakeholders and project team members can also use electronic communications (including e-mail, texting, instant messaging, social media, video and web conferencing, and other forms of electronic media) to communicate with the project manager formally or informally.

2.1.3 Organizational Structures

Organizational structure is an enterprise environmental factor, which can affect the availability of resources and influence how projects are conducted (see also Section 2.1.5). Organizational structures range from functional to projectized, with a variety of matrix structures in between. Table 2-1 shows key project-related characteristics of the major types of organizational structures.

Table 2-1. Influence of Organizational Structures on Projects

Organization Structure / Project Characteristics	Functional	Matrix			Projectized
		Weak Matrix	Balanced Matrix	Strong Matrix	
Project Manager's Authority	Little or None	Low	Low to Moderate	Moderate to High	High to Almost Total
Resource Availability	Little or None	Low	Low to Moderate	Moderate to High	High to Almost Total
Who manages the project budget	Functional Manager	Functional Manager	Mixed	Project Manager	Project Manager
Project Manager's Role	Part-time	Part-time	Full-time	Full-time	Full-time
Project Management Administrative Staff	Part-time	Part-time	Part-time	Full-time	Full-time

The classic functional organization, shown in Figure 2-1, is a hierarchy where each employee has one clear superior. Staff members are grouped by specialty, such as production, marketing, engineering, and accounting at the top level. Specialties may be further subdivided into focused functional units, such as mechanical and electrical engineering. Each department in a functional organization will do its project work independently of other departments.

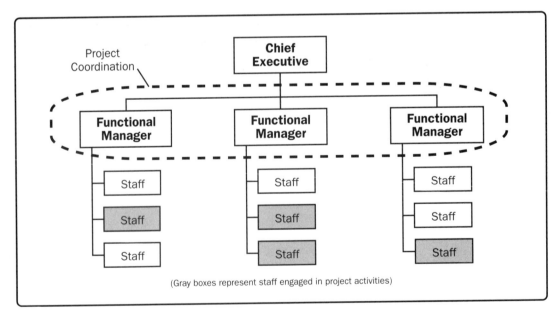

(Gray boxes represent staff engaged in project activities)

Figure 2-1. Functional Organization

Matrix organizations, as shown in Figures 2-2 through 2-4, reflect a blend of functional and projectized characteristics. Matrix organizations can be classified as weak, balanced, or strong depending on the relative level of power and influence between functional and project managers. Weak matrix organizations maintain many of the characteristics of a functional organization, and the role of the project manager is more of a coordinator or expediter. A project expediter works as staff assistant and communications coordinator. The expediter cannot personally make or enforce decisions. Project coordinators have power to make some decisions, have some authority, and report to a higher-level manager. Strong matrix organizations have many of the characteristics of the projectized organization, and have full-time project managers with considerable authority and full-time project administrative staff. While the balanced matrix organization recognizes the need for a project manager, it does not provide the project manager with the full authority over the project and project funding. Table 2-1 provides additional details of the various matrix organizational structures.

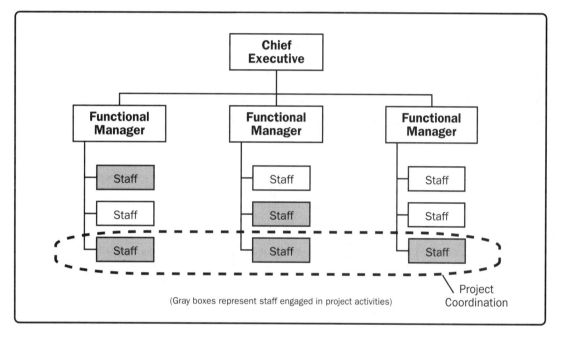

Figure 2-2. Weak Matrix Organization

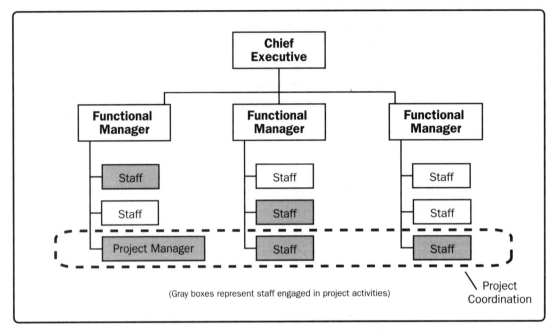

Figure 2-3. Balanced Matrix Organization

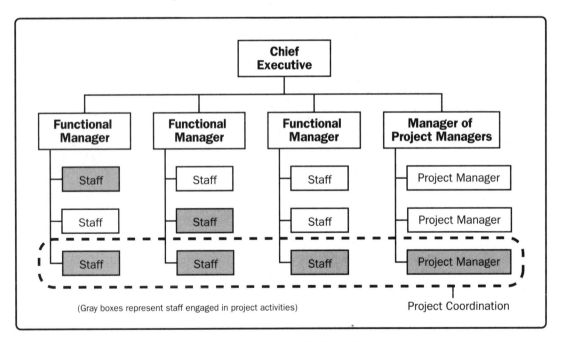

Figure 2-4. Strong Matrix Organization

At the opposite end of the spectrum to the functional organization is the projectized organization, shown in Figure 2-5. In a projectized organization, team members are often colocated. Most of the organization's resources are involved in project work, and project managers have a great deal of independence and authority. Virtual collaboration techniques are often used to accomplish the benefits of colocated teams. Projectized organizations often have organizational units called departments, but they can either report directly to the project manager or provide support services to the various projects.

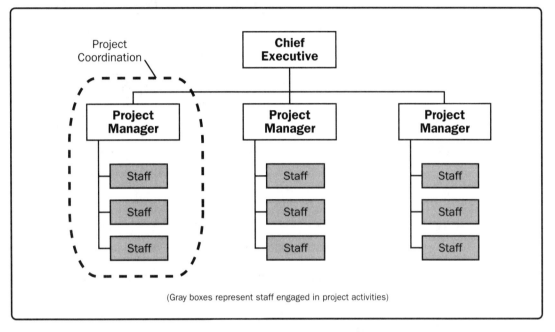

(Gray boxes represent staff engaged in project activities)

Figure 2-5. Projectized Organization

Many organizations involve all these structures at various levels, often referred to as a composite organization, as shown in Figure 2-6. For example, even a fundamentally functional organization may create a special project team to handle a critical project. Such a team may have many of the characteristics of a project team in a projectized organization. The team may include full-time staff from different functional departments, may develop its own set of operating procedures, and may even operate outside of the standard, formalized reporting structure during the project. Also, an organization may manage most of its projects in a strong matrix, but allow small projects to be managed by functional departments.

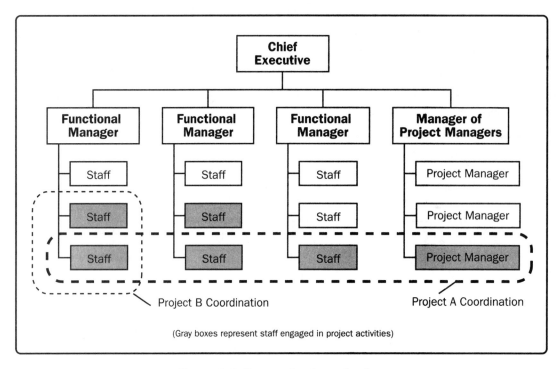

Figure 2-6. Composite Organization

Many organizational structures include strategic, middle management, and operational levels. The project manager may interact with all three levels depending on factors such as:

- Strategic importance of the project,
- Capacity of stakeholders to exert influence on the project,
- Degree of project management maturity,
- Project management systems, and
- Organizational communications.

This interaction determines project characteristics such as:

- Project manager's level of authority,
- Resource availability and management,
- Entity controlling the project budget,
- Project manager's role, and
- Project team composition.

2.1.4 Organizational Process Assets

Organizational process assets are the plans, processes, policies, procedures, and knowledge bases specific to and used by the performing organization. They include any artifact, practice, or knowledge from any or all of the organizations involved in the project that can be used to perform or govern the project. These process assets include formal and informal plans, processes, policies, procedures, and knowledge bases, specific to and used by the performing organization. The process assets also include the organization's knowledge bases such as lessons learned and historical information. Organizational process assets may include completed schedules, risk data, and earned value data. Organizational process assets are inputs to most planning processes. Throughout the project, the project team members may update and add to the organizational process assets as necessary. Organizational process assets may be grouped into two categories: (1) processes and procedures, and (2) corporate knowledge base.

2.1.4.1 Processes and Procedures

The organization's processes and procedures for conducting project work include, but are not limited to:

- *Initiating and Planning:*
  - Guidelines and criteria for tailoring the organization's set of standard processes and procedures to satisfy the specific needs of the project;
  - Specific organizational standards such as policies (e.g., human resources policies, health and safety policies, ethics policies, and project management policies), product and project life cycles, and quality policies and procedures (e.g., process audits, improvement targets, checklists, and standardized process definitions for use in the organization); and
  - Templates (e.g., risk register, work breakdown structure, project schedule network diagram, and contract templates).

- *Executing, Monitoring and Controlling:*
  - Change control procedures, including the steps by which performing organization standards, policies, plans, and procedures or any project documents will be modified, and how any changes will be approved and validated;
  - Financial controls procedures (e.g., time reporting, required expenditure and disbursement reviews, accounting codes, and standard contract provisions);
  - Issue and defect management procedures defining issue and defect controls, issue and defect identification and resolution, and action item tracking;

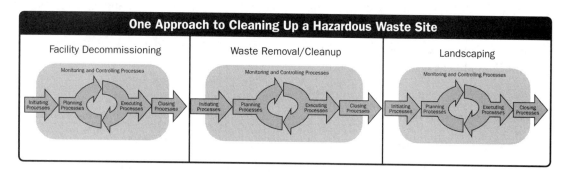

Figure 2-11. Example of a Three-Phase Project

- **Overlapping relationship.** In an overlapping relationship, a phase starts prior to completion of the previous one (see Figure 2-12). This can sometimes be applied as an example of the schedule compression technique called fast tracking. Overlapping phases may require additional resources to allow work to be done in parallel, may increase risk, and can result in rework if a subsequent phase progresses before accurate information is available from the previous phase.

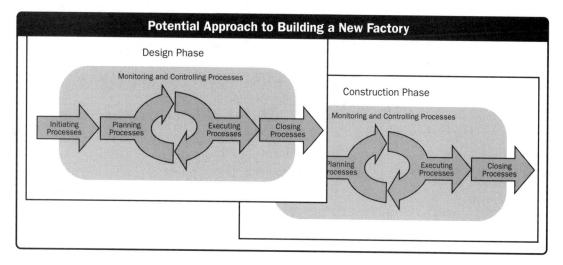

Figure 2-12. Example of a Project with Overlapping Phases

For projects with more than one phase, there may be different relationships (overlapping, sequential, parallel) between individual phases. Considerations such as level of control required, effectiveness, and degree of uncertainty determine the relationship to be applied between phases. Based on those considerations, both relationships could occur between different phases of a single project.

2.4.2.2 Predictive Life Cycles

Predictive life cycles (also known as fully plan-driven) are ones in which the project scope, and the time and cost required to deliver that scope, are determined as early in the project life cycle as practically possible. As shown in Figure 2-13, these projects proceed through a series of sequential or overlapping phases, with each phase generally focusing on a subset of project activities and project management processes. The work performed in each phase is usually different in nature to that in the preceding and subsequent phases, therefore, the makeup and skills required of the project team may vary from phase to phase.

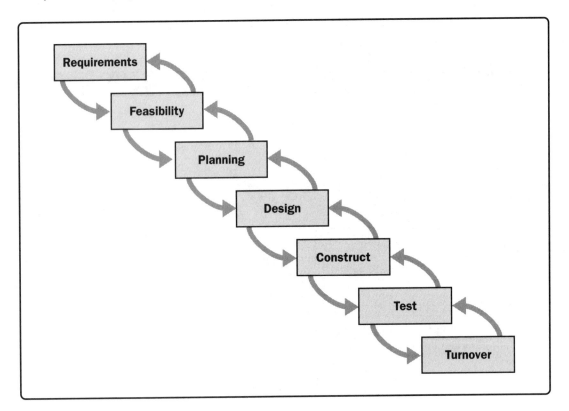

Figure 2-13. Example of Predictive Life Cycle

When the project is initiated, the project team will focus on defining the overall scope for the product and project, develop a plan to deliver the product (and any associated deliverables), and then proceed through phases to execute the plan within that scope. Changes to the project scope are carefully managed and require re planning and formal acceptance of the new scope.

Predictive life cycles are generally preferred when the product to be delivered is well understood, there is a substantial base of industry practice, or where a product is required to be delivered in full to have value to stakeholder groups.

Even projects with predictive life cycles may use the concept of rolling wave planning, where a more general, high-level plan is available and more detailed planning is executed for appropriate time windows, as new work activities are approaching and resources are to be assigned.

2.4.2.3 Iterative and Incremental Life Cycles

Iterative and incremental life cycles are ones in which project phases (also called iterations) intentionally repeat one or more project activities as the project team's understanding of the product increases. Iterations develop the product through a series of repeated cycles, while increments successively add to the functionality of the product. These life cycles develop the product both iteratively and incrementally.

Iterative and incremental projects may proceed in phases, and the iterations themselves will be performed in a sequential or overlapping fashion. During an iteration, activities from all Project Management Process Groups will be performed. At the end of each iteration, a deliverable or set of deliverables will be completed. Future iterations may enhance those deliverables or create new ones. Each iteration incrementally builds the deliverables until the exit criteria for the phase are met, allowing the project team to incorporate feedback.

In most iterative life cycles, a high-level vision will be developed for the overall undertaking, but the detailed scope is elaborated one iteration at a time. Often the planning for the next iteration is carried out as work progresses on the current iteration's scope and deliverables. The work required for a given set of deliverables may vary in duration and effort, and the project team may change between or during iterations. Those deliverables that are not addressed within the scope of the current iteration are typically scoped at a high level only and may be tentatively assigned to a specific future iteration. Changes to the scope of an iteration are carefully managed once work begins.

Iterative and incremental life cycles are generally preferred when an organization needs to manage changing objectives and scope, to reduce the complexity of a project, or when the partial delivery of a product is beneficial and provides value for one or more stakeholder groups without impact to the final deliverable or set of deliverables. Large and complex projects are frequently executed in an iterative fashion to reduce risk by allowing the team to incorporate feedback and lessons learned between iterations.

2.4.2.4 Adaptive Life Cycles

Adaptive life cycles (also known as change-driven or agile methods) are intended to respond to high levels of change and ongoing stakeholder involvement. Adaptive methods are also iterative and incremental, but differ in that iterations are very rapid (usually with a duration of 2 to 4 weeks) and are fixed in time and cost. Adaptive projects generally perform several processes in each iteration, although early iterations may concentrate more on planning activities.

The overall scope of the project will be decomposed into a set of requirements and work to be performed, sometimes referred to as a product backlog. At the beginning of an iteration, the team will work to determine how many of the highest priority items on the backlog list can be delivered within the next iteration. At the end of each iteration, the product should be ready for review by the customer. This does not mean that the customer is required to accept delivery, just that the product should not include unfinished, incomplete, or unusable features. The sponsor and customer representatives should be continuously engaged with the project to provide feedback on deliverables as they are created and to ensure that the product backlog reflects their current needs.

Adaptive methods are generally preferred when dealing with a rapidly changing environment, when requirements and scope are difficult to define in advance, and when it is possible to define small incremental improvements that will deliver value to stakeholders.

3

PROJECT MANAGEMENT PROCESSES

Project management is the application of knowledge, skills, tools, and techniques to project activities to meet the project requirements. This application of knowledge requires the effective management of the project management processes.

A process is a set of interrelated actions and activities performed to create a pre-specified product, service, or result. Each process is characterized by its inputs, the tools and techniques that can be applied, and the resulting outputs. As explained in Section 2, the project manager needs to consider organizational process assets and enterprise environmental factors. These should be taken into account for every process, even if they are not explicitly listed as inputs in the process specification. Organizational process assets provide guidelines and criteria for tailoring the organization's processes to the specific needs of the project. Enterprise environmental factors may constrain the project management options.

In order for a project to be successful, the project team should:

- Select appropriate processes required to meet the project objectives;
- Use a defined approach that can be adapted to meet requirements;
- Establish and maintain appropriate communication and engagement with stakeholders;
- Comply with requirements to meet stakeholder needs and expectations; and
- Balance the competing constraints of scope, schedule, budget, quality, resources, and risk to produce the specified product, service, or result.

The project processes are performed by the project team with stakeholder interaction and generally fall into one of two major categories:

- **Project management processes.** These processes ensure the effective flow of the project throughout its life cycle. These processes encompass the tools and techniques involved in applying the skills and capabilities described in the Knowledge Areas (Sections 4 through 13).

- **Product-oriented processes.** These processes specify and create the project's product. Product-oriented processes are typically defined by the project life cycle (as discussed in Section 2.4) and vary by application area as well as the phase of the product life cycle. The scope of the project cannot be defined without some basic understanding of how to create the specified product. For example, various construction techniques and tools need to be considered when determining the overall complexity of the house to be built.

The *PMBOK® Guide* describes only the project management processes. Although product-oriented processes are outside the scope of this document, they should not be ignored by the project manager and project team. Project management processes and product-oriented processes overlap and interact throughout the life of a project.

Project management processes apply globally and across industry groups. Good practice means there is general agreement that the application of project management processes has been shown to enhance the chances of success over a wide range of projects. Good practice does not mean that the knowledge, skills, and processes described should always be applied uniformly on all projects. For any given project, the project manager, in collaboration with the project team, is always responsible for determining which processes are appropriate, and the appropriate degree of rigor for each process.

Project managers and their teams should carefully address each process and its inputs and outputs and determine which are applicable to the project they are working on. The *PMBOK® Guide* may be used as a resource in managing a project while considering the overall approach and methodology to be followed for the project. This effort is known as tailoring.

Project management is an integrative undertaking that requires each project and product process to be appropriately aligned and connected with the other processes to facilitate coordination. Actions taken during one process typically affect that process and other related processes. For example, a scope change typically affects project cost, but it may not affect the communications management plan or level of risk. These process interactions often require tradeoffs among project requirements and objectives, and the specific performance tradeoffs will vary from project to project and organization to organization. Successful project management includes actively managing these interactions to meet sponsor, customer, and other stakeholder requirements. In some circumstances, a process or set of processes will need to be iterated several times in order to achieve the required outcome.

Projects exist within an organization and do not operate as a closed system. They require input data from the organization and beyond, and deliver capabilities back to the organization. The project processes may generate information to improve the management of future projects and organizational process assets.

The *PMBOK® Guide* describes the nature of project management processes in terms of the integration between the processes, their interactions, and the purposes they serve. Project management processes are grouped into five categories known as Project Management Process Groups (or Process Groups):

- **Initiating Process Group.** Those processes performed to define a new project or a new phase of an existing project by obtaining authorization to start the project or phase.

- **Planning Process Group.** Those processes required to establish the scope of the project, refine the objectives, and define the course of action required to attain the objectives that the project was undertaken to achieve.

- **Executing Process Group.** Those processes performed to complete the work defined in the project management plan to satisfy the project specifications.

- **Monitoring and Controlling Process Group.** Those processes required to track, review, and regulate the progress and performance of the project; identify any areas in which changes to the plan are required; and initiate the corresponding changes.

- **Closing Process Group.** Those processes performed to finalize all activities across all Process Groups to formally close the project or phase.

The remainder of this section provides information for project management of a single project organized as a network of interlinked processes, details the project management processes, and includes the following major sections:

3.1 Common Project Management Process Interactions

3.2 Project Management Process Groups

3.3 Initiating Process Group

3.4 Planning Process Group

3.5 Executing Process Group

3.6 Monitoring and Controlling Process Group

3.7 Closing Process Group

3.8 Project Information

3.9 Role of the Knowledge Areas

3.10 The Standard for Project Management of a Project

3.1 Common Project Management Process Interactions

The project management processes are presented as discrete elements with well-defined interfaces. However, in practice they overlap and interact in ways that are not completely detailed in this document. Most experienced project management practitioners recognize there is more than one way to manage a project. The required Process Groups and their processes are guides for applying appropriate project management knowledge and skills during the project. The application of the project management processes is iterative, and many processes are repeated during the project.

The integrative nature of project management requires the Monitoring and Controlling Process Group to interact with the other Process Groups, as shown in Figure 3-1. Monitoring and Controlling processes occur at the same time as processes contained within other Process Groups. Thus, the Monitoring and Controlling Process is pictured as a "background" Process Group for the other four Process Groups shown in Figure 3-1.

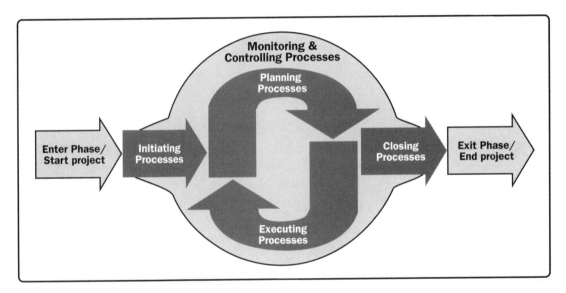

Figure 3-1. Project Management Process Groups

Project Management Process Groups are linked by the outputs which are produced. The Process Groups are seldom either discrete or one-time events; they are overlapping activities that occur throughout the project. The output of one process generally becomes an input to another process or is a deliverable of the project, subproject, or project phase. Deliverables at the subproject or project level may be called incremental deliverables. The Planning Process Group provides the Executing Process Group with the project management plan and project documents, and, as the project progresses, it often creates updates to the project management plan and the project documents. Figure 3-2 illustrates how the Process Groups interact and shows the level of overlap at various times. If the project is divided into phases, the Process Groups interact within each phase.

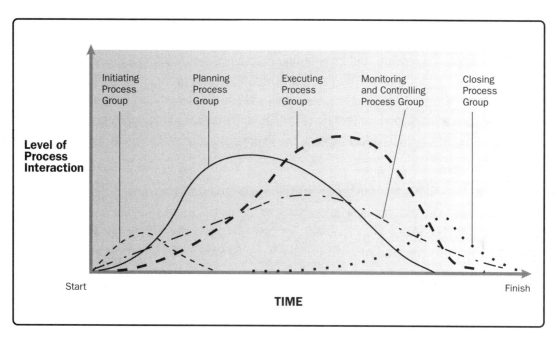

Figure 3-2. Process Groups Interact in a Phase or Project

An example of this interaction is the exit of a design phase, which requires sponsor acceptance of the design document. Once it is available, the design document provides the product description for the Planning and Executing Process Groups in one or more subsequent phases. When a project is divided into phases, the Process Groups are used, as appropriate, to effectively drive the project to completion in a controlled manner. In multiphase projects, processes are repeated within each phase until the criteria for phase completion have been satisfied. Additional information on project organization, life cycles, and project phases is provided in Section 2.

3.2 Project Management Process Groups

The following sections identify and describe the five Project Management Process Groups required for any project. These five Process Groups have clear dependencies and are typically performed in each project and highly interact with one another. These five Process Groups are independent of application areas or industry focus. Individual Process Groups and individual processes are often iterated prior to completing the project and can have interactions within a Process Group and among Process Groups. The nature of these interactions varies from project to project and may or may not be performed in a particular order.

The process flow diagram, Figure 3-3, provides an overall summary of the basic flow and interactions among Process Groups and specific stakeholders. The project management processes are linked by specific inputs and outputs where the result or outcome of one process becomes the input to another process but not necessarily in the same Process Group. **The Process Groups are not project life cycle phases**. In fact, it is possible that all Process Groups could be conducted within a phase. As projects are separated into distinct phases or subcomponents, such as concept development feasibility study, design, prototype, build, or test, etc., all of the Process Groups would normally be repeated for each phase or subcomponent along the lines explained previously and illustrated in Figure 3-2.

The project management processes are shown in the Process Group in which most of the related activities takes place. For example, a process that normally takes place in the planning phase is put into the Planning Process Group. When this process is updated by an Executing Process Group process or activity, it is not considered a new process within the Executing Process Group but is still a Planning Process Group process or activity. The iterative nature of project management means that processes from any group may be reused throughout the project life cycle. For example, in response to a risk event, executing a risk response may trigger further analysis, which leads to another iteration of the Identify Risks process and the associated Perform Quantitative Risk Analysis and Perform Quantitative Risk Analysis processes to evaluate the impact.

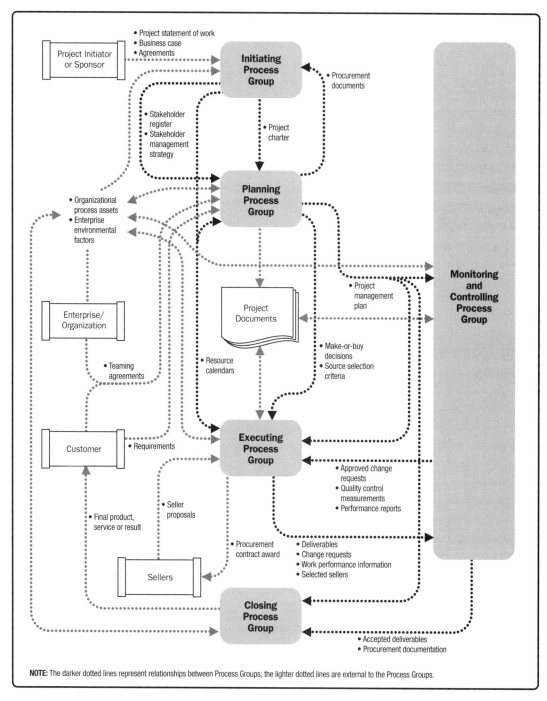

NOTE: The darker dotted lines represent relationships between Process Groups; the lighter dotted lines are external to the Process Groups.

Figure 3-3. Project Management Process Interactions

3.3 Initiating Process Group

The Initiating Process Group consists of those processes performed to define a new project or a new phase of an existing project by obtaining authorization to start the project or phase. Within the Initiating processes, the initial scope is defined and initial financial resources are committed. Internal and external stakeholders who will interact and influence the overall outcome of the project are identified. If not already assigned, the project manager will be selected. This information is captured in the project charter and stakeholder register. When the project charter is approved, the project becomes officially authorized. Although the project management team may help write the project charter, this standard assumes that business case assessment, approval, and funding are handled externally to the project boundaries (Figure 3-4). A project boundary is defined as the point in time that a project or project phase is authorized to its completion. The key purpose of this Process Group is to align the stakeholders' expectations with the project's purpose, give them visibility about the scope and objectives, show how their participation in the project and it associated phases can ensure that their expectations are achieved. These processes help set the vision of the project—what is needed to be accomplished.

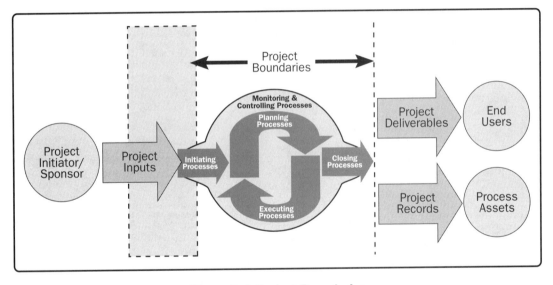

Figure 3-4. Project Boundaries

Large complex projects should be divided into separate phases. In such projects, the Initiating processes are carried out during subsequent phases to validate the decisions made during the original Develop Project Charter and Identify Stakeholders processes. Performing the Initiating processes at the start of each phase helps to keep the project focused on the business need that the project was undertaken to address. The success criteria are verified, and the influence, drivers and objectives of the project stakeholders are reviewed. A decision is then made as to whether the project should be continued, delayed, or discontinued.

Involving the sponsors, customers, and other stakeholders during initiation creates a shared understanding of success criteria, reduces the overhead of involvement, and generally improves deliverable acceptance, customer satisfaction, and other stakeholder satisfaction.

Initiating processes may be performed at the organizational, program, or portfolio level and therefore, would be outside of the project's level of control. For example, prior to commencing a project, the need for high-level requirements may be documented as part of a larger organizational initiative. A process of evaluating alternatives may be utilized to determine the feasibility of the new undertaking. Clear descriptions of the project objectives may be developed, including the reasons why a specific project is the best alternative to satisfy the requirements. The documentation for this decision may also contain the initial project scope statement, deliverables, project duration, and a forecast of the resources for the organization's investment analysis. As part of the Initiating processes, the project manager is given the authority to apply organizational resources to the subsequent project activities.

3.4 Planning Process Group

The Planning Process Group consists of those processes performed to establish the total scope of the effort, define and refine the objectives, and develop the course of action required to attain those objectives. The Planning processes develop the project management plan and the project documents that will be used to carry out the project. The complex nature of project management may require the use of repeated feedback loops for additional analysis. As more project information or characteristics are gathered and understood, additional planning will likely be required. Significant changes occurring throughout the project life cycle trigger a need to revisit one or more of the planning processes and possibly some of the initiating processes. This progressive detailing of the project management plan is called progressive elaboration, indicating that planning and documentation are iterative and ongoing activities. The key benefit of this Process Group is to delineate the strategy and tactics as well as the course of action or path to successfully complete the project or phase. When the Planning Process Group is well managed, it is much easier to get stakeholder buy-in and engagement. These processes express how this will be done, setting the route to the desired objective.

The project management plan and project documents developed as outputs from the Planning Process Group will explore all aspects of the scope, time, cost, quality, communications, human resources, risks, procurements, and stakeholder engagement.

Updates arising from approved changes during the project (generally during Monitoring and Controlling processes and specifically during the Direct and Manage Project Work Process) may significantly impact parts of the project management plan and the project documents. Updates to these documents provide greater precision with respect to schedule, costs, and resource requirements to meet the defined project scope.

The project team seeks input and encourages involvement from all stakeholders when planning the project and developing the project management plan and project documents. While the act of collecting feedback and refining the documents cannot continue indefinitely, procedures set by the organization dictate when the initial planning ends. These procedures will be affected by the nature of the project, the established project boundaries, appropriate monitoring and controlling activities, as well as the environment in which the project will be performed.

Other interactions among the processes within the Planning Process Group are dependent upon the nature of the project. For example, for some projects there will be little or no identifiable risks until after a significant amount of planning has been done. At that time, the team might recognize that the cost and schedule targets are overly aggressive, thus involving considerably more risk than previously understood. The results of the iterations are documented as updates to the project management plan or to various project documents.

3.5 Executing Process Group

The Executing Process Group consists of those processes performed to complete the work defined in the project management plan to satisfy the project specifications. This Process Group involves coordinating people and resources, managing stakeholder expectations, as well as integrating and performing the activities of the project in accordance with the project management plan.

During project execution, results may require planning updates and rebaselining. This may include changes to expected activity durations, changes in resource productivity and availability, and unanticipated risks. Such variances may affect the project management plan or project documents and may require detailed analysis and development of appropriate project management responses. The results of the analysis can trigger change requests that, if approved, may modify the project management plan or other project documents and possibly require establishing new baselines. A large portion of the project's budget will be expended in performing the Executing Process Group processes.

3.6 Monitoring and Controlling Process Group

The Monitoring and Controlling Process Group consists of those processes required to track, review, and orchestrate the progress and performance of the project; identify any areas in which changes to the plan are required; and initiate the corresponding changes. The key benefit of this Process Group is that project performance is measured and analyzed at regular intervals, appropriate events, or exception conditions to identify variances from the project management plan. The Monitoring and Controlling Process Group also involves:

- Controlling changes and recommending corrective or preventive action in anticipation of possible problems,

- Monitoring the ongoing project activities against the project management plan and the project performance measurement baseline, and

- Influencing the factors that could circumvent integrated change control or configuration management so only approved changes are implemented.

This continuous monitoring provides the project team insight into the health of the project and identifies any areas requiring additional attention. The Monitoring and Controlling Process Group not only monitors and controls the work being done within a Process Group, but also monitors and controls the entire project effort. In multiphase projects, the Monitoring and Controlling Process Group coordinates project phases in order to implement corrective or preventive actions to bring the project into compliance with the project management plan. This review can result in recommended and approved updates to the project management plan. For example, a missed activity finish date may require adjustments and trade-offs between budget and schedule objectives. In order to reduce or control overhead, management-by-exception procedures and other techniques can be appropriately considered.

3.7 Closing Process Group

The Closing Process Group consists of those processes performed to conclude all activities across all Project Management Process Groups to formally complete the project, phase, or contractual obligations. This Process Group, when completed, verifies that the defined processes are completed within all of the Process Groups to close the project or a project phase, as appropriate, and formally establishes that the project or project phase is complete.

This Process Group also formally establishes the premature closure of the project. Prematurely closed projects may include, for example: aborted projects, cancelled projects, and projects having a critical situation. In specific cases, when some contracts cannot be formally closed (e.g. claims, termination clauses, etc.) or some activities are to be transferred to other organizational units, specific hand-over procedures may be arranged and finalized.

At project or phase closure, the following may occur:

- Obtain acceptance by the customer or sponsor to formally close the project or phase,
- Conduct post-project or phase-end review,
- Record impacts of tailoring to any process,
- Document lessons learned,
- Apply appropriate updates to organizational process assets,
- Archive all relevant project documents in the project management information system (PMIS) to be used as historical data,
- Close out all procurement activities ensuring termination of all relevant agreements, and
- Perform team members' assessments and release project resources.

3.8 Project Information

Throughout the life cycle of the project, a significant amount of data and information is collected, analyzed, transformed, and distributed in various formats to project team members and other stakeholders. Project data are collected as a result of various Executing processes and are shared within the project team. The collected data are analyzed in context, and aggregated and transformed to become project information during various Controlling processes. The information may then be communicated verbally or stored and distributed as reports in various formats.

The project data are continuously collected and analyzed during the dynamic context of the project execution. As a result, the terms data and information are often used interchangeably in practice. The indiscriminate use of these terms can lead to confusion and misunderstandings by the various project stakeholders. The following guidelines help minimize miscommunication and help the project team use appropriate terminology:

- **Work performance data.** The raw observations and measurements identified during activities performed to carry out the project work. Examples include reported percent of work physically completed, quality and technical performance measures, start and finish dates of schedule activities, number of change requests, number of defects, actual costs, actual durations, etc.

- **Work performance information.** The performance data collected from various controlling processes, analyzed in context and integrated based on relationships across areas. Examples of performance information are status of deliverables, implementation status for change requests, and forecasted estimates to complete.

- **Work performance reports.** The physical or electronic representation of work performance information compiled in project documents, intended to generate decisions or raise issues, actions, or awareness. Examples include status reports, memos, justifications, information notes, electronic dashboards, recommendations, and updates.

Figure 3-5 illustrates the flow of project information across the various processes used to manage the project.

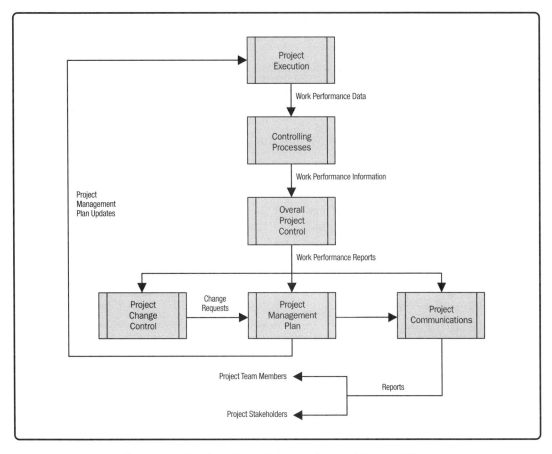

Figure 3-5. Project Data, Information and Report Flow

3.9 Role of the Knowledge Areas

The 47 project management processes identified in the *PMBOK® Guide* are further grouped into ten separate Knowledge Areas. A Knowledge Area represents a complete set of concepts, terms, and activities that make up a professional field, project management field, or area of specialization. These ten Knowledge Areas are used on most projects most of the time. Project teams should utilize these ten Knowledge Areas and other Knowledge Areas, as appropriate, for their specific project. The Knowledge Areas are: Project Integration Management, Project Scope Management, Project Time Management, Project Quality Management, Project Human Resource Management, Project Communications Management, Project Risk Management, Project Procurement Management and Project Stakeholder Management. Each Knowledge Area within the *PMBOK® Guide* is contained in a separate section.

The *PMBOK® Guide* defines the important aspects of each Knowledge Area and how it integrates with the five Process Groups. As supporting elements, the Knowledge Areas provide a detailed description of the process inputs and outputs along with a descriptive explanation of tools and techniques most frequently used within the project management processes to produce each outcome. A data flow diagram is provided in each Knowledge Area (Sections 4 through 8). The data flow diagram is a summary level depiction of the process inputs and process outputs that flow down through all the processes within a specific Knowledge Area (see Figure 3-6 for data flow diagram legend). Although the processes are presented here as discrete elements with well-defined interfaces, in practice they are iterative and can overlap and interact in ways not detailed here.

Table 3-1 reflects the mapping of the 47 project management processes within the 5 Project Management Process Groups and the 10 Knowledge Areas.

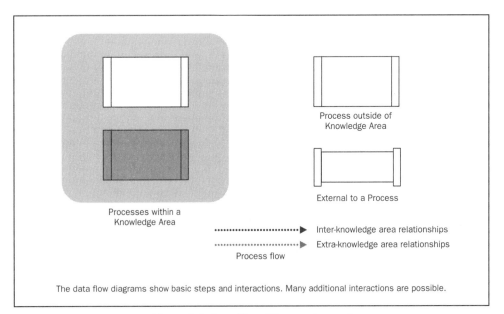

Figure 3-6. Data Flow Diagram Legend

Table 3-1. Project Management Process Group and Knowledge Area Mapping

Knowledge Areas	Project Management Process Groups				
	Initiating Process Group	Planning Process Group	Executing Process Group	Monitoring and Controlling Process Group	Closing Process Group
4. Project Integration Management	4.1 Develop Project Charter	4.2 Develop Project Management Plan	4.3 Direct and Manage Project Work	4.4 Monitor and Control Project Work 4.5 Perform Integrated Change Control	4.6 Close Project or Phase
5. Project Scope Management		5.1 Plan Scope Management 5.2 Collect Requirements 5.3 Define Scope 5.4 Create WBS		5.5 Validate Scope 5.6 Control Scope	
6. Project Time Management		6.1 Plan Schedule Management 6.2 Define Activities 6.3 Sequence Activities 6.4 Estimate Activity Resources 6.5 Estimate Activity Durations 6.6 Develop Schedule		6.7 Control Schedule	
7. Project Cost Management		7.1 Plan Cost Management 7.2 Estimate Costs 7.3 Determine Budget		7.4 Control Costs	
8. Project Quality Management		8.1 Plan Quality Management	8.2 Perform Quality Assurance	8.3 Control Quality	
9. Project Human Resource Management		9.1 Plan Human Resource Management	9.2 Acquire Project Team 9.3 Develop Project Team 9.4 Manage Project Team		
10. Project Communications Management		10.1 Plan Communications Management	10.2 Manage Communications	10.3 Control Communications	
11. Project Risk Management		11.1 Plan Risk Management 11.2 Identify Risks 11.3 Perform Qualitative Risk Analysis 11.4 Perform Quantitative Risk Analysis 11.5 Plan Risk Responses		11.6 Control Risks	
12. Project Procurement Management		12.1 Plan Procurement Management	12.2 Conduct Procurements	12.3 Control Procurements	12.4 Close Procurements
13. Project Stakeholder Management	13.1 Identify Stakeholders	13.2 Plan Stakeholder Management	13.3 Manage Stakeholder Engagement	13.4 Control Stakeholder Engagement	

3

PROJECT INTEGRATION MANAGEMENT

Project Integration Management includes the processes and activities to identify, define, combine, unify, and coordinate the various processes and project management activities within the Project Management Process Groups. In the project management context, integration includes characteristics of unification, consolidation, communication, and integrative actions that are crucial to controlled project execution through completion, successfully managing stakeholder expectations, and meeting requirements. Project Integration Management includes making choices about resource allocation, making trade-offs among competing objectives and alternatives, and managing the interdependencies among the project management Knowledge Areas. The project management processes are usually presented as discrete processes with defined interfaces while, in practice, they overlap and interact in ways that cannot be completely detailed in the *PMBOK® Guide*.

Figure 4-1 provides an overview of the Project Integration Management processes, which are as follows:

4.1 Develop Project Charter—The process of developing a document that formally authorizes the existence of a project and provides the project manager with the authority to apply organizational resources to project activities.

4.2 Develop Project Management Plan—The process of defining, preparing, and coordinating all subsidiary plans and integrating them into a comprehensive project management plan. The project's integrated baselines and subsidiary plans may be included within the project management plan.

4.3 Direct and Manage Project Work—The process of leading and performing the work defined in the project management plan and implementing approved changes to achieve the project's objectives.

4.4 Monitor and Control Project Work—The process of tracking, reviewing, and reporting project progress against the performance objectives defined in the project management plan.

4.5 Perform Integrated Change Control—The process of reviewing all change requests; approving changes and managing changes to deliverables, organizational process assets, project documents, and the project management plan; and communicating their disposition.

4.6 Close Project or Phase—The process of finalizing all activities across all of the Project Management Process Groups to formally complete the phase or project.

These processes interact with each other and with processes in other Knowledge Areas as described in detail in Section 3 and Annex A1.

The need for Project Integration Management is necessary in situations where individual processes interact. For example, a cost estimate needed for a contingency plan involves integrating the processes in the Project Cost, Time, and Risk Management Knowledge Areas. When additional risks associated with various staffing alternatives are identified, then one or more of those processes may be revisited. The project deliverables may also need integrating with ongoing operations of the performing organization, the requesting organization, and with the long-term strategic planning that takes future problems and opportunities into consideration. Project Integration Management also includes the activities needed to manage project documents to ensure consistency with the project management plan and product, service, or capability deliverables.

Most experienced project management practitioners know there is no single way to manage a project. They apply project management knowledge, skills, and required processes in a preferred order and with varying rigor to achieve the desired project performance. However, the determination that a particular process is not required does not mean that it should not be addressed. The project manager and project team need to address every process and the project environment to determine the level of implementation for each process within the project. If a project has more than one phase, the level of rigor applied within each of the project phases should be appropriate for each phase. This determination is also addressed by the project manager and project team.

The integrative nature of projects and project management can be understood by thinking of other types of activities performed while completing a project. Examples of some activities performed by the project management team are:

- Develop, review, analyze, and understand the scope. This includes the project and product requirements, criteria, assumptions, constraints, and other influences related to a project, and how each will be managed or addressed within the project;
- Transform the collected project information into a project management plan using a structured approach as described in the *PMBOK® Guide*;
- Perform activities to produce project deliverables; and
- Measure and monitor the project's progress and take appropriate action to meet project objectives.

The links among the processes in the Project Management Process Groups are often iterative in nature. For example, the Planning Process Group provides the Executing Process Group with a documented project management plan early in the project and then updates the project management plan if changes occur as the project progresses.

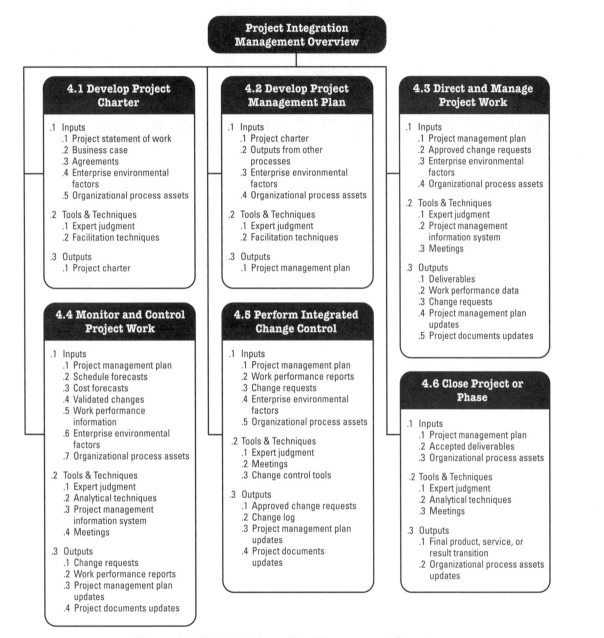

Figure 4-1. Project Integration Management Overview

4.1 Develop Project Charter

Develop Project Charter is the process of developing a document that formally authorizes the existence of a project and provides the project manager with the authority to apply organizational resources to project activities. The key benefit of this process is a well-defined project start and project boundaries, creation of a formal record of the project, and a direct way for senior management to formally accept and commit to the project. The inputs, tools and techniques, and outputs for this process are shown in Figure 4-2. Figure 4-3 depicts the data flow diagram of the process.

Inputs	Tools & Techniques	Outputs
.1 Project statement of work	.1 Expert judgment	.1 Project charter
.2 Business case	.2 Facilitation techniques	
.3 Agreements		
.4 Enterprise environmental factors		
.5 Organizational process assets		

Figure 4-2. Develop Project Charter: Inputs, Tools and Techniques, and Outputs

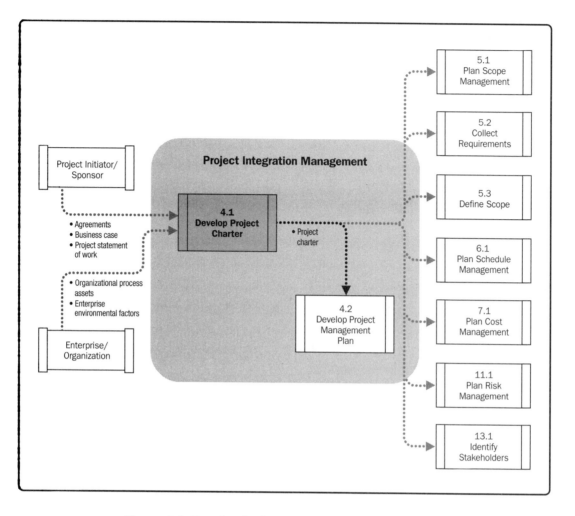

Figure 4-3. Develop Project Charter Data Flow Diagram

The project charter establishes a partnership between the performing and requesting organizations. In the case of external projects, a formal contract is typically the preferred way to establish an agreement. In this case, the project team becomes the seller responding to conditions of an offer to buy from an outside entity. A project charter is still used to establish internal agreements within an organization to assure proper delivery under the contract. The approved project charter formally initiates the project. A project manager is identified and assigned as early in the project as is feasible, preferably while the project charter is being developed and always prior to the start of planning. The project charter should be authored by the sponsoring entity. The project charter provides the project manager with the authority to plan and execute the project. It is recommended that the project manager participate in the development of the project charter to obtain a foundational understanding of the project requirements. This understanding will better allow for efficient resources allocation to project activities.

Projects are initiated by an entity external to the project such as a sponsor, program or project management office (PMO) staff person, or a portfolio governing body chairperson or authorized representative. The project initiator or sponsor should be at the level that is appropriate to procure funding and commit resources to the project. Projects are initiated due to internal business needs or external influences. These needs or influences often trigger the creation of a needs analysis, feasibility study, business case, or description of the situation that the project will address. Chartering a project validates alignment of the project to the strategy and ongoing work of the organization. A project charter is not considered to be a contract, because there is no consideration or money promised or exchanged in its creation.

4.1.1 Develop Project Charter: Inputs

4.1.1.1 Project Statement of Work

The project statement of work (SOW) is a narrative description of products, services, or results to be delivered by a project. For internal projects, the project initiator or sponsor provides the statement of work based on business needs, product, or service requirements. For external projects, the statement of work can be received from the customer as part of a bid document, (e.g., a request for proposal, request for information, or request for bid) or as part of a contract. The SOW references the following:

- **Business need.** An organization's business need may be based on a market demand, technological advance, legal requirement, government regulation, or environmental consideration. Typically, the business need and the cost-benefit analysis are contained in the business case to justify the project.

- **Product scope description.** The product scope description documents the characteristics of the product, service, or results that the project will be undertaken to create. The description should also document the relationship between the products, services, or results being created and the business need that the project will address.

- **Strategic plan.** The strategic plan documents the organization's strategic vision, goals, and objectives and may contain a high-level mission statement. All projects should be aligned with their organization's strategic plan. Strategic plan alignment ensures that each project contributes to the overall objections of the organization.

4.1.1.2 Business Case

The business case or similar document describes the necessary information from a business standpoint to determine whether or not the project is worth the required investment. It is commonly used for decision making by managers or executives above the project level. Typically, the business need and the cost-benefit analysis are contained in the business case to justify and establish boundaries for the project, and such analysis is usually completed by a business analyst using various stakeholder inputs. The sponsor should agree to the scope and limitations of the business case. The business case is created as a result of one or more of the following:

- Market demand (e.g., a car company authorizing a project to build more fuel-efficient cars in response to gasoline shortages),

- Organizational need (e.g., due to high overhead costs a company may combine staff functions and streamline processes to reduce costs.),

- Customer request (e.g., an electric utility authorizing a project to build a new substation to serve a new industrial park),

- Technological advance (e.g., an airline authorizing a new project to develop electronic tickets instead of paper tickets based on technological advances),

- Legal requirement (e.g., a paint manufacturer authorizing a project to establish guidelines for handling toxic materials),

- Ecological impacts (e.g., a company authorizing a project to lessen its environmental impact), or

- Social need (e.g., a nongovernmental organization in a developing country authorizing a project to provide potable water systems, latrines, and sanitation education to communities suffering from high rates of cholera).

Each of the examples in this list may contain elements of risk that should be addressed. In the case of multiphase projects, the business case may be periodically reviewed to ensure that the project is on track to deliver the business benefits. In the early stages of the project life cycle, periodic review of the business case by the sponsoring organization also helps to confirm that the project is still aligned with the business case. The project manager is responsible for ensuring that the project effectively and efficiently meets the goals of the organization and those requirements of a broad set of stakeholders, as defined in the business case.

4.1.1.3 Agreements

Agreements are used to define initial intentions for a project. Agreements may take the form of contracts, memorandums of understanding (MOUs), service level agreements (SLA), letter of agreements, letters of intent, verbal agreements, email, or other written agreements. Typically, a contract is used when a project is being performed for an external customer.

4.1.1.4 Enterprise Environmental Factors

Described in Section 2.1.5. The enterprise environmental factors that can influence the Develop Project Charter process include, but are not limited to:

- Governmental standards, industry standards, or regulations (e.g. codes of conduct, quality standards, or worker protection standards),
- Organizational culture and structure, and
- Marketplace conditions.

4.1.1.5 Organizational Process Assets

Described in Section 2.1.4. The organizational process assets that can influence the Develop Project Charter process include, but are not limited to:

- Organizational standard processes, policies, and process definitions,
- Templates (e.g., project charter template), and
- Historical information and lessons learned knowledge base (e.g., projects, records, and documents; all project closure information and documentation; information about both the results of previous project selection decisions and previous project performance information; and information from the risk management activity).

4.1.2 Develop Project Charter: Tools and Techniques

4.1.2.1 Expert Judgment

Expert judgment is often used to assess the inputs used to develop the project charter. Expert judgment is applied to all technical and management details during this process. Such expertise is provided by any group or individual with specialized knowledge or training and is available from many sources, including:

- Other units within the organization,
- Consultants,
- Stakeholders, including customers or sponsors,
- Professional and technical associations,
- Industry groups,
- Subject matter experts (SME), and
- Project management office (PMO).

4.1.2.2 Facilitation Techniques

Facilitation techniques have broad application within project management processes and guide the development of the project charter. Brainstorming, conflict resolution, problem solving, and meeting management are examples of key techniques used by facilitators to help teams and individuals accomplish project activities.

4.1.3 Develop Project Charter: Outputs

4.1.3.1 Project Charter

The project charter is the document issued by the project initiator or sponsor that formally authorizes the existence of a project and provides the project manager with the authority to apply organizational resources to project activities. It documents the business needs, assumptions, constraints, the understanding of the customer's needs and high-level requirements, and the new product, service, or result that it is intended to satisfy, such as:

- Project purpose or justification,

- Measurable project objectives and related success criteria,

- High-level requirements,

- Assumptions and constraints,

- High-level project description and boundaries,

- High-level risks,

- Summary milestone schedule,

- Summary budget,

- Stakeholder list,

- Project approval requirements (i.e., what constitutes project success, who decides the project is successful, and who signs off on the project),

- Assigned project manager, responsibility, and authority level, and

- Name and authority of the sponsor or other person(s) authorizing the project charter.

4.2 Develop Project Management Plan

Develop Project Management Plan is the process of defining, preparing, and coordinating all subsidiary plans and integrating them into a comprehensive project management plan. The key benefit of this process is a central document that defines the basis of all project work. The inputs, tools and techniques, and outputs for this process are depicted in Figure 4-4. Figure 4-5 depicts the data flow diagram of the process.

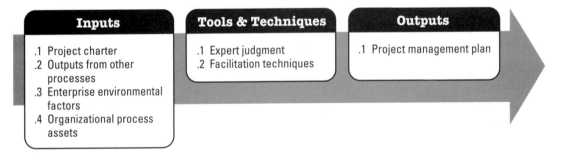

Inputs	Tools & Techniques	Outputs
.1 Project charter .2 Outputs from other processes .3 Enterprise environmental factors .4 Organizational process assets	.1 Expert judgment .2 Facilitation techniques	.1 Project management plan

Figure 4-3. Develop Project Charter Data Flow Diagram

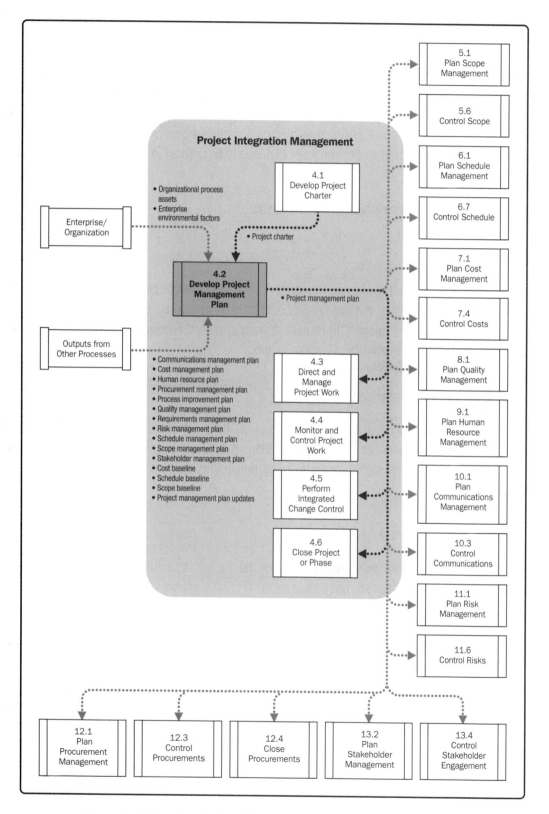

Figure 4-5. Develop Project Management Plan Data Flow Diagram

The project management plan defines how the project is executed, monitored and controlled, and closed. The project management plan's content varies depending upon the application area and complexity of the project. It is developed through a series of integrated processes extending through project closure. This process results in a project management plan that is progressively elaborated by updates, and controlled and approved through the Perform Integrated Change Control (Section 4.5) process. Projects that exist in the context of a program should develop a project management plan that is consistent with the program management plan. For example, if the program management plan indicates all changes exceeding a specified cost need to be reviewed by the change control board (CCB), then this process and cost threshold needs to be defined in the project management plan.

4.2.1 Develop Project Management Plan: Inputs

4.2.1.1 Project Charter

Described in Section 4.1.3.1. The size of the project charter varies depending on the complexity of the project and the information known at the time of its creation. At a minimum, the project charter should define the high-level boundaries of the project. The project manager uses the project charter as the starting point for initial planning throughout the Initiating Process Group.

4.2.1.2 Outputs from Other Processes

Outputs from many of the other processes described in Sections 5 through 13 are integrated to create the project management plan. Any baselines and subsidiary plans that are an output from other planning processes are inputs to this process. In addition, changes to these documents may necessitate updates to the project management plan.

4.2.1.3 Enterprise Environmental Factors

Described in Section 2.1.5. The enterprise environmental factors that can influence the Develop Project Management Plan process include, but are not limited to:

- Governmental or industry standards;
- Project management body of knowledge for vertical market (e.g., construction) and/or focus area (e.g. environmental, safety, risk, or agile software development);
- Project management information system (e.g., an automated tool, such as a scheduling software tool, a configuration management system, an information collection and distribution system, or web interfaces to other online automated systems);

- Organizational structure, culture, management practices, and sustainability;

- Infrastructure (e.g., existing facilities and capital equipment); and

- Personnel administration (e.g., hiring and termination guidelines, employee performance reviews, and employee development and training records).

4.2.1.4 Organizational Process Assets

Described in Section 2.1.4. The organizational process assets that can influence the Develop Project Management Plan process include, but are not limited to:

- Standardized guidelines, work instructions, proposal evaluation criteria, and performance measurement criteria;

- Project management plan template, including:

  ○ Guidelines and criteria for tailoring the organization's set of standard processes to satisfy the specific needs of the project, and

  ○ Project closure guidelines or requirements such as the product validation and acceptance criteria;

- Change control procedures, including the steps by which official organization standards, policies, plans, and procedures, or any project documents will be modified and how any changes will be approved and validated;

- Project files from previous projects (e.g., scope, cost, schedule and performance measurement baselines, project calendars, project schedule network diagrams, and risk registers,);

- Historical information and lessons learned knowledge base; and

- Configuration management knowledge base containing the versions and baselines of all official organization standards, policies, procedures, and any project documents.

4.2.2 Develop Project Management Plan: Tools and Techniques

4.2.2.1 Expert Judgment

When developing the project management plan, expert judgment is utilized to:

- Tailor the process to meet the project needs,
- Develop technical and management details to be included in the project management plan,
- Determine resources and skill levels needed to perform project work,
- Define the level of configuration management to apply on the project,
- Determine which project documents will be subject to the formal change control process, and
- Prioritize the work on the project to ensure the project resources are allocated to the appropriate work at the appropriate time.

4.2.2.2 Facilitation Techniques

Described in Section 4.1.2.2. Facilitation techniques have broad application within project management processes and are used to guide the development of the project management plan. Brainstorming, conflict resolution, problem solving, and meeting management are key techniques used by facilitators to help teams and individuals achieve agreement to accomplish project activities.

4.2.3 Develop Project Management Plan: Outputs

4.2.3.1 Project Management Plan

The project management plan is the document that describes how the project will be executed, monitored, and controlled. It integrates and consolidates all of the subsidiary plans and baselines from the planning processes.

Project baselines include, but are not limited to:

- Scope baseline (Section 5.4.3.1),
- Schedule baseline (Section 6.6.3.1), and
- Cost baseline (Section 7.3.3.1).

4.4.1.7 Organizational Process Assets

Described in Section 2.1.4. The organizational process assets that can influence the Monitor and Control Project Work process include, but are not limited to:

- Organizational communication requirements;

- Financial controls procedures (e.g., time reporting, required expenditure and disbursement reviews, accounting codes, and standard contract provisions);

- Issue and defect management procedures defining issue and defect controls, issue and defect identification, and resolution and action item tracking;

- Change control procedures, including those for scope, schedule, cost, and quality variances;

- Risk control procedures including risk categories, probability definition and impact, and probability and impact matrix;

- Process measurement database used to make available measurement data on processes and products; and

- Lessons learned database.

4.4.2 Monitor and Control Project Work: Tools and Techniques

4.4.2.1 Expert Judgment

Expert judgment is used by the project management team to interpret the information provided by the monitor and control processes. The project manager, in collaboration with the team, determines the actions required to ensure that project performance matches expectations.

4.4.2.2 Analytical Techniques

Analytical techniques are applied in project management to forecast potential outcomes based on possible variations of project or environmental variables and their relationships with other variables. Examples of analytical techniques used in projects are:

- Regression analysis,

- Grouping methods,

- Causal analysis,

- Root cause analysis,

- Forecasting methods (e.g., time series, scenario building, simulation, etc.),

- Failure mode and effect analysis (FMEA),

- Fault tree analysis (FTA),

- Reserve analysis,

- Trend analysis,

- Earned value management, and

- Variance analysis.

4.4.2.3 Project Management Information System

The project management information system, which is part of enterprise environmental factors, provides access to automated tools, such as scheduling, cost, and resourcing tools, performance indicators, databases, project records, and financials used during the Monitor and Control Project Work process.

4.4.2.4 Meetings

Described in Section 4.3.2.3. Meetings may be face-to-face, virtual, formal, or informal. They may include project team members, stakeholders, and others involved in or affected by the project. Types of meetings include, but are not limited to, user groups and review meetings.

4.4.3 Monitor and Control Project Work: Outputs

4.4.3.1 Change Requests

As a result of comparing planned results to actual results, change requests may be issued to expand, adjust, or reduce project scope, product scope, or quality requirements and schedule or cost baselines. Change requests may necessitate the collection and documentation of new requirements. Changes can impact the project management plan, project documents, or product deliverables. Changes that meet the project's change control criteria should go through the integrated change control process established for the project. Changes may include, but are not limited to, the following:

- **Corrective action**—An intentional activity that realigns the performance of the project work with the project management plan;

- **Preventive action**—An intentional activity that ensures the future performance of the project work is aligned with the project management plan; and

- **Defect repair**—An intentional activity to modify a nonconforming product or product component.

4.4.3.2 Work Performance Reports

Work performance reports are the physical or electronic representation of work performance information compiled in project documents, intended to generate decisions, actions, or awareness. Project information may be communicated verbally from person to person. However, in order to record, store, and sometimes distribute work performance information, a physical or electronic representation in the form of project documents is required. Work performance reports are a subset of project documents, which are intended to create awareness and generate decisions or actions. Specific work performance metrics may be defined at the start of the project and included in the normal work performance reports provided to key stakeholders.

Examples of work performance reports include status reports, memos, justifications, information notes, recommendations, and updates.

4.4.3.3 Project Management Plan Updates

Changes identified during the Monitor and Control Project Work process may affect the overall project management plan. These changes, after being processed through the appropriate change control process can lead to project management plan updates. Project management plan elements that may be updated include, but are not limited to:

- Scope management plan (Section 5.1.3.1),

- Requirements management plan (Section 5.1.3.2),

- Schedule management plan (Section 6.1.3.1),

- Cost management plan (Section 7.1.3.1),

- Quality management plan (Section 8.1.3.1),

- Scope baseline (Section 5.4.3.1),

- Schedule baseline (Section 6.6.3.1), and

- Cost baseline (Section 7.3.3.1).

4.4.3.4 Project Documents Updates

Project documents that may be updated include, but are not limited to:

- Schedule and cost forecasts,
- Work performance reports, and
- Issue log.

4.5 Perform Integrated Change Control

Perform Integrated Change Control is the process of reviewing all change requests; approving changes and managing changes to deliverables, organizational process assets, project documents, and the project management plan; and communicating their disposition. It reviews all requests for changes or modifications to project documents, deliverables, baselines, or the project management plan and approves or rejects the changes. The key benefit of this process is that it allows for documented changes within the project to be considered in an integrated fashion while reducing project risk, which often arises from changes made without consideration to the overall project objectives or plans. The inputs, tools and techniques, and outputs of this process are depicted in Figure 4-10. Figure 4-11 depicts the data flow diagram of the process.

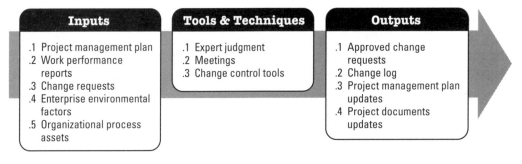

Inputs	Tools & Techniques	Outputs
.1 Project management plan .2 Work performance reports .3 Change requests .4 Enterprise environmental factors .5 Organizational process assets	.1 Expert judgment .2 Meetings .3 Change control tools	.1 Approved change requests .2 Change log .3 Project management plan updates .4 Project documents updates

Figure 4-10. Perform Integrated Change Control: Inputs, Tools & Techniques, and Outputs

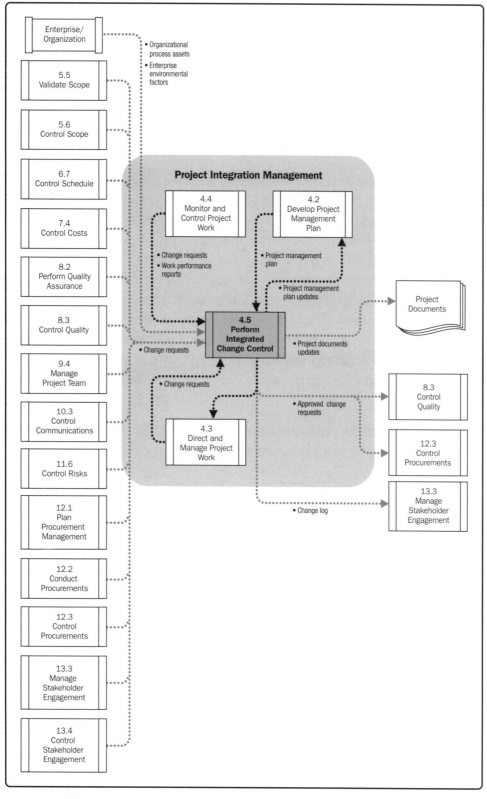

Figure 4-11. Perform Integrated Change Control Data Flow Diagram

The Perform Integrated Change Control process is conducted from project inception through completion and is the ultimate responsibility of the project manager. The project management plan, the project scope statement, and other deliverables are maintained by carefully and continuously managing changes, either by rejecting changes or by approving changes, thereby assuring that only approved changes are incorporated into a revised baseline.

Changes may be requested by any stakeholder involved with the project. Although changes may be initiated verbally, they should be recorded in written form and entered into the change management and/or configuration management system. Change requests are subject to the process specified in the change control and configuration control systems. Those change request processes may require information on estimated time impacts and estimated cost impacts.

Every documented change request needs to be either approved or rejected by a responsible individual, usually the project sponsor or project manager. The responsible individual will be identified in the project management plan or by organizational procedures. When required, the Perform Integrated Change Control process includes a change control board (CCB), which is a formally chartered group responsible for reviewing, evaluating, approving, delaying, or rejecting changes to the project, and for recording and communicating such decisions. Approved change requests can require new or revised cost estimates, activity sequences, schedule dates, resource requirements, and analysis of risk response alternatives. These changes can require adjustments to the project management plan and other project documents. The applied level of change control is dependent upon the application area, complexity of the specific project, contract requirements, and the context and environment in which the project is performed. Customer or sponsor approval may be required for certain change requests after CCB approval, unless they are part of the CCB.

Configuration control is focused on the specification of both the deliverables and the processes; while change control is focused on identifying, documenting, and approving or rejecting changes to the project documents, deliverables, or baselines.

Some of the configuration management activities included in the Perform Integrated Change Control process are as follows:

- **Configuration identification.** Identification and selection of a configuration item to provide the basis for which the product configuration is defined and verified, products and documents are labeled, changes are managed, and accountability is maintained.

- **Configuration status accounting.** Information is recorded and reported as to when appropriate data about the configuration item should be provided. This information includes a listing of approved configuration identification, status of proposed changes to the configuration, and the implementation status of approved changes.

- **Configuration verification and audit.** Configuration verification and configuration audits ensure the composition of a project's configuration items is correct and that corresponding changes are registered, assessed, approved, tracked, and correctly implemented. This ensures the functional requirements defined in the configuration documentation have been met.

4.5.1 Perform Integrated Change Control: Inputs

4.5.1.1 Project Management Plan

Described in Section 4.2.3.1. Elements of the project management plan that may be used include, but are not limited to:

- Scope management plan, which contains the procedures for scope changes;

- Scope baseline, which provides product definition; and

- Change management plan, which provides the direction for managing the change control process and documents the formal change control board (CCB).

Changes are documented and updated within the project management plan as part of the change and configuration management processes.

4.5.1.2 Work Performance Reports

Described in Section 4.4.3.2. Work performance reports of particular interest to the Perform Integrated Change Control process include resource availability, schedule and cost data, and earned value management (EVM) reports, burnup or burndown charts.

4.5.1.3 Change Requests

All of the Monitoring and Controlling processes and many of the Executing processes produce change requests as an output. Change requests may include corrective action, preventive action, and defect repairs. However, corrective and preventive actions do not normally affect the project baselines—only the performance against the baselines.

4.5.1.4 Enterprise Environmental Factors

Described in Section 2.1.5. The following enterprise environmental factor can influence the Perform Integrated Change Control process: project management information system. The project management information system may include the scheduling software tool, a configuration management system, an information collection and distribution system, or web interfaces to other online automated systems.

4.5.1.5 Organizational Process Assets

Described in Section 2.1.4. The organizational process assets that can influence the Perform Integrated Change Control process include, but are not limited to:

- Change control procedures, including the steps by which official organization standards, policies, plans, and other project documents will be modified, and how any changes will be approved, validated, and implemented;

- Procedures for approving and issuing change authorizations;

- Process measurement database used to collect and make available measurement data on processes and products;

- Project documents (e.g., scope, cost, and schedule baselines, project calendars, project schedule network diagrams, risk registers, planned response actions, and defined risk impact); and

- Configuration management knowledge base containing the versions and baselines of all official organization standards, policies, procedures, and any project documents.

4.5.2 Perform Integrated Change Control: Tools and Techniques

4.5.2.1 Expert Judgment

In addition to the project management team's expert judgment, stakeholders may be asked to provide their expertise and may be asked to sit on the change control board (CCB). Such judgment and expertise are applied to any technical and management details during this process and may be provided by various sources, for example:

- Consultants,
- Stakeholders, including customers or sponsors,
- Professional and technical associations,
- Industry groups,
- Subject matter experts (SMEs), and
- Project management office (PMO).

4.5.2.2 Meetings

In this case, these meetings are usually referred to as change control meetings. When needed for the project, a change control board (CCB) is responsible for meeting and reviewing the change requests and approving, rejecting, or other disposition of those changes. The CCB may also review configuration management activities. The roles and responsibilities of these boards are clearly defined and agreed upon by appropriate stakeholders and documented in the change management plan. CCB decisions are documented and communicated to the stakeholders for information and follow-up actions.

4.5.2.3 Change Control Tools

In order to facilitate configuration and change management, manual or automated tools may be used. Tool selection should be based on the needs of the project stakeholders including organizational and environmental considerations and/or constraints.

Tools are used to manage the change requests and the resulting decisions. Additional considerations should be made for communication to assist the CCB members in their duties as well as distribute the decisions to the appropriate stakeholders.

4.5.3 Perform Integrated Change Control: Outputs

4.5.3.1 Approved Change Requests

Change requests are processed according to the change control system by the project manager, CCB, or by an assigned team member. Approved change requests will be implemented through the Direct and Manage Project Work process. The disposition of all change requests, approved or not, will be updated in the change log as part of updates to the project documents.

4.5.3.2 Change Log

A change log is used to document changes that occur during a project. These changes and their impact to the project in terms of time, cost, and risk, are communicated to the appropriate stakeholders. Rejected change requests are also captured in the change log.

4.5.3.3 Project Management Plan Updates

Elements of the project management plan that may be updated include, but are not limited to:

- Any subsidiary plans, and
- Baselines that are subject to the formal change control process.

Changes to baselines should only show the changes from the current time forward. Past performance may not be changed. This protects the integrity of the baselines and the historical data of past performance.

4.5.3.4 Project Documents Updates

Project documents that may be updated as a result of the Perform Integrated Change Control process include all documents specified as being subject to the project's formal change control process.

4.6 Close Project or Phase

Close Project or Phase is the process of finalizing all activities across all of the Project Management Process Groups to formally complete the project or phase. The key benefit of this process is that it provides lessons learned, the formal ending of project work, and the release of organization resources to pursue new endeavors. The inputs, tools and techniques, and outputs of this process are depicted in Figure 4-12. Figure 4-13 depicts the data flow diagram of the process.

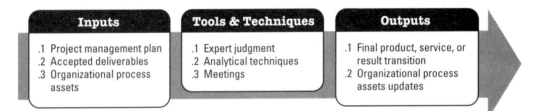

Inputs	Tools & Techniques	Outputs
.1 Project management plan .2 Accepted deliverables .3 Organizational process assets	.1 Expert judgment .2 Analytical techniques .3 Meetings	.1 Final product, service, or result transition .2 Organizational process assets updates

Figure 4-12. Close Project or Phase: Inputs, Tools & Techniques, and Outputs

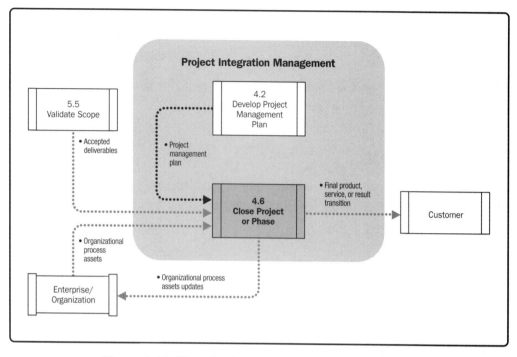

Figure 4-13. Close Project or Phase Data Flow Diagram

When closing the project, the project manager reviews all prior information from the previous phase closures to ensure that all project work is completed and that the project has met its objectives. Since project scope is measured against the project management plan, the project manager reviews the scope baseline to ensure completion before considering the project closed. The Close Project or Phase process also establishes the procedures to investigate and document the reasons for actions taken if a project is terminated before completion. In order to successfully achieve this, the project manager needs to engage all the proper stakeholders in the process.

This includes all planned activities necessary for administrative closure of the project or phase, including step-by-step methodologies that address:

- Actions and activities necessary to satisfy completion or exit criteria for the phase or project;

- Actions and activities necessary to transfer the project's products, services, or results to the next phase or to production and/or operations; and

- Activities needed to collect project or phase records, audit project success or failure, gather lessons learned and archive project information for future use by the organization.

4.6.1 Close Project or Phase: Inputs

4.6.1.1 Project Management Plan

Described in Section 4.2.3.1. The project management plan becomes the agreement between the project manager and project sponsor, defining what constitutes project completion.

4.6.1.2 Accepted Deliverables

Described in Section 5.5. Accepted deliverables may include approved product specifications, delivery receipts, and work performance documents. Partial or interim deliverables may also be included for phased or cancelled projects.

4.6.1.3 Organizational Process Assets

Described in Section 2.1.4. The organizational process assets that can influence the Close Project or Phase process include, but are not limited to:

- Project or phase closure guidelines or requirements (e.g., administrative procedures, project audits, project evaluations, and transition criteria); and
- Historical information and lessons learned knowledge base (e.g., project records and documents, all project closure information and documentation, information about both the results of previous project selection decisions and previous project performance information, and information from risk management activities).

4.6.2 Close Project or Phase: Tools and Techniques

4.6.2.1 Expert Judgment

Expert judgment is applied when performing administrative closure activities. These experts ensure the project or phase closure is performed to the appropriate standards. Expertise is available from many sources, including but not limited to

- Other project managers within the organization,
- Project management office (PMO), and
- Professional and technical associations.

4.6.2.2 Analytical Techniques

Described in Section 4.4.2.2. Examples of analytical techniques used in project closeout are:

- Regression analysis, and
- Trend analysis.

4.6.2.3 Meetings

Described in Section 4.3.2.3. Meetings may be face-to-face, virtual, formal, or informal. This may include project team members and other stakeholders, involved in or affected by the project. Types of meetings include, but are not limited to lessons learned, closeout, user group, and review meetings.

4.6.3 Close Project or Phase: Outputs

4.6.3.1 Final Product, Service, or Result Transition

This output refers to the transition of the final product, service, or result that the project was authorized to produce (or in the case of phase closure, the intermediate product, service, or result of that phase).

4.6.3.2 Organizational Process Assets Updates

The organizational process assets that are updated as a result of the Close Project or Phase process include, but are not limited to:

- **Project files**—Documentation resulting from the project's activities, for example, project management plan; scope, cost, schedule, and project calendars; risk registers and other registers; change management documentation; planned risk response actions; and risk impact.

- **Project or phase closure documents**—Project or phase closure documents, consisting of formal documentation that indicates completion of the project or phase and the transfer of the completed project or phase deliverables to others, such as an operations group or to the next phase. During project closure, the project manager reviews prior phase documentation, customer acceptance documentation from the Validate Scope process (Section 5.4), and the contract (if applicable), to ensure that all project requirements are completed prior to finalizing the closure of the project. If the project was terminated prior to completion, the formal documentation indicates why the project was terminated and formalizes the procedures for the transfer of the finished and unfinished deliverables of the cancelled project to others.

- **Historical information**—Historical information and lessons learned information are transferred to the lessons learned knowledge base for use by future projects or phases. This can include information on issues and risks as well as techniques that worked well that can be applied to future projects.

 ©2013 Project Management Institute. *A Guide to the Project Management Body of Knowledge (PMBOK® Guide) – Fifth Edition*

5

PROJECT SCOPE MANAGEMENT

Project Scope Management includes the processes required to ensure that the project includes all the work required, and only the work required, to complete the project successfully. Managing the project scope is primarily concerned with defining and controlling what is and is not included in the project.

Figure 5-1 provides an overview of the Project Scope Management processes, which include the following:

5.1 Plan Scope Management—The process of creating a scope management plan that documents how the project scope will be defined, validated, and controlled.

5.2 Collect Requirements—The process of determining, documenting, and managing stakeholder needs and requirements to meet project objectives.

5.3 Define Scope—The process of developing a detailed description of the project and product.

5.4 Create WBS—The process of subdividing project deliverables and project work into smaller, more manageable components.

5.5 Validate Scope—The process of formalizing acceptance of the completed project deliverables.

5.6 Control Scope—The process of monitoring the status of the project and product scope and managing changes to the scope baseline.

These processes interact with each other and with processes in other Knowledge Areas as described in detail in Section 3 and Annex A1.

In the project context, the term scope can refer to:

- **Product scope.** The features and functions that characterize a product, service, or result; and/or

- **Project scope.** The work performed to deliver a product, service, or result with the specified features and functions. The term project scope is sometimes viewed as including product scope.

The processes used to manage project scope, as well as the supporting tools and techniques, can vary by project. The scope baseline for the project is the approved version of the project scope statement, work breakdown structure (WBS), and its associated WBS dictionary. A baseline can be changed only through formal change control procedures and is used as a basis for comparison while performing Validate Scope and Control Scope processes as well as other controlling processes.

Completion of the project scope is measured against the project management plan (Section 4.2.3.1). Completion of the product scope is measured against the product requirements (Section 5.2). The Project Scope Management processes need to be well integrated with the other Knowledge Area processes, so that the work of the project will result in delivery of the specified product scope.

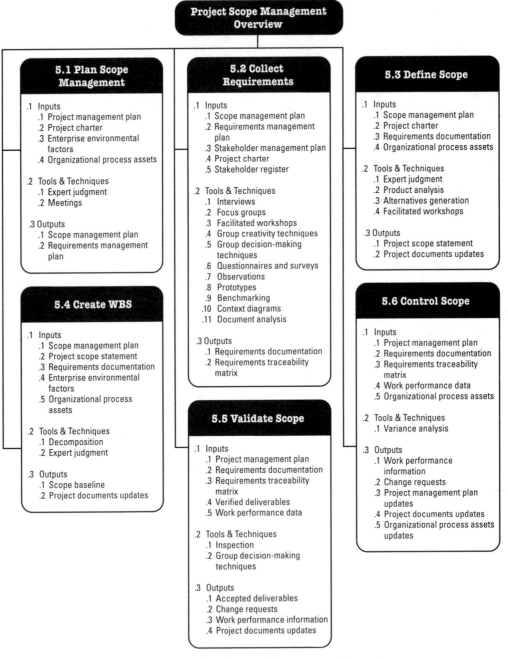

Figure 5-1. Project Scope Management Overview

5.1 Plan Scope Management

Plan Scope Management is the process of creating a scope management plan that documents how the project scope will be defined, validated, and controlled. The key benefit of this process is that it provides guidance and direction on how scope will be managed throughout the project. The inputs, tools and techniques, and outputs of this process are depicted in Figure 5-2. Figure 5-3 depicts the data flow diagram of the process.

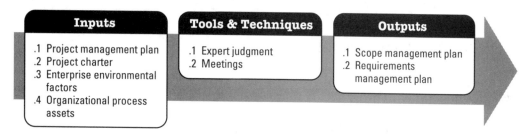

Inputs	Tools & Techniques	Outputs
.1 Project management plan .2 Project charter .3 Enterprise environmental factors .4 Organizational process assets	.1 Expert judgment .2 Meetings	.1 Scope management plan .2 Requirements management plan

Figure 5-2. Plan Scope Management: Inputs, Tools & Techniques, and Outputs

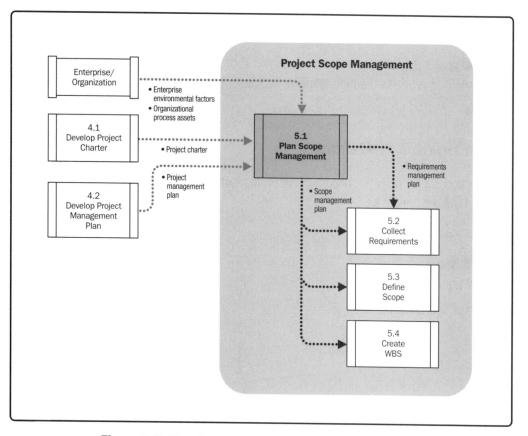

Figure 5-3. Plan Scope Management Data Flow Diagram

The scope management plan is a component of the project or program management plan that describes how the scope will be defined, developed, monitored, controlled, and verified. The development of the scope management plan and the detailing of the project scope begin with the analysis of information contained in the project charter (Section 4.1.3.1), the latest approved subsidiary plans of the project management plan (Section 4.2.3.1), historical information contained in the organizational process assets (Section 2.1.4), and any other relevant enterprise environmental factors (Section 2.1.5). This plan helps reduce the risk of project scope creep.

5.1.1 Plan Scope Management: Inputs

5.1.1.1 Project Management Plan

Described in Section 4.2.3.1. Approved subsidiary plans of the project management plan are used to create the scope management plan and influence the approach taken for planning scope and managing project scope.

5.1.1.2 Project Charter

Described in Section 4.1.3.1. The project charter is used to provide the project context needed to plan the scope management processes. It provides the high-level project description and product characteristics from the project statement of work.

5.1.1.3 Enterprise Environmental Factors

Described in Section 2.1.5. The enterprise environmental factors that can influence the Plan Scope Management process include, but are not limited to:

- Organization's culture,
- Infrastructure,
- Personnel administration, and
- Marketplace conditions.

5.1.1.4 Organizational Process Assets

Described in Section 2.1.4. The organizational process assets that can influence the Plan Scope Management process include, but are not limited to:

- Policies and procedures, and
- Historical information and lessons learned knowledge base.

5.1.2 Plan Scope Management: Tools and Techniques

5.1.2.1 Expert Judgment

Expert judgment refers to input received from knowledgeable and experienced parties. Expertise may be provided by any group or person with specialized education, knowledge, skill, experience, or training in developing scope management plans.

5.1.2.2 Meetings

Project teams may attend project meetings to develop the scope management plan. Attendees at these meetings may include the project manager, the project sponsor, selected project team members, selected stakeholders, anyone with responsibility for any of the scope management processes, and others as needed.

5.1.3 Plan Scope Management: Outputs

5.1.3.1 Scope Management Plan

The scope management plan is a component of the project or program management plan that describes how the scope will be defined, developed, monitored, controlled, and verified. The scope management plan is a major input into the Develop Project Management Plan process, and the other scope management processes. The components of a scope management plan include:

- Process for preparing a detailed project scope statement;
- Process that enables the creation of the WBS from the detailed project scope statement;
- Process that establishes how the WBS will be maintained and approved;
- Process that specifies how formal acceptance of the completed project deliverables will be obtained; and
- Process to control how requests for changes to the detailed project scope statement will be processed. This process is directly linked to the Perform Integrated Change Control process (Section 4.5).

The scope management plan can be formal or informal, broadly framed or highly detailed, based on the needs of the project.

5.1.3.2 Requirements Management Plan

The requirements management plan is a component of the project management plan that describes how requirements will be analyzed, documented, and managed. The phase-to-phase relationship, described in Section 2.4.2.1, strongly influences how requirements are managed. The project manager chooses the most effective relationship for the project and documents this approach in the requirements management plan. Many of the requirements management plan components are based on that relationship.

Components of the requirements management plan can include, but are not limited to:

- How requirements activities will be planned, tracked, and reported;
- Configuration management activities such as: how changes to the product will be initiated, how impacts will be analyzed, how they will be traced, tracked, and reported, as well as the authorization levels required to approve these changes;
- Requirements prioritization process;
- Product metrics that will be used and the rationale for using them; and
- Traceability structure to reflect which requirement attributes will be captured on the traceability matrix.

5.2 Collect Requirements

Collect Requirements is the process of determining, documenting, and managing stakeholder needs and requirements to meet project objectives. The key benefit of this process is that it provides the basis for defining and managing the project scope including product scope. The inputs, tools and techniques, and outputs of this process are depicted in Figure 5-4. Figure 5-5 depicts the data flow diagram of the process.

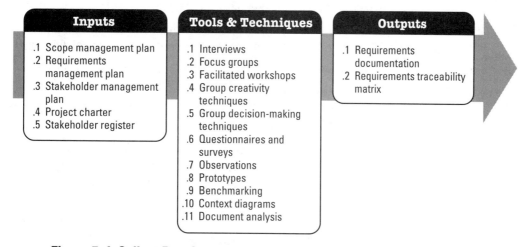

Figure 5-4. Collect Requirements: Inputs, Tools & Techniques, and Outputs

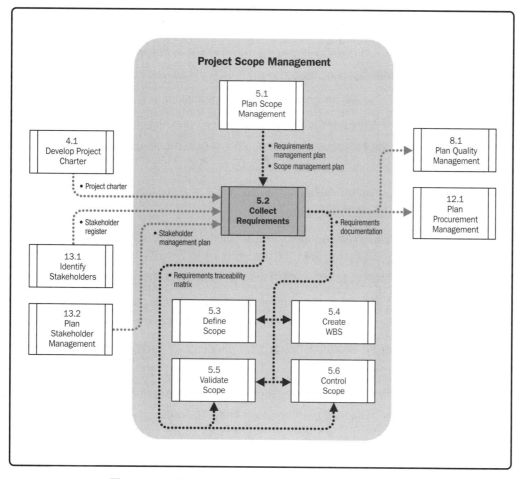

Figure 5-5. Collect Requirements Data Flow Diagram

The project's success is directly influenced by active stakeholder involvement in the discovery and decomposition of needs into requirements and by the care taken in determining, documenting, and managing the requirements of the product, service, or result of the project. Requirements include conditions or capabilities that are to be met by the project or present in the product, service, or result to satisfy an agreement or other formally imposed specification. Requirements include the quantified and documented needs and expectations of the sponsor, customer, and other stakeholders. These requirements need to be elicited, analyzed, and recorded in enough detail to be included in the scope baseline and to be measured once project execution begins. Requirements become the foundation of the WBS. Cost, schedule, quality planning, and sometimes procurement are all based upon these requirements. The development of requirements begins with an analysis of the information contained in the project charter (Section 4.1.3.1), the stakeholder register (Section 13.1.3.1) and the stakeholder management plan (Section 13.2.3.1).

Many organizations categorize requirements into different types, such as business and technical solutions, the former referring to stakeholder needs and the latter as to how those needs will be implemented. Requirements can be grouped into classifications allowing for further refinement and detail as the requirements are elaborated. These classifications include:

- Business requirements, which describe the higher-level needs of the organization as a whole, such as the business issues or opportunities, and reasons why a project has been undertaken.

- Stakeholder requirements, which describe needs of a stakeholder or stakeholder group.

- Solution requirements, which describe features, functions, and characteristics of the product, service, or result that will meet the business and stakeholder requirements. Solution requirements are further grouped into functional and nonfunctional requirements:

  o Functional requirements describe the behaviors of the product. Examples include processes, data, and interactions with the product.

  o Nonfunctional requirements supplement functional requirements and describe the environmental conditions or qualities required for the product to be effective. Examples include: reliability, security, performance, safety, level of service, supportability, retention/purge, etc.

- Transition requirements describe temporary capabilities, such as data conversion and training requirements, needed to transition from the current "as-is" state to the future "to-be" state.

- Project requirements, which describe the actions, processes, or other conditions the project needs to meet.

- Quality requirements, which capture any condition or criteria needed to validate the successful completion of a project deliverable or fulfillment of other project requirements.

5.2.1 Collect Requirements: Inputs

5.2.1.1 Scope Management Plan

Described in Section 5.1.3.1. The scope management plan provides clarity as to how project teams will determine which type of requirements need to be collected for the project.

5.2.1.2 Requirements Management Plan

Described in Section 5.1.3.2. The requirements management plan provides the processes that will be used throughout the Collect Requirements process to define and document the stakeholder needs.

5.2.1.3 Stakeholder Management Plan

Described in Section 13.2.3.1. The stakeholder management plan is used to understand stakeholder communication requirements and the level of stakeholder engagement in order to assess and adapt to the level of stakeholder participation in requirements activities.

5.2.1.4 Project Charter

Described in Section 4.1.3.1. The project charter is used to provide the high-level description of the product, service, or result of the project so that detailed requirements can be developed.

5.2.1.5 Stakeholder Register

Described in Section 13.1.3.1. The stakeholder register is used to identify stakeholders who can provide information on the requirements. The stakeholder register also captures major requirements and main expectations stakeholders may have for the project.

5.2.2 Collect Requirements: Tools and Techniques

5.2.2.1 Interviews

An interview is a formal or informal approach to elicit information from stakeholders by talking to them directly. It is typically performed by asking prepared and spontaneous questions and recording the responses. Interviews are often conducted on an individual basis between an interviewer and an interviewee, but may involve multiple interviewers and/or multiple interviewees. Interviewing experienced project participants, sponsors and other executives, and subject matter experts can aid in identifying and defining the features and functions of the desired product deliverables. Interviews are also useful for obtaining confidential information.

5.2.2.2 Focus Groups

Focus groups bring together prequalified stakeholders and subject matter experts to learn about their expectations and attitudes about a proposed product, service, or result. A trained moderator guides the group through an interactive discussion, designed to be more conversational than a one-on-one interview.

5.2.2.3 Facilitated Workshops

Facilitated workshops are focused sessions that bring key stakeholders together to define product requirements. Workshops are considered a primary technique for quickly defining cross-functional requirements and reconciling stakeholder differences. Because of their interactive group nature, well-facilitated sessions can build trust, foster relationships, and improve communication among the participants, which can lead to increased stakeholder consensus. In addition, issues can be discovered earlier and resolved more quickly than in individual sessions.

For example, facilitated workshops called joint application design/development (JAD) sessions are used in the software development industry. These facilitated sessions focus on bringing business subject matter experts and the development team together to improve the software development process. In the manufacturing industry, quality function deployment (QFD) is another example of a facilitated workshop technique that helps determine critical characteristics for new product development. QFD starts by collecting customer needs, also known as voice of the customer (VOC). These needs are then objectively sorted and prioritized, and goals are set for achieving them. User stories, which are short, textual descriptions of required functionality, are often developed during a requirements workshop. User stories describe the stakeholder who benefits from the feature (role), what the stakeholder needs to accomplish (goal), and the benefit to the stakeholder (motivation). User stories are widely used with agile methods.

5.2.2.4 Group Creativity Techniques

Several group activities can be organized to identify project and product requirements. Some of the group creativity techniques that can be used are:

- **Brainstorming.** A technique used to generate and collect multiple ideas related to project and product requirements. Although brainstorming by itself does not include voting or prioritization, it is often used with other group creativity techniques that do.

- **Nominal group technique.** A technique that enhances brainstorming with a voting process used to rank the most useful ideas for further brainstorming or for prioritization.

- **Idea/mind mapping.** A technique in which ideas created through individual brainstorming sessions are consolidated into a single map to reflect commonality and differences in understanding, and generate new ideas.

- **Affinity diagram.** A technique that allows large numbers of ideas to be classified into groups for review and analysis.

- **Multicriteria decision analysis.** A technique that utilizes a decision matrix to provide a systematic analytical approach for establishing criteria, such as risk levels, uncertainty, and valuation, to evaluate and rank many ideas.

5.2.2.5 Group Decision-Making Techniques

A group decision-making technique is an assessment process having multiple alternatives with an expected outcome in the form of future actions. These techniques can be used to generate, classify, and prioritize product requirements.

There are various methods of reaching a group decision, such as:

- **Unanimity.** A decision that is reached whereby everyone agrees on a single course of action. One way to reach unanimity is the Delphi technique, in which a selected group of experts answers questionnaires and provides feedback regarding the responses from each round of requirements gathering. The responses are only available to the facilitator to maintain anonymity.

- **Majority.** A decision that is reached with support obtained from more than 50 % of the members of the group. Having a group size with an uneven number of participants can ensure that a decision will be reached, rather than resulting in a tie.

- **Plurality.** A decision that is reached whereby the largest block in a group decides, even if a majority is not achieved. This method is generally used when the number of options nominated is more than two.

- **Dictatorship.** In this method, one individual makes the decision for the group.

All of these group decision-making techniques can be applied to the group creativity techniques used in the Collect Requirements process.

5.2.2.6 Questionnaires and Surveys

Questionnaires and surveys are written sets of questions designed to quickly accumulate information from a large number of respondents. Questionnaires and/or surveys are most appropriate with varied audiences, when a quick turnaround is needed, when respondents are geographically dispersed, and where statistical analysis is appropriate.

5.2.2.7 Observations

Observations provide a direct way of viewing individuals in their environment and how they perform their jobs or tasks and carry out processes. It is particularly helpful for detailed processes when the people that use the product have difficulty or are reluctant to articulate their requirements. Observation is also known as "job shadowing." It is usually done externally by an observer viewing a business expert performing a job. It can also be done by a "participant observer" who actually performs a process or procedure to experience how it is done to uncover hidden requirements.

5.2.2.8 Prototypes

Prototyping is a method of obtaining early feedback on requirements by providing a working model of the expected product before actually building it. Since a prototype is tangible, it allows stakeholders to experiment with a model of the final product rather than being limited to discussing abstract representations of their requirements. Prototypes support the concept of progressive elaboration in iterative cycles of mock-up creation, user experimentation, feedback generation, and prototype revision. When enough feedback cycles have been performed, the requirements obtained from the prototype are sufficiently complete to move to a design or build phase. Storyboarding is a prototyping technique showing sequence or navigation through a series of images or illustrations. Storyboards are used on a variety of projects in a variety of industries, such as film, advertising, instructional design, and on agile and other software development projects. In software development, storyboards use mock-ups to show navigation paths through webpages, screens, or other user interfaces.

5.2.2.9 Benchmarking

Benchmarking involves comparing actual or planned practices, such as processes and operations, to those of comparable organizations to identify best practices, generate ideas for improvement, and provide a basis for measuring performance. The organizations compared during benchmarking can be internal or external.

5.2.2.10 Context Diagrams

The context diagram is an example of a scope model. Context diagrams visually depict the product scope by showing a business system (process, equipment, computer system, etc.), and how people and other systems (actors) interact with it. Context diagrams show inputs to the business system, the actor(s) providing the input, the outputs from the business system, and the actor(s) receiving the output.

5.2.2.11 Document Analysis

Document analysis is used to elicit requirements by analyzing existing documentation and identifying information relevant to the requirements. There are a wide range of documents that may be analyzed to help elicit relevant requirements. Examples of documents that may be analyzed include, but are not limited to: business plans, marketing literature, agreements, requests for proposal, current process flows, logical data models, business rules repositories, application software documentation, business process or interface documentation, use cases, other requirements documentation, problem/issue logs, policies, procedures, and regulatory documentation such as laws, codes, or ordinances, etc.

5.2.3 Collect Requirements: Outputs

5.2.3.1 Requirements Documentation

Requirements documentation describes how individual requirements meet the business need for the project. Requirements may start out at a high level and become progressively more detailed as more about the requirements is known. Before being baselined, requirements need to be unambiguous (measurable and testable), traceable, complete, consistent, and acceptable to key stakeholders. The format of a requirements document may range from a simple document listing all the requirements categorized by stakeholder and priority, to more elaborate forms containing an executive summary, detailed descriptions, and attachments.

Components of requirements documentation can include, but, are not limited to:

- Business requirements, including:
  - Business and project objectives for traceability;
  - Business rules for the performing organization; and
  - Guiding principles of the organization.

- Stakeholder requirements, including:
  - Impacts to other organizational areas;
  - Impacts to other entities inside or outside the performing organization; and
  - Stakeholder communication and reporting requirements.
- Solution requirements, including:
  - Functional and nonfunctional requirements;
  - Technology and standard compliance requirements;
  - Support and training requirements;
  - Quality requirements; and
  - Reporting requirements, etc. (solution requirements can be documented textually, in models, or both).
- Project requirements, such as:
  - Levels of service, performance, safety, compliance, etc.; and
  - Acceptance criteria.
- Transition requirements.
- Requirements assumptions, dependencies, and constraints.

5.2.3.2 Requirements Traceability Matrix

The requirements traceability matrix is a grid that links product requirements from their origin to the deliverables that satisfy them. The implementation of a requirements traceability matrix helps ensure that each requirement adds business value by linking it to the business and project objectives. It provides a means to track requirements throughout the project life cycle, helping to ensure that requirements approved in the requirements documentation are delivered at the end of the project. Finally, it provides a structure for managing changes to the product scope.

Tracing includes, but is not limited to, tracing requirements for the following:

- Business needs, opportunities, goals, and objectives;

- Project objectives;

- Project scope/WBS deliverables;

- Product design;

- Product development;

- Test strategy and test scenarios; and

- High-level requirements to more detailed requirements.

Attributes associated with each requirement can be recorded in the requirements traceability matrix. These attributes help to define key information about the requirement. Typical attributes used in the requirements traceability matrix may include: a unique identifier, a textual description of the requirement, the rationale for inclusion, owner, source, priority, version, current status (such as active, cancelled, deferred, added, approved, assigned, completed), and status date. Additional attributes to ensure that the requirement has met stakeholders' satisfaction may include stability, complexity, and acceptance criteria. Figure 5-6 provides an example of a requirements traceability matrix with its associated attributes.

Requirements Traceability Matrix								
Project Name:								
Cost Center:								
Project Description:								
ID	Associate ID	Requirements Description	Business Needs, Opportunities, Goals, Objectives	Project Objectives	WBS Deliverables	Product Design	Product Development	Test Cases
001	1.0							
	1.1							
	1.2							
	1.2.1							
002	2.0							
	2.1							
	2.1.1							
003	3.0							
	3.1							
	3.2							
004	4.0							
005	5.0							

Figure 5-6. Example of a Requirements Traceability Matrix

5.3 Define Scope

Define Scope is the process of developing a detailed description of the project and product. The key benefit of this process is that it describes the project, service, or result boundaries by defining which of the requirements collected will be included in and excluded from the project scope. The inputs, tools and techniques, and outputs of this process are depicted in Figure 5-7. Figure 5-8 depicts the data flow diagram of the process.

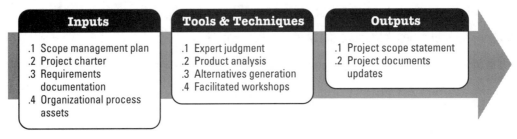

Figure 5-7. Define Scope: Inputs, Tools & Techniques, and Outputs

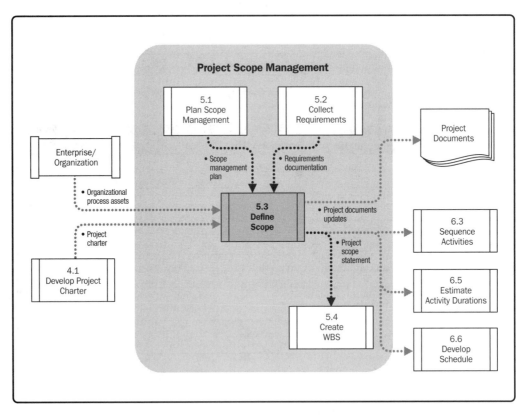

Figure 5-8. Define Scope Data Flow Diagram

Since all of the requirements identified in Collect Requirements may not be included in the project, the Define Scope process selects the final project requirements from the requirements documentation delivered during the Collect Requirements process. It then develops a detailed description of the project and product, service, or result.

The preparation of a detailed project scope statement is critical to project success and builds upon the major deliverables, assumptions, and constraints that are documented during project initiation. During project planning, the project scope is defined and described with greater specificity as more information about the project is known. Existing risks, assumptions, and constraints are analyzed for completeness and added or updated as necessary. The Define Scope process can be highly iterative. In iterative life cycle projects, a high-level vision will be developed for the overall project, but the detailed scope is determined one iteration at a time and the detailed planning for the next iteration is carried out as work progresses on the current project scope and deliverables.

5.3.1 Define Scope: Inputs

5.3.1.1 Scope Management Plan

Described in Section 5.1.3.1. The scope management plan is a component of the project management plan that establishes the activities for developing, monitoring, and controlling the project scope.

5.3.1.2 Project Charter

Described in Section 4.1.3.1. The project charter provides the high-level project description and product characteristics. It also contains project approval requirements. If a project charter is not used in the performing organization, then comparable information needs to be acquired or developed, and used as a basis for the detailed project scope statement. Organizations that do not produce a formal project charter will usually perform an informal analysis to identify the content necessary for further scope planning.

5.3.1.3 Requirements Documentation

Described in Section 5.2.3.1. This documentation will be used to select the requirements that will be included in the project.

5.3.1.4 Organizational Process Assets

Described in Section 2.1.4. Organizational process assets can influence how scope is defined. Examples include, but are not limited to:

- Policies, procedures, and templates for a project scope statement;
- Project files from previous projects; and
- Lessons learned from previous phases or projects.

5.3.2 Define Scope: Tools and Techniques

5.3.2.1 Expert Judgment

Expert judgment is often used to analyze the information needed to develop the project scope statement. Such judgment and expertise is applied to any technical detail. Such expertise is provided by any group or individual with specialized knowledge or training, and is available from many sources, including but not limited to:

- Other units within the organization;
- Consultants;
- Stakeholders, including customers or sponsors;
- Professional and technical associations;
- Industry groups; and
- Subject matter experts.

5.3.2.2 Product Analysis

For projects that have a product as a deliverable, as opposed to a service or result, product analysis can be an effective tool. Each application area has one or more generally accepted methods for translating high-level product descriptions into tangible deliverables. Product analysis includes techniques such as product breakdown, systems analysis, requirements analysis, systems engineering, value engineering, and value analysis.

5.3.2.3 Alternatives Generation

Alternatives generation is a technique used to develop as many potential options as possible in order to identify different approaches to execute and perform the work of the project. A variety of general management techniques can be used, such as brainstorming, lateral thinking, analysis of alternatives, etc.

5.3.2.4 Facilitated Workshops

Described in Section 5.2.2.3. The participation of key players with a variety of expectations and/or fields of expertise in these intensive working sessions helps to reach a cross-functional and common understanding of the project objectives and its limits.

5.3.3 Define Scope: Outputs

5.3.3.1 Project Scope Statement

The project scope statement is the description of the project scope, major deliverables, assumptions, and constraints. The project scope statement documents the entire scope, including project and product scope. It describes, in detail, the project's deliverables and the work required to create those deliverables. It also provides a common understanding of the project scope among project stakeholders. It may contain explicit scope exclusions that can assist in managing stakeholder expectations. It enables the project team to perform more detailed planning, guides the project team's work during execution, and provides the baseline for evaluating whether requests for changes or additional work are contained within or outside the project's boundaries.

The degree and level of detail to which the project scope statement defines the work that will be performed and the work that is excluded can help determine how well the project management team can control the overall project scope. The detailed project scope statement, either directly, or by reference to other documents, includes the following:

- **Product scope description.** Progressively elaborates the characteristics of the product, service, or result described in the project charter and requirements documentation.

- **Acceptance criteria.** A set of conditions that is required to be met before deliverables are accepted.

- **Deliverable.** Any unique and verifiable product, result, or capability to perform a service that is required to be produced to complete a process, phase, or project. Deliverables also include ancillary results, such as project management reports and documentation. These deliverables may be described at a summary level or in great detail.

- **Project exclusion.** Generally identifies what is excluded from the project. Explicitly stating what is out of scope for the project helps to manage stakeholders' expectations.

- **Constraints.** A limiting factor that affects the execution of a project or process. Constraints identified with the project scope statement list and describe the specific internal or external restrictions or limitations associated with the project scope that affect the execution of the project, for example, a predefined budget or any imposed dates or schedule milestones that are issued by the customer or performing organization. When a project is performed under an agreement, contractual provisions will generally be constraints. Information on constraints may be listed in the project scope statement or in a separate log.

- **Assumptions.** A factor in the planning process that is considered to be true, real, or certain, without proof or demonstration. Also describes the potential impact of those factors if they prove to be false. Project teams frequently identify, document, and validate assumptions as part of their planning process. Information on assumptions may be listed in the project scope statement or in a separate log.

Although the project charter and the project scope statement are sometimes perceived as containing a certain degree of redundancy, they are different in the level of detail contained in each. The project charter contains high-level information, while the project scope statement contains a detailed description of the scope elements. These elements are progressively elaborated throughout the project. Table 5-1 describes some of the key elements for each document.

Table 5-1. Elements of the Project Charter and Project Scope Statement

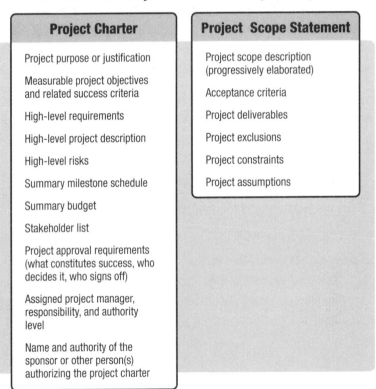

Project Charter	Project Scope Statement
Project purpose or justification	Project scope description (progressively elaborated)
Measurable project objectives and related success criteria	Acceptance criteria
High-level requirements	Project deliverables
High-level project description	Project exclusions
High-level risks	Project constraints
Summary milestone schedule	Project assumptions
Summary budget	
Stakeholder list	
Project approval requirements (what constitutes success, who decides it, who signs off)	
Assigned project manager, responsibility, and authority level	
Name and authority of the sponsor or other person(s) authorizing the project charter	

5.3.3.2 Project Documents Updates

Project documents that may be updated include, but are not limited to:

- Stakeholder register,
- Requirements documentation, and
- Requirements traceability matrix.

5.4 Create WBS

Create WBS is the process of subdividing project deliverables and project work into smaller, more manageable components. The key benefit of this process is that it provides a structured vision of what has to be delivered. The inputs, tools and techniques, and outputs of this process are depicted in Figure 5-9. Figure 5-10 depicts the data flow diagram of the process.

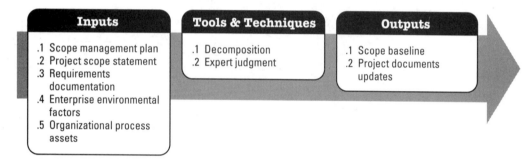

Inputs	Tools & Techniques	Outputs
.1 Scope management plan .2 Project scope statement .3 Requirements documentation .4 Enterprise environmental factors .5 Organizational process assets	.1 Decomposition .2 Expert judgment	.1 Scope baseline .2 Project documents updates

Figure 5-9. Create WBS: Inputs, Tools & Techniques, and Outputs

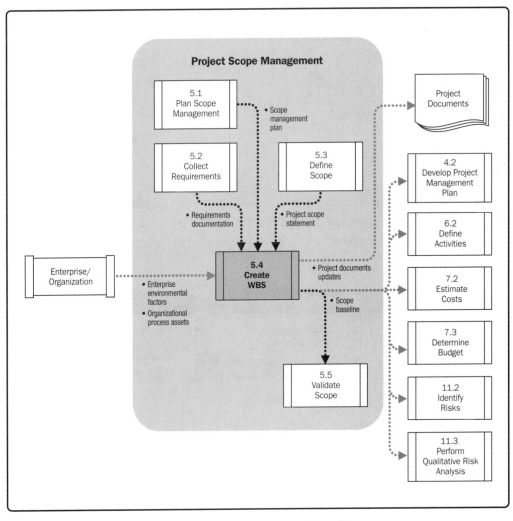

Figure 5-10. Create WBS Data Flow Diagram

The WBS is a hierarchical decomposition of the total scope of work to be carried out by the project team to accomplish the project objectives and create the required deliverables. The WBS organizes and defines the total scope of the project, and represents the work specified in the current approved project scope statement.

The planned work is contained within the lowest level of WBS components, which are called work packages. A work package can be used to group the activities where work is scheduled and estimated, monitored, and controlled. In the context of the WBS, work refers to work products or deliverables that are the result of activity and not to the activity itself.

5.4.1 Create WBS: Inputs

5.4.1.1 Scope Management Plan

Described in Section 5.1.3.1. The scope management plan specifies how to create the WBS from the detailed project scope statement and how the WBS will be maintained and approved.

5.4.1.2 Project Scope Statement

Described in Section 5.3.3.1. The project scope statement describes the work that will be performed and the work that is excluded. It also lists and describes the specific internal or external restrictions or limitations that may affect the execution of the project.

5.4.1.3 Requirements Documentation

Described in Section 5.2.3.1. Detailed requirements documentation is essential for understanding what needs to be produced as the result of the project and what needs to be done to deliver the project and its final products.

5.4.1.4 Enterprise Environmental Factors

Described in Section 2.1.5. Industry-specific WBS standards, relevant to the nature of the project, may serve as external reference sources for creation of the WBS. For example, engineering projects may reference ISO/IEC 15288 on Systems Engineering – System Life Cycle Processes [6], to create a WBS for a new project.

5.4.1.5 Organizational Process Assets

Described in Section 2.1.4. The organizational process assets that can influence the Create WBS process include, but are not limited to:

- Policies, procedures, and templates for the WBS;
- Project files from previous projects; and
- Lessons learned from previous projects.

5.4.2 Create WBS: Tools and Techniques

5.4.2.1 Decomposition

Decomposition is a technique used for dividing and subdividing the project scope and project deliverables into smaller, more manageable parts. The work package is the work defined at the lowest level of the WBS for which cost and duration can be estimated and managed. The level of decomposition is often guided by the degree of control needed to effectively manage the project. The level of detail for work packages will vary with the size and complexity of the project. Decomposition of the total project work into work packages generally involves the following activities:

- Identifying and analyzing the deliverables and related work;
- Structuring and organizing the WBS;
- Decomposing the upper WBS levels into lower-level detailed components;
- Developing and assigning identification codes to the WBS components; and
- Verifying that the degree of decomposition of the deliverables is appropriate.

A portion of a WBS with some branches of the WBS decomposed down through the work package level is shown in Figure 5-11.

5.4.2.2 Expert Judgment

Expert judgment is often used to analyze the information needed to decompose the project deliverables down into smaller component parts in order to create an effective WBS. Such judgment and expertise is applied to technical details of the project's scope and used to reconcile differences in opinion on how to best break down the overall scope of the project. This level of expertise is provided by any group or individual with relevant training, knowledge, or experience with similar projects or business areas. Expert judgment can also come in the form of predefined templates that provide guidance on how to effectively break down common deliverables. Such templates may be industry or discipline specific or may come from experience gained in similar projects. The project manager, in collaboration with the project team, then determines the final decomposition of the project scope into the discrete work packages that will be used to effectively manage the work of the project.

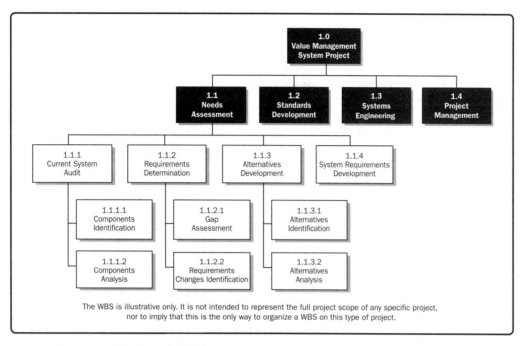

The WBS is illustrative only. It is not intended to represent the full project scope of any specific project, nor to imply that this is the only way to organize a WBS on this type of project.

Figure 5-11. Sample WBS Decomposed Down Through Work Packages

A WBS structure may be created through various approaches. Some of the popular methods include the top-down approach, the use of organization-specific guidelines, and the use of WBS templates. A bottom-up approach can be used during the integration of subcomponents. The WBS structure can be represented in a number of forms, such as:

- Using phases of the project life cycle as the second level of decomposition, with the product and project deliverables inserted at the third level, as shown in Figure 5-12;

- Using major deliverables as the second level of decomposition, as shown in Figure 5-13; and

- Incorporating subcomponents which may be developed by organizations outside the project team, such as contracted work. The seller then develops the supporting contract WBS as part of the contracted work.

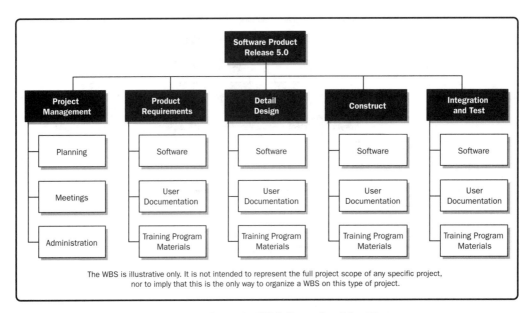

Figure 5-12. Sample WBS Organized by Phase

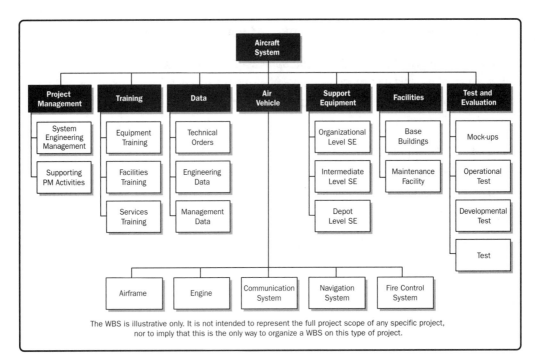

Figure 5-13. Sample WBS with Major Deliverables

6.2.1.2 Scope Baseline

Described in Section 5.4.3.1. The project WBS, deliverables, constraints, and assumptions documented in the scope baseline are considered explicitly while defining activities.

6.2.1.3 Enterprise Environmental Factors

Described in Section 2.1.5. Enterprise environmental factors that influence the Define Activities process include, but are not limited to:

- Organizational cultures and structure,

- Published commercial information from commercial databases, and

- Project management information system (PMIS).

6.2.1.4 Organizational Process Assets

Described in Section 2.1.4. The organizational process assets that can influence the Define Activities process include, but are not limited to:

- Lessons learned knowledge base containing historical information regarding activity lists used by previous similar projects,

- Standardized processes,

- Templates that contain a standard activity list or a portion of an activity list from a previous project, and

- Existing formal and informal activity planning-related policies, procedures, and guidelines, such as the scheduling methodology, that are considered in developing the activity definitions.

6.2.2 Define Activities: Tools and Techniques

6.2.2.1 Decomposition

Decomposition is a technique used for dividing and subdividing the project scope and project deliverables into smaller, more manageable parts. Activities represent the effort needed to complete a work package. The Define Activities process defines the final outputs as activities rather than deliverables, as done in the Create WBS process (Section 5.4).

The activity list, WBS, and WBS dictionary can be developed either sequentially or concurrently, with the WBS and WBS dictionary as the basis for development of the final activity list. Each work package within the WBS is decomposed into the activities required to produce the work package deliverables. Involving team members in the decomposition can lead to better and more accurate results.

6.2.2.2 Rolling Wave Planning

Rolling wave planning is an iterative planning technique in which the work to be accomplished in the near term is planned in detail, while the work in the future is planned at a higher level. It is a form of progressive elaboration. Therefore, work can exist at various levels of detail depending on where it is in the project life cycle. During early strategic planning, when information is less defined, work packages may be decomposed to the known level of detail. As more is known about the upcoming events in the near term, work packages can be decomposed into activities.

6.2.2.3 Expert Judgment

Project team members or other experts, who are experienced and skilled in developing detailed project scope statements, the WBS, and project schedules, can provide expertise in defining activities.

6.2.3 Define Activities: Outputs

6.2.3.1 Activity List

The activity list is a comprehensive list that includes all schedule activities required on the project. The activity list also includes the activity identifier and a scope of work description for each activity in sufficient detail to ensure that project team members understand what work is required to be completed. Each activity should have a unique title that describes its place in the schedule, even if that activity title is displayed outside the context of the project schedule.

6.2.3.2 Activity Attributes

Activities, distinct from milestones, have durations, during which the work of that activity is performed, and may have resources and costs associated with that work. Activity attributes extend the description of the activity by identifying the multiple components associated with each activity. The components for each activity evolve over time. During the initial stages of the project, they include the activity identifier (ID), WBS ID, and activity label or name, and when completed, may include activity codes, activity description, predecessor activities, successor activities, logical relationships, leads and lags (Section 6.3.2.3), resource requirements, imposed dates, constraints, and assumptions. Activity attributes can be used to identify the person responsible for executing the work, geographic area, or place where the work has to be performed, the project calendar the activity is assigned to, and activity type such as level of effort (often abbreviated as LOE), discrete effort, and apportioned effort. Activity attributes are used for schedule development and for selecting, ordering, and sorting the planned schedule activities in various ways within reports. The number of attributes varies by application area.

6.2.3.3 Milestone List

A milestone is a significant point or event in a project. A milestone list is a list identifying all project milestones and indicates whether the milestone is mandatory, such as those required by contract, or optional, such as those based upon historical information. Milestones are similar to regular schedule activities, with the same structure and attributes, but they have zero duration because milestones represent a moment in time.

6.3 Sequence Activities

Sequence Activities is the process of identifying and documenting relationships among the project activities. The key benefit of this process is that it defines the logical sequence of work to obtain the greatest efficiency given all project constraints. The inputs, tools and techniques, and outputs of this process are depicted in Figure 6-7. Figure 6-8 depicts the data flow diagram of the process.

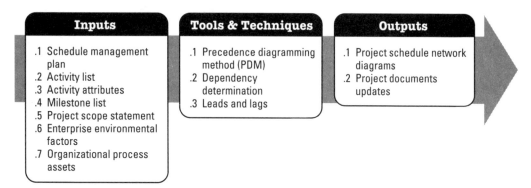

Inputs	Tools & Techniques	Outputs
.1 Schedule management plan	.1 Precedence diagramming method (PDM)	.1 Project schedule network diagrams
.2 Activity list	.2 Dependency determination	.2 Project documents updates
.3 Activity attributes	.3 Leads and lags	
.4 Milestone list		
.5 Project scope statement		
.6 Enterprise environmental factors		
.7 Organizational process assets		

Figure 6-7. Sequence Activities: Inputs, Tools & Techniques, and Outputs

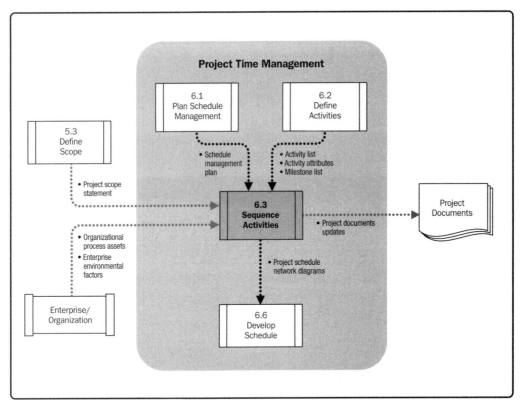

Figure 6-8. Sequence Activities Data Flow Diagram

Every activity and milestone except the first and last should be connected to at least one predecessor with a finish-to-start or start-to-start logical relationship and at least one successor with a finish-to-start or finish-to-finish logical relationship. Logical relationships should be designed to create a realistic project schedule. It may be necessary to use lead or lag time between activities to support a realistic and achievable project schedule. Sequencing can be performed by using project management software or by using manual or automated techniques.

6.3.1 Sequence Activities: Inputs

6.3.1.1 Schedule Management Plan

Described in Section 6.1.3.1. The schedule management plan identifies the scheduling method and tool to be used for the project, which will guide how the activities may be sequenced.

6.3.1.2 Activity List

Described in Section 6.2.3.1. The activity list contains all schedule activities required on the project, which are to be sequenced. Dependencies and other constraints for these activities can influence the sequencing of the activities.

6.3.1.3 Activity Attributes

Described in Section 6.2.3.2. Activity attributes may describe a necessary sequence of events or defined predecessor or successor relationships.

6.3.1.4 Milestone List

Described in Section 6.2.3.3. The milestone list may have scheduled dates for specific milestones, which may influence the way activities are sequenced.

6.3.1.5 Project Scope Statement

Described in Section 5.3.3.1. The project scope statement contains the product scope description, which includes product characteristics that may affect activity sequencing, such as the physical layout of a plant to be constructed or subsystem interfaces on a software project. Other information from the project scope statement including project deliverables, project constraints, and project assumptions may also affect activity sequencing. While these effects are often apparent in the activity list, the product scope description is generally reviewed to ensure accuracy.

6.3.1.6 Enterprise Environmental Factors

Described in Section 2.1.5. Enterprise environmental factors that influence the Sequence Activities process include, but are not limited to:

- Government or industry standards,
- Project management information system (PMIS),
- Scheduling tool, and
- Company work authorization systems.

6.3.1.7 Organizational Process Assets

Described in Section 2.1.4. The organizational process assets that can influence the Sequence Activities process include, but are not limited to: project files from the corporate knowledge base used for scheduling methodology, existing formal and informal activity planning-related policies, procedures, and guidelines, such as the scheduling methodology that are considered in developing logical relationships, and templates that can be used to expedite the preparation of networks of project activities. Related activity attributes information in templates can also contain additional descriptive information useful in sequencing activities.

6.3.2 Sequence Activities: Tools and Techniques

6.3.2.1 Precedence Diagramming Method

The precedence diagramming method (PDM) is a technique used for constructing a schedule model in which activities are represented by nodes and are graphically linked by one or more logical relationships to show the sequence in which the activities are to be performed. Activity-on-node (AON) is one method of representing a precedence diagram. This is the method used by most project management software packages.

PDM includes four types of dependencies or logical relationships. A predecessor activity is an activity that logically comes before a dependent activity in a schedule. A successor activity is a dependent activity that logically comes after another activity in a schedule. These relationships are defined below and are illustrated in Figure 6-9:

- **Finish-to-start (FS).** A logical relationship in which a successor activity cannot start until a predecessor activity has finished. Example: The awards ceremony (successor) cannot start until the race (predecessor) has finished.

- **Finish-to-finish (FF).** A logical relationship in which a successor activity cannot finish until a predecessor activity has finished. Example: Writing a document (predecessor) is required to finish before editing the document (successor) can finish.

- **Start-to-start (SS).** A logical relationship in which a successor activity cannot start until a predecessor activity has started. Example: Level concrete (successor) cannot begin until pour foundation (predecessor) begins.

- **Start-to-finish (SF).** A logical relationship in which a successor activity cannot finish until a predecessor activity has started. Example: The first security guard shift (successor) cannot finish until the second security guard shift (predecessor) starts.

In PDM, finish-to-start is the most commonly used type of precedence relationship. The start-to-finish relationship is very rarely used but is included to present a complete list of the PDM relationship types.

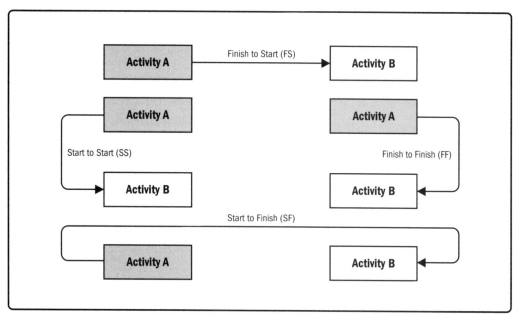

Figure 6-9. Precedence Diagramming Method (PDM) Relationship Types

6.3.2.2 Dependency Determination

Dependencies may be characterized by the following attributes: mandatory or discretionary, internal or external, as described below. Dependency has four attributes, but two can be applicable at the same time in following ways: mandatory external dependencies, mandatory internal dependencies, discretionary external dependencies, or discretionary internal dependencies.

- **Mandatory dependencies.** Mandatory dependencies are those that are legally or contractually required or inherent in the nature of the work. Mandatory dependencies often involve physical limitations, such as on a construction project, where it is impossible to erect the superstructure until after the foundation has been built, or on an electronics project, where a prototype has to be built before it can be tested. Mandatory dependencies are also sometimes referred to as hard logic or hard dependencies. Technical dependencies may not be mandatory. The project team determines which dependencies are mandatory during the process of sequencing the activities. Mandatory dependencies should not be confused with assigning schedule constraints in the scheduling tool.

- **Discretionary dependencies.** Discretionary dependencies are sometimes referred to as preferred logic, preferential logic, or soft logic. Discretionary dependencies are established based on knowledge of best practices within a particular application area or some unusual aspect of the project where a specific sequence is desired, even though there may be other acceptable sequences. Discretionary dependencies should be fully documented since they can create arbitrary total float values and can limit later scheduling options. When fast tracking techniques are employed, these discretionary dependencies should be reviewed and considered for modification or removal. The project team determines which dependencies are discretionary during the process of sequencing the activities.

- **External dependencies.** External dependencies involve a relationship between project activities and non-project activities. These dependencies are usually outside the project team's control. For example, the testing activity in a software project may be dependent on the delivery of hardware from an external source, or governmental environmental hearings may need to be held before site preparation can begin on a construction project. The project management team determines which dependencies are external during the process of sequencing the activities.

- **Internal dependencies.** Internal dependencies involve a precedence relationship between project activities and are generally inside the project team's control. For example, if the team cannot test a machine until they assemble it, this is an internal mandatory dependency. The project management team determines which dependencies are internal during the process of sequencing the activities.

6.3.2.3 Leads and Lags

A lead is the amount of time whereby a successor activity can be advanced with respect to a predecessor activity. For example, on a project to construct a new office building, the landscaping could be scheduled to start two weeks prior to the scheduled punch list completion. This would be shown as a finish-to-start with a two-week lead as shown in Figure 6-10. Lead is often represented as a negative value for lag in scheduling software.

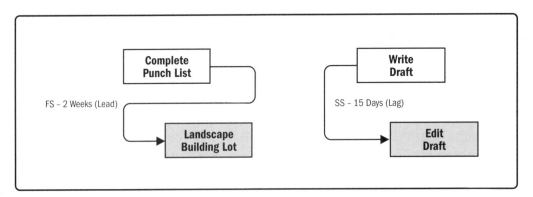

Figure 6-10. Examples of Lead and Lag

A lag is the amount of time whereby a successor activity will be delayed with respect to a predecessor activity. For example, a technical writing team may begin editing the draft of a large document 15 days after they begin writing it. This can be shown as a start-to-start relationship with a 15-day lag as shown in Figure 6-10. Lag can also be represented in project schedule network diagrams as shown in Figure 6-11 in the relationship between activities H and I, as indicated by the nomenclature SS+10 (start-to-start plus 10 days lag) even though offset is not shown relative to a timescale.

The project management team determines the dependencies that may require a lead or a lag to accurately define the logical relationship. The use of leads and lags should not replace schedule logic. Activities and their related assumptions should be documented.

6.3.3 Sequence Activities: Outputs

6.3.3.1 Project Schedule Network Diagrams

A project schedule network diagram is a graphical representation of the logical relationships, also referred to as dependencies, among the project schedule activities. Figure 6-11 illustrates a project schedule network diagram. A project schedule network diagram is produced manually or by using project management software. It can include full project details, or have one or more summary activities. A summary narrative can accompany the diagram and describe the basic approach used to sequence the activities. Any unusual activity sequences within the network should be fully described within the narrative.

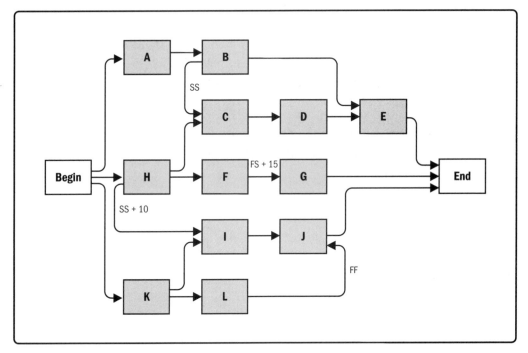

Figure 6-11. Project Schedule Network Diagram

6.3.3.2 Project Documents Updates

Project documents that may be updated include, but are not limited to:

- Activity lists,
- Activity attributes,
- Milestone list, and
- Risk register.

6.4 Estimate Activity Resources

Estimate Activity Resources is the process of estimating the type and quantities of material, human resources, equipment, or supplies required to perform each activity. The key benefit of this process is that it identifies the type, quantity, and characteristics of resources required to complete the activity which allows more accurate cost and duration estimates. The inputs, tools and techniques, and outputs of this process are depicted in Figure 6-12. Figure 6-13 depicts the data flow diagram of the process.

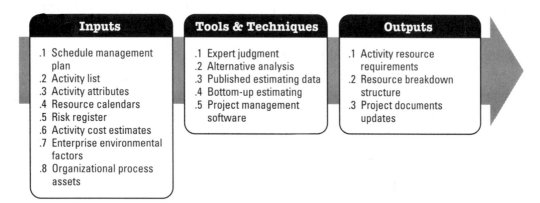

Figure 6-12. Estimate Activity Resources: Inputs, Tools & Techniques, and Outputs

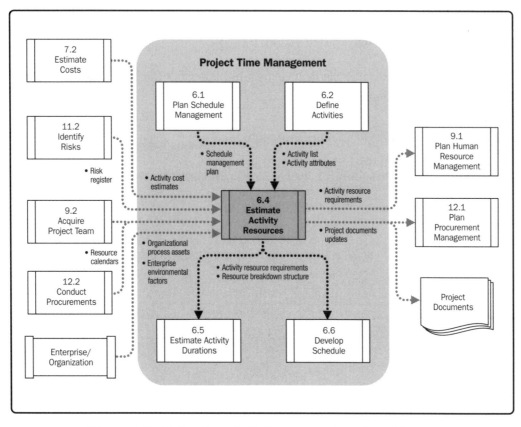

Figure 6-13. Estimate Activity Resources Data Flow Diagram

The Estimate Activity Resources process is closely coordinated with the Estimate Costs process (Section 7.2). For example:

- A construction project team will need to be familiar with local building codes. Such knowledge is often readily available from local sellers. However, if the local labor pool lacks experience with unusual or specialized construction techniques, the additional cost for a consultant may be the most effective way to secure knowledge of the local building codes.

- An automotive design team will need to be familiar with the latest in automated assembly techniques. The requisite knowledge might be obtained by hiring a consultant, by sending a designer to a seminar on robotics, or by including someone from manufacturing as a member of the project team.

6.4.1 Estimate Activity Resources: Inputs

6.4.1.1 Schedule Management Plan

Described in Section 6.1.3.1. The schedule management plan identifies the level of accuracy and the units of measure for the resources to be estimated.

6.4.1.2 Activity List

Described in Section 6.2.3.1. The activity list identifies the activities which will need resources.

6.4.1.3 Activity Attributes

Described in Section 6.2.3.2. The activity attributes provide the primary data input for use in estimating those resources required for each activity in the activity list.

6.4.1.4 Resource Calendars

Described in Sections 9.2.3.2 and 12.2.3.3. A resource calendar is a calendar that identifies the working days and shifts on which each specific resource is available. Information on which resources (such as human resources, equipment, and material) are potentially available during a planned activity period, is used for estimating resource utilization. Resource calendars specify when and how long identified project resources will be available during the project. This information may be at the activity or project level. This knowledge includes consideration of attributes such as resource experience and/or skill level, as well as various geographical locations from which the resources originate and when they may be available.

6.4.1.5 Risk Register

Described in Section 11.2.3.1. Risk events may impact resource selection and availability. Updates to the risk register are included with project documents updates, described in Section 11.5.3.2, from Plan Risk Responses.

6.4.1.6 Activity Cost Estimates

Described in Section 7.2.3.1. The cost of resources may impact resource selection.

6.4.1.7 Enterprise Environmental Factors

Described in Section 2.1.5. The enterprise environmental factors that can influence the Estimate Activity Resources process include, but are not limited to, resource location, availability, and skills.

6.4.1.8 Organizational Process Assets

Described in Section 2.1.4. The organizational process assets that can influence the Estimate Activity Resources process include, but are not limited to:

- Policies and procedures regarding staffing,
- Policies and procedures relating to rental and purchase of supplies and equipment, and
- Historical information regarding types of resources used for similar work on previous projects.

6.4.2 Estimate Activity Resources: Tools and Techniques

6.4.2.1 Expert Judgment

Expert judgment is often required to assess the resource-related inputs to this process. Any group or person with specialized knowledge in resource planning and estimating can provide such expertise.

6.4.2.2 Alternative Analysis

Many schedule activities have alternative methods of accomplishment. They include using various levels of resource capability or skills, different size or type of machines, different tools (hand versus automated), and make-rent-or-buy decisions regarding the resource (Section 12.1.3.5).

6.4.2.3 Published Estimating Data

Several organizations routinely publish updated production rates and unit costs of resources for an extensive array of labor trades, material, and equipment for different countries and geographical locations within countries.

6.4.2.4 Bottom-Up Estimating

Bottom-up estimating is a method of estimating project duration or cost by aggregating the estimates of the lower-level components of the WBS. When an activity cannot be estimated with a reasonable degree of confidence, the work within the activity is decomposed into more detail. The resource needs are estimated. These estimates are then aggregated into a total quantity for each of the activity's resources. Activities may or may not have dependencies between them that can affect the application and use of resources. If there are dependencies, this pattern of resource usage is reflected and documented in the estimated requirements of the activity.

6.4.2.5 Project Management Software

Project management software, such as a scheduling software tool, has the capability to help plan, organize, and manage resource pools and develop resource estimates. Depending on the sophistication of the software, resource breakdown structures, resource availability, resource rates, and various resource calendars can be defined to assist in optimizing resource utilization.

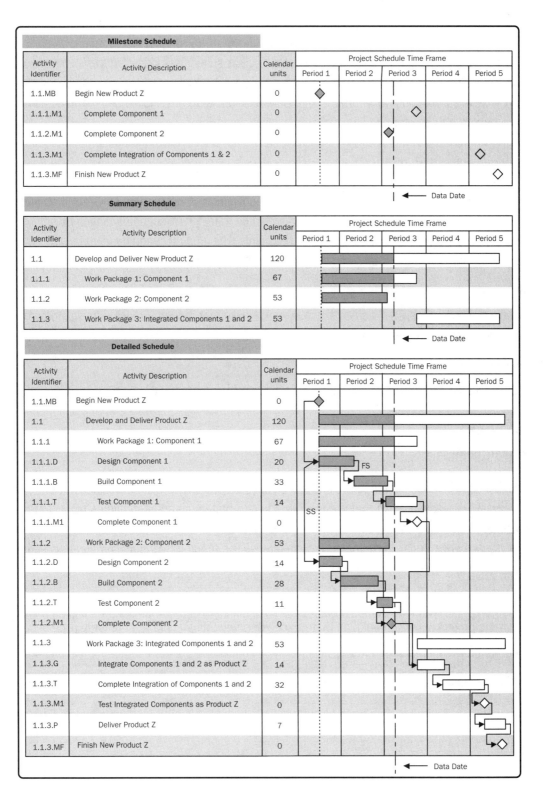

Figure 6-21. Project Schedule Presentations —Examples

Figure 6-21 shows schedule presentations for a sample project being executed, with the work in progress reported through the data date, a point in time when the status of the project is recorded, which is sometimes also called the as-of date or status date. For a simple project schedule model, Figure 6-21 reflects schedule presentations in the forms of (1) a milestone schedule as a milestone chart, (2) a summary schedule as a bar chart, and (3) a detailed schedule as a project schedule network diagram. Figure 6-21 also visually shows the relationships among the three different levels of schedule presentation.

6.6.3.3 Schedule Data

The schedule data for the project schedule model is the collection of information for describing and controlling the schedule. The schedule data includes at least the schedule milestones, schedule activities, activity attributes, and documentation of all identified assumptions and constraints. The amount of additional data varies by application area. Information frequently supplied as supporting detail includes, but is not limited to:

- Resource requirements by time period, often in the form of a resource histogram;
- Alternative schedules, such as best-case or worst-case, not resource-leveled, or resource-leveled, with or without imposed dates; and
- Scheduling of contingency reserves.

Schedule data could also include such items as resource histograms, cash-flow projections, and order and delivery schedules.

6.6.3.4 Project Calendars

A project calendar identifies working days and shifts that are available for scheduled activities. It distinguishes time periods in days or parts of days that are available to complete scheduled activities from time periods that are not available. A schedule model may require more than one project calendar to allow for different work periods for some activities to calculate the project schedule. The project calendars may be updated.

6.6.3.5 Project Management Plan Updates

Elements of the project management plan that may be updated include, but are not limited to:

- Schedule baseline (Section 6.6.3.1),
- Schedule management plan (Section 6.1.3.1).

6.6.3.6 Project Documents Updates

Project documents that may be updated include, but are not limited to:

- **Activity resource requirements.** Resource leveling can have a significant effect on preliminary estimates for the types and quantities of resources required. If the resource-leveling analysis changes the project resource requirements, then the project resource requirements are updated.

- **Activity attributes.** Activity attributes (Section 6.2.3.2) are updated to include any revised resource requirements and any other revisions generated by the Develop Schedule process.

- **Calendars.** The calendar for each project may consist of multiple calendars, project calendars, individual resource calendars etc., as the basis for scheduling the project.

- **Risk register.** The risk register may need to be updated to reflect opportunities or threats perceived through scheduling assumptions.

6.7 Control Schedule

Control Schedule is the process of monitoring the status of project activities to update project progress and manage changes to the schedule baseline to achieve the plan. The key benefit of this process is that it provides the means to recognize deviation from the plan and take corrective and preventive actions and thus minimize risk. The inputs, tools and techniques, and outputs of this process are depicted in Figure 6-22. Figure 6-23 depicts the data flow diagram of the process.

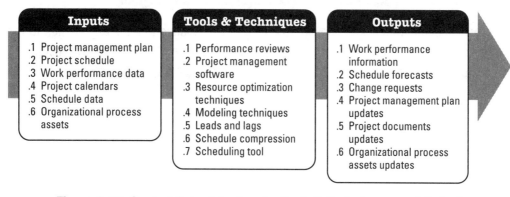

Inputs	Tools & Techniques	Outputs
.1 Project management plan .2 Project schedule .3 Work performance data .4 Project calendars .5 Schedule data .6 Organizational process assets	.1 Performance reviews .2 Project management software .3 Resource optimization techniques .4 Modeling techniques .5 Leads and lags .6 Schedule compression .7 Scheduling tool	.1 Work performance information .2 Schedule forecasts .3 Change requests .4 Project management plan updates .5 Project documents updates .6 Organizational process assets updates

Figure 6-22. Control Schedule: Inputs, Tools & Techniques, and Outputs

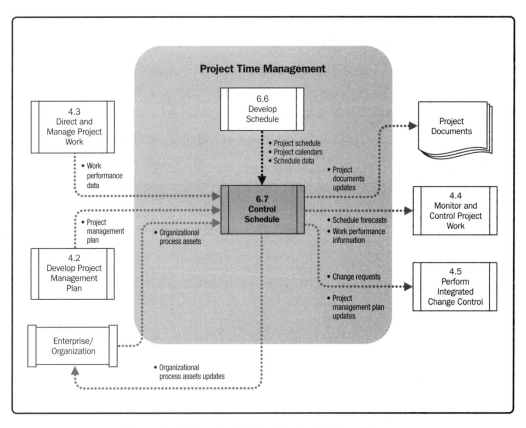

Figure 6-23. Control Schedule Data Flow Diagram

Updating the schedule model requires knowing the actual performance to date. Any change to the schedule baseline can only be approved through the Perform Integrated Change Control process (Section 4.5). Control Schedule, as a component of the Perform Integrated Change Control process, is concerned with:

- Determining the current status of the project schedule,
- Influencing the factors that create schedule changes,
- Determining if the project schedule has changed, and
- Managing the actual changes as they occur.

If any agile approach is utilized, control schedule is concerned with:

- Determining the current status of the project schedule by comparing the total amount of work delivered and accepted against the estimates of work completed for the elapsed time cycle,

- Conducting retrospective reviews (scheduled reviews to record lessons learned) for correcting processes and improving, if required,

- Reprioritizing the remaining work plan (backlog),

- Determining the rate at which the deliverables are produced, validated, and accepted (velocity) in given time per iteration (agreed work cycle duration, typically two weeks or one month),

- Determining that the project schedule has changed, and

- Managing the actual changes as they occur.

6.7.1 Control Schedule: Inputs

6.7.1.1 Project Management Plan

Described in Section 4.2.3.1. The project management plan contains the schedule management plan and the schedule baseline. The schedule management plan describes how the schedule will be managed and controlled. The schedule baseline is used as a reference to compare with actual results to determine if a change, corrective action, or preventive action is necessary.

6.7.1.2 Project Schedule

Described in Section 6.6.3.2. Project schedule refers to the most recent version with notations to indicate updates, completed activities, and started activities as of the indicated data date.

6.7.1.3 Work Performance Data

Described in Section 4.3.3.2. Work performance data refers to information about project progress such as which activities have started, their progress (e.g., actual duration, remaining duration, and physical percent complete), and which activities have finished.

6.7.1.4 Project Calendars

Described in Section 6.6.3.4. A schedule model may require more than one project calendar to allow for different work periods for some activities to calculate the schedule forecasts.

6.7.1.5 Schedule Data

Described in Section 6.6.3.3. Schedule data will be reviewed and updated in the Control Schedule process.

6.7.1.6 Organizational Process Assets

Described in Section 2.1.4. The organizational process assets that influence the Control Schedule process include, but are not limited to:

- Existing formal and informal schedule control-related policies, procedures, and guidelines;
- Schedule control tools; and
- Monitoring and reporting methods to be used.

6.7.2 Control Schedule: Tools and Techniques

6.7.2.1 Performance Reviews

Performance reviews measure, compare, and analyze schedule performance such as actual start and finish dates, percent complete, and remaining duration for work in progress. Various techniques may be used, among them:

- **Trend analysis.** Trend analysis examines project performance over time to determine whether performance is improving or deteriorating. Graphical analysis techniques are valuable for understanding performance to date and for comparison to future performance goals in the form of completion dates.
- **Critical path method (Section 6.6.2.2).** Comparing the progress along the critical path can help determine schedule status. The variance on the critical path will have a direct impact on the project end date. Evaluating the progress of activities on near critical paths can identify schedule risk.

- **Critical chain method (Section 6.6.2.3).** Comparing the amount of buffer remaining to the amount of buffer needed to protect the delivery date can help determine schedule status. The difference between the buffer needed and the buffer remaining can determine whether corrective action is appropriate.

- **Earned value management (Section 7.4.2.1).** Schedule performance measurements such as schedule variance (SV) and schedule performance index (SPI), are used to assess the magnitude of variation to the original schedule baseline. The total float and early finish variances are also essential planning components to evaluate project time performance. Important aspects of schedule control include determining the cause and degree of variance relative to the schedule baseline (Section 6.6.3.1), estimating the implications of those variances for future work to completion, and deciding whether corrective or preventive action is required. For example, a major delay on any activity not on the critical path may have little effect on the overall project schedule, while a much shorter delay on a critical or near-critical activity may require immediate action. For projects not using earned value management, similar variance analysis can be performed by comparing planned activity start or finish dates against actual start or finish dates to identify variances between the schedule baseline and actual project performance. Further analysis can be performed to determine the cause and degree of variance relative to the schedule baseline and any corrective or preventative actions needed.

6.7.2.2 Project Management Software

Project management software for scheduling provides the ability to track planned dates versus actual dates, to report variances to and progress made against the schedule baseline, and to forecast the effects of changes to the project schedule model.

6.7.2.3 Resource Optimization Techniques

Described in Section 6.6.2.4. Resource optimization techniques involve the scheduling of activities and the resources required by those activities while taking into consideration both the resource availability and the project time.

6.7.2.4 Modeling Techniques

Described in Section 6.6.2.5. Modeling techniques are used to review various scenarios guided by risk monitoring to bring the schedule model into alignment with the project management plan and approved baseline.

6.7.2.5 Leads and Lags

Adjusting leads and lags is applied during network analysis to find ways to bring project activities that are behind into alignment with the plan. For example, on a project to construct a new office building, the landscaping can be adjusted to start before the exterior work of the building is complete by increasing the lead time in the relationship. Or, a technical writing team can adjust the start of editing the draft of a large document immediately after the document is completed by eliminating or decreasing lag time.

6.7.2.6 Schedule Compression

Described in Section 6.6.2.7. Schedule compression techniques are used to find ways to bring project activities that are behind into alignment with the plan by fast tracking or crashing schedule for the remaining work.

6.7.2.7 Scheduling Tool

Schedule data is updated and compiled into the schedule model to reflect actual progress of the project and remaining work to be completed. The scheduling tool (Section 6.6.2.8) and the supporting schedule data are used in conjunction with manual methods or other project management software to perform schedule network analysis to generate an updated project schedule.

6.7.3 Control Schedule: Outputs

6.7.3.1 Work Performance Information

The calculated SV and SPI time performance indicators for WBS components, in particular the work packages and control accounts, are documented and communicated to stakeholders.

6.7.3.2 Schedule Forecasts

Schedule forecasts are estimates or predictions of conditions and events in the project's future based on information and knowledge available at the time of the forecast. Forecasts are updated and reissued based on work performance information provided as the project is executed. The information is based on the project's past performance and expected future performance, and includes earned value performance indicators that could impact the project in the future.

6.7.3.3 Change Requests

Schedule variance analysis, along with review of progress reports, results of performance measures, and modifications to the project scope or project schedule may result in change requests to the schedule baseline, scope baseline, and/or other components of the project management plan. Change requests are processed for review and disposition through the Perform Integrated Change Control process (Section 4.5). Preventive actions may include recommended changes to eliminate or reduce the probability of negative schedule variances.

6.7.3.4 Project Management Plan Updates

Elements of the project management plan that may be updated include, but are not limited to:

- **Schedule baseline.** Changes to the schedule baseline are incorporated in response to approved change requests (Section 4.4.3.1) related to project scope changes, activity resources, or activity duration estimates. The schedule baseline may be updated to reflect changes caused by schedule compression techniques.

- **Schedule management plan.** The schedule management plan may be updated to reflect a change in the way the schedule is managed.

- **Cost baseline.** The cost baseline may be updated to reflect approved change requests or changes caused by compression techniques.

6.7.3.5 Project Documents Updates

Project documents that may be updated include, but are not limited to:

- **Schedule Data.** New project schedule network diagrams may be developed to display approved remaining durations and approved modifications to the schedule. In some cases, project schedule delays can be so severe that development of a new target schedule with forecasted start and finish dates is needed to provide realistic data for directing the work, measuring performance, and measuring progress.

- **Project Schedule.** An updated project schedule will be generated from the schedule model populated with updated schedule data to reflect the schedule changes and manage the project.

- **Risk Register.** The risk register, and risk response plans within it, may also be updated based on the risks that may arise due to schedule compression techniques.

6.7.3.6 Organizational Process Assets Updates

Organizational process assets that may be updated include, but are not limited to:

- Causes of variances,
- Corrective action chosen and the reasons, and
- Other types of lessons learned from project schedule control.

7

PROJECT COST MANAGEMENT

Project Cost Management includes the processes involved in planning, estimating, budgeting, financing, funding, managing, and controlling costs so that the project can be completed within the approved budget.

Figure 7-1 provides an overview of the following Project Cost Management processes:

7.1 **Plan Cost Management**—The process that establishes the policies, procedures, and documentation for planning, managing, expending, and controlling project costs.

7.2 **Estimate Costs**—The process of developing an approximation of the monetary resources needed to complete project activities.

7.3 **Determine Budget**—The process of aggregating the estimated costs of individual activities or work packages to establish an authorized cost baseline.

7.4 **Control Costs**—The process of monitoring the status of the project to update the project costs and managing changes to the cost baseline.

These processes interact with each other and with processes in other Knowledge Areas as described in detail in Section 3 and Annex A1.

On some projects, especially those of smaller scope, cost estimating and cost budgeting are tightly linked and can be viewed as a single process that can be performed by a single person over a relatively short period of time. These are presented here as distinct processes because the tools and techniques for each are different. The ability to influence cost is greatest at the early stages of the project, making early scope definition critical (Section 5.3).

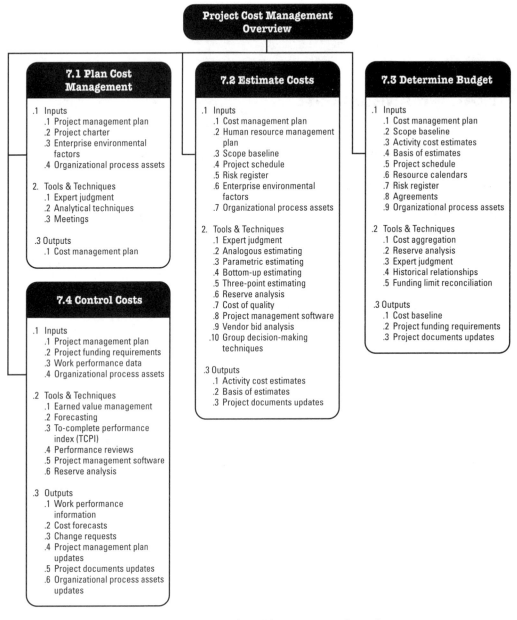

Figure 7-1. Project Cost Management Overview

Project Cost Management should consider the stakeholder requirements for managing costs. Different stakeholders will measure project costs in different ways and at different times. For example, the cost of an acquired item may be measured when the acquisition decision is made or committed, the order is placed, the item is delivered, or the actual cost is incurred or recorded for project accounting purposes.

Project Cost Management is primarily concerned with the cost of the resources needed to complete project activities. Project Cost Management should also consider the effect of project decisions on the subsequent recurring cost of using, maintaining, and supporting the product, service, or result of the project. For example, limiting the number of design reviews can reduce the cost of the project but could increase the resulting product's operating costs.

In many organizations, predicting and analyzing the prospective financial performance of the project's product is performed outside of the project. In others, such as a capital facilities project, Project Cost Management can include this work. When such predictions and analyses are included, Project Cost Management may address additional processes and numerous general financial management techniques such as return on investment, discounted cash flow, and investment payback analysis.

The cost management planning effort occurs early in project planning and sets the framework for each of the cost management processes so that performance of the processes will be efficient and coordinated.

7.1 Plan Cost Management

Plan Cost Management is the process that establishes the policies, procedures, and documentation for planning, managing, expending, and controlling project costs. The key benefit of this process is that it provides guidance and direction on how the project costs will be managed throughout the project. The inputs, tools and techniques, and outputs of this process are depicted in Figure 7-2. Figure 7-3 depicts the data flow diagram of the process.

Inputs	Tools & Techniques	Outputs
.1 Project management plan	.1 Expert judgment	.1 Cost management plan
.2 Project charter	.2 Analytical techniques	
.3 Enterprise environmental factors	.3 Meetings	
.4 Organizational process assets		

Figure 7-2. Plan Cost Management: Inputs, Tools & Techniques, and Outputs

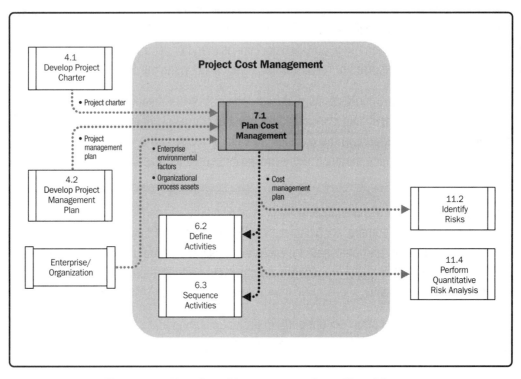

Figure 7-3. Plan Cost Management: Data Flow Diagram

The cost management processes and their associated tools and techniques are documented in the cost management plan. The cost management plan is a component of the project management plan.

7.1.1 Plan Cost Management: Inputs

7.1.1.1 Project Management Plan

Described in Section 4.2.3.1. The project management plan contains information used to develop the cost management plan, which contains, but is not limited to:

- **Scope baseline.** The scope baseline includes the project scope statement and WBS detail for cost estimation and management.

- **Schedule baseline.** The schedule baseline defines when the project costs will be incurred.

- **Other information.** Other cost-related scheduling, risk, and communications decisions from the project management plan.

7.1.1.2 Project Charter

Described in Section 4.1.3.1. The project charter provides the summary budget from which the detailed project costs are developed. The project charter also defines the project approval requirements that will influence the management of the project costs.

7.1.1.3 Enterprise Environmental Factors

Described in Section 2.1.5. The enterprise environmental factors that influence the Plan Cost Management process include, but are not limited to:

- Organizational culture and structure can all influence cost management;
- Market conditions describe what products, services, and results are available in the regional and global market;
- Currency exchange rates for project costs sourced from more than one country;
- Published commercial information such as resource cost rate information is often available from commercial databases that track skills and human resource costs, and provide standard costs for material and equipment. Published seller price lists are another source of information; and
- Project management information system, which provides alternative possibilities for managing cost.

7.1.1.4 Organizational Process Assets

Described in Section 2.1.4. The organizational process assets that influence the Plan Cost Management process include, but are not limited to:

- Financial controls procedures (e.g., time reporting, required expenditure and disbursement reviews, accounting codes, and standard contract provisions);
- Historical information and lessons learned knowledge bases;
- Financial databases; and
- Existing formal and informal cost estimating and budgeting-related policies, procedures, and guidelines.

7.1.2 Plan Cost Management: Tools and Techniques

7.1.2.1 Expert Judgment

Expert judgment, guided by historical information, provides valuable insight about the environment and information from prior similar projects. Expert judgment can also suggest whether to combine methods and how to reconcile differences between them.

Judgment based upon expertise in an application area, Knowledge Area, discipline, industry, etc., as appropriate for the activity being performed should be used in developing the cost management plan.

7.1.2.2 Analytical Techniques

Developing the cost management plan may involve choosing strategic options to fund the project such as: self-funding, funding with equity, or funding with debt. The cost management plan may also detail ways to finance project resources such as making, purchasing, renting, or leasing. These decisions, like other financial decisions affecting the project, may affect project schedule and/or risks.

Organizational policies and procedures may influence which financial techniques are employed in these decisions. Techniques may include (but are not limited to): payback period, return on investment, internal rate of return, discounted cash flow, and net present value.

7.1.2.3 Meetings

Project teams may hold planning meetings to develop the cost management plan. Attendees at these meetings may include the project manager, the project sponsor, selected project team members, selected stakeholders, anyone with responsibility for project costs, and others as needed.

7.1.3 Plan Cost Management: Outputs

7.1.3.1 Cost Management Plan

The cost management plan is a component of the project management plan and describes how the project costs will be planned, structured, and controlled. The cost management processes and their associated tools and techniques are documented in the cost management plan.

For example, the cost management plan can establish the following:

- **Units of measure.** Each unit used in measurements (such as staff hours, staff days, weeks for time measures; or meters, liters, tons, kilometers, or cubic yards for quantity measures; or lump sum in currency form) is defined for each of the resources.

- **Level of precision.** The degree to which activity cost estimates will be rounded up or down (e.g., US$100.49 to US$100, or US$995.59 to US$1,000), based on the scope of the activities and magnitude of the project.

- **Level of accuracy.** The acceptable range (e.g., ±10%) used in determining realistic activity cost estimates is specified, and may include an amount for contingencies;

- **Organizational procedures links.** The work breakdown structure (WBS) (Section 5.4) provides the framework for the cost management plan, allowing for consistency with the estimates, budgets, and control of costs. The WBS component used for the project cost accounting is called the control account. Each control account is assigned a unique code or account number(s) that links directly to the performing organization's accounting system.

- **Control thresholds.** Variance thresholds for monitoring cost performance may be specified to indicate an agreed-upon amount of variation to be allowed before some action needs to be taken. Thresholds are typically expressed as percentage deviations from the baseline plan.

- **Rules of performance measurement.** Earned value management (EVM) rules of performance measurement are set. For example, the cost management plan may:

  o Define the points in the WBS at which measurement of control accounts will be performed;

  o Establish the earned value measurement techniques (e.g., weighted milestones, fixed-formula, percent complete, etc.) to be employed; and

  o Specify tracking methodologies and the earned value management computation equations for calculating projected estimate at completion (EAC) forecasts to provide a validity check on the bottom-up EAC.

For more specific information regarding earned value management, refer to the *Practice Standard for Earned Value Management – Second Edition.*

7

- **Reporting formats.** The formats and frequency for the various cost reports are defined.

- **Process descriptions.** Descriptions of each of the other cost management processes are documented.

- **Additional details.** Additional details about cost management activities include, but are not limited to:

    o Description of strategic funding choices,

    o Procedure to account for fluctuations in currency exchange rates, and

    o Procedure for project cost recording.

7.2 Estimate Costs

Estimate Costs is the process of developing an approximation of the monetary resources needed to complete project activities. The key benefit of this process is that it determines the amount of cost required to complete project work. The inputs, tools and techniques, and outputs of this process are depicted in Figure 7-4. Figure 7-5 depicts the data flow diagram of the process.

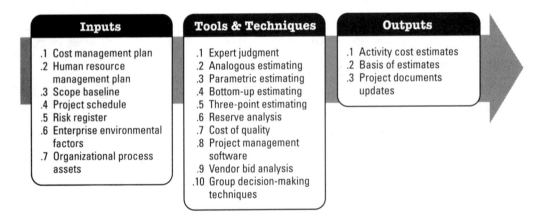

Inputs	Tools & Techniques	Outputs
.1 Cost management plan	.1 Expert judgment	.1 Activity cost estimates
.2 Human resource management plan	.2 Analogous estimating	.2 Basis of estimates
.3 Scope baseline	.3 Parametric estimating	.3 Project documents updates
.4 Project schedule	.4 Bottom-up estimating	
.5 Risk register	.5 Three-point estimating	
.6 Enterprise environmental factors	.6 Reserve analysis	
.7 Organizational process assets	.7 Cost of quality	
	.8 Project management software	
	.9 Vendor bid analysis	
	.10 Group decision-making techniques	

Figure 7-4. Estimate Costs: Inputs, Tools & Techniques, and Outputs

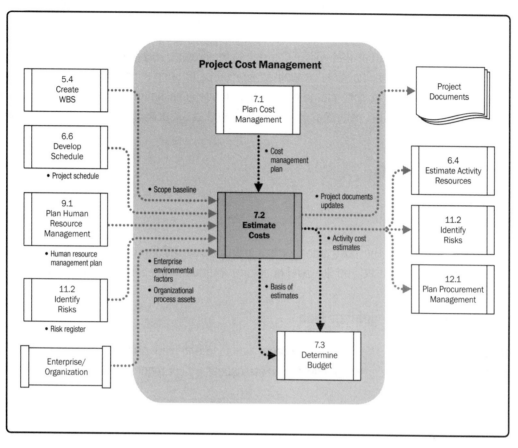

Figure 7-5. Estimate Costs Data Flow Diagram

Cost estimates are a prediction that is based on the information known at a given point in time. Cost estimates include the identification and consideration of costing alternatives to initiate and complete the project. Cost trade-offs and risks should be considered, such as make versus buy, buy versus lease, and the sharing of resources in order to achieve optimal costs for the project.

Cost estimates are generally expressed in units of some currency (i.e., dollars, euros, yen, etc.), although in some instances other units of measure, such as staff hours or staff days, are used to facilitate comparisons by eliminating the effects of currency fluctuations.

Cost estimates should be reviewed and refined during the course of the project to reflect additional detail as it becomes available and assumptions are tested. The accuracy of a project estimate will increase as the project progresses through the project life cycle. For example, a project in the initiation phase may have a rough order of magnitude (ROM) estimate in the range of −25% to +75%. Later in the project, as more information is known, definitive estimates could narrow the range of accuracy to -5% to +10%. In some organizations, there are guidelines for when such refinements can be made and the degree of confidence or accuracy that is expected.

Sources of input information are derived from the outputs of processes in other Knowledge Areas. Once received, all of this information will remain available as inputs to all of the cost management processes.

Costs are estimated for all resources that will be charged to the project. This includes, but is not limited to, labor, materials, equipment, services, and facilities, as well as special categories such as an inflation allowance, cost of financing, or contingency costs. A cost estimate is a quantitative assessment of the likely costs for resources required to complete the activity. Cost estimates may be presented at the activity level or in summary form.

7.2.1 Estimate Costs: Inputs

7.2.1.1 Cost Management Plan

Described in Section 7.1.3.1. The cost management plan defines how project costs will be managed and controlled. It includes the method used and the level of accuracy required to estimate activity cost.

7.2.1.2 Human Resource Management Plan

Described in Section 9.1.3.1. The human resource management plan provides project staffing attributes, personnel rates, and related rewards/recognition, which are necessary components for developing the project cost estimates.

7.2.1.3 Scope Baseline

The scope baseline is comprised of the following:

- **Project scope statement.** The project scope statement (Section 5.3.3.1) provides the product description, acceptance criteria, key deliverables, project boundaries, assumptions, and constraints about the project. One basic assumption that needs to be made when estimating project costs is whether the estimates will be limited to direct project costs only or whether the estimates will also include indirect costs. Indirect costs are those costs that cannot be directly traced to a specific project and therefore will be accumulated and allocated equitably over multiple projects by some approved and documented accounting procedure. One of the most common constraints for many projects is a limited project budget. Examples of other constraints are required delivery dates, available skilled resources, and organizational policies.

- **Work breakdown structure.** The WBS (Section 5.4) provides the relationships among all the components of the project and the project deliverables.

- **WBS dictionary.** The WBS dictionary (Section 5.4.3.1) provides detailed information about the deliverables and a description of the work for each component in the WBS required to produce each deliverable.

Additional information that may be found in the scope baseline with contractual and legal implications, such as health, safety, security, performance, environmental, insurance, intellectual property rights, licenses, and permits. All of this information should be considered when developing the cost estimates.

7.2.1.4 Project Schedule

Described in Section 6.6.3.2. The type and quantity of resources and the amount of time which those resources are applied to complete the work of the project are major factors in determining the project cost. Schedule activity resources and their respective durations are used as key inputs to this process. Estimate Activity Resources (Section 6.4) involves determining the availability of staff, the number of staff hours required, and quantities of material and equipment needed to perform schedule activities. It is closely coordinated with cost estimating. Activity duration estimates (Section 6.5.3.1) will affect cost estimates on any project where the project budget includes an allowance for the cost of financing (including interest charges) and where resources are applied per unit of time for the duration of the activity. Activity duration estimates can also affect cost estimates that have time-sensitive costs included in them, such as union labor with regularly expiring collective bargaining agreements or materials with seasonal cost variations.

7.2.1.5 Risk Register

Described in Section 11.2.3.1. The risk register should be reviewed to consider risk response costs. Risks, which can be either threats or opportunities, typically have an impact on both activity and overall project costs. As a general rule, when the project experiences a negative risk event, the near-term cost of the project will usually increase, and there will sometimes be a delay in the project schedule. In a similar way, the project team should be sensitive to potential opportunities that can benefit the business either by directly reducing activity costs or by accelerating the schedule.

7.2.1.6 Enterprise Environmental Factors

Described in Section 2.1.5. The enterprise environmental factors that influence the Estimate Costs process include, but are not limited to:

- **Market conditions.** These conditions describe what products, services, and results are available in the market, from whom, and under what terms and conditions. Regional and/or global supply and demand conditions greatly influence resource costs.

- **Published commercial information.** Resource cost rate information is often available from commercial databases that track skills and human resource costs, and provide standard costs for material and equipment. Published seller price lists are another source of information.

7.2.1.7 Organizational Process Assets

Described in Section 2.1.4. The organizational process assets that influence the Estimate Costs process include, but are not limited to:

- Cost estimating policies,
- Cost estimating templates,
- Historical information, and
- Lessons learned.

7.2.2 Estimate Costs: Tools and Techniques

7.2.2.1 Expert Judgment

Expert judgment, guided by historical information, provides valuable insight about the environment and information from prior similar projects. Expert judgment can also be used to determine whether to combine methods of estimating and how to reconcile differences between them.

7.2.2.2 Analogous Estimating

Analogous cost estimating uses the values such as scope, cost, budget, and duration or measures of scale such as size, weight, and complexity from a previous, similar project as the basis for estimating the same parameter or measurement for a current project. When estimating costs, this technique relies on the actual cost of previous, similar projects as the basis for estimating the cost of the current project. It is a gross value estimating approach, sometimes adjusted for known differences in project complexity.

Analogous cost estimating is frequently used to estimate a value when there is a limited amount of detailed information about the project, for example, in the early phases of a project. Analogous cost estimating uses historical information and expert judgment.

Analogous cost estimating is generally less costly and less time consuming than other techniques, but it is also generally less accurate. Analogous cost estimates can be applied to a total project or to segments of a project, in conjunction with other estimating methods. Analogous estimating is most reliable when the previous projects are similar in fact and not just in appearance, and the project team members preparing the estimates have the needed expertise.

7.2.2.3 Parametric Estimating

Parametric estimating uses a statistical relationship between relevant historical data and other variables (e.g., square footage in construction) to calculate a cost estimate for project work. This technique can produce higher levels of accuracy depending upon the sophistication and underlying data built into the model. Parametric cost estimates can be applied to a total project or to segments of a project, in conjunction with other estimating methods.

7.2.2.4 Bottom-Up Estimating

Bottom-up estimating is a method of estimating a component of work. The cost of individual work packages or activities is estimated to the greatest level of specified detail. The detailed cost is then summarized or "rolled up" to higher levels for subsequent reporting and tracking purposes. The cost and accuracy of bottom-up cost estimating are typically influenced by the size and complexity of the individual activity or work package.

7.2.2.5 Three-Point Estimating

The accuracy of single-point activity cost estimates may be improved by considering estimation uncertainty and risk and using three estimates to define an approximate range for an activity's cost:

- **Most likely** (cM). The cost of the activity, based on realistic effort assessment for the required work and any predicted expenses.

- **Optimistic** (cO). The activity cost based on analysis of the best-case scenario for the activity.

- **Pessimistic** (cP). The activity cost based on analysis of the worst-case scenario for the activity.

Depending on the assumed distribution of values within the range of the three estimates the expected cost, cE, can be calculated using a formula. Two commonly used formulas are triangular and beta distributions. The formulas are:

- **Triangular Distribution.** $cE = (cO + cM + cP) / 3$
- **Beta Distribution** (from a traditional PERT analysis). $cE = (cO + 4cM + cP) / 6$

Cost estimates based on three points with an assumed distribution provide an expected cost and clarify the range of uncertainty around the expected cost.

7.2.2.6 Reserve Analysis

Cost estimates may include contingency reserves (sometimes called contingency allowances) to account for cost uncertainty. Contingency reserves are the budget within the cost baseline that is allocated for identified risks, which are accepted and for which contingent or mitigating responses are developed. Contingency reserves are often viewed as the part of the budget intended to address the "known-unknowns" that can affect a project. For example, rework for some project deliverables could be anticipated, while the amount of this rework is unknown. Contingency reserves may be estimated to account for this unknown amount of rework. Contingency reserves can provide for a specific activity, for the whole project, or both. The contingency reserve may be a percentage of the estimated cost, a fixed number, or may be developed by using quantitative analysis methods.

As more precise information about the project becomes available, the contingency reserve may be used, reduced, or eliminated. Contingency should be clearly identified in cost documentation. Contingency reserves are part of the cost baseline and the overall funding requirements for the project.

Estimates may also be produced for the amount of management reserve to be funded for the project. Management reserves are an amount of the project budget withheld for management control purposes and are reserved for unforeseen work that is within scope of the project. Management reserves are intended to address the "unknown unknowns" that can affect a project. The management reserve is not included in the cost baseline but is part of the overall project budget and funding requirements. When an amount of management reserves is used to fund unforeseen work, the amount of management reserve used is added to the cost baseline, thus requiring an approved change to the cost baseline.

7.2.2.7 Cost of Quality (COQ)

Assumptions about costs of quality (Section 8.1.2.2) may be used to prepare the activity cost estimate.

7.2.2.8 Project Management Software

Project management software applications, computerized spreadsheets, simulation, and statistical tools are used to assist with cost estimating. Such tools can simplify the use of some cost-estimating techniques and thereby facilitate rapid consideration of cost estimate alternatives.

7.2.2.9 Vendor Bid Analysis

Cost estimating methods may include analysis of what the project should cost, based on the responsive bids from qualified vendors. When projects are awarded to a vendor under competitive processes, additional cost estimating work may be required of the project team to examine the price of individual deliverables and to derive a cost that supports the final total project cost.

7.2.2.10 Group Decision-Making Techniques

Team-based approaches, such as brainstorming, the Delphi or nominal group techniques, are useful for engaging team members to improve estimate accuracy and commitment to the emerging estimates. By involving a structured group of people who are close to the technical execution of work in the estimation process, additional information is gained and more accurate estimates are obtained. Additionally, when people are involved in the estimation process, their commitment towards meeting the resulting estimates increases.

7.2.3 Estimate Costs: Outputs

7.2.3.1 Activity Cost Estimates

Activity cost estimates are quantitative assessments of the probable costs required to complete project work. Cost estimates can be presented in summary form or in detail. Costs are estimated for all resources that are applied to the activity cost estimate. This includes, but is not limited to, direct labor, materials, equipment, services, facilities, information technology, and special categories such as cost of financing (including interest charges), an inflation allowance, exchange rates, or a cost contingency reserve. Indirect costs, if they are included in the project estimate, can be included at the activity level or at higher levels.

7.2.3.2 Basis of Estimates

The amount and type of additional details supporting the cost estimate vary by application area. Regardless of the level of detail, the supporting documentation should provide a clear and complete understanding of how the cost estimate was derived.

Supporting detail for activity cost estimates may include:

- Documentation of the basis of the estimate (i.e., how it was developed),
- Documentation of all assumptions made,
- Documentation of any known constraints,
- Indication of the range of possible estimates (e.g., €10,000 (±10%) to indicate that the item is expected to cost between a range of values), and
- Indication of the confidence level of the final estimate.

7.2.3.3 Project Documents Updates

Project documents that may be updated include, but are not limited to, the risk register.

7.3 Determine Budget

Determine Budget is the process of aggregating the estimated costs of individual activities or work packages to establish an authorized cost baseline. The key benefit of this process is that it determines the cost baseline against which project performance can be monitored and controlled. The inputs, tools and techniques, and outputs of this process are depicted in Figure 7-6. Figure 7-7 depicts the data flow diagram of the process.

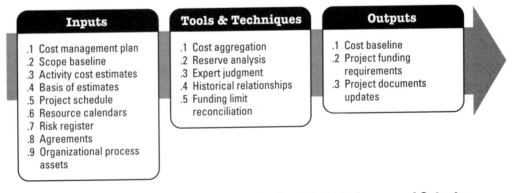

Inputs	Tools & Techniques	Outputs
.1 Cost management plan .2 Scope baseline .3 Activity cost estimates .4 Basis of estimates .5 Project schedule .6 Resource calendars .7 Risk register .8 Agreements .9 Organizational process assets	.1 Cost aggregation .2 Reserve analysis .3 Expert judgment .4 Historical relationships .5 Funding limit reconciliation	.1 Cost baseline .2 Project funding requirements .3 Project documents updates

Figure 7-6. Determine Budget: Inputs, Tools & Techniques, and Outputs

 ©2013 Project Management Institute. *A Guide to the Project Management Body of Knowledge (PMBOK® Guide) – Fifth Edition*

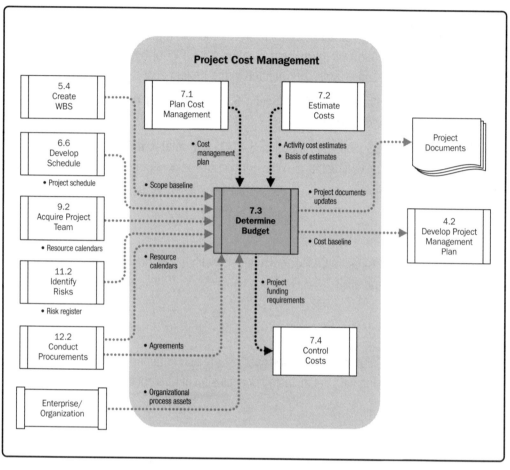

Figure 7-7. Determine Budget Data Flow Diagram

A project budget includes all the funds authorized to execute the project. The cost baseline is the approved version of the time-phased project budget, but excludes management reserves.

7.3.1 Determine Budget: Inputs

7.3.1.1 Cost Management Plan

Described in Section 7.1.3.1. The cost management plan describes how the project costs will be managed and controlled.

7.3.1.2 Scope Baseline

- **Project scope statement.** Formal limitations by period for the expenditure of project funds can be mandated by the organization, by agreement (Section 12.2.3.2), or by other entities such as government agencies. These funding constraints are reflected in the project scope statement.
- **Work breakdown structure.** The WBS (Section 5.4) provides the relationships among all the project deliverables and their various components.
- **WBS dictionary.** The WBS dictionary (Section 5.4.3.1) and related detailed statements of work provide an identification of the deliverables and a description of the work in each WBS component required to produce each deliverable.

7.3.1.3 Activity Cost Estimates

Described in Section 7.2.3.1. Cost estimates for each activity within a work package are aggregated to obtain a cost estimate for each work package.

7.3.1.4 Basis of Estimates

Described in Section 7.2.3.2. Supporting detail for cost estimates contained in the basis for estimates should specify any basic assumptions dealing with the inclusion or exclusion of indirect or other costs in the project budget.

7.3.1.5 Project Schedule

Described in Section 6.6.3.2. The project schedule includes planned start and finish dates for the project's activities, milestones, work packages, and control accounts. This information can be used to aggregate costs to the calendar periods in which the costs are planned to be incurred.

7.3.1.6 Resource Calendars

Described in Sections 9.2.3.2 and 12.2.3.3. Resource calendars provide information on which resources are assigned to the project and when they are assigned. This information can be used to indicate resource costs over the duration of the project.

7.3.1.7 Risk Register

Described in Section 11.2.3.1. The risk register should be reviewed to consider how to aggregate the risk response costs. Updates to the risk register are included with project document updates described in Section 11.5.3.2.

7.3.1.8 Agreements

Described in Section 12.2.3.2. Applicable agreement information and costs relating to products, services, or results that have been or will be purchased are included when determining the budget.

7.3.1.9 Organizational Process Assets

Described in Section 2.1.4. The organizational process assets that influence the Determine Budget process include, but are not limited to:

- Existing formal and informal cost budgeting-related policies, procedures, and guidelines;
- Cost budgeting tools; and
- Reporting methods.

7.3.2 Determine Budget: Tools and Techniques

7.3.2.1 Cost Aggregation

Cost estimates are aggregated by work packages in accordance with the WBS. The work package cost estimates are then aggregated for the higher component levels of the WBS (such as control accounts) and ultimately for the entire project.

7.3.2.2 Reserve Analysis

Budget reserve analysis can establish both the contingency reserves and the management reserves for the project. Management and contingency reserves are addressed in more detail in Section 7.2.2.6.

7.3.2.3 Expert Judgment

Expert judgment, guided by experience in an application area, Knowledge Area, discipline, industry, or similar project, aids in determining the budget. Such expertise may be provided by any group or person with specialized education, knowledge, skill, experience, or training. Expert judgment is available from many sources, including, but not limited to:

- Other units within the performing organization,

- Consultants,

- Stakeholders, including customers,

- Professional and technical associations, and

- Industry groups.

7.3.2.4 Historical Relationships

Any historical relationships that result in parametric estimates or analogous estimates involve the use of project characteristics (parameters) to develop mathematical models to predict total project costs. Such models may be simple (e.g., residential home construction is based on a certain cost per square foot of space) or complex (e.g., one model of software development costing uses multiple separate adjustment factors, each of which has numerous points within it).

Both the cost and accuracy of analogous and parametric models can vary widely. They are most likely to be reliable when:

- Historical information used to develop the model is accurate,

- Parameters used in the model are readily quantifiable, and

- Models are scalable, such that they work for large projects, small projects, and phases of a project.

7.3.2.5 Funding Limit Reconciliation

The expenditure of funds should be reconciled with any funding limits on the commitment of funds for the project. A variance between the funding limits and the planned expenditures will sometimes necessitate the rescheduling of work to level out the rate of expenditures. This is accomplished by placing imposed date constraints for work into the project schedule.

7.3.3 Determine Budget: Outputs

7.3.3.1 Cost Baseline

The cost baseline is the approved version of the time-phased project budget, excluding any management reserves, which can only be changed through formal change control procedures and is used as a basis for comparison to actual results. It is developed as a summation of the approved budgets for the different schedule activities.

Figure 7-8 illustrates the various components of the project budget and cost baseline. Activity cost estimates for the various project activities along with any contingency reserves (Section 7.2.2.6) for these activities are aggregated into their associated work package costs. The work package cost estimates, along with any contingency reserves estimated for the work packages, are aggregated into control accounts. The summation of the control accounts make up the cost baseline. Since the cost estimates that make up the cost baseline are directly tied to the schedule activities, this enables a time-phased view of the cost baseline, which is typically displayed in the form of an S-curve, as is illustrated in Figure 7-9.

Management reserves (Section 7.2.2.6) are added to the cost baseline to produce the project budget. As changes warranting the use of management reserves arise, the change control process is used to obtain approval to move the applicable management reserve funds into the cost baseline.

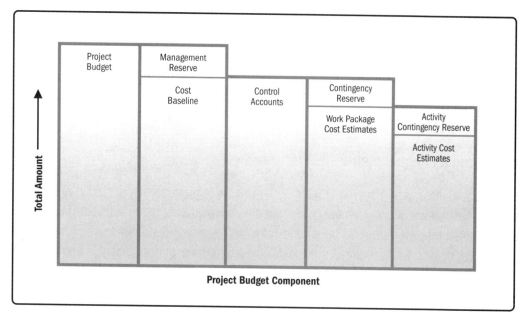

Figure 7-8. Project Budget Components

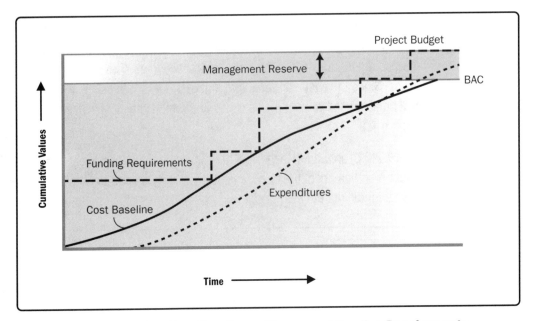

Figure 7-9. Cost Baseline, Expenditures, and Funding Requirements

7.3.3.2 Project Funding Requirements

Total funding requirements and periodic funding requirements (e.g., quarterly, annually) are derived from the cost baseline. The cost baseline will include projected expenditures plus anticipated liabilities. Funding often occurs in incremental amounts that are not continuous, and may not be evenly distributed, which appear as steps as shown in Figure 7-9. The total funds required are those included in the cost baseline, plus management reserves, if any. Funding requirements may include the source(s) of the funding.

7.3.3.3 Project Documents Updates

Project documents that may be updated include, but are not limited to:

- Risk register,
- Activity cost estimates, and
- Project schedule.

8.2.2.2 Quality Audits

A quality audit is a structured, independent process to determine if project activities comply with organizational and project policies, processes, and procedures. The objectives of a quality audit may include:

- Identify all good and best practices being implemented;

- Identify all nonconformity, gaps, and shortcomings;

- Share good practices introduced or implemented in similar projects in the organization and/or industry;

- Proactively offer assistance in a positive manner to improve implementation of processes to help the team raise productivity; and

- Highlight contributions of each audit in the lessons learned repository of the organization.

The subsequent effort to correct any deficiencies should result in a reduced cost of quality and an increase in sponsor or customer acceptance of the project's product. Quality audits may be scheduled or random, and may be conducted by internal or external auditors.

Quality audits can confirm the implementation of approved change requests including updates, corrective actions, defect repairs, and preventive actions.

8.2.2.3 Process Analysis

Process analysis follows the steps outlined in the process improvement plan to identify needed improvements. This analysis also examines problems experienced, constraints experienced, and non-value-added activities identified during process operation. Process analysis includes root cause analysis—a specific technique used to identify a problem, discover the underlying causes that lead to it, and develop preventive actions.

8.2.3 Perform Quality Assurance: Outputs

8.2.3.1 Change Requests

Change requests are created and used as input into the Perform Integrated Change Control process (Section 4.5) to allow full consideration of the recommended improvements. Change requests are used to take corrective action, preventive action, or to perform defect repair.

8.2.3.2 Project Management Plan Updates

Elements of the project management plan that may be updated include, but are not limited to:

- Quality management plan (Section 8.1.3.1),
- Scope management plan (Section 5.1.3.1),
- Schedule management plan (Section 6.1.3.1), and
- Cost management plan (7.1.3.1).

8.2.3.3 Project Documents Updates

Project documents that may be updated include, but are not limited to:

- Quality audit reports,
- Training plans, and
- Process documentation.

8.2.3.4 Organizational Process Assets Updates

Elements of the organizational process assets that may be updated include, but are not limited to, the organization's quality standards and the quality management system.

8.3 Control Quality

Control Quality is the process of monitoring and recording results of executing the quality activities to assess performance and recommend necessary changes. The key benefits of this process include: (1) identifying the causes of poor process or product quality and recommending and/or taking action to eliminate them; and (2) validating that project deliverables and work meet the requirements specified by key stakeholders necessary for final acceptance. The inputs, tools and techniques, and outputs of this process are depicted in Figure 8-11. Figure 8-12 depicts the data flow diagram of the process.

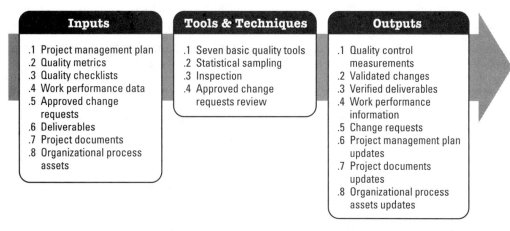

Figure 8-11. Control Quality: Inputs, Tools & Techniques, and Outputs

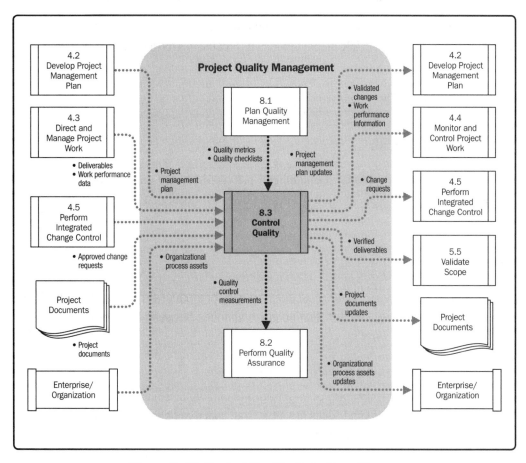

Figure 8-12. Control Quality Data Flow Diagram

The Control Quality process uses a set of operational techniques and tasks to verify that the delivered output will meet the requirements. Quality assurance should be used during the project's planning and executing phases to provide confidence that the stakeholder's requirements will be met and quality control should be used during the project executing and closing phases to formally demonstrate, with reliable data, that the sponsor and/or customer's acceptance criteria have been met.

The project management team may have a working knowledge of statistical control processes to evaluate data contained in the control quality outputs. Among other subjects, the team may find it useful to know the differences between the following pairs of terms:

- *Prevention* (keeping errors out of the process) and *inspection* (keeping errors out of the hands of the customer).

- *Attribute sampling* (the result either conforms or does not conform) and *variables sampling* (the result is rated on a continuous scale that measures the degree of conformity).

- *Tolerances* (specified range of acceptable results) and *control limits* (that identify the boundaries of common variation in a statistically stable process or process performance).

8.3.1 Control Quality: Inputs

8.3.1.1 Project Management Plan

Described in Section 8.1.3.1. The project management plan contains the quality management plan, which is used to control quality. The quality management plan describes how quality control will be performed within the project.

8.3.1.2 Quality Metrics

Described in Section 4.2.3.1. A quality metric describes a project or product attribute and how it will be measured. Some examples of quality metrics include: function points, mean time between failure (MTBF), and mean time to repair (MTTR).

8.3.1.3 Quality Checklists

Described in Section 8.1.3.4. Quality checklists are structured lists that help to verify that the work of the project and its deliverables fulfill a set of requirements.

8.3.1.4 Work Performance Data

Described in Section 4.3.3.2. Work performance data can include:

- Planned vs. actual technical performance,
- Planned vs. actual schedule performance, and
- Planned vs. actual cost performance.

8.3.1.5 Approved Change Requests

As part of the Perform Integrated Change Control process, a change log update indicates that some changes are approved and some are not. Approved change requests may include modifications such as defect repairs, revised work methods, and revised schedule. The timely implementation of approved changes needs to be verified.

8.3.1.6 Deliverables

Described in Section 4.3.3.1. A deliverable is any unique and verifiable product, result, or capability that results in a validated deliverable required by the project.

8.3.1.7 Project Documents

Project documents may include, but are not limited to:

- Agreements,
- Quality audit reports and change logs supported with corrective action plans,
- Training plans and assessments of effectiveness, and
- Process documentation such as those obtained using either the seven basic quality tools or the quality management and control tools shown in Figures 8-7 and 8-10.

8.3.1.8 Organizational Process Assets

Described in Section 2.1.4. The organizational process assets that influence the Control Quality process include, but are not limited to:

- The organization's quality standards and policies,
- Standard work guidelines, and
- Issue and defect reporting procedures and communication policies.

8.3.2 Control Quality: Tools and Techniques

8.3.2.1 Seven Basic Quality Tools

Described in Section 8.1.2.3. The seven basic quality tools are illustrated conceptually in Figure 8-7.

8.3.2.2 Statistical Sampling

Described in Section 8.1.2.6. Samples are selected and tested as defined in the quality management plan.

8.3.2.3 Inspection

An inspection is the examination of a work product to determine if it conforms to documented standards. The results of an inspection generally include measurements and may be conducted at any level. For example, the results of a single activity can be inspected, or the final product of the project can be inspected. Inspections may be called reviews, peer reviews, audits, or walkthroughs. In some application areas, these terms have narrow and specific meanings. Inspections also are used to validate defect repairs.

8.3.2.4 Approved Change Requests Review

All approved change requests should be reviewed to verify that they were implemented as approved.

8.3.3 Control Quality: Outputs

8.3.3.1 Quality Control Measurements

Quality control measurements are the documented results of control quality activities. They should be captured in the format that was specified through the Plan Quality Management process (Section 8.1).

8.3.3.2 Validated Changes

Any changed or repaired items are inspected and will be either accepted or rejected before notification of the decision is provided. Rejected items may require rework.

8.3.3.3 Verified Deliverables

A goal of the Control Quality process is to determine the correctness of deliverables. The results of performing the Control Quality process are verified deliverables. Verified deliverables are an input to Validate Scope (5.5.1.4) for formalized acceptance.

8.3.3.4 Work Performance Information

Work performance information is the performance data collected from various controlling processes, analyzed in context and integrated based on relationships across areas. Examples include information about the project requirements fulfillment such as causes for rejections, rework required, or the need for process adjustments.

8.3.3.5 Change Requests

If the recommended corrective or preventive actions or a defect repair requires a change to the project management plan, a change request (Section 4.4.3.1) should be initiated in accordance with the defined Perform Integrated Change Control (4.5) process.

8.3.3.6 Project Management Plan Updates

Elements of the project management plan that may be updated include, but are not limited to:

- Quality management plan (Section 8.1.3.1), and
- Process improvement plan (Section 8.1.3.2).

8.3.3.7 Project Documents Updates

Project documents that may be updated include, but are not limited to,

- Quality standards;
- Agreements;
- Quality audit reports and change logs supported with corrective action plans;
- Training plans and assessments of effectiveness; and
- Process documentation, such as information obtained using the seven basic quality tools or the quality management and control tools.

8.3.3.8 Organizational Process Assets Updates

Elements of the organizational process assets that may be updated include, but are not limited to:

- **Completed checklists.** When checklists are used, the completed checklists become part of the project documents and organizational process assets (Section 4.1.1.5).

- **Lessons learned documentation.** The causes of variances, the reasoning behind the corrective action chosen, and other types of lessons learned from control quality are documented so they become part of the historical database for both the project and the performing organization.

9

PROJECT HUMAN RESOURCE MANAGEMENT

Project Human Resource Management includes the processes that organize, manage, and lead the project team. The project team is comprised of the people with assigned roles and responsibilities for completing the project. Project team members may have varied skill sets, may be assigned full or part-time, and may be added or removed from the team as the project progresses. Project team members may also be referred to as the project's staff. Although specific roles and responsibilities for the project team members are assigned, the involvement of all team members in project planning and decision making is beneficial. Participation of team members during planning adds their expertise to the process and strengthens their commitment to the project.

Figure 9-1 provides an overview of the Project Human Resource Management processes, which are as follows:

9.1 Plan Human Resource Management—The process of identifying and documenting project roles, responsibilities, required skills, reporting relationships, and creating a staffing management plan.

9.2 Acquire Project Team—The process of confirming human resource availability and obtaining the team necessary to complete project activities.

9.3 Develop Project Team—The process of improving competencies, team member interaction, and overall team environment to enhance project performance.

9.4 Manage Project Team—The process of tracking team member performance, providing feedback, resolving issues, and managing changes to optimize project performance.

These processes interact with each other and with processes in other Knowledge Areas as described in detail in Section 3 and Annex A1.

As a result of these interactions additional planning may be required throughout the project. For example:

- After initial team members create a work breakdown structure, additional team members may need to be added to the team.

- As additional team members are added to the team, their experience levels, or lack thereof, could decrease or increase project risk, creating the need for additional risk planning.

- When activity durations are estimated, budgeted, scoped, or planned prior to identifying all project team members and their competency levels, the activity durations may change.

The project management team is a subset of the project team and is responsible for the project management and leadership activities such as initiating, planning, executing, monitoring, controlling, and closing the various project phases. This group can also be referred to as the core, executive, or leadership team. For smaller projects, the project management responsibilities may be shared by the entire team or administered solely by the project manager. The project sponsor works with the project management team, typically assisting with matters such as project funding, clarifying scope, monitoring progress, and influencing stakeholders in both the requesting and performing organization for the project benefit.

Managing and leading the project team includes, but is not limited to:

- **Influencing the project team.** The project manager needs to be aware of and influence, when possible, human resource factors that may impact the project. These factors includes team environment, geographical locations of team members, communications among stakeholders, internal and external politics, cultural issues, organizational uniqueness, and others factors that may alter project performance.

- **Professional and ethical behavior.** The project management team should be aware of, subscribe to, and ensure that all team members follow professional and ethical behavior.

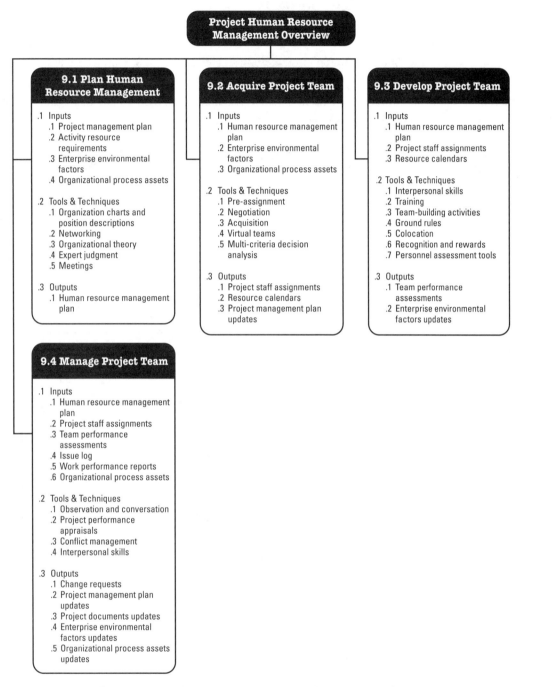

Figure 9-1. Project Human Resource Management Overview

9.1 Plan Human Resource Management

Plan Human Resource Management is the process of identifying and documenting project roles, responsibilities, required skills, reporting relationships, and creating a staffing management plan. The key benefit of this process is that it establishes project roles and responsibilities, project organization charts, and the staffing management plan including the timetable for staff acquisition and release. The inputs, tools and techniques, and outputs of this process are depicted in Figure 9-2. Figure 9-3 depicts the data flow diagram of the process.

Figure 9-2. Plan Human Resource Management: Inputs, Tools & Techniques, and Outputs

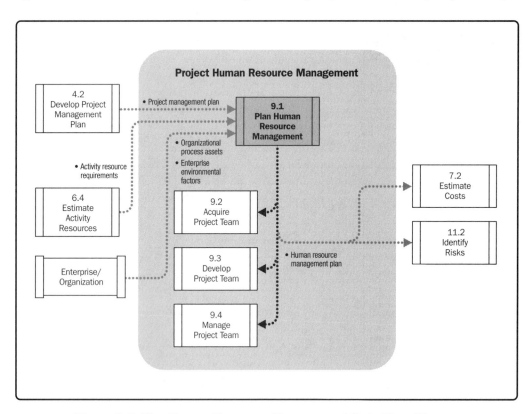

Figure 9-3. Plan Human Resource Management Data Flow Diagram

Human resource planning is used to determine and identify human resources with the necessary skills required for project success. The human resource management plan describes how the roles and responsibilities, reporting relationships, and staffing management will be addressed and structured within a project. It also contains the staffing management plan including timetables for staff acquisition and release, identification of training needs, team-building strategies, plans for recognition and rewards programs, compliance considerations, safety issues, and the impact of the staffing management plan on the organization.

Effective human resource planning should consider and plan for the availability of or competition for scarce resources. Project roles can be designated for teams or team members. Those teams or team members can be from inside or outside the organization performing the project. Other projects may be competing for human resources with the same competencies or skill sets. Given these factors, project costs, schedules, risks, quality, and other project areas may be significantly affected.

9.1.1 Plan Human Resource Management: Inputs

9.1.1.1 Project Management Plan

Described in Section 4.2.3.1. The project management plan is used to develop the human resource management plan as described in Section 9.1.3.1. The information used for the development of the human resource management plan includes, but is not limited to:

- The project life cycle and the processes that will be applied to each phase,
- How work will be executed to accomplish the project objectives,
- A change management plan that documents how changes will be monitored and controlled,
- A configuration management plan that documents how configuration management will be performed,
- How integrity of the project baselines will be maintained, and
- Needs and methods of communication among stakeholders.

9.1.1.2 Activity Resource Requirements

Described in Section 6.4.3.1. Human resource planning uses activity resource requirements to determine the human resource needs for the project. The preliminary requirements regarding the required project team members and their competencies are progressively elaborated as part of the Plan Human Resource Management process.

9.1.1.3 Enterprise Environmental Factors

Described in Section 2.1.5. The enterprise environmental factors that can influence the Plan Human Resource Management process include, but are not limited to:

- Organizational culture and structure,
- Existing human resources,
- Geographical dispersion of team members,
- Personnel administration policies, and
- Marketplace conditions.

9.1.1.4 Organizational Process Assets

Described in Section 2.1.4. The organizational process assets that can influence the Plan Human Resource Management process include, but are not limited to:

- Organizational standard processes, policies, and role descriptions;
- Templates for organizational charts and position descriptions;
- Lessons learned on organizational structures that have worked in previous projects; and
- Escalation procedures for handling issues within the team and within the performing organization.

9.1.2 Plan Human Resource Management: Tools and Techniques

9.1.2.1 Organization Charts and Position Descriptions

Various formats exist to document team member roles and responsibilities. Most of the formats fall into one of three types (Figure 9-4): hierarchical, matrix, and text-oriented. Additionally, some project assignments are listed in subsidiary plans, such as the risk, quality, or communications management plans. Regardless of the method utilized, the objective is to ensure that each work package has an unambiguous owner and that all team members have a clear understanding of their roles and responsibilities. For example, a hierarchical format may be used to represent high-level roles, while a text-based format may be better suited to document the detailed responsibilities.

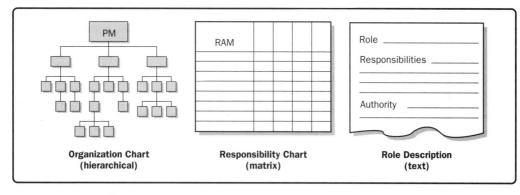

Figure 9-4. Roles and Responsibility Definition Formats

- **Hierarchical-type charts.** The traditional organization chart structure can be used to show positions and relationships in a graphical, top-down format. Work breakdown structures (WBS) designed to show how project deliverables are broken down into work packages provide a way of showing high-level areas of responsibility. While the WBS shows a breakdown of project deliverables, the organizational breakdown structure (OBS) is arranged according to an organization's existing departments, units, or teams with the project activities or work packages listed under each department. An operational department such as information technology or purchasing can see all of its project responsibilities by looking at its portion of the OBS. The resource breakdown structure (RBS) is a hierarchical list of resources related by category and resource type that is used to facilitate planning and controlling of project work. Each descending (lower) level represents an increasingly detailed description of the resource until small enough to be used in conjunction with the work breakdown structure (WBS) to allow the work to be planned, monitored and controlled. The resource breakdown structure is helpful in tracking project costs and can be aligned with the organization's accounting system. It can contain resource categories other than human resources.

- **Matrix-based charts.** A responsibility assignment matrix (RAM) is a grid that shows the project resources assigned to each work package. It is used to illustrate the connections between work packages or activities and project team members. On larger projects, RAMs can be developed at various levels. For example, a high-level RAM can define what a project team group or unit is responsible for within each component of the WBS, while lower-level RAMs are used within the group to designate roles, responsibilities, and levels of authority for specific activities. The matrix format shows all activities associated with one person and all people associated with one activity. This also ensures that there is only one person accountable for any one task to avoid confusion of responsibility. One example of a RAM is a RACI (responsible, accountable, consult, and inform) chart, shown in Figure 9-5. The sample chart shows the work to be done in the left column as activities. The assigned resources can be shown as individuals or groups. The project manager can select other options such as "lead" and "resource" designations or others, as appropriate for the project. A RACI chart is a useful tool to use when the team consists of internal and external resources in order to ensure clear divisions of roles and expectations.

RACI Chart	Person				
Activity	Ann	Ben	Carlos	Dina	Ed
Create charter	A	R	I	I	I
Collect requirements	I	A	R	C	C
Submit change request	I	A	R	R	C
Develop test plan	A	C	I	I	R

R = Responsible   A = Accountable   C = Consult   I = Inform

Figure 9-5. RACI Matrix

- **Text-oriented formats.** Team member responsibilities that require detailed descriptions can be specified in text-oriented formats. Usually in outline form, the documents provide information such as responsibilities, authority, competencies, and qualifications. The documents are known by various names including position descriptions and role-responsibility-authority forms. These documents can be used as templates for future projects, especially when the information is updated throughout the current project by applying lessons learned.

9.1.2.2 Networking

Networking is the formal and informal interaction with others in an organization, industry, or professional environment. It is a constructive way to understand political and interpersonal factors that will impact the effectiveness of various staffing management options. Human resource management benefits from successful networking by improving knowledge of and access to human resource assets such as strong competencies, specialized experience, and external partnership opportunities. Examples of human resources networking activities include proactive correspondence, luncheon meetings, informal conversations including meetings and events, trade conferences, and symposia. Networking can be a useful technique at the beginning of a project. It can also be an effective way to enhance project management professional development during the project and after the project ends.

9.1.2.3 Organizational Theory

Organizational theory provides information regarding the way in which people, teams, and organizational units behave. Effective use of common themes identified in organizational theory can shorten the amount of time, cost, and effort needed to create the Plan Human Resource Management process outputs and improve planning efficiency. It is important to recognize that different organizational structures have different individual response, individual performance, and personal relationship characteristics. Also, applicable organizational theories may recommend exercising a flexible leadership style that adapts to the changes in a team's maturity level throughout the project life cycle.

9.1.2.4 Expert Judgment

When developing the human resource management plan, expert judgment is used to:

- List the preliminary requirements for the required skills;
- Assess the roles required for the project based on standardized role descriptions within the organization;
- Determine the preliminary effort level and number of resources needed to meet project objectives;
- Determine reporting relationships needed based on the organizational culture;
- Provide guidelines on lead time required for staffing, based on lessons learned and market conditions;
- Identify risks associated with staff acquisition, retention, and release plans; and
- Identify and recommend programs for complying with applicable government and union contracts.

9.1.2.5 Meetings

When planning human resource management of the project, the project management team will hold planning meetings. These meetings leverage a combination of other tools and techniques to allow for all project management team members to reach consensus on the human resource management plan.

9.1.3 Plan Human Resource Management: Outputs

9.1.3.1 Human Resource Management Plan

The human resource management plan, a part of the project management plan, provides guidance on how project human resources should be defined, staffed, managed, and eventually released. The human resource management plan and any subsequent revisions are also inputs into the Develop Project Management Plan process.

The human resource management plan includes, but is not limited to, the following:

- **Roles and responsibilities.** The following should be addressed when listing the roles and responsibilities needed to complete a project:
    - *Role*. The function assumed by or assigned to a person in the project. Examples of project roles are civil engineer, business analyst, and testing coordinator. Role clarity concerning authority, responsibilities, and boundaries should also be documented.
    - *Authority*. The right to apply project resources, make decisions, sign approvals, accept deliverables, and influence others to carry out the work of the project. Examples of decisions that need clear authority include the selection of a method for completing an activity, quality acceptance, and how to respond to project variances. Team members operate best when their individual levels of authority match their individual responsibilities.
    - *Responsibility*. The assigned duties and work that a project team member is expected to perform in order to complete the project's activities.
    - *Competency*. The skill and capacity required to complete assigned activities within the project constraints. If project team members do not possess required competencies, performance can be jeopardized. When such mismatches are identified, proactive responses such as training, hiring, schedule changes, or scope changes are initiated.

- **Project organization charts.** A project organization chart is a graphic display of project team members and their reporting relationships. It can be formal or informal, highly detailed or broadly framed, based on the needs of the project. For example, the project organization chart for a 3,000-person disaster response team will have greater detail than a project organization chart for an internal, twenty-person project.

- **Staffing management plan.** The staffing management plan is a component of the human resource management plan that describes when and how project team members will be acquired and how long they will be needed. It describes how human resource requirements will be met. The staffing management plan can be formal or informal, highly detailed, or broadly framed, depending upon the needs of the project. The plan is updated continually during the project to direct ongoing team member acquisition and development actions. Information in the staffing management plan varies by application area and project size, but items to consider include:

  - *Staff acquisition.* A number of questions arise when planning the acquisition of project team members. For example, whether the human resources come from within the organization or from external, contracted sources; whether the team members need to work in a central location or may work from distant locations; costs associated with each level of expertise needed for the project; and level of assistance that the organization's human resource department and functional managers are able to provide to the project management team.

  - *Resource calendars.* Calendars that identify the working days and shifts on which each specific resource is available. The staffing management plan describes necessary time frames for project team members, either individually or collectively, as well as when acquisition activities such as recruiting should start. One tool for charting human resources is a resource histogram, used by the project management team as a means of providing a visual representation or resources allocation to all interested parties. This chart illustrates the number of hours a person, department, or entire project team that will be needed each week or month over the course of the project. The chart can include a horizontal line that represents the maximum number of hours available from a particular resource. Bars that extend beyond the maximum available hours identify the need for a resource optimization strategy (Section 6.6.2.4), such as adding more resources or modifying the schedule. An example of a resource histogram is illustrated in Figure 9-6.

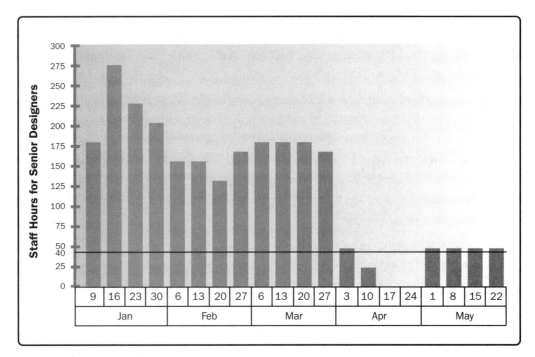

Figure 9-6. Illustrative Resource Histogram

- ○ *Staff release plan*. Determining the method and timing of releasing team members benefits both the project and team members. When team members are released from a project, the costs associated with those resources are no longer charged to the project, thus reducing project costs. Morale is improved when smooth transitions to upcoming projects are already planned. A staff release plan also helps mitigate human resource risks that may occur during or at the end of a project.

- ○ *Training needs*. If it is expected that the team members to be assigned will not have the required competencies, a training plan can be developed as part of the project. The plan can also include ways to help team members obtain certifications that would support their ability to benefit the project.

- ○ *Recognition and rewards*. Clear criteria for rewards and a planned system for their use help promote and reinforce desired behaviors. To be effective, recognition and rewards should be based on activities and performance under a person's control. For example, a team member who is to be rewarded for meeting cost objectives should have an appropriate level of control over decisions that affect expenses. Creating a plan with established times for distribution of rewards ensures that recognition takes place and is not forgotten. Recognition and rewards are part of the Develop Project Team process (Section 9.3).

○ *Compliance.* The staffing management plan can include strategies for complying with applicable government regulations, union contracts, and other established human resource policies.

○ *Safety.* Policies and procedures that protect team members from safety hazards can be included in the staffing management plan as well as in the risk register.

9.2 Acquire Project Team

Acquire Project Team is the process of confirming human resource availability and obtaining the team necessary to complete project activities. The key benefit of this process consists of outlining and guiding the team selection and responsibility assignment to obtain a successful team. The inputs, tools and techniques, and outputs of this process are depicted in Figure 9-7. Figure 9-8 depicts the data flow diagram of the process.

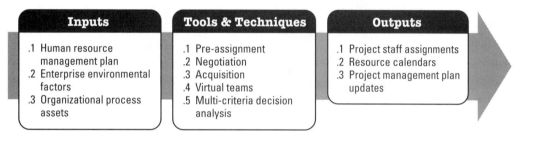

Inputs	Tools & Techniques	Outputs
.1 Human resource management plan .2 Enterprise environmental factors .3 Organizational process assets	.1 Pre-assignment .2 Negotiation .3 Acquisition .4 Virtual teams .5 Multi-criteria decision analysis	.1 Project staff assignments .2 Resource calendars .3 Project management plan updates

Figure 9-7. Acquire Project Team: Inputs, Tools & Techniques, and Outputs

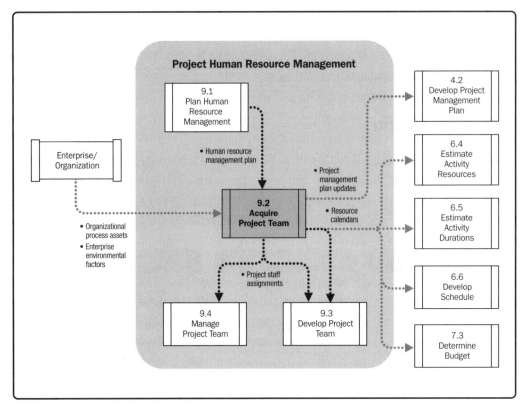

Figure 9-8. Acquire Project Team Data Flow Diagram

The project management team may or may not have direct control over team member selection because of collective bargaining agreements, use of subcontractor personnel, matrix project environment, internal or external reporting relationships, or other various reasons. It is important that the following factors are considered during the process of acquiring the project team:

- The project manager or project management team should effectively negotiate and influence others who are in a position to provide the required human resources for the project.

- Failure to acquire the necessary human resources for the project may affect project schedules, budgets, customer satisfaction, quality, and risks. Insufficient human resources or capabilities decrease the probability of success and, in a worst case scenario, could result in project cancellation.

- If the human resources are not available due to constraints, such as economic factors or previous assignments to other projects, the project manager or project team may be required to assign alternative resources, perhaps with lower competencies, provided there is no violation of legal, regulatory, mandatory, or other specific criteria.

These factors should be considered and planned for in the planning stages of the project. The project manager or project management team will be required to reflect the impact of any unavailability of required human resources in the project schedule, project budget, project risks, project quality, training plans, and the other project management plans.

9.2.1 Acquire Project Team: Inputs

9.2.1.1 Human Resource Management Plan

Described in Section 9.1.3.1. The human resource management plan provides guidance on how project human resources should be identified, staffed, managed, and eventually released. It includes:

- Roles and responsibilities defining the positions, skills, and competencies that the project demands;
- Project organization charts indicating the number of people needed for the project; and
- Staffing management plan delineating the time periods each project team member will be needed and other information important to engage the project team.

9.2.1.2 Enterprise Environmental Factors

Described in Section 2.1.5. The enterprise environmental factors that influence the Acquire Project Team process include, but are not limited to:

- Existing information on human resources including availability, competency levels, prior experience, interest in working on the project and their cost rate;
- Personnel administration policies such as those that affect outsourcing;
- Organizational structure as described in Section 2.3.1; and
- Colocation or multiple locations.

9.2.1.3 Organizational Process Assets

Described in Section 2.1.4. The organizational process assets that influence the Acquire Project Team process include, but are not limited to, organizational standard policies, processes, and procedures.

9

9.2.2 Acquire Project Team: Tools and Techniques

9.2.2.1 Pre-assignment

When project team members are selected in advance, they are considered pre-assigned. This situation can occur if the project is the result of specific people being identified as part of a competitive proposal, if the project is dependent upon the expertise of particular persons, or if some staff assignments are defined within the project charter.

9.2.2.2 Negotiation

Staff assignments are negotiated on many projects. For example, the project management team may need to negotiate with:

- Functional managers, to ensure that the project receives appropriately competent staff in the required time frame and that the project team members will be able, willing, and authorized to work on the project until their responsibilities are completed;
- Other project management teams within the performing organization, to appropriately assign scarce or specialized human resources; and
- External organizations, vendors, suppliers, contractors, etc., for appropriate, scarce, specialized, qualified, certified, or other such specified human resources. Special consideration should be given to external negotiating policies, practices, processes, guidelines, legal, and other such criteria.

The project management team's ability to influence others plays an important role in negotiating staff assignments, as do the politics of the organizations involved. For example, a functional manager will weigh the benefits and visibility of competing projects when determining where to assign exceptional performers requested by various project teams.

9.2.2.3 Acquisition

When the performing organization is unable to provide the staff needed to complete a project, the required services may be acquired from outside sources. This can involve hiring individual consultants or subcontracting work to another organization.

9.2.2.4 Virtual Teams

The use of virtual teams creates new possibilities when acquiring project team members. Virtual teams can be defined as groups of people with a shared goal who fulfill their roles with little or no time spent meeting face to face. The availability of communication technology such as e-mail, audio conferencing, social media, web-based meetings and video conferencing has made virtual teams feasible. The virtual team model makes it possible to:

- Form teams of people from the same organization who live in widespread geographic areas;
- Add special expertise to a project team even though the expert is not in the same geographic area;
- Incorporate employees who work from home offices;
- Form teams of people who work different shifts, hours, or days;
- Include people with mobility limitations or disabilities; and
- Move forward with projects that would have been ignored due to travel expenses.

There are some disadvantages related to virtual teams, such as possibility for misunderstandings, feeling of isolation, difficulties in sharing knowledge and experience between team members, and cost of appropriate technology. Communication planning becomes increasingly important in a virtual team environment. Additional time may be needed to set clear expectations, facilitate communications, develop protocols for resolving conflict, include people in decision making, understand cultural differences, and share credit in successes.

9.2.2.5 Multi-Criteria Decision Analysis

Selection criteria are often used as a part of acquiring the project team. By use of a multi-criteria decision analysis tool, criteria are developed and used to rate or score potential team members. The criteria are weighted according to the relative importance of the needs within the team. Some examples of selection criteria that can be used to score team members are shown as follows:

- **Availability.** Identify whether the team member is available to work on the project within the time period needed. If there are there any concerns for availability during the project timeline.
- **Cost.** Verify if the cost of adding the team member is within the prescribed budget.
- **Experience.** Verify that the team member has the relevant experience that will contribute to the project success.
- **Ability.** Verify that the team member has the competencies needed by the project.

- **Knowledge.** Consider if the team member has relevant knowledge of the customer, similar implemented projects, and nuances of the project environment.
- **Skills.** Determine whether the member has the relevant skills to use a project tool, implementation, or training.
- **Attitude.** Determine whether the member has the ability to work with others as a cohesive team.
- **International factors.** Consider team member location, time zone and communication capabilities.

9.2.3 Acquire Project Team: Outputs

9.2.3.1 Project Staff Assignments

The project is staffed when appropriate people have been assigned to the team. The documentation of these assignments can include a project team directory, memos to team members, and names inserted into other parts of the project management plan, such as project organization charts and schedules.

9.2.3.2 Resource Calendars

Resource calendars document the time periods that each project team member is available to work on the project. Creating a reliable schedule (Section 6.6.3.1) depends on having a good understanding of each person's availability and schedule constraints, including time zones, work hours, vacation time, local holidays, and commitments to other projects.

9.2.3.3 Project Management Plan Updates

Elements of the project management plan that may be updated include, but are not limited to, the human resource management plan. For example, the person assigned to a predefined role may not fulfill all staffing requirements outlined in the human resource management plan. When gaps occur, the project management plan needs to be updated to change the team structure, roles, or responsibilities.

9.3 Develop Project Team

Develop Project Team is the process of improving competencies, team member interaction, and overall team environment to enhance project performance. The key benefit of this process is that it results in improved teamwork, enhanced people skills and competencies, motivated employees, reduced staff turnover rates, and improved overall project performance. The inputs, tools and techniques, and outputs of this process are depicted in Figure 9-9. Figure 9-10 depicts the data flow diagram of the process.

Inputs	Tools & Techniques	Outputs
.1 Human resource management plan .2 Project staff assignments .3 Resource calendars	.1 Interpersonal skills .2 Training .3 Team-building activities .4 Ground rules .5 Colocation .6 Recognition and rewards .7 Personnel assessment tools	.1 Team performance assessments .2 Enterprise environmental factors updates

Figure 9-9. Develop Project Team: Inputs, Tools & Techniques, and Outputs

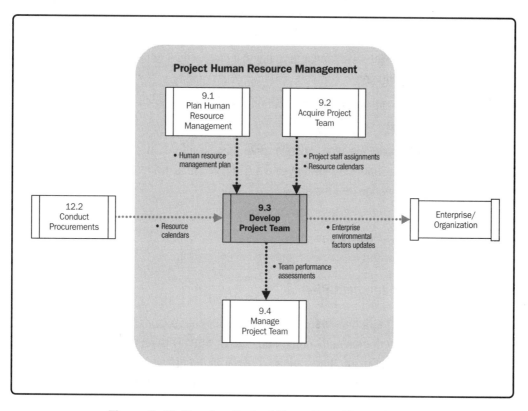

Figure 9-10. Develop Project Team Data Flow Diagram

Project managers should acquire skills to identify, build, maintain, motivate, lead, and inspire project teams to achieve high team performance and to meet the project's objectives. Teamwork is a critical factor for project success, and developing effective project teams is one of the primary responsibilities of the project manager. Project managers should create an environment that facilitates teamwork. Project managers should continually motivate their team by providing challenges and opportunities, by providing timely feedback and support as needed, and by recognizing and rewarding good performance. High team performance can be achieved by using open and effective communication, creating team building opportunities, developing trust among team members, managing conflicts in a constructive manner, and encouraging collaborative problem solving and decision making. The project manager should request management support and/or influence the appropriate stakeholders to acquire the resources needed to develop effective project teams.

Project managers operate in a global environment and work on projects characterized by cultural diversity. Team members often have diverse industry experience, know multiple languages, and sometimes operate in the "team language" that may be a different language or norm than their native one. The project management team should capitalize on cultural differences, focus on developing and sustaining the project team throughout the project life cycle, and promote working together interdependently in a climate of mutual trust. Developing the project team improves the people skills, technical competencies, and overall team environment and project performance. It requires clear, timely, effective, and efficient communication between team members throughout the life of the project. Objectives of developing a project team include, but are not limited to:

- Improving knowledge and skills of team members to increase their ability to complete project deliverables, while lowering costs, reducing schedules, and improving quality;

- Improving feelings of trust and agreement among team members to raise morale, lower conflict, and increase team work; and

- Creating a dynamic, cohesive, and collaborative team culture to (1) improve individual and team productivity, team spirit, and cooperation and (2) allow cross training and mentoring between team members to share knowledge and expertise.

9.3.1 Develop Project Team: Inputs

9.3.1.1 Human Resource Management Plan

Described in Section 9.1.3.1. The human resource management plan provides guidance on how project human resources should be defined, staffed, managed, controlled, and eventually released. It identifies training strategies and plans for developing the project team. Items such as rewards, feedback, additional training, and disciplinary actions can be added to the plan as a result of ongoing team performance assessments and other forms of project team management.

9.3.1.2 Project Staff Assignments

Described in Section 9.2.3.1. Team development starts with a list of the project team members. Project staff assignment documents identify the people who are on the team.

9.3.1.3 Resource Calendars

Described in Section 9.2.3.2. Resource calendars identify times when the project team members can participate in team development activities.

9.3.2 Develop Project Team: Tools and Techniques

9.3.2.1 Interpersonal Skills

Interpersonal skills, sometimes known as "soft skills," are behavioral competencies that include proficiencies such as communication skills, emotional intelligence, conflict resolution, negotiation, influence, team building, and group facilitation. These soft skills are valuable assets when developing the project team. For example, the project management team can use emotional intelligence to reduce tension and increase cooperation by identifying, assessing, and controlling the sentiments of project team members, anticipating their actions, acknowledging their concerns, and following up on their issues.

9.3.2.2 Training

Training includes all activities designed to enhance the competencies of the project team members. Training can be formal or informal. Examples of training methods include classroom, online, computer-based, on-the-job training from another project team member, mentoring, and coaching. If project team members lack the necessary management or technical skills, such skills can be developed as part of the project work. Scheduled training takes place as stated in the human resource management plan. Unplanned training takes place as a result of observation, conversation, and project performance appraisals conducted during the controlling process of managing the project team. Training costs could be included in the project budget, or supported by performing organization if the added skills may be useful for future projects. It could be performed by in-house or external trainers.

9

9.3.2.3 Team-Building Activities

Team-building activities can vary from a 5-minute agenda item in a status review meeting to an off-site, professionally facilitated experience designed to improve interpersonal relationships. The objective of team-building activities is to help individual team members work together effectively. Team-building strategies are particularly valuable when team members operate from remote locations without the benefit of face-to-face contact. Informal communication and activities can help in building trust and establishing good working relationships.

As an ongoing process, team building is crucial to project success. While team building is essential during the initial stages of a project, it is a never-ending process. Changes in a project environment are inevitable, and to manage them effectively, a continued or a renewed team-building effort should be applied. The project manager should continually monitor team functionality and performance to determine if any actions are needed to prevent or correct various team problems.

One of the models used to describe team development is the Tuckman ladder (Tuckman, 1965; Tuckman & Jensen, 1977), which includes five stages of development that teams may go through. Although it's common for these stages to occur in order, it's not uncommon for a team to get stuck in a particular stage or slip to an earlier stage. Projects with team members who worked together in the past may skip a stage.

- **Forming.** This phase is where the team meets and learns about the project and their formal roles and responsibilities. Team members tend to be independent and not as open in this phase.

- **Storming.** During this phase, the team begins to address the project work, technical decisions, and the project management approach. If team members are not collaborative and open to differing ideas and perspectives, the environment can become counterproductive.

- **Norming.** In the norming phase, team members begin to work together and adjust their work habits and behaviors to support the team. The team learns to trust each other.

- **Performing.** Teams that reach the performing stage function as a well-organized unit. They are interdependent and work through issues smoothly and effectively.

- **Adjourning.** In the adjourning phase, the team completes the work and moves on from the project. This typically occurs when staff is released from the project as deliverables are completed or as part of carrying out the Close Project or Phase process (Section 4.6).

The duration of a particular stage depends upon team dynamics, team size, and team leadership. Project managers should have a good understanding of team dynamics in order to move their team members through all stages in an effective manner.

9.3.2.4 Ground Rules

Ground rules establish clear expectations regarding acceptable behavior by project team members. Early commitment to clear guidelines decreases misunderstandings and increases productivity. Discussing ground rules in areas such as code of conduct, communication, working together, or meeting etiquette allows team members to discover values that are important to one another. All project team members share responsibility for enforcing the rules once they are established.

9.3.2.5 Colocation

Colocation, also referred to as "tight matrix," involves placing many or all of the most active project team members in the same physical location to enhance their ability to perform as a team. Colocation can be temporary, such as at strategically important times during the project, or for the entire project. Colocation strategies can include a team meeting room (sometimes called "war room"), places to post schedules, and other conveniences that enhance communication and a sense of community. While colocation is considered a good strategy, the use of virtual teams can bring benefits such as the use of more skilled resources, reduced costs, less travel, and relocation expenses and the proximity of team members to suppliers, customers, or other key stakeholders.

9.3.2.6 Recognition and Rewards

Part of the team development process involves recognizing and rewarding desirable behavior. The original plans concerning ways in which to reward people are developed during the Plan Human Resource Management process. It is important to recognize that a particular reward given to any individual will be effective only if it satisfies a need which is valued by that individual. Award decisions are made, formally or informally, during the process of managing the project team through project performance appraisals (Section 9.4.2.2). Cultural differences should be considered when determining recognition and rewards.

People are motivated if they feel they are valued in the organization and this value is demonstrated by the rewards given to them. Generally, money is viewed as a tangible aspect of any reward system, but intangible rewards could be equally or even more effective. Most project team members are motivated by an opportunity to grow, accomplish, and apply their professional skills to meet new challenges. A good strategy for project managers is to give the team recognition throughout the life cycle of the project rather than waiting until the project is completed.

9.3.2.7 Personnel Assessment Tools

Personnel assessment tools give the project manager and the project team insight into areas of strength and weakness. These tools help project managers assess the team preferences, aspirations, how they process and organize information, how they tend to make decisions, and how they prefer to interact with people.

Various tools are available such as attitudinal surveys, specific assessments, structured interviews, ability tests, and focus groups. These tools can provide improved understanding, trust, commitment, and communications among team members and facilitate more productive teams throughout the project.

9.3.3 Develop Project Team: Outputs

9.3.3.1 Team Performance Assessments

As project team development efforts such as training, team building, and colocation are implemented, the project management team makes formal or informal assessments of the project team's effectiveness. Effective team development strategies and activities are expected to increase the team's performance, which increases the likelihood of meeting project objectives. Team performance assessment criteria should be determined by all appropriate parties and incorporated in the Develop Project Team inputs.

The performance of a successful team is measured in terms of technical success according to agreed-upon project objectives (including quality levels), performance on project schedule (finished on time), and performance on budget (finished within financial constraints). High-performance teams are characterized by these task-oriented and results-oriented outcomes.

The evaluation of a team's effectiveness may include indicators such as:

- Improvements in skills that allow individuals to perform assignments more effectively,
- Improvements in competencies that help the team perform better as a team,
- Reduced staff turnover rate, and
- Increased team cohesiveness where team members share information and experiences openly and help each other to improve the overall project performance.

As a result of conducting an evaluation of the team's overall performance, the project management team can identify the specific training, coaching, mentoring, assistance, or changes required to improve the team's performance. This should also include identification of the appropriate or required resources necessary to achieve and implement the improvements identified in the assessment. These resources and recommendations for team improvement should be well documented and forwarded to the relevant parties.

9.3.3.2 Enterprise Environmental Factors Updates

The enterprise environmental factors that may be updated as a result of the Develop Project Team process include, but are not limited to, personnel administration, employee training records, and skill assessments.

9.4 Manage Project Team

Manage Project Team is the process of tracking team member performance, providing feedback, resolving issues, and managing team changes to optimize project performance. The key benefit of this process is that it influences team behavior, manages conflict, resolves issues, and appraises team member performance. The inputs, tools and techniques, and outputs of this process are depicted in Figure 9-11. Figure 9-12 depicts the data flow diagram of the process.

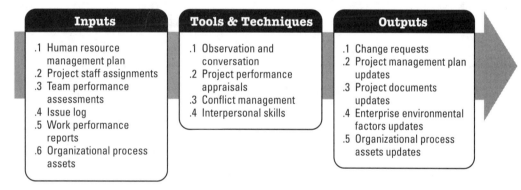

Inputs	Tools & Techniques	Outputs
.1 Human resource management plan .2 Project staff assignments .3 Team performance assessments .4 Issue log .5 Work performance reports .6 Organizational process assets	.1 Observation and conversation .2 Project performance appraisals .3 Conflict management .4 Interpersonal skills	.1 Change requests .2 Project management plan updates .3 Project documents updates .4 Enterprise environmental factors updates .5 Organizational process assets updates

Figure 9-11. Manage Project Team: Inputs, Tools & Techniques, and Outputs

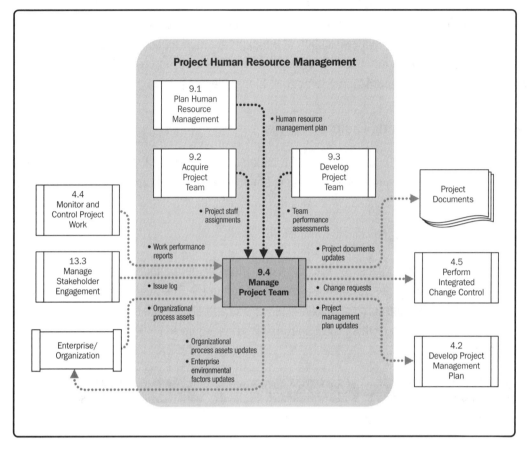

Figure 9-12. Manage Project Team Data Flow Diagram

As a result of managing the project team, change requests are submitted, the human resource management plan is updated, issues are resolved, input is provided for performance appraisals, and lessons learned are added to the organization's database.

Managing the project team requires a variety of management skills for fostering teamwork and integrating the efforts of team members to create high-performance teams. Team management involves a combination of skills with special emphasis on communication, conflict management, negotiation, and leadership. Project managers should provide challenging assignments to team members and provide recognition for high performance.

9.4.1 Manage Project Team: Inputs

9.4.1.1 Human Resource Management Plan

Described in Section 9.1.3.1. The human resource management plan provides guidance on how project human resources should be defined, staffed, managed, controlled, and eventually released. It includes, but is not limited to:

- Roles and responsibilities,
- Project organization, and
- Staffing management plan.

9.4.1.2 Project Staff Assignments

Described in Section 9.2.3.1. Project staff assignments provide documentation, which includes the list of project team members.

9.4.1.3 Team Performance Assessments

Described in Section 9.3.3.1. The project management team makes ongoing formal or informal assessments of the project team's performance. By continually assessing the project team's performance, actions can be taken to resolve issues, modify communication, address conflict, and improve team interaction.

9.4.1.4 Issue Log

Issues arise in the course of managing the project team. An issue log can be used to document and monitor who is responsible for resolving specific issues by a target date.

9.4.1.5 Work Performance Reports

Described in Section 4.4.3.2. Work performance reports provide documentation about the current project status compared to project forecasts. Performance areas that can help with project team management include results from schedule control, cost control, quality control, and scope validation. The information from performance reports and related forecasts assists in determining future human resource requirements, recognition and rewards, and updates to the staffing management plan.

9.4.1.6 Organizational Process Assets

Described in Section 2.1.4. The organizational process assets that can influence the Manage Project Team process include, but are not limited to:

- Certificates of appreciation,
- Newsletters,
- Websites,
- Bonus structures,
- Corporate apparel, and
- Other organizational perquisites.

9.4.2 Manage Project Team: Tools and Techniques

9.4.2.1 Observation and Conversation

Observation and conversation are used to stay in touch with the work and attitudes of project team members. The project management team monitors progress toward project deliverables, accomplishments that are a source of pride for team members, and interpersonal issues.

9.4.2.2 Project Performance Appraisals

Objectives for conducting performance appraisals during the course of a project can include clarification of roles and responsibilities, constructive feedback to team members, discovery of unknown or unresolved issues, development of individual training plans, and the establishment of specific goals for future time periods.

The need for formal or informal project performance appraisals depends on the length of the project, complexity of the project, organizational policy, labor contract requirements, and the amount and quality of regular communication.

9.4.2.3 Conflict Management

Conflict is inevitable in a project environment. Sources of conflict include scarce resources, scheduling priorities, and personal work styles. Team ground rules, group norms, and solid project management practices, like communication planning and role definition, reduce the amount of conflict.

Successful conflict management results in greater productivity and positive working relationships. When managed properly, differences of opinion can lead to increased creativity and better decision making. If the differences become a negative factor, project team members are initially responsible for their resolution. If conflict escalates, the project manager should help facilitate a satisfactory resolution. Conflict should be addressed early and usually in private, using a direct, collaborative approach. If disruptive conflict continues, formal procedures may be used, including disciplinary actions.

The success of project managers in managing their project teams often depends a great deal on their ability to resolve conflict. Different project managers may utilize different conflict resolution methods. Factors that influence conflict resolution methods include:

- Relative importance and intensity of the conflict,
- Time pressure for resolving the conflict,
- Position taken by persons involved, and
- Motivation to resolve conflict on a long-term or a short-term basis.

There are five general techniques for resolving conflict. As each one has its place and use, these are not given in any particular order:

- **Withdraw/Avoid.** Retreating from an actual or potential conflict situation; postponing the issue to be better prepared or to be resolved by others.
- **Smooth/Accommodate.** Emphasizing areas of agreement rather than areas of difference; conceding one's position to the needs of others to maintain harmony and relationships.
- **Compromise/Reconcile.** Searching for solutions that bring some degree of satisfaction to all parties in order to temporarily or partially resolve the conflict.
- **Force/Direct.** Pushing one's viewpoint at the expense of others; offering only win-lose solutions, usually enforced through a power position to resolve an emergency.
- **Collaborate/Problem Solve.** Incorporating multiple viewpoints and insights from differing perspectives; requires a cooperative attitude and open dialogue that typically leads to consensus and commitment.

9.4.2.4 Interpersonal Skills

Project managers use a combination of technical, personal, and conceptual skills to analyze situations and interact appropriately with team members. Using appropriate interpersonal skills allows project managers to capitalize on the strengths of all team members.

Examples of interpersonal skills that a project manager uses most often include:

- **Leadership.** Successful projects require strong leadership skills. Leadership is important through all phases of the project life cycle. There are multiple leadership theories defining leadership styles that should be used as needed for each situation or team. It is especially important to communicate the vision and inspire the project team to achieve high performance.

- **Influencing.** Because project managers often have little or no direct authority over team members in a matrix environment, their ability to influence stakeholders on a timely basis is critical to project success. Key influencing skills include:

  o Ability to be persuasive and clearly articulate points and positions;

  o High levels of active and effective listening skills;

  o Awareness of, and consideration for, the various perspectives in any situation; and

  o Gathering relevant and critical information to address important issues and reach agreements while maintaining mutual trust.

- **Effective decision making.** This involves the ability to negotiate and influence the organization and the project management team. Some guidelines for decision making include:

  o Focus on goals to be served,

  o Follow a decision-making process,

  o Study the environmental factors,

  o Analyze available information,

  o Develop personal qualities of the team members,

  o Stimulate team creativity, and

  o Manage risk.

9.4.3 Manage Project Team: Outputs

9.4.3.1 Change Requests

Staffing changes, whether by choice or by uncontrollable events, can affect the rest of the project management plan. When staffing issues disrupt the project team from adhering to the project management plan such as causing the schedule to be extended or the budget to be exceeded, a change request can be processed through the Perform Integrated Change Control process. Staffing changes may include moving people to different assignments, outsourcing some of the work, and replacing team members who leave.

Preventive actions are those actions that are developed to reduce the probability and/or impact of problems before they occur. These actions may include cross training to reduce problems during project team member absences and additional role clarification to ensure all responsibilities are fulfilled.

9.4.3.2 Project Management Plan Updates

Elements of the project management plan that may be updated include, but are not limited to, the human resource management plan.

9.4.3.3 Project Documents Updates

Project documents that may indirectly be updated include, but are not limited to:

- Issue log,
- Roles description, and
- Project staff assignments.

9.4.3.4 Enterprise Environmental Factors Updates

Enterprise environmental factors that may require updates as a result of the Manage Project Team process include, but are not limited to:

- Input to organizational performance appraisals, and
- Personnel skill updates.

9.4.3.5 Organizational Process Assets Updates

Organizational process assets that may require updates as a result of the Manage Project Team process include, but are not limited to:

- Historical information and lessons learned documentation,
- Templates, and
- Organizational standard processes.

10

PROJECT COMMUNICATIONS MANAGEMENT

Project Communications Management includes the processes that are required to ensure timely and appropriate planning, collection, creation, distribution, storage, retrieval, management, control, monitoring, and the ultimate disposition of project information. Project managers spend most of their time communicating with team members and other project stakeholders, whether they are internal (at all organizational levels) or external to the organization. Effective communication creates a bridge between diverse stakeholders who may have different cultural and organizational backgrounds, different levels of expertise, and different perspectives and interests, which impact or have an influence upon the project execution or outcome.

Figure 10-1 provides an overview of the Project Communications Management processes, which are as follows:

10.1 Plan Communications Management—The process of developing an appropriate approach and plan for project communications based on stakeholder's information needs and requirements, and available organizational assets.

10.2 Manage Communications—The process of creating, collecting, distributing, storing, retrieving and the ultimate disposition of project information in accordance with the communications management plan.

10.3 Control Communications—The process of monitoring and controlling communications throughout the entire project life cycle to ensure the information needs of the project stakeholders are met.

These processes interact with each other and with processes in other Knowledge Areas as described in detail in Section 3 and Annex A1.

The communication activities involved in these processes may often have many potential dimensions that need to be considered, including, but not limited to:

- Internal (within the project) and external (customer, vendors, other projects, organizations, the public);
- Formal (reports, minutes, briefings) and informal (emails, memos, ad-hoc discussions);
- Vertical (up and down the organization) and horizontal (with peers);
- Official (newsletters, annual report) and unofficial (off the record communications); and
- Written and oral, and verbal (voice inflections) and nonverbal (body language).

Most communication skills are common for both general management and project management, such as, but not limited to:

- Listening actively and effectively;

- Questioning and probing ideas and situations to ensure better understanding;

- Educating to increase team's knowledge so that they can be more effective;

- Fact-finding to identify or confirm information;

- Setting and managing expectations;

- Persuading a person, a team, or an organization to perform an action;

- Motivating to provide encouragement or reassurance;

- Coaching to improve performance and achieve desired results;

- Negotiating to achieve mutually acceptable agreements between parties;

- Resolving conflict to prevent disruptive impacts; and

- Summarizing, recapping, and identifying the next steps.

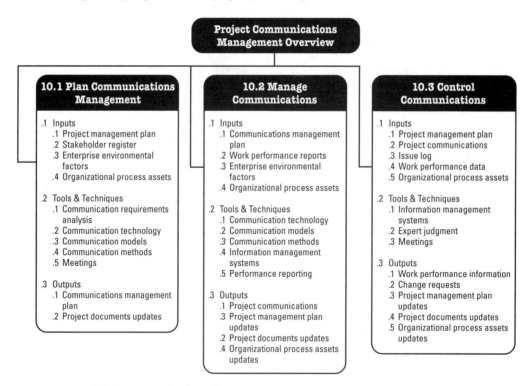

Figure 10-1. Project Communications Management Overview

©2013 Project Management Institute. *A Guide to the Project Management Body of Knowledge (PMBOK® Guide) – Fifth Edition*

10.1 Plan Communications Management

Plan Communications Management is the process of developing an appropriate approach and plan for project communications based on stakeholder's information needs and requirements, and available organizational assets. The key benefit of this process is that it identifies and documents the approach to communicate most effectively and efficiently with stakeholders. The inputs, tools and techniques, and outputs of this process are depicted in Figure 10-2. Figure 10-3 depicts the data flow diagram of the Plan Communications Management process.

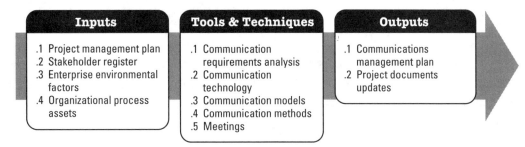

Figure 10-2. Plan Communications Management: Inputs, Tools & Techniques, and Outputs

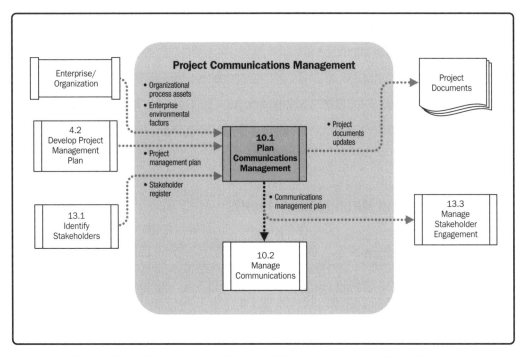

Figure 10-3. Plan Communications Management Data Flow Diagram

Planning the project communications is important to the ultimate success of any project. Inadequate communications planning may lead to problems such as delay in message delivery, communication of information to the wrong audience, or insufficient communication to the stakeholders and misunderstanding or misinterpretation of the message communicated.

On most projects, communication planning is performed very early, such as during project management plan development. This allows appropriate resources, such as time and budget, to be allocated to communication activities. Effective communication means that the information is provided in the right format, at the right time, to the right audience, and with the right impact. Efficient communication means providing only the information that is needed.

While all projects share the need to communicate project information, the information needs and methods of distribution may vary widely. In addition, the methods of storage, retrieval, and ultimate disposition of the project information need to be considered and appropriately documented during this process. Important considerations that may need to be taken into account include, but are not limited to:

- Who needs what information, and who is authorized to access that information;
- When they will need the information;
- Where the information should be stored;
- What format the information should be stored in;
- How the information can be retrieved; and
- Whether time zone, language barriers, and cross-cultural considerations need to be taken into account.

The results of the Plan Communications Management process should be reviewed regularly throughout the project and revised as needed to ensure continued applicability.

10.1.1 Plan Communications Management: Inputs

10.1.1.1 Project Management Plan

Described in Section 4.2.3.1. The project management plan provides information on how the project will be executed, monitored, controlled, and closed.

10.1.1.2 Stakeholder Register

Described in Section 13.1.3.1. The stakeholder register provides the information needed to plan the communication with project stakeholders.

10.1.1.3 Enterprise Environmental Factors

Described in Section 2.1.5. The Plan Communications Management process is tightly linked with enterprise environmental factors, since the structure of an organization will have a major effect on the project's communication requirements. All enterprise environmental factors described in Section 2.1.5 are used as inputs for this process, since communications need to be adapted to the project environment.

10.1.1.4 Organizational Process Assets

Described in Section 2.1.4. All organizational process assets described in Section 2.1.4 are used as inputs to the Plan Communications Management process. Of these, lessons learned and historical information are of particular importance because they can provide insights on both the decisions taken regarding communications issues and the results of those decisions in previous similar projects. These can be used as guiding information to plan the communication activities for the current project.

10.1.2 Plan Communications Management: Tools and Techniques

10.1.2.1 Communication Requirements Analysis

The analysis of the communication requirements determines the information needs of the project stakeholders. These requirements are defined by combining the type and format of information needed with an analysis of the value of that information. Project resources should be expended only on communicating information that contributes to the success of the project or where a lack of communication can lead to failure.

The project manager should also consider the number of potential communication channels or paths as an indicator of the complexity of a project's communications. The total number of potential communication channels is $n(n-1)/2$, where n represents the number of stakeholders. For example, a project with 10 stakeholders has $10(10-1)/2 = 45$ potential communication channels. As a result, a key component of planning the project's actual communications is to determine and limit who will communicate with whom and who will receive what information.

Sources of information typically used to identify and define project communication requirements include, but are not limited to:

- Organizational charts;
- Project organization and stakeholder responsibility relationships;
- Disciplines, departments, and specialties involved in the project;
- Logistics of how many persons will be involved with the project and at which locations;
- Internal information needs (e.g., when communicating within organizations);
- External information needs (e.g., when communicating with the media, public, or contractors); and
- Stakeholder information and communication requirements from within the stakeholder register.

10.1.2.2 Communication Technology

The methods used to transfer information among project stakeholders may vary significantly. For example, a project team may use techniques from brief conversations to extended meetings, or from simple written documents to extensive materials (e.g., schedules, databases, and websites), which are accessible online as methods of communication.

Factors that can affect the choice of communication technology include:

- **Urgency of the need for information.** There is a need to consider the urgency, frequency, and format of the information to be communicated as they may vary from project to project and also within different stages of a project.
- **Availability of technology.** There is a need to ensure that the technology that is required to facilitate communication is compatible, available, and accessible for all stakeholders throughout the life of the project.

- **Ease of Use.** There is a need to ensure that the choice of communication technologies is suitable for project participants and that appropriate training events are planned for, where appropriate.

- **Project environment.** There is a need to determine if the team will meet and operate on a face-to-face basis or in a virtual environment; whether they will be located in one or multiple time zones; whether they will use multiple languages for communication; and finally, whether there are any other project environmental factors, such as culture, which may affect communications.

- **Sensitivity and confidentiality of the information.** There is a need to determine if the information to be communicated is sensitive or confidential and whether or not additional security measures need to be taken. Also, the most appropriate way to communicate the information should be considered.

10.1.2.3 Communication Models

The communication models used to facilitate communications and the exchange of information may vary from project to project and also within different stages of the same project. A basic communication model, shown in Figure 10-4, consists of two parties, defined as the sender and receiver. Medium is the technology medium and includes the mode of communication while noise includes any interference or barriers that might compromise the delivery of the message. The sequence of steps in a basic communication model is:

- **Encode.** Thoughts or ideas are translated (encoded) into language by the sender.

- **Transmit Message.** This information is then sent by the sender using communication channel (medium). The transmission of this message may be compromised by various factors (e.g., distance, unfamiliar technology, inadequate infrastructure, cultural difference, and lack of background information). These factors are collectively termed as noise.

- **Decode.** The message is translated by the receiver back into meaningful thoughts or ideas.

- **Acknowledge.** Upon receipt of a message, the receiver may signal (acknowledge) receipt of the message but this does not necessarily mean agreement with or comprehension of the message.

- **Feedback/Response.** When the received message has been decoded and understood, the receiver encodes thoughts and ideas into a message and then transmits this message to the original sender.

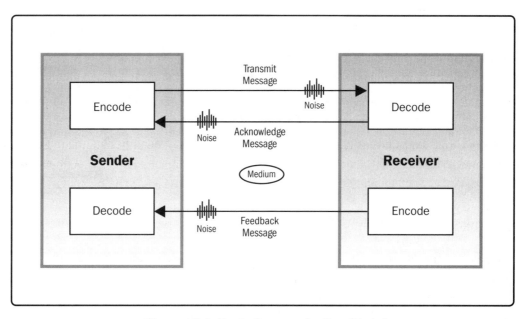

Figure 10-4. Basic Communication Model

The components of the basic communication model need to be considered when project communications are discussed. As part of the communications process, the sender is responsible for the transmission of the message, ensuring the information being communicated is clear and complete, and confirming the communication is correctly understood. The receiver is responsible for ensuring that the information is received in its entirety, understood correctly, and acknowledged or responded to appropriately.

There are many challenges in using these components to effectively communicate with project stakeholders, such as in a highly technical, multinational project team. Successful communication of a technical concept from one team member to another team member in a different country could involve encoding the message in the appropriate language, sending the message using a variety of technologies, and having the receiver decode the message into his or her native language and then reply or provide feedback. Any noise introduced along the way may compromise the original meaning of the message. In this example, there are multiple factors that may lead to the intended meaning of the message being misunderstood or misinterpreted.

10.1.2.4 Communication Methods

There are several communication methods that are used to share information among project stakeholders. These methods are broadly classified as follows:

- **Interactive communication.** Between two or more parties performing a multidirectional exchange of information. It is the most efficient way to ensure a common understanding by all participants on specified topics, and includes meetings, phone calls, instant messaging, video conferencing, etc.

- **Push communication.** Sent to specific recipients who need to receive the information. This ensures that the information is distributed but does not ensure that it actually reached or was understood by the intended audience. Push communications include letters, memos, reports, emails, faxes, voice mails, blogs, press releases, etc.

- **Pull communication.** Used for very large volumes of information, or for very large audiences, and requires the recipients to access the communication content at their own discretion. These methods include intranet sites, e-learning, lessons learned databases, knowledge repositories, etc.

The choices of communication methods that are used for a project may need to be discussed and agreed upon by the project stakeholders based on communication requirements; cost and time constraints; and familiarity and availability of the required tools and resources that may be applicable to the communications process.

10.1.2.5 Meetings

Described in Section 4.3.2.3. The Plan Communications Management process requires discussion and dialogue with the project team to determine the most appropriate way to update and communicate project information, and to respond to requests from various stakeholders for that information. These discussions and dialogue are commonly facilitated through meetings, which may be conducted face to face or online and in different locations, such as the project site or the customer's site.

There are several types of project-related meetings where project communications may occur. Most project meetings consist of stakeholders coming together for the purpose of resolving problems or making decisions. Although casual discussions may be construed as a meeting, most project meetings are more formal with a prearranged time, place, and agenda. Typical meetings begin with a defined list of issues to be discussed, which are circulated in advance with minutes and other information documented specifically for the meeting. This information is then disseminated to other appropriate stakeholders on an as-needed basis.

10.1.3 Plan Communications Management: Outputs

10.1.3.1 Communications Management Plan

The communications management plan is a component of the project management plan that describes how project communications will be planned, structured, monitored, and controlled. The plan contains the following information:

- Stakeholder communication requirements;

- Information to be communicated, including language, format, content, and level of detail;

- Reason for the distribution of that information;

- Time frame and frequency for the distribution of required information and receipt of acknowledgment or response, if applicable;

- Person responsible for communicating the information;

- Person responsible for authorizing release of confidential information;

- Person or groups who will receive the information;

- Methods or technologies used to convey the information, such as memos, e-mail, and/or press releases;

- Resources allocated for communication activities, including time and budget;

- Escalation process identifying time frames and the management chain (names) for escalation of issues that cannot be resolved at a lower staff level;

- Method for updating and refining the communications management plan as the project progresses and develops;

- Glossary of common terminology;

- Flow charts of the information flow in the project, workflows with possible sequence of authorization, list of reports, and meeting plans, etc.; and

- Communication constraints usually derived from a specific legislation or regulation, technology, and organizational policies, etc.

The communications management plan can also include guidelines and templates for project status meetings, project team meetings, e-meetings, and e-mail messages. The use of a project website and project management software can also be included if these are to be used in the project.

10.1.3.2 Project Documents Updates

Project documents that may be updated include, but are not limited to:

- Project schedule, and
- Stakeholder register.

10.2 Manage Communications

Manage Communications is the process of creating, collecting, distributing, storing, retrieving, and the ultimate disposition of project information in accordance to the communications management plan. The key benefit of this process is that it enables an efficient and effective communications flow between project stakeholders. The inputs, tools and techniques, and outputs of this process are depicted in Figure 10-5. Figure 10-6 depicts the data flow diagram of the Manage Communications process.

10

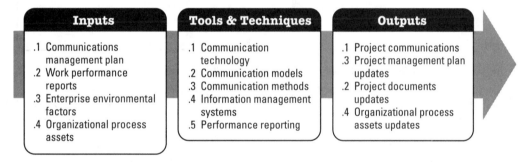

Inputs	Tools & Techniques	Outputs
.1 Communications management plan	.1 Communication technology	.1 Project communications
.2 Work performance reports	.2 Communication models	.3 Project management plan updates
.3 Enterprise environmental factors	.3 Communication methods	.2 Project documents updates
.4 Organizational process assets	.4 Information management systems	.4 Organizational process assets updates
	.5 Performance reporting	

Figure 10-5. Manage Communications: Inputs, Tools & Techniques, and Outputs

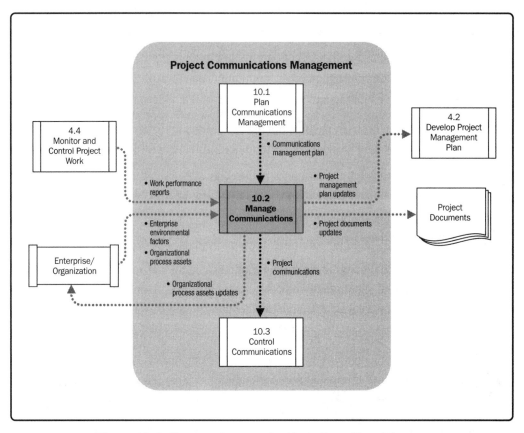

Figure 10-6. Manage Communications Data Flow Diagram

This process goes beyond the distribution of relevant information and seeks to ensure that the information being communicated to project stakeholders has been appropriately generated, as well as received and understood. It also provides opportunities for stakeholders to make requests for further information, clarification, and discussion. Techniques and considerations for effective communications management include, but are not limited to, the following:

- **Sender-receiver models.** Incorporating feedback loops to provide opportunities for interaction/ participation and remove barriers to communication.

- **Choice of media.** Situation specifics as to when to communicate in writing versus orally, when to prepare an informal memo versus a formal report, and when to communicate face to face versus by e-mail.

- **Writing style.** Appropriate use of active versus passive voice, sentence structure, and word choice.

- **Meeting management techniques.** Preparing an agenda and dealing with conflicts.

- **Presentation techniques.** Awareness of the impact of body language and design of visual aids.

- **Facilitation techniques.** Building consensus and overcoming obstacles.

- **Listening techniques.** Listening actively (acknowledging, clarifying, and confirming understanding) and removal of barriers that adversely affect comprehension.

10.2.1 Manage Communications: Inputs

10.2.1.1 Communications Management Plan

Described in Section 10.1.3.1. The communications management plan describes how project communications will be planned, structured, monitored, and controlled.

10.2.1.2 Work Performance Reports

Described in Section 4.4.3.2. Work performance reports are a collection of project performance and status information that may be used to facilitate discussion and to create communications. To optimize this process, it is important that reports be comprehensive, accurate, and available in a timely manner.

10.2.1.3 Enterprise Environmental Factors

Described in Section 2.1.5. Specific enterprise environmental factors that can influence the Manage Communications process include, but are not limited to:

- Organizational culture and structure,

- Government or industry standards and regulations, and

- Project management information system.

10.2.1.4 Organizational Process Assets

Described in Section 2.1.4. Organizational process assets that can influence the Manage Communications process include, but are not limited to:

- Policies, procedures, processes, and guidelines regarding communications management;
- Templates; and
- Historical information and lessons learned.

10.2.2 Manage Communications: Tools and Techniques

10.2.2.1 Communication Technology

Described in Section 10.1.2.2. The choice of communication technology is an important consideration in the Manage Communications process. As this can vary significantly from project to project and also throughout the life of a project, the focus is to ensure that the choice is appropriate for the information that is being communicated.

10.2.2.2 Communication Models

Described in Section 10.1.2.3. The choice of communication models is an important consideration in this process. As the components in the communications all contribute toward an effective and efficient communications process, the focus is to ensure that the choice of the communication model is appropriate for the project that is undertaken and that any barriers (noise) are identified and managed.

10.2.2.3 Communication Methods

Described in Section 10.1.2.4. The choice of communication methods is an important consideration in this process. As there can be many potential barriers and challenges during this process, the focus is to ensure that the information that has been created and distributed has been received and understood to enable response and feedback.

10.2.2.4 Information Management Systems

Project information is managed and distributed using a variety of tools, including:

- Hard-copy document management: letters, memos, reports, and press releases;
- Electronic communications management: e-mail, fax, voice mail, telephone, video and web conferencing, websites, and web publishing; and
- Electronic project management tools: web interfaces to scheduling and project management software, meeting and virtual office support software, portals, and collaborative work management tools.

10.2.2.5 Performance Reporting

Performance reporting is the act of collecting and distributing performance information, including status reports, progress measurements, and forecasts. Performance reporting involves the periodic collection and analysis of baseline versus actual data to understand and communicate the project progress and performance as well as to forecast the project results.

Performance reporting needs to provide information at an appropriate level for each audience. The format may range from a simple status report to more elaborate reports and may be prepared regularly or on an exception basis. A simple status report might show performance information, such as percent complete or status dashboards for each area (i.e., scope, schedule, cost, and quality). More elaborate reports may include:

- Analysis of past performance,
- Analysis of project forecasts (including time and cost),
- Current status of risks and issues,
- Work completed during the period,
- Work to be completed in the next period,
- Summary of changes approved in the period, and
- Other relevant information, which is reviewed and discussed.

10.2.3 Manage Communications: Outputs

10.2.3.1 Project Communications

The Manage Communications process involves the activities that are required for information to be created, distributed, received, acknowledged, and understood. Project communications may include but are not limited to: performance reports, deliverables status, schedule progress, and cost incurred. Project communications can vary significantly and are influenced by factors such as, but not limited to, the urgency and impact of the message, its method of delivery, and level of confidentiality.

10.2.3.2 Project Management Plan Updates

The project management plan provides information on project baselines, communications management, and stakeholder management. Each of these areas may require updates based upon the current performance of the project against the performance measurement baseline (PMB). The performance measurement baseline is an approved plan for the project work to which the project execution is compared, and deviations are measured for management control. The performance measurement baseline typically integrates scope, schedule, and cost parameters of a project, but may also include technical and quality parameters.

10.2.3.3 Project Documents Updates

Project documents that may be updated include, but are not limited to:

- Issue log,
- Project schedule, and
- Project funding requirements.

10.2.3.4 Organizational Process Assets Updates

The organizational process assets, which may be updated include, but are not limited to:

- **Stakeholder notifications.** Information may be provided to stakeholders about resolved issues, approved changes, and general project status.

- **Project reports.** Formal and informal project reports describe project status and include lessons learned, issue logs, project closure reports, and outputs from other Knowledge Areas (Sections 4-13).

- **Project presentations.** The project team provides information formally or informally to any or all of the project stakeholders. The information and presentation method should be relevant to the needs of the audience.

- **Project records.** Project records may include correspondence, memos, meeting minutes, and other documents describing the project. This information should, to the extent possible and appropriate, be maintained in an organized manner. Project team members can also maintain records in a project notebook or register, which could be physical or electronic.

- **Feedback from stakeholders.** Information received from stakeholders concerning project operations is distributed and used to modify or improve future performance of the project.

- **Lessons learned documentation.** Documentation includes the causes of issues, reasoning behind the corrective action chosen, and other types of lessons learned about communications management. Lessons learned need to be documented and distributed so that it becomes part of the historical database for both the project and the performing organization.

10.3 Control Communications

Control Communications is the process of monitoring and controlling communications throughout the entire project life cycle to ensure the information needs of the project stakeholders are met. The key benefit of this process is that it ensures an optimal information flow among all communication participants, at any moment in time. The inputs, tools and techniques, and outputs of this process are depicted in Figure 10-7. Figure 10-8 depicts the data flow diagram of the Control Communications process.

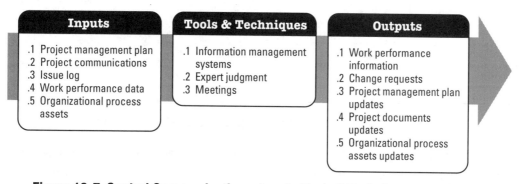

Inputs	Tools & Techniques	Outputs
.1 Project management plan .2 Project communications .3 Issue log .4 Work performance data .5 Organizational process assets	.1 Information management systems .2 Expert judgment .3 Meetings	.1 Work performance information .2 Change requests .3 Project management plan updates .4 Project documents updates .5 Organizational process assets updates

Figure 10-7. Control Communications: Inputs, Tools & Techniques, and Outputs

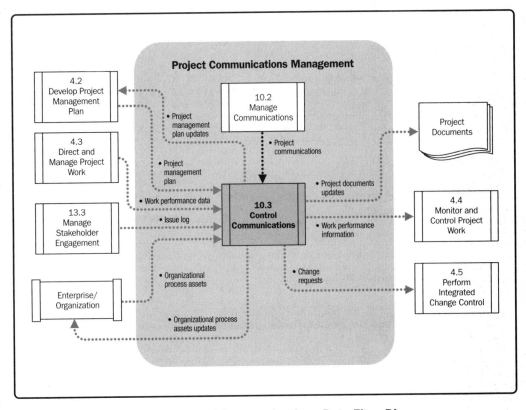

Figure 10-8. Control Communications Data Flow Diagram

The Control Communications process can trigger an iteration of the Plan Communications Management and/or Manage Communications processes. This iteration illustrates the continuous nature of the Project Communications Management processes. Specific communication elements, such as issues or key performance indicators (e.g., actual vs. planned schedule, cost, and quality), may trigger an immediate revision, while others may not. The impact and repercussions of project communications should be carefully evaluated and controlled to ensure that the right message is delivered to the right audience at the right time.

10.3.1 Control Communications: Inputs

10.3.1.1 Project Management Plan

Described in Section 4.2.3.1. The project management plan describes how the project will be executed, monitored, controlled, and closed. It provides valuable information for the Control Communications process such as, but not limited to:

- Stakeholder communication requirements,
- Reason for the distribution of the information,
- Timeframe and frequency for the distribution of required information,
- Individual or group responsible for communication of the information, and
- Individual or group receiving the information.

10.3.1.2 Project Communications

Described in Section 10.2.3.1. The Control Communications process involves the activities that are required for information and communications to be monitored, acted upon, and released to stakeholders. Project communications come from multiple sources and may vary significantly in their format, level of detail, degree of formality and confidentiality. Project communications may include but are not limited to:

- Deliverables status,
- Schedule progress, and
- Costs incurred.

10.3.1.3 Issue Log

Described in Section 13.3.3.1. An issue log is used to document and monitor the resolution of issues. It may be used to facilitate communication and ensure a common understanding of issues. A written log documents and helps to monitor who is responsible for resolving specific issues by a target date. Issue resolution addresses obstacles that can block the team from achieving its goals. This information is important to the Control Communications process as it provides both a repository for what has already happened in the project and a platform for subsequent communications to be delivered.

10.3.1.4 Work Performance Data

Described in Section 4.3.3.2. Work performance data organizes and summarizes the information gathered, and presents the results of comparative analysis to the performance measurement baseline.

10.3.1.5 Organizational Process Assets

Described in Section 2.1.4. The organizational process assets that may influence the Control Communications process include, but are not limited to:

- Report templates;
- Policies, standards, and procedures that define communications;
- Specific communication technologies available;
- Allowed communication media;
- Record retention policies; and
- Security requirements.

10.3.2 Control Communications: Tools and Techniques

10.3.2.1 Information Management Systems

An information management system provides a set of standard tools for the project manager to capture, store, and distribute information to stakeholders about the project's costs, schedule progress, and performance. Some software packages allow the project manager to consolidate reports from several systems and facilitate report distribution to the project stakeholders. Examples of distribution formats may include table reporting, spreadsheet analysis, and presentations. Graphic capabilities can be used to create visual representations of project performance information.

10.3.2.2 Expert Judgment

Expert judgment is often relied upon by the project team to assess the impact of the project communications, need for action or intervention, actions that should be taken, responsibility for taking such actions, and the timeframe for taking action. Expert judgment may need to be applied to technical and/or management details and may be provided by any group or individual with specialized knowledge or training, such as:

- Other units within the organization,
- Consultants,
- Stakeholders, including customers or sponsors,
- Professional and technical associations,
- Industry groups,
- Subject matter experts, and
- Project management office (PMO).

The project manager, in collaboration with the project team, then determines the actions required to ensure that the right message is communicated to the right audience at the right time.

10.3.2.3 Meetings

The Control Communications process requires discussion and dialogue with the project team to determine the most appropriate way to update and communicate project performance, and to respond to requests from stakeholders for information. These discussions and dialogues are commonly facilitated through meetings, which may be conducted face to face or online and in different locations, such as the project site or the client's site. Project meetings also include discussions and dialog with suppliers, vendors, and other project stakeholders.

10.3.3 Control Communications: Outputs

10.3.3.1 Work Performance Information

Described in Section 4.4.1.5. Work performance information organizes and summarizes the performance data gathered. This performance data typically provides status and progress information on the project at the level of detail required by the various stakeholders. This information is then communicated to the appropriate stakeholders.

10.3.3.2 Change Requests

Described in Section 4.3.3.3. The Control Communications process often results in the need for adjustment, action, and intervention. As a result, change requests will be generated as an output. These change requests are processed through the Perform Integrated Change Control process (Section 4.5) and may result in:

- New or revised cost estimates, activity sequences, schedule dates, resource requirements, and analysis of risk response alternatives;

- Adjustments to the project management plan and documents;

- Recommendations of corrective actions that may bring the expected future performance of the project back in line with the project management plan; and

- Recommendations of preventive actions that may reduce the probability of incurring future negative project performance.

10.3.3.3 Project Management Plan Updates

Control Communications process may trigger updates to the communications management plan as well as other components of the project management plan (e.g. stakeholders and human resource management plans).

10.3.3.4 Project Documents Updates

Project documents may be updated as a result of the Control Communications process. These updates may include, but are not limited to:

- Forecasts,

- Performance reports, and

- Issue log.

10.3.3.5 Organizational Process Assets Updates

The organizational process assets that may be updated include, but are not limited to, report formats and lessons learned documentation. This documentation may become part of the historical database for both this project and the performing organization and may include the causes of issues, reasons behind the corrective action chosen, and other types of lessons learned during the project.

11

PROJECT RISK MANAGEMENT

Project Risk Management includes the processes of conducting risk management planning, identification, analysis, response planning, and controlling risk on a project. The objectives of project risk management are to increase the likelihood and impact of positive events, and decrease the likelihood and impact of negative events in the project.

Figure 11-1 provides an overview of the Project Risk Management processes, which are as follows:

11.1 Plan Risk Management—The process of defining how to conduct risk management activities for a project.

11.2 Identify Risks—The process of determining which risks may affect the project and documenting their characteristics.

11.3 Perform Qualitative Risk Analysis—The process of prioritizing risks for further analysis or action by assessing and combining their probability of occurrence and impact.

11.4 Perform Quantitative Risk Analysis—The process of numerically analyzing the effect of identified risks on overall project objectives.

11.5 Plan Risk Responses—The process of developing options and actions to enhance opportunities and to reduce threats to project objectives.

11.6 Control Risks—The process of implementing risk response plans, tracking identified risks, monitoring residual risks, identifying new risks, and evaluating risk process effectiveness throughout the project.

These processes interact with each other and with processes in other Knowledge Areas as described in detail in Section 3 and Annex A1.

11

Project risk is an uncertain event or condition that, if it occurs, has a positive or negative effect on one or more project objectives such as scope, schedule, cost, and quality. A risk may have one or more causes and, if it occurs, it may have one or more impacts. A cause may be a given or potential requirement, assumption, constraint, or condition that creates the possibility of negative or positive outcomes. For example, causes could include the requirement of an environmental permit to do work, or having limited personnel assigned to design the project. The risk is that the permitting agency may take longer than planned to issue a permit; or, in the case of an opportunity, additional development personnel may become available who can participate in design, and they can be assigned to the project. If either of these uncertain events occurs, there may be an impact on the project, scope, cost, schedule, quality, or performance. Risk conditions may include aspects of the project's or organization's environment that contribute to project risk, such as immature project management practices, lack of integrated management systems, concurrent multiple projects, or dependency on external participants who are outside the project's direct control.

Project risk has its origins in the uncertainty present in all projects. Known risks are those that have been identified and analyzed, making it possible to plan responses for those risks. Known risks that cannot be managed proactively, should be assigned a contingency reserve. Unknown risks cannot be managed proactively and therefore may be assigned a management reserve. A negative project risk that has occurred is considered an issue.

Individual project risks are different from overall project risk. Overall project risk represents the effect of uncertainty on the project as a whole. It is more than the sum of the individual risks within a project, since it includes all sources of project uncertainty. It represents the exposure of stakeholders to the implications of variations in project outcome, both positive and negative.

Organizations perceive risk as the effect of uncertainty on projects and organizational objectives. Organizations and stakeholders are willing to accept varying degrees of risk depending on their risk attitude. The risk attitudes of both the organization and the stakeholders may be influenced by a number of factors, which are broadly classified into three themes:

- *Risk appetite*, which is the degree of uncertainty an entity is willing to take on in anticipation of a reward.

- *Risk tolerance*, which is the degree, amount, or volume of risk that an organization or individual will withstand.

- *Risk threshold*, which refers to measures along the level of uncertainty or the level of impact at which a stakeholder may have a specific interest. Below that risk threshold, the organization will accept the risk. Above that risk threshold, the organization will not tolerate the risk.

For example, an organization's risk attitude may include its appetite for uncertainty, its threshold for risk levels that are unacceptable, or its risk tolerance at which point the organization may select a different risk response.

Positive and negative risks are commonly referred to as opportunities and threats. The project may be accepted if the risks are within tolerances and are in balance with the rewards that may be gained by taking the risks. Positive risks that offer opportunities within the limits of risk tolerances may be pursued in order to generate enhanced value. For example, adopting an aggressive resource optimization technique is a risk taken in anticipation of a reward for using fewer resources.

Individuals and groups adopt attitudes toward risk that influence the way they respond. These risk attitudes are driven by perception, tolerances, and other biases, which should be made explicit wherever possible. A consistent approach to risk should be developed for each project, and communication about risk and its handling should be open and honest. Risk responses reflect an organization's perceived balance between risk taking and risk avoidance.

To be successful, an organization should be committed to address risk management proactively and consistently throughout the project. A conscious choice should be made at all levels of the organization to actively identify and pursue effective risk management during the life of the project. Project risk could exist at the moment a project is initiated. Moving forward on a project without a proactive focus on risk management is likely to lead to more problems arising from unmanaged threats.

11

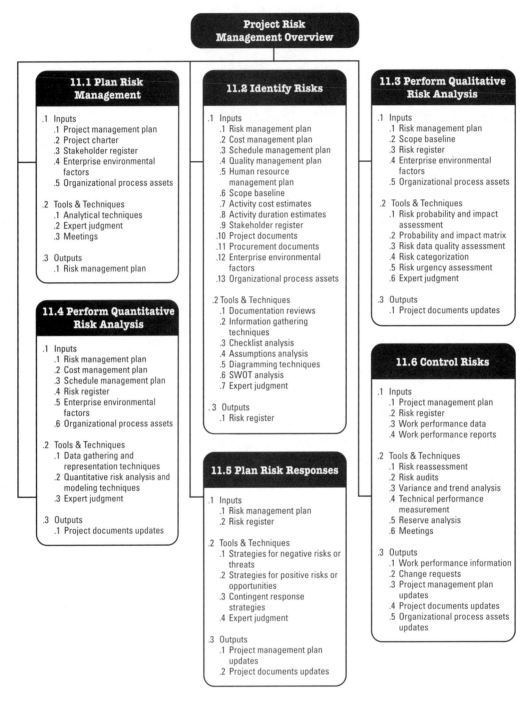

Figure 11-1. Project Risk Management Overview

11.1 Plan Risk Management

Plan Risk Management is the process of defining how to conduct risk management activities for a project. The key benefit of this process is it ensures that the degree, type, and visibility of risk management are commensurate with both the risks and the importance of the project to the organization. The risk management plan is vital to communicate with and obtain agreement and support from all stakeholders to ensure the risk management process is supported and performed effectively over the project life cycle. The inputs, tools and techniques, and outputs of this process are depicted in Figure 11-2. Figure 11-3 depicts the data flow diagram of the process.

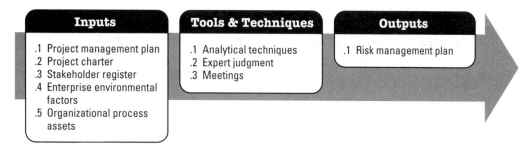

Inputs	Tools & Techniques	Outputs
.1 Project management plan .2 Project charter .3 Stakeholder register .4 Enterprise environmental factors .5 Organizational process assets	.1 Analytical techniques .2 Expert judgment .3 Meetings	.1 Risk management plan

Figure 11-2. Plan Risk Management: Inputs, Tools & Techniques, and Outputs

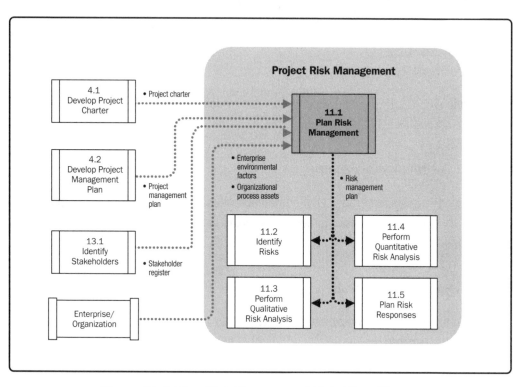

Figure 11-3. Plan Risk Management Data Flow Diagram

Careful and explicit planning enhances the probability of success for other risk management processes. Planning is also important to provide sufficient resources and time for risk management activities and to establish an agreed-upon basis for evaluating risks. The Plan Risk Management process should begin when a project is conceived and should be completed early during project planning.

11.1.1 Plan Risk Management: Inputs

11.1.1.1 Project Management Plan

In planning risk management, all approved subsidiary management plans and baselines should be taken into consideration in order to make the risk management plan consistent with them. The risk management plan is also a component of the project management plan. The project management plan provides baseline or current state of risk-affected areas including scope, schedule, and cost.

11.1.1.2 Project Charter

Described in Section 4.1.3.1. The project charter can provide various inputs such as high-level risks, high-level project descriptions, and high-level requirements.

11.1.1.3 Stakeholder Register

Described in Section 13.1.3.1. The stakeholder register, which contains all details related to the project's stakeholders, provides an overview of their roles.

11.1.1.4 Enterprise Environmental Factors

Described in Section 2.1.5. The enterprise environmental factors that can influence the Plan Risk Management process include, but are not limited to, risk attitudes, thresholds, and tolerances that describe the degree of risk that an organization will withstand.

11.1.1.5 Organizational Process Assets

Described in Section 2.1.4. The organizational process assets that can influence the Plan Risk Management process include, but are not limited to:

- Risk categories,
- Common definitions of concepts and terms,
- Risk statement formats,
- Standard templates,
- Roles and responsibilities,
- Authority levels for decision making, and
- Lessons learned.

11.1.2 Plan Risk Management: Tools and Techniques

11.1.2.1 Analytical Techniques

Analytical techniques are used to understand and define the overall risk management context of the project. Risk management context is a combination of stakeholder risk attitudes and the strategic risk exposure of a given project based on the overall project context. For example, a stakeholder risk profile analysis may be performed to grade and qualify the project stakeholder risk appetite and tolerance. Other techniques, such as the use of strategic risk scoring sheets, are used to provide a high-level assessment of the risk exposure of the project based on the overall project context. Depending on these assessments, the project team can allocate appropriate resources and focus on the risk management activities.

11.1.2.2 Expert Judgment

To ensure a comprehensive establishment of the risk management plan, judgment, and expertise should be considered from groups or individuals with specialized training or knowledge on the subject area, such as:

- Senior management,
- Project stakeholders,
- Project managers who have worked on projects in the same area (directly or through lessons learned),
- Subject matter experts (SMEs) in business or project area,
- Industry groups and consultants, and
- Professional and technical associations.

11.1.2.3 Meetings

Project teams hold planning meetings to develop the risk management plan. Attendees at these meetings may include the project manager, selected project team members and stakeholders, anyone in the organization with responsibility to manage the risk planning and execution activities, and others, as needed.

High-level plans for conducting the risk management activities are defined in these meetings. Risk management cost elements and schedule activities should be developed for inclusion in the project budget and schedule, respectively. Risk contingency reserve application approaches may be established or reviewed. Risk management responsibilities should be assigned. General organizational templates for risk categories and definitions of terms such as levels of risk, probability by type of risk, impact by type of objectives, and the probability and impact matrix will be tailored to the specific project. If templates for other steps in the process do not exist, they may be generated in these meetings. The outputs of these activities are summarized in the risk management plan.

11.1.3 Plan Risk Management: Outputs

11.1.3.1 Risk Management Plan

The risk management plan is a component of the project management plan and describes how risk management activities will be structured and performed. The risk management plan includes the following:

- **Methodology.** Defines the approaches, tools, and data sources that will be used to perform risk management on the project.

- **Roles and responsibilities.** Defines the lead, support, and risk management team members for each type of activity in the risk management plan, and clarifies their responsibilities.

- **Budgeting.** Estimates funds needed, based on assigned resources, for inclusion in the cost baseline and establishes protocols for application of contingency and management reserves.

- **Timing.** Defines when and how often the risk management processes will be performed throughout the project life cycle, establishes protocols for application of schedule contingency reserves, and establishes risk management activities for inclusion in the project schedule.

- **Risk categories.** Provide a means for grouping potential causes of risk. Several approaches can be used, for example, a structure based on project objectives by category. A risk breakdown structure (RBS) helps the project team to look at many sources from which project risk may arise in a risk identification exercise. Different RBS structures will be appropriate for different types of projects. An organization can use a previously prepared custom categorization framework, which may take the form of a simple list of categories or may be structured into an RBS. The RBS is a hierarchical representation of risks according to their risk categories. An example is shown in Figure 11-4.

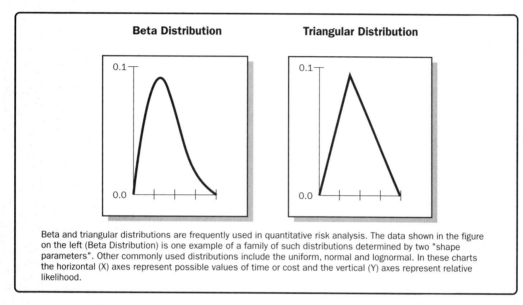

Beta and triangular distributions are frequently used in quantitative risk analysis. The data shown in the figure on the left (Beta Distribution) is one example of a family of such distributions determined by two "shape parameters". Other commonly used distributions include the uniform, normal and lognormal. In these charts the horizontal (X) axes represent possible values of time or cost and the vertical (Y) axes represent relative likelihood.

Figure 11-4. Example of a Risk Breakdown Structure (RBS)

- **Definitions of risk probability and impact.** The quality and credibility of the risk analysis requires that different levels of risk probability and impact be defined that are specific to the project context. General definitions of probability levels and impact levels are tailored to the individual project during the Plan Risk Management process for use in subsequent processes. Table 11-1 is an example of definitions of negative impacts that could be used in evaluating risk impacts related to four project objectives. (Similar tables may be established with a positive impact perspective). Table 11-1 illustrates both relative and numerical (in this case, nonlinear) approaches.

Table 11-1. Definition of Impact Scales for Four Project Objectives

Defined Conditions for Impact Scales of a Risk on Major Project Objectives (Examples are shown for negative impacts only)					
	Relative or numerical scales are shown				
Project Objective	Very low /0.05	Low /0.10	Moderate /0.20	High /0.40	Very high /0.80
Cost	Insignificant cost increase	< 10% cost increase	10 – 20% cost increase	20 – 40% cost increase	> 40% cost increase
Time	Insignificant time increase	< 5% time increase	5 – 10% time increase	10 – 20% time increase	> 20% time increase
Scope	Scope decrease barely noticeable	Minor areas of scope affected	Major areas of scope affected	Scope reduction unacceptable to sponsor	Project end item is effectively useless
Quality	Quality degradation barely noticeable	Only very demanding applications are affected	Quality reduction requires sponsor approval	Quality reduction unacceptable to sponsor	Project end item is effectively useless

This table presents examples of risk impact definitions for four different project objectives. They should be tailored in the Risk Management Planning process to the individual project and to the organization's risk thresholds. Impact definitions can be developed for opportunities in a similar way.

- **Probability and impact matrix.** A probability and impact matrix is a grid for mapping the probability of each risk occurrence and its impact on project objectives if that risk occurs. Risks are prioritized according to their potential implications for having an effect on the project's objectives. A typical approach to prioritizing risks is to use a look-up table or a probability and impact matrix. The specific combinations of probability and impact that lead to a risk being rated as "high," "moderate," or "low" importance are usually set by the organization.

- **Revised stakeholders' tolerances.** Stakeholders' tolerances, as they apply to the specific project, may be revised in the Plan Risk Management process.

- **Reporting formats.** Reporting formats define how the outcomes of the risk management process will be documented, analyzed, and communicated. It describes the content and format of the risk register as well as any other risk reports required.

- **Tracking.** Tracking documents how risk activities will be recorded for the benefit of the current project and how risk management processes will be audited.

11.2 Identify Risks

Identify Risks is the process of determining which risks may affect the project and documenting their characteristics. The key benefit of this process is the documentation of existing risks and the knowledge and ability it provides to the project team to anticipate events. The inputs, tools and techniques, and outputs of this process are depicted in Figure 11-5. Figure 11-6 depicts the data flow diagram of the process.

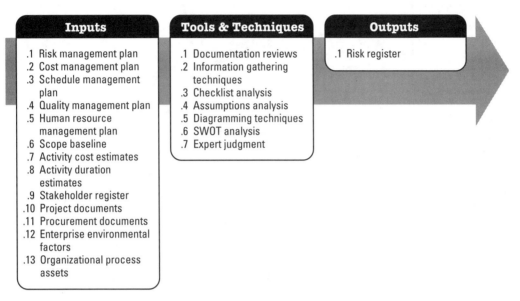

Inputs	Tools & Techniques	Outputs
.1 Risk management plan .2 Cost management plan .3 Schedule management plan .4 Quality management plan .5 Human resource management plan .6 Scope baseline .7 Activity cost estimates .8 Activity duration estimates .9 Stakeholder register .10 Project documents .11 Procurement documents .12 Enterprise environmental factors .13 Organizational process assets	.1 Documentation reviews .2 Information gathering techniques .3 Checklist analysis .4 Assumptions analysis .5 Diagramming techniques .6 SWOT analysis .7 Expert judgment	.1 Risk register

Figure 11-5. Identify Risks: Inputs, Tools & Techniques, and Outputs

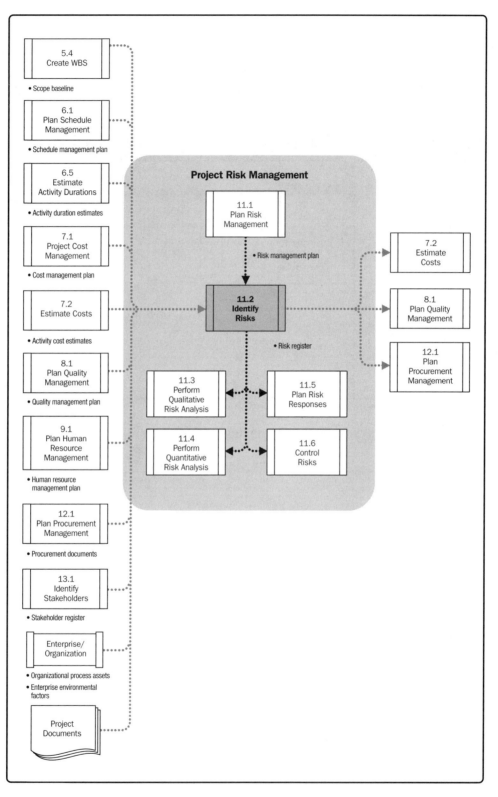

Figure 11-6. Identify Risks Data Flow Diagram

Participants in risk identification activities may include the following: project manager, project team members, risk management team (if assigned), customers, subject matter experts from outside the project team, end users, other project managers, stakeholders, and risk management experts. While these personnel are often key participants for risk identification, all project personnel should be encouraged to identify potential risks.

Identify risks is an iterative process, because new risks may evolve or become known as the project progresses through its life cycle. The frequency of iteration and participation in each cycle will vary by situation. The format of the risk statements should be consistent to ensure that each risk is understood clearly and unambiguously in order to support effective analysis and response development. The risk statement should support the ability to compare the relative effect of one risk against others on the project. The process should involve the project team so they can develop and maintain a sense of ownership and responsibility for the risks and associated risk response actions. Stakeholders outside the project team may provide additional objective information.

11.2.1 Identify Risks: Inputs

11.2.1.1 Risk Management Plan

Described in Section 11.1.3.1. Key elements of the risk management plan that contribute to the Identify Risks process are the assignments of roles and responsibilities, provision for risk management activities in the budget and schedule, and categories of risk, which are sometimes expressed as a risk breakdown structure (Figure 11-4).

11.2.1.2 Cost Management Plan

Described in Section 7.1.3.1. The cost management plan provides processes and controls that can be used to help identify risks across the project.

11.2.1.3 Schedule Management Plan

Described in Section 6.1.3.1. The schedule management plan provides insight to project time/schedule objectives and expectations which may be impacted by risks (known and unknown).

11.2.1.4 Quality Management Plan

Described in Section 8.1.3.1. The quality management plan provides a baseline of quality measures and metrics for use in identifying risks.

11.2.1.5 Human Resource Management Plan

Described in Section 9.1.3.1. The human resource management plan provides guidance on how project human resources should be defined, staffed, managed, and eventually released. It can also contain roles and responsibilities, project organization charts, and the staffing management plan, which form a key input to identify risk process.

11.2.1.6 Scope Baseline

Described in Section 5.4.3.1. Project assumptions are found in the project scope statement. Uncertainty in project assumptions should be evaluated as potential causes of project risk.

The WBS is a critical input to identifying risks as it facilitates an understanding of the potential risks at both the micro and macro levels. Risks can be identified and subsequently tracked at summary, control account, and/or work package levels.

11.2.1.7 Activity Cost Estimates

Described in Section 7.2.3.1. Activity cost estimate reviews are useful in identifying risks as they provide a quantitative assessment of the likely cost to complete scheduled activities and ideally are expressed as a range, with the width of the range indicating the degree(s) of risk. The review may result in projections indicating the estimate is either sufficient or insufficient to complete the activity (i.e., pose a risk to the project).

11.2.1.8 Activity Duration Estimates

Described in Section 6.5.3.1. Activity duration estimate reviews are useful in identifying risks related to the time allowances for the activities or project as a whole, again with the width of the range of such estimates indicating the relative degree(s) of risk.

11.2.1.9 Stakeholder Register

Described in Section 13.1.3.1. Information about the stakeholders is useful for soliciting inputs to identify risks, as this will ensure that key stakeholders, especially the stakeholder, sponsor, and customer are interviewed or otherwise participate during the Identify Risks process.

11.2.1.10 Project Documents

Project documents provide the project team with information about decisions that help better identify project risks. Project documents improve cross-team and stakeholder communications and include, but are not limited to:

- Project charter,
- Project schedule,
- Schedule network diagrams,
- Issue log,
- Quality checklist, and
- Other information proven to be valuable in identifying risks.

11.2.1.11 Procurement Documents

Defined in Section 12.1.3.3. If the project requires external procurement of resources, procurement documents become a key input to the Identify Risks process. The complexity and the level of detail of the procurement documents should be consistent with the value of, and risks associated with, planned procurement.

11.2.1.12 Enterprise Environmental Factors

Described in Section 2.1.5. Enterprise environmental factors that can influence the Identify Risks process include, but are not limited to:

- Published information, including commercial databases,
- Academic studies,
- Published checklists,
- Benchmarking,
- Industry studies, and
- Risk attitudes.

11

11.2.1.13 Organizational Process Assets

Described in Section 2.1.4. Organizational process assets that can influence the Identify Risks process include, but are not limited to:

- Project files, including actual data,
- Organizational and project process controls,
- Risk statement formats or templates, and
- Lessons learned.

11.2.2 Identify Risks: Tools and Techniques

11.2.2.1 Documentation Reviews

A structured review of the project documentation may be performed, including plans, assumptions, previous project files, agreements, and other information. The quality of the plans, as well as consistency between those plans and the project requirements and assumptions, may be indicators of risk in the project.

11.2.2.2 Information Gathering Techniques

Examples of information gathering techniques used in identifying risks can include:

- **Brainstorming.** The goal of brainstorming is to obtain a comprehensive list of project risks. The project team usually performs brainstorming, often with a multidisciplinary set of experts who are not part of the team. Ideas about project risk are generated under the leadership of a facilitator, either in a traditional free-form brainstorm session or structured mass interviewing techniques. Categories of risk, such as in a risk breakdown structure, can be used as a framework. Risks are then identified and categorized by type of risk and their definitions are refined.

- **Delphi technique.** The Delphi technique is a way to reach a consensus of experts. Project risk experts participate in this technique anonymously. A facilitator uses a questionnaire to solicit ideas about the important project risks. The responses are summarized and are then recirculated to the experts for further comment. Consensus may be reached in a few rounds of this process. The Delphi technique helps reduce bias in the data and keeps any one person from having undue influence on the outcome.

- **Interviewing.** Interviewing experienced project participants, stakeholders, and subject matter experts helps to identify risks.

- **Root cause analysis.** Root-cause analysis is a specific technique used to identify a problem, discover the underlying causes that lead to it, and develop preventive action.

11.2.2.3 Checklist Analysis

Risk identification checklists are developed based on historical information and knowledge that has been accumulated from previous similar projects and from other sources of information. The lowest level of the RBS can also be used as a risk checklist. While a checklist may be quick and simple, it is impossible to build an exhaustive one, and care should be taken to ensure the checklist is not used to avoid the effort of proper risk identification. The team should also explore items that do not appear on the checklist. Additionally, the checklist should be pruned from time to time to remove or archive related items. The checklist should be reviewed during project closure to incorporate new lessons learned and improve it for use on future projects.

11.2.2.4 Assumptions Analysis

Every project and its plan is conceived and developed based on a set of hypotheses, scenarios, or assumptions. Assumptions analysis explores the validity of assumptions as they apply to the project. It identifies risks to the project from inaccuracy, instability, inconsistency, or incompleteness of assumptions.

11.2.2.5 Diagramming Techniques

Risk diagramming techniques may include:

- **Cause and effect diagrams.** These are also known as Ishikawa or fishbone diagrams and are useful for identifying causes of risks.

- **System or process flow charts.** These show how various elements of a system interrelate and the mechanism of causation.

- **Influence diagrams.** These are graphical representations of situations showing causal influences, time ordering of events, and other relationships among variables and outcomes, as shown in Figure 11-7.

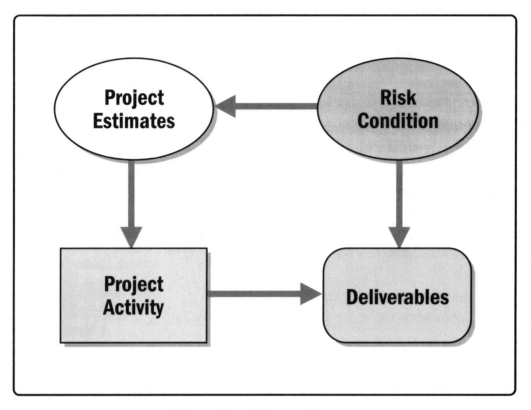

Figure 11-7. Influence Diagram

11.2.2.6 SWOT Analysis

This technique examines the project from each of the strengths, weaknesses, opportunities, and threats (SWOT) perspectives to increase the breadth of identified risks by including internally generated risks. The technique starts with identification of strengths and weaknesses of the organization, focusing on either the project, organization, or the business area in general. SWOT analysis then identifies any opportunities for the project that arise from organizational strengths, and any threats arising from organizational weaknesses. The analysis also examines the degree to which organizational strengths offset threats, as well as identifying opportunities that may serve to overcome weaknesses.

11.2.2.7 Expert Judgment

Risks may be identified directly by experts with relevant experience with similar projects or business areas. Such experts should be identified by the project manager and invited to consider all aspects of the project and suggest possible risks based on their previous experience and areas of expertise. The experts' bias should be taken into account in this process.

11.2.3 Identify Risks: Outputs

11.2.3.1 Risk Register

The primary output from Identify Risks is the initial entry into the risk register. The risk register is a document in which the results of risk analysis and risk response planning are recorded. It contains the outcomes of the other risk management processes as they are conducted, resulting in an increase in the level and type of information contained in the risk register over time. The preparation of the risk register begins in the Identify Risks process with the following information, and then becomes available to other project management and risk management processes:

- **List of identified risks.** The identified risks are described in as much detail as is reasonable. A structure for describing risks using risk statements may be applied, for example, EVENT may occur causing IMPACT, or If CAUSE exists, EVENT may occur leading to EFFECT. In addition to the list of identified risks, the root causes of those risks may become more evident. These are the fundamental conditions or events that may give rise to one or more identified risks. They should be recorded and used to support future risk identification for this and other projects.

- **List of potential responses.** Potential responses to a risk may sometimes be identified during the Identify Risks process. These responses, if identified in this process, should be used as inputs to the Plan Risk Responses process.

11.3 Perform Qualitative Risk Analysis

Perform Qualitative Risk Analysis is the process of prioritizing risks for further analysis or action by assessing and combining their probability of occurrence and impact. The key benefit of this process is that it enables project managers to reduce the level of uncertainty and to focus on high-priority risks. The inputs, tools and techniques, and outputs of this process are depicted in Figure 11-8. Figure 11-9 depicts the data flow diagram of the process.

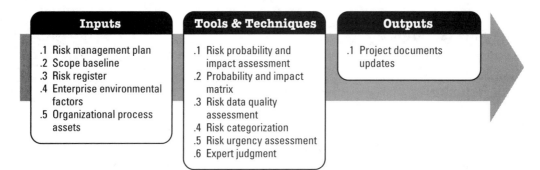

Figure 11-8. Perform Qualitative Risk Analysis: Inputs, Tools & Techniques, and Outputs

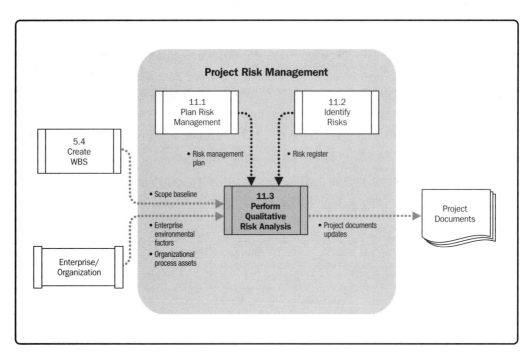

Figure 11-9. Perform Qualitative Risk Analysis Data Flow Diagram

Perform Qualitative Risk Analysis assesses the priority of identified risks using their relative probability or likelihood of occurrence, the corresponding impact on project objectives if the risks occur, as well as other factors such as the time frame for response and the organization's risk tolerance associated with the project constraints of cost, schedule, scope, and quality. Such assessments reflect the risk attitude of the project team and other stakeholders. Effective assessment therefore requires explicit identification and management of the risk approaches of key participants in the Perform Qualitative Risk Analysis process. Where these risk approaches introduce bias into the assessment of identified risks, attention should be paid to identifying bias and correcting for it.

Establishing definitions of the levels of probability and impact can reduce the influence of bias. The time criticality of risk-related actions may magnify the importance of a risk. An evaluation of the quality of the available information on project risks also helps to clarify the assessment of the risk's importance to the project.

Perform Qualitative Risk Analysis is usually a rapid and cost-effective means of establishing priorities for Plan Risk Responses and lays the foundation for Perform Quantitative Risk Analysis, if required. The Perform Qualitative Risk Analysis process is performed regularly throughout the project life cycle, as defined in the project's risk management plan. This process can lead into Perform Quantitative Risk Analysis (Section 11.4) or directly into Plan Risk Responses (Section 11.5).

11.3.1 Perform Qualitative Risk Analysis: Inputs

11.3.1.1 Risk Management Plan

Described in Section 11.1.3.1. Key elements of the risk management plan used in the Perform Qualitative Risk Analysis process include roles and responsibilities for conducting risk management, budgets, schedule activities for risk management, risk categories, definitions of probability and impact, the probability and impact matrix, and revised stakeholders' risk tolerances. These inputs are usually tailored to the project during the Plan Risk Management process. If they are not available, they may be developed during the Perform Qualitative Risk Analysis process.

11.3.1.2 Scope Baseline

Described in Section 5.4.3.1. Projects of a common or recurrent type tend to have more well-understood risks. Projects using state-of-the-art or first-of-its-kind technology, and highly complex projects, tend to have more uncertainty. This can be evaluated by examining the scope baseline.

11.3.1.3 Risk Register

Described in Section 11.2.3.1. The risk register contains the information that will be used to assess and prioritize risks.

11.3.1.4 Enterprise Environmental Factors

Described in Section 2.1.5. Enterprise environmental factors may provide insight and context to the risk assessment, such as:

- Industry studies of similar projects by risk specialists, and
- Risk databases that may be available from industry or proprietary sources.

11.3.1.5 Organizational Process Assets

Described in Section 2.1.4. The organizational process assets that can influence the Perform Qualitative Risk Analysis process include information on prior, similar completed projects.

11.3.2 Perform Qualitative Risk Analysis: Tools and Techniques

11.3.2.1 Risk Probability and Impact Assessment

Risk probability assessment investigates the likelihood that each specific risk will occur. Risk impact assessment investigates the potential effect on a project objective such as schedule, cost, quality, or performance, including both negative effects for threats and positive effects for opportunities.

Probability and impact are assessed for each identified risk. Risks can be assessed in interviews or meetings with participants selected for their familiarity with the risk categories on the agenda. Project team members and knowledgeable persons external to the project are included.

The level of probability for each risk and its impact on each objective is evaluated during the interview or meeting. Explanatory detail, including assumptions justifying the levels assigned, are also recorded. Risk probabilities and impacts are rated according to the definitions given in the risk management plan. Risks with low ratings of probability and impact will be included within the risk register as part of the watch list for future monitoring.

11.3.2.2 Probability and Impact Matrix

Risks can be prioritized for further quantitative analysis and planning risk responses based on their risk rating. Ratings are assigned to risks based on their assessed probability and impact. Evaluation of each risk's importance and priority for attention is typically conducted using a look-up table or a probability and impact matrix. Such a matrix specifies combinations of probability and impact that lead to rating the risks as low, moderate, or high priority. Descriptive terms or numeric values can be used depending on organizational preference.

Each risk is rated on its probability of occurrence and impact on an objective if it does occur. The organization should determine which combinations of probability and impact result in a classification of high risk, moderate risk, and low risk. In a black-and-white matrix, these conditions are denoted using different shades of gray. Specifically in Figure 11-10, the dark gray area (with the largest numbers) represents high risk: the medium gray area (with the smallest numbers) represents low risk, and the light gray area (with in-between numbers) represents moderate risk. Usually, these risk-rating rules are specified by the organization in advance of the project and included in organizational process assets. Risk rating rules can be tailored in the Plan Risk Management process to the specific project.

Probability and Impact Matrix

Probability	Threats					Opportunities				
0.90	0.05	0.09	0.18	0.36	0.72	0.72	0.36	0.18	0.09	0.05
0.70	0.04	0.07	0.14	0.28	0.56	0.56	0.28	0.14	0.07	0.04
0.50	0.03	0.05	0.10	0.20	0.40	0.40	0.20	0.10	0.05	0.03
0.30	0.02	0.03	0.06	0.12	0.24	0.24	0.12	0.06	0.03	0.02
0.10	0.01	0.01	0.02	0.04	0.08	0.08	0.04	0.02	0.01	0.01
	0.05/ Very Low	0.10/ Low	0.20/ Moderate	0.40/ High	0.80/ Very High	0.80/ Very High	0.40/ High	0.20/ Moderate	0.10/ Low	0.05/ Very Low

Impact (numerical scale) on an objective (e.g., cost, time, scope or quality)

Each risk is rated on its probability of occurring and impact on an objective if it does occur. The organization's thresholds for low, moderate or high risks are shown in the matrix and determine whether the risk is scored as high, moderate or low for that objective.

Figure 11-10. Probability and Impact Matrix

11

As illustrated in Figure 11-10, an organization can rate a risk separately for each objective (e.g., cost, time, and scope). In addition, it may develop ways to determine one overall rating for each risk. Finally, opportunities and threats are handled in the same matrix using definitions of the different levels of impact that are appropriate for each.

The risk score helps guide risk responses. For example, risks that have a negative impact on objectives, otherwise known as threats if they occur, and that are in the high-risk (dark gray) zone of the matrix, may require priority action and aggressive response strategies. Threats found in the low-risk (medium gray) zone may not require proactive management action beyond being placed in the risk register as part of the watch list or adding a contingency reserve. Similarly for opportunities, those in the high-risk (dark gray) zone, which may be obtained most easily and offer the greatest benefit, should be targeted first. Opportunities in the low-risk (medium gray) zone should be monitored.

11.3.2.3 Risk Data Quality Assessment

Risk data quality assessment is a technique to evaluate the degree to which the data about risks is useful for risk management. It involves examining the degree to which the risk is understood and the accuracy, quality, reliability, and integrity of the data about the risk.

The use of low-quality risk data may lead to a qualitative risk analysis of little use to the project. If data quality is unacceptable, it may be necessary to gather better data. Often, the collection of information about risks is difficult, and consumes more time and resources than originally planned. The values used in the example in Figure 11-10 are representative. The numbers of steps in the scale are usually established when defining the risk attitude of the organization.

11.3.2.4 Risk Categorization

Risks to the project can be categorized by sources of risk (e.g., using the RBS), the area of the project affected (e.g., using the WBS), or other useful categories (e.g., project phase) to determine the areas of the project most exposed to the effects of uncertainty. Risks can also be categorized by common root causes. This technique helps determine work packages, activities, project phases or even roles in the project, which can lead to the development of effective risk responses.

©2013 Project Management Institute. *A Guide to the Project Management Body of Knowledge (PMBOK® Guide) – Fifth Edition*

11.3.2.5 Risk Urgency Assessment

Risks requiring near-term responses may be considered more urgent to address. Indicators of priority may include probability of detecting the risk, time to affect a risk response, symptoms and warning signs, and the risk rating. In some qualitative analyses, the assessment of risk urgency is combined with the risk ranking that is determined from the probability and impact matrix to give a final risk severity rating.

11.3.2.6 Expert Judgment

Expert judgment is required to assess the probability and impact of each risk to determine its location in the matrix shown in Figure 11-10. Experts generally are those having experience with similar, recent projects. Gathering expert judgment is often accomplished with the use of risk facilitation workshops or interviews. The experts' bias should be taken into account in this process.

11.3.3 Perform Qualitative Risk Analysis: Outputs

11.3.3.1 Project Documents Updates

Project documents that may be updated include, but are not limited to:

- **Risk register updates.** As new information becomes available through the qualitative risk assessment, the risk register is updated. Updates to the risk register may include assessments of probability and impacts for each risk, risk ranking or scores, risk urgency information or risk categorization, and a watch list for low probability risks or risks requiring further analysis.

- **Assumptions log updates.** As new information becomes available through the qualitative risk assessment, assumptions could change. The assumptions log needs to be revisited to accommodate this new information. Assumptions may be incorporated into the project scope statement or in a separate assumptions log.

11.4 Perform Quantitative Risk Analysis

Perform Quantitative Risk Analysis is the process of numerically analyzing the effect of identified risks on overall project objectives. The key benefit of this process is that it produces quantitative risk information to support decision making in order to reduce project uncertainty. The inputs, tools and techniques, and outputs of this process are depicted in Figure 11-11. Figure 11-12 depicts the data flow diagram of the process.

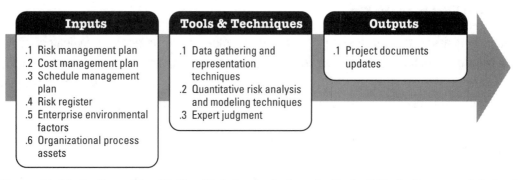

Figure 11-11. Perform Quantitative Risk Analysis: Inputs, Tools & Techniques, and Outputs

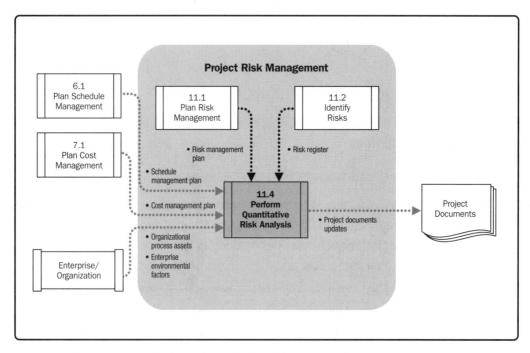

Figure 11-12. Perform Quantitative Risk Analysis Data Flow Diagram

Perform Quantitative Risk Analysis is performed on risks that have been prioritized by the Perform Qualitative Risk Analysis process as potentially and substantially impacting the project's competing demands. The Perform Quantitative Risk Analysis process analyzes the effect of those risks on project objectives. It is used mostly to evaluate the aggregate effect of all risks affecting the project. When the risks drive the quantitative analysis, the process may be used to assign a numerical priority rating to those risks individually.

Perform Quantitative Risk Analysis generally follows the Perform Qualitative Risk Analysis process. In some cases, it may not be possible to execute the Perform Quantitative Risk Analysis process due to lack of sufficient data to develop appropriate models. The project manager should exercise expert judgment to determine the need for and the viability of quantitative risk analysis. The availability of time and budget, and the need for qualitative or quantitative statements about risk and impacts, will determine which method(s) to use on any particular project. Perform Quantitative Risk Analysis should be repeated, as needed, as part of the Control Risks process to determine if the overall project risk has been satisfactorily decreased. Trends may indicate the need for more or less focus on appropriate risk management activities.

11.4.1 Perform Quantitative Risk Analysis: Inputs

11.4.1.1 Risk Management Plan

Described in Section 11.1.3.1. The risk management plan provides guidelines, methods, and tools to be used in quantitative risk analysis.

11.4.1.2 Cost Management Plan

Described in Section 7.1.3.1. The cost management plan provides guidelines on establishing and managing risk reserves.

11.4.1.3 Schedule Management Plan

Described in Section 6.1.3.1. The schedule management plan provides guidelines on establishing and managing risk reserves.

11.4.1.4 Risk Register

Described in Section 11.2.3.1. The risk register is used as a reference point for performing quantitative risk analysis.

11.4.1.5 Enterprise Environmental Factors

Described in Section 2.1.5. Enterprise environmental factors may provide insight and context to the risk analysis, such as:

- Industry studies of similar projects by risk specialists, and
- Risk databases that may be available from industry or proprietary sources.

11.4.1.6 Organizational Process Assets

Described in Section 2.1.4. The organizational process assets that can influence the Perform Quantitative Risk Analysis process include information from prior, similar completed projects.

11.4.2 Perform Quantitative Risk Analysis: Tools and Techniques

11.4.2.1 Data Gathering and Representation Techniques

- **Interviewing.** Interviewing techniques draw on experience and historical data to quantify the probability and impact of risks on project objectives. The information needed depends upon the type of probability distributions that will be used. For instance, information would be gathered on the optimistic (low), pessimistic (high), and most likely scenarios for some commonly used distributions. Examples of three-point estimates for cost are shown in Figure 11-13. Additional information on three-point estimates appears in Estimate Activity Durations (Section 6.5) and Estimate Costs (Section 7.2). Documenting the rationale of the risk ranges and the assumptions behind them are important components of the risk interview because they can provide insight on the reliability and credibility of the analysis.

Range of Project Cost Estimates

WBS Element	Low	Most Likely	High
Design	$4M	$6M	$10M
Build	$16M	$20M	$35M
Test	$11M	$15M	$23M
Total Project	$31M	$41M	$68M

Interviewing relevant stakeholders helps determine the three-point estimates for each WBS element for triangular, beta or other distributions. In this example, the likelihood of completing the project at or below the most likely estimate of $41 million is relatively small as shown in the simulation results in Figure 11-17 (Cost Risk Simulation Results).

Figure 11-13. Range of Project Cost Estimates Collected During the Risk Interview

- **Probability distributions.** Continuous probability distributions, which are used extensively in modeling and simulation, represent the uncertainty in values such as durations of schedule activities and costs of project components. Discrete distributions can be used to represent uncertain events, such as the outcome of a test or a possible scenario in a decision tree. Two examples of widely used continuous distributions are shown in Figure 11-14. These distributions depict shapes that are compatible with the data typically developed during the quantitative risk analysis. Uniform distributions can be used if there is no obvious value that is more likely than any other between specified high and low bounds, such as in the early concept stage of design.

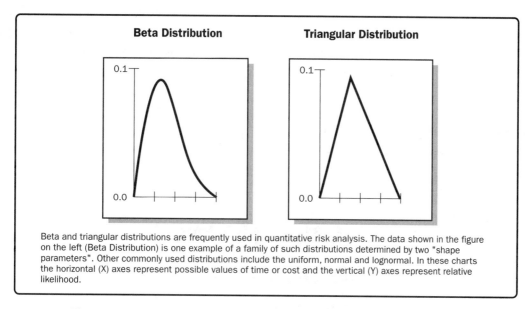

Beta and triangular distributions are frequently used in quantitative risk analysis. The data shown in the figure on the left (Beta Distribution) is one example of a family of such distributions determined by two "shape parameters". Other commonly used distributions include the uniform, normal and lognormal. In these charts the horizontal (X) axes represent possible values of time or cost and the vertical (Y) axes represent relative likelihood.

Figure 11-14. Examples of Commonly Used Probability Distributions

11.4.2.2 Quantitative Risk Analysis and Modeling Techniques

Commonly used techniques use both event-oriented and project-oriented analysis approaches, including:

- **Sensitivity analysis.** Sensitivity analysis helps to determine which risks have the most potential impact on the project. It helps to understand how the variations in project's objectives correlate with variations in different uncertainties. Conversely, it examines the extent to which the uncertainty of each project element affects the objective being studied when all other uncertain elements are held at their baseline values. One typical display of sensitivity analysis is the tornado diagram (Figure 11-15), which is useful for comparing relative importance and impact of variables that have a high degree of uncertainty to those that are more stable. The Tornado diagram is also helpful in analyzing risk-taking scenarios enabled on specific risks whose quantitative analysis highlights possible benefits greater than corresponding identified negative impacts. A tornado diagram is a special type of bar chart used in sensitivity analysis for comparing the relative importance of the variables. In a tornado diagram, the Y-axis contains each type of uncertainty at base values, and the X-axis contains the spread or correlation of the uncertainty to the studied output. In this figure, each uncertainty contains a horizontal bar and is ordered vertically to show uncertainties with a decreasing spread from the base values.

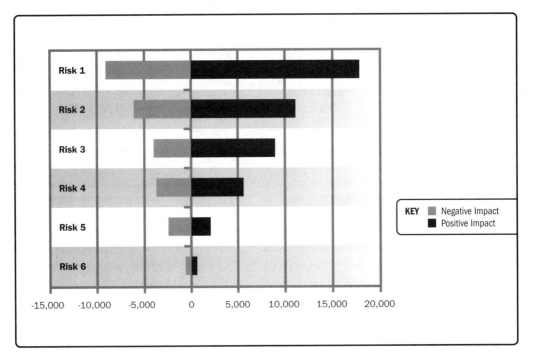

Figure 11-15. Example of Tornado Diagram

- **Expected monetary value analysis.** Expected monetary value (EMV) analysis is a statistical concept that calculates the average outcome when the future includes scenarios that may or may not happen (i.e., analysis under uncertainty). The EMV of opportunities are generally expressed as positive values, while those of threats are expressed as negative values. EMV requires a risk-neutral assumption—neither risk averse nor risk seeking. EMV for a project is calculated by multiplying the value of each possible outcome by its probability of occurrence and adding the products together. A common use of this type of analysis is a decision tree analysis (Figure 11-16).

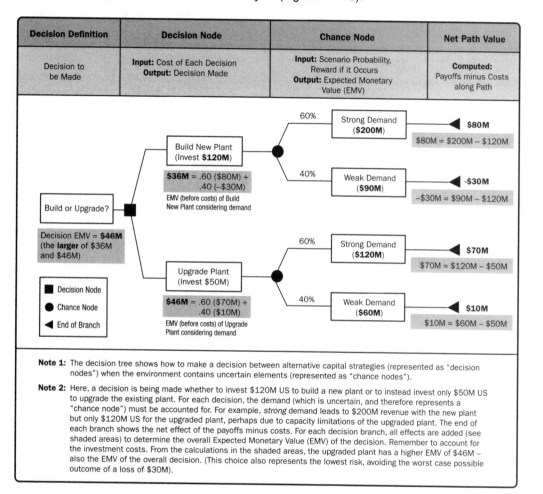

Figure 11-16. Decision Tree Diagram

- **Modeling and simulation.** A project simulation uses a model that translates the specified detailed uncertainties of the project into their potential impact on project objectives. Simulations are typically performed using the Monte Carlo technique. In a simulation, the project model is computed many times (iterated), with the input values (e.g., cost estimates or activity durations) chosen at random for each iteration from the probability distributions of these variables. A histogram (e.g., total cost or completion date) is calculated from the iterations. For a cost risk analysis, a simulation uses cost estimates. For a schedule risk analysis, the schedule network diagram and duration estimates are used. The output from a cost risk simulation using the three-element model and risk ranges is shown in Figure 11-17. It illustrates the respective probability of achieving specific cost targets. Similar curves can be developed for other project objectives.

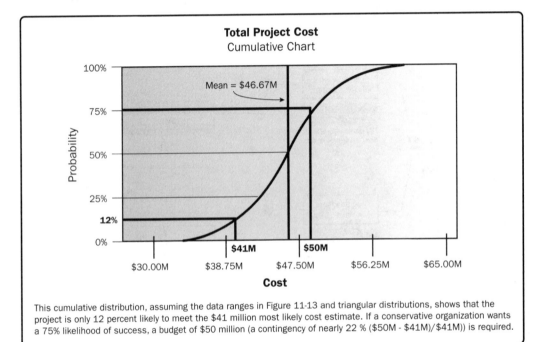

This cumulative distribution, assuming the data ranges in Figure 11-13 and triangular distributions, shows that the project is only 12 percent likely to meet the $41 million most likely cost estimate. If a conservative organization wants a 75% likelihood of success, a budget of $50 million (a contingency of nearly 22 % ($50M - $41M)/$41M)) is required.

Figure 11-17. Cost Risk Simulation Results

11.4.2.3 Expert Judgment

Expert judgment (ideally using experts with relevant, recent experience) is required to identify potential cost and schedule impacts, to evaluate probability, and to define inputs such as probability distributions into the tools.

Expert judgment also comes into play in the interpretation of the data. Experts should be able to identify the weaknesses of the tools as well as their strengths. Experts may determine when a specific tool may or may not be more appropriate given the organization's capabilities and culture.

11.4.3 Perform Quantitative Risk Analysis: Outputs

11.4.3.1 Project Documents Updates

Project documents are updated with information resulting from quantitative risk analysis. For example, risk register updates could include:

- **Probabilistic analysis of the project.** Estimates are made of potential project schedule and cost outcomes listing the possible completion dates and costs with their associated confidence levels. This output, often expressed as a cumulative frequency distribution, is used with stakeholder risk tolerances to permit quantification of the cost and time contingency reserves. Such contingency reserves are needed to bring the risk of overrunning stated project objectives to a level acceptable to the organization.

- **Probability of achieving cost and time objectives.** With the risks facing the project, the probability of achieving project objectives under the current plan can be estimated using quantitative risk analysis results. For instance, in Figure 11-17, the likelihood of achieving the cost estimate of US$41 million is about 12%.

- **Prioritized list of quantified risks.** This list includes those risks that pose the greatest threat or present the greatest opportunity to the project. These include the risks that may have the greatest effect on cost contingency and those that are most likely to influence the critical path. These risks may be evaluated, in some cases, through a tornado diagram generated as a result of the simulation analysis.

- **Trends in quantitative risk analysis results.** As the analysis is repeated, a trend may become apparent that leads to conclusions affecting risk responses. Organizational historical information on project schedule, cost, quality, and performance should reflect new insights gained through the Perform Quantitative Risk Analysis process. Such history may take the form of a quantitative risk analysis report. This report may be separate from, or linked to, the risk register.

11.5 Plan Risk Responses

Plan Risk Responses is the process of developing options and actions to enhance opportunities and to reduce threats to project objectives. The key benefit of this process is that it addresses the risks by their priority, inserting resources and activities into the budget, schedule and project management plan as needed. The inputs, tools and techniques, and outputs of this process are depicted in Figure 11-18. Figure 11-19 depicts the data flow diagram of the process.

Inputs	Tools & Techniques	Outputs
.1 Risk management plan .2 Risk register	.1 Strategies for negative risks or threats .2 Strategies for positive risks or opportunities .3 Contingent response strategies .4 Expert judgment	.1 Project management plan updates .2 Project documents updates

Figure 11-18. Plan Risk Responses: Inputs, Tools & Techniques, and Outputs

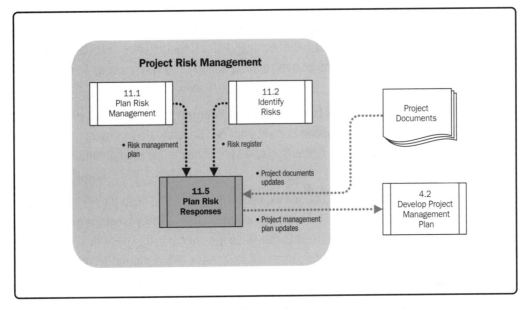

Figure 11-19. Plan Risk Responses Data Flow Diagram

The Plan Risk Responses process follows the Perform Quantitative Risk Analysis process (if used). Each risk response requires an understanding of the mechanism by which it will address the risk. This is the mechanism used to analyze if the risk response plan is having the desired effect. It includes the identification and assignment of one person (an owner for risk response) to take responsibility for each agreed-to and funded risk response. Risk responses should be appropriate for the significance of the risk, cost-effective in meeting the challenge, realistic within the project context, agreed upon by all parties involved, and owned by a responsible person. Selecting the optimum risk response from several options is often required.

The Plan Risk Responses process presents commonly used approaches to planning responses to the risks. Risks include threats and opportunities that can affect project success, and responses are discussed for each.

11.5.1 Plan Risk Responses: Inputs

11.5.1.1 Risk Management Plan

Important components of the risk management plan include roles and responsibilities, risk analysis definitions, timing for reviews (and for eliminating risks from review), and risk thresholds for low, moderate, and high risks. Risk thresholds help identify those risks for which specific responses are needed.

11.5.1.2 Risk Register

The risk register refers to identified risks, root causes of risks, lists of potential responses, risk owners, symptoms and warning signs, the relative rating or priority list of project risks, risks requiring responses in the near term, risks for additional analysis and response, trends in qualitative analysis results, and a watch list, which is a list of low-priority risks within the risk register.

11.5.2 Plan Risk Responses: Tools and Techniques

Several risk response strategies are available. The strategy or mix of strategies most likely to be effective should be selected for each risk. Risk analysis tools, such as decision tree analysis (Section 11.4.2.2), can be used to choose the most appropriate responses. Specific actions are developed to implement that strategy, including primary and backup strategies, as necessary. A fallback plan can be developed for implementation if the selected strategy turns out not to be fully effective or if an accepted risk occurs. Secondary risks should also be reviewed. Secondary risks are risks that arise as a direct result of implementing a risk response. A contingency reserve is often allocated for time or cost. If developed, it may include identification of the conditions that trigger its use.

11.5.2.1 Strategies for Negative Risks or Threats

Three strategies, which typically deal with threats or risks that may have negative impacts on project objectives if they occur, are: *avoid*, *transfer*, and *mitigate*. The fourth strategy, *accept*, can be used for negative risks or threats as well as positive risks or opportunities. Each of these risk response strategies have varied and unique influence on the risk condition. These strategies should be chosen to match the risk's probability and impact on the project's overall objectives. Avoidance and mitigation strategies are usually good strategies for critical risks with high impact, while transference and acceptance are usually good strategies for threats that are less critical and with low overall impact. The four strategies for dealing with negative risks or threats are further described as follows:

- **Avoid.** Risk avoidance is a risk response strategy whereby the project team acts to eliminate the threat or protect the project from its impact. It usually involves changing the project management plan to eliminate the threat entirely. The project manager may also isolate the project objectives from the risk's impact or change the objective that is in jeopardy. Examples of this include extending the schedule, changing the strategy, or reducing scope. The most radical avoidance strategy is to shut down the project entirely. Some risks that arise early in the project can be avoided by clarifying requirements, obtaining information, improving communication, or acquiring expertise.

- **Transfer.** Risk transference is a risk response strategy whereby the project team shifts the impact of a threat to a third party, together with ownership of the response. Transferring the risk simply gives another party responsibility for its management—it does not eliminate it. Transferring does not mean disowning the risk by transferring it to a later project or another person without his or her knowledge or agreement. Risk transference nearly always involves payment of a risk premium to the party taking on the risk. Transferring liability for risk is most effective in dealing with financial risk exposure. Transference tools can be quite diverse and include, but are not limited to, the use of insurance, performance bonds, warranties, guarantees, etc. Contracts or agreements may be used to transfer liability for specified risks to another party. For example, when a buyer has capabilities that the seller does not possess, it may be prudent to transfer some work and its concurrent risk contractually back to the buyer. In many cases, use of a cost-plus contract may transfer the cost risk to the buyer, while a fixed-price contract may transfer risk to the seller.

- **Mitigate.** Risk mitigation is a risk response strategy whereby the project team acts to reduce the probability of occurrence or impact of a risk. It implies a reduction in the probability and/or impact of an adverse risk to be within acceptable threshold limits. Taking early action to reduce the probability and/or impact of a risk occurring on the project is often more effective than trying to repair the damage after the risk has occurred. Adopting less complex processes, conducting more tests, or choosing a more stable supplier are examples of mitigation actions. Mitigation may require prototype development to reduce the risk of scaling up from a bench-scale model of a process or product. Where it is not possible to reduce probability, a mitigation response might address the risk impact by targeting linkages that determine the severity. For example, designing redundancy into a system may reduce the impact from a failure of the original component.

- **Accept.** Risk acceptance is a risk response strategy whereby the project team decides to acknowledge the risk and not take any action unless the risk occurs. This strategy is adopted where it is not possible or cost-effective to address a specific risk in any other way. This strategy indicates that the project team has decided not to change the project management plan to deal with a risk, or is unable to identify any other suitable response strategy. This strategy can be either passive or active. Passive acceptance requires no action except to document the strategy, leaving the project team to deal with the risks as they occur, and to periodically review the threat to ensure that it does not change significantly. The most common active acceptance strategy is to establish a contingency reserve, including amounts of time, money, or resources to handle the risks.

11.5.2.2 Strategies for Positive Risks or Opportunities

Three of the four responses are suggested to deal with risks with potentially positive impacts on project objectives. The fourth strategy, *accept*, can be used for negative risks or threats as well as positive risks or opportunities. These strategies, described below, are to exploit, share, enhance, and accept.

- **Exploit.** The exploit strategy may be selected for risks with positive impacts where the organization wishes to ensure that the opportunity is realized. This strategy seeks to eliminate the uncertainty associated with a particular upside risk by ensuring the opportunity definitely happens. Examples of directly exploiting responses include assigning an organization's most talented resources to the project to reduce the time to completion or using new technologies or technology upgrades to reduce cost and duration required to realize project objectives.

- **Enhance.** The enhance strategy is used to increase the probability and/or the positive impacts of an opportunity. Identifying and maximizing key drivers of these positive-impact risks may increase the probability of their occurrence. Examples of enhancing opportunities include adding more resources to an activity to finish early.

- **Share.** Sharing a positive risk involves allocating some or all of the ownership of the opportunity to a third party who is best able to capture the opportunity for the benefit of the project. Examples of sharing actions include forming risk-sharing partnerships, teams, special-purpose companies, or joint ventures, which can be established with the express purpose of taking advantage of the opportunity so that all parties gain from their actions.

- **Accept.** Accepting an opportunity is being willing to take advantage of the opportunity if it arises, but not actively pursuing it.

11.5.2.3 Contingent Response Strategies

Some responses are designed for use only if certain events occur. For some risks, it is appropriate for the project team to make a response plan that will only be executed under certain predefined conditions, if it is believed that there will be sufficient warning to implement the plan. Events that trigger the contingency response, such as missing intermediate milestones or gaining higher priority with a supplier, should be defined and tracked. Risk responses identified using this technique are often called contingency plans or fallback plans and include identified triggering events that set the plans in effect.

11.5.2.4 Expert Judgment

Expert judgment is input from knowledgeable parties pertaining to the actions to be taken on a specific and defined risk. Expertise may be provided by any group or person with specialized education, knowledge, skill, experience, or training in establishing risk responses.

11.5.3 Plan Risk Responses: Outputs

11.5.3.1 Project Management Plan Updates

Elements of the project management plan that may be updated as a result of carrying out this process include, but are not limited to:

- **Schedule management plan.** The schedule management plan is updated to reflect changes in process and practice driven by the risk responses. This may include changes in tolerance or behavior related to resource loading and leveling, as well as updates to the schedule strategy.

- **Cost management plan.** The cost management plan is updated to reflect changes in process and practice driven by the risk responses. This may include changes in tolerance or behavior related to cost accounting, tracking, and reports, as well as updates to the budget strategy and how contingency reserves are consumed.

- **Quality management plan.** The quality management plan is updated to reflect changes in process and practice driven by the risk responses. This may include changes in tolerance or behavior related to requirements, quality assurance, or quality control, as well as updates to the requirements documentation.

- **Procurement management plan.** The procurement management plan may be updated to reflect changes in strategy, such as alterations in the make-or-buy decision or contract type(s) driven by the risk responses.

- **Human resource management plan.** The staffing management plan, part of the human resource management plan, is updated to reflect changes in project organizational structure and resource applications driven by the risk responses. This may include changes in tolerance or behavior related to staff allocation, as well as updates to the resource loading.

- **Scope baseline.** Because of new, modified or omitted work generated by the risk responses, the scope baseline may be updated to reflect those changes.

- **Schedule baseline.** Because of new work (or omitted work) generated by the risk responses, the schedule baseline may be updated to reflect those changes.

- **Cost baseline.** Because of new work (or omitted work) generated by the risk responses, the cost baseline may be updated to reflect those changes.

11.5.3.2 Project Documents Updates

In the Plan Risk Responses process, several project documents are updated as needed. For example, when appropriate risk responses are chosen and agreed upon, they are included in the risk register. The risk register should be written to a level of detail that corresponds with the priority ranking and the planned response. Often, the high and moderate risks are addressed in detail. Risks judged to be of low priority are included in a watch list for periodic monitoring. Updates to the risk register can include, but are not limited to:

- Risk owners and assigned responsibilities;

- Agreed-upon response strategies;

- Specific actions to implement the chosen response strategy;

- Trigger conditions, symptoms, and warning signs of a risk occurrence;

- Budget and schedule activities required to implement the chosen responses;

- Contingency plans and triggers that call for their execution;

- Fallback plans for use as a reaction to a risk that has occurred and the primary response proves to be inadequate;

- Residual risks that are expected to remain after planned responses have been taken, as well as those that have been deliberately accepted;

- Secondary risks that arise as a direct outcome of implementing a risk response; and

- Contingency reserves that are calculated based on the quantitative risk analysis of the project and the organization's risk thresholds.

Other project documents updated could include:

- **Assumptions log updates.** As new information becomes available through the application of risk responses, assumptions could change. The assumptions log needs to be revisited to accommodate this new information.

- **Technical documentation updates.** As new information becomes available through the application of risk responses, technical approaches and physical deliverables may change. Any supporting documentation needs to be revisited to accommodate this new information.

- **Change requests.** Planning for possible risk responses can often result in recommendations for changes to the resources, activities, cost estimates, and other items identified during other planning processes. When such recommendations are identified, change requests are generated and processed through the Perform Integrated Change Control process.

11.6 Control Risks

Control Risks is the process of implementing risk response plans, tracking identified risks, monitoring residual risks, identifying new risks, and evaluating risk process effectiveness throughout the project. The key benefit of this process is that it improves efficiency of the risk approach throughout the project life cycle to continuously optimize risk responses. The inputs, tools and techniques, and outputs of this process are depicted in Figure 11-20. Figure 11-21 depicts the data flow diagram of the process.

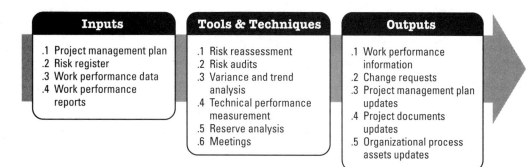

Inputs	Tools & Techniques	Outputs
.1 Project management plan .2 Risk register .3 Work performance data .4 Work performance reports	.1 Risk reassessment .2 Risk audits .3 Variance and trend analysis .4 Technical performance measurement .5 Reserve analysis .6 Meetings	.1 Work performance information .2 Change requests .3 Project management plan updates .4 Project documents updates .5 Organizational process assets updates

Figure 11-20. Control Risks: Inputs, Tools & Techniques, and Outputs

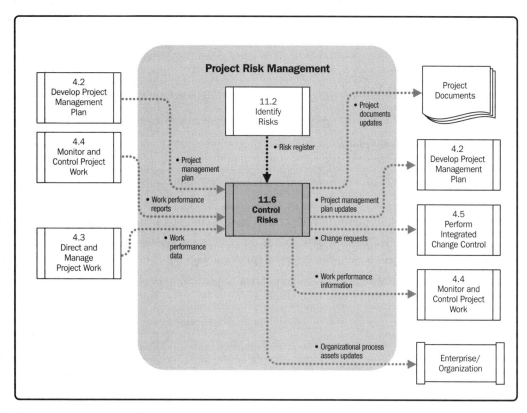

Figure 11-21. Control Risks Data Flow Diagram

Planned risk responses that are included in the risk register are executed during the life cycle of the project, but the project work should be continuously monitored for new, changing, and outdated risks.

The Control Risks process applies techniques, such as variance and trend analysis, which require the use of performance information generated during project execution. Other purposes of the Control Risks process are to determine if:

- Project assumptions are still valid,
- Analysis shows an assessed risk has changed or can be retired,
- Risk management policies and procedures are being followed, and
- Contingency reserves for cost or schedule should be modified in alignment with the current risk assessment.

Control Risks can involve choosing alternative strategies, executing a contingency or fallback plan, taking corrective action, and modifying the project management plan. The risk response owner reports periodically to the project manager on the effectiveness of the plan, any unanticipated effects, and any correction needed to handle the risk appropriately. Control Risks also includes updating the organizational process assets, including project lessons learned databases and risk management templates, for the benefit of future projects.

11.6.1 Control Risks: Inputs

11.6.1.1 Project Management Plan

Described in Section 4.2.3.1. The project management plan, which includes the risk management plan, provides guidance for risk monitoring and controlling.

11.6.1.2 Risk Register

The risk register has key inputs that include identified risks and risk owners, agreed-upon risk responses, control actions for assessing the effectiveness of response plans, risk responses, specific implementation actions, symptoms and warning signs of risk, residual and secondary risks, a watch list of low-priority risks, and the time and cost contingency reserves. The watch list is within the risk register and provides a list of low-priority risks.

11.6.1.3 Work Performance Data

Described in Section 4.3.3.2. Work performance data related to various performance results possibly impacted by risks includes, but is not limited to:

- Deliverable status,
- Schedule progress, and
- Costs incurred.

11.6.1.4 Work Performance Reports

Described in Section 4.4.3.2. Work performance reports take information from performance measurements and analyze it to provide project work performance information including variance analysis, earned value data, and forecasting data. These data points could be impactful in controlling performance related risks.

11.6.2 Control Risks: Tools and Techniques

11.6.2.1 Risk Reassessment

Control Risks often results in identification of new risks, reassessment of current risks, and the closing of risks that are outdated. Project risk reassessments should be regularly scheduled. The amount and detail of repetition that are appropriate depends on how the project progresses relative to its objectives.

11.6.2.2 Risk Audits

Risk audits examine and document the effectiveness of risk responses in dealing with identified risks and their root causes, as well as the effectiveness of the risk management process. The project manager is responsible for ensuring that risk audits are performed at an appropriate frequency, as defined in the project's risk management plan. Risk audits may be included during routine project review meetings, or the team may choose to hold separate risk audit meetings. The format for the audit and its objectives should be clearly defined before the audit is conducted.

11

11.6.2.3 Variance and Trend Analysis

Many control processes employ variance analysis to compare the planned results to the actual results. For the purposes of controlling risks, trends in the project's execution should be reviewed using performance information. Earned value analysis and other methods of project variance and trend analysis may be used for monitoring overall project performance. Outcomes from these analyses may forecast potential deviation of the project at completion from cost and schedule targets. Deviation from the baseline plan may indicate the potential impact of threats or opportunities.

11.6.2.4 Technical Performance Measurement

Technical performance measurement compares technical accomplishments during project execution to the schedule of technical achievement. It requires the definition of objective, quantifiable measures of technical performance, which can be used to compare actual results against targets. Such technical performance measures may include weight, transaction times, number of delivered defects, storage capacity, etc. Deviation, such as demonstrating more or less functionality than planned at a milestone, can help to forecast the degree of success in achieving the project's scope.

11.6.2.5 Reserve Analysis

Throughout execution of the project, some risks may occur with positive or negative impacts on budget or schedule contingency reserves. Reserve analysis compares the amount of the contingency reserves remaining to the amount of risk remaining at any time in the project in order to determine if the remaining reserve is adequate.

11.6.2.6 Meetings

Project risk management should be an agenda item at periodic status meetings. The amount of time required for that item will vary, depending upon the risks that have been identified, their priority, and difficulty of response. The more often risk management is practiced, the easier it becomes. Frequent discussions about risk make it more likely that people will identify risks and opportunities.

11.6.3 Control Risks: Outputs

11.6.3.1 Work Performance Information

Work performance information, as a Control Risks output, provides a mechanism to communicate and support project decision making.

11.6.3.2 Change Requests

Implementing contingency plans or workarounds sometimes results in a change request. Change requests are prepared and submitted to the Perform Integrated Change Control process (Section 4.5). Change requests can include recommended corrective and preventive actions as well.

- **Recommended corrective actions.** These are activities that realign the performance of the project work with the project management plan. They include contingency plans and workarounds. The latter are responses that were not initially planned, but are required to deal with emerging risks that were previously unidentified or accepted passively.

- **Recommended preventive actions.** These are activities that ensure that future performance of the project work is aligned with the project management plan.

11.6.3.3 Project Management Plan Updates

If the approved change requests have an effect on the risk management processes, the corresponding component documents of the project management plan are revised and reissued to reflect the approved changes. The elements of the project management plan that may be updated are the same as those in the Plan Risk Responses process.

11

11.6.3.4 Project Documents Updates

Project documents that may be updated as a result of the Control Risk process include, but are not limited to the risk register. Risk register updates may include:

- **Outcomes of risk reassessments, risk audits, and periodic risk reviews.** These outcomes may include identification of new risks, updates to probability, impact, priority, response plans, ownership, and other elements of the risk register. Outcomes can also include closing risks that are no longer applicable and releasing their associated reserves.

- **Actual outcomes of the project's risks and of the risk responses.** This information can help project managers to plan for risk throughout their organizations, as well as on future projects.

11.6.3.5 Organizational Process Assets Updates

The risk management processes produce information that may be used for future projects, and should be captured in the organizational process assets. The organizational process assets that may be updated include, but are not limited to:

- Templates for the risk management plan, including the probability and impact matrix and risk register,

- Risk breakdown structure, and

- Lessons learned from the project risk management activities.

These documents should be updated as needed and at project closure. Final versions of the risk register and the risk management plan templates, checklists, and risk breakdown structure are included.

12.3.2 Control Procurements: Tools and Techniques

12.3.2.1 Contract Change Control System

A contract change control system defines the process by which the procurement can be modified. It includes the paperwork, tracking systems, dispute resolution procedures, and approval levels necessary for authorizing changes. The contract change control system is integrated with the integrated change control system.

12.3.2.2 Procurement Performance Reviews

A procurement performance review is a structured review of the seller's progress to deliver project scope and quality, within cost and on schedule, as compared to the contract. It can include a review of seller-prepared documentation and buyer inspections, as well as quality audits conducted during seller's execution of the work. The objective of a performance review is to identify performance successes or failures, progress with respect to the procurement statement of work, and contract noncompliance, which allow the buyer to quantify the seller's demonstrated ability or inability to perform work. Such reviews may take place as a part of project status reviews, which would include key suppliers.

12.3.2.3 Inspections and Audits

Inspections and audits required by the buyer and supported by the seller, as specified in the procurement contract, can be conducted during execution of the project to verify compliance in the seller's work processes or deliverables. If authorized by contract, some inspection and audit teams can include buyer procurement personnel.

12.3.2.4 Performance Reporting

Work performance data and reports supplied by sellers are evaluated against the agreement requirements. Work performance information from this evaluation is then reported as appropriate. Performance reporting provides management with information about how effectively the seller is achieving the contractual objectives.

12.3.2.5 Payment Systems

Payments to the seller are typically processed by the accounts payable system of the buyer after certification of satisfactory work by an authorized person on the project team. All payments should be made and documented in strict accordance with the terms of the contract.

12

12.3.2.6 Claims Administration

Contested changes and potential constructive changes are those requested changes where the buyer and seller cannot reach an agreement on compensation for the change or cannot agree that a change has occurred. These contested changes are variously called claims, disputes, or appeals. Claims are documented, processed, monitored, and managed throughout the contract life cycle, usually in accordance with the terms of the contract. If the parties themselves do not resolve a claim, it may have to be handled in accordance with alternative dispute resolution (ADR) typically following procedures established in the contract. Settlement of all claims and disputes through negotiation is the preferred method.

12.3.2.7 Records Management System

A records management system is used by the project manager to manage contract and procurement documentation and records. It consists of a specific set of processes, related control functions, and automation tools that are consolidated and combined as part of the project management information system (Section 4.4.2.3). The system contains a retrievable archive of contract documents and correspondence.

12.3.3 Control Procurements: Outputs

12.3.3.1 Work Performance Information

Work performance information provides a basis for identification of current or potential problems to support later claims or new procurements. By reporting on the performance of a vendor, the organization increases knowledge of the performance of the procurement, which supports improved forecasting, risk management, and decision making. Performance reports also assist in the event there is a dispute with the vendor.

Work performance information includes reporting compliance of contracts, which provides procuring organizations a mechanism to track specific deliverables expected and received from vendors. Contract compliance reports support improved communications with vendors so that potential issues are addressed promptly to the satisfaction of all parties.

12.3.3.2 Change Requests

Change requests to the project management plan, its subsidiary plans, and other components, such as the cost baseline, schedule baseline, and procurement management plan, may result from the Control Procurements process. Change requests are processed for review and approval through the Perform Integrated Change Control process.

Requested but unresolved changes can include direction provided by the buyer or actions taken by the seller, which the other party considers a constructive change to the contract. Since any of these constructive changes may be disputed by one party and can lead to a claim against the other party, such changes are uniquely identified and documented by project correspondence.

12.3.3.3 Project Management Plan Updates

Elements of the project management plan that may be updated include, but are not limited to:

- **Procurement management plan.** The procurement management plan is updated to reflect any approved change requests that affect procurement management, including impacts to costs or schedules.

- **Schedule baseline.** If there are slippages that impact overall project performance, the schedule baseline may need to be updated to reflect the current expectations.

- **Cost baseline.** If there are changes that impact overall project costs, the cost baseline may need to be updated to reflect the current expectations.

12.3.3.4 Project Documents Updates

Project documents that may be updated include, but are not limited to, procurement documentation. Procurement documentation may include the procurement contract with all supporting schedules, requested unapproved contract changes, and approved change requests. Procurement documentation also includes any seller-developed technical documentation and other work performance information, such as deliverables, seller performance reports and warranties, financial documents including invoices and payment records, and the results of contract-related inspections.

12.3.3.5 Organizational Process Assets Updates

Elements of the organizational process assets that may be updated include, but are not limited to:

12

- **Correspondence.** Contract terms and conditions often require written documentation of certain aspects of buyer/seller communications, such as the need for warnings of unsatisfactory performance and requests for contract changes or clarification. This can include the reported results of buyer audits and inspections that indicate weaknesses the seller needs to correct. In addition to specific contract requirements for documentation, a complete and accurate written record of all written and oral contract communications, as well as actions taken and decisions made, are maintained by both parties.

- **Payment schedules and requests.** All payments should be made in accordance with the procurement contract terms and conditions.

- **Seller performance evaluation documentation.** Seller performance evaluation documentation is prepared by the buyer. Such performance evaluations document the seller's ability to continue to perform work on the current contract, indicate if the seller can be allowed to perform work on future projects, or rate how well the seller is performing the project work. These documents may form the basis for early termination of the seller's contract or determine how contract penalties, fees, or incentives are administered. The results of these performance evaluations can also be included in the appropriate qualified seller lists.

12.4 Close Procurements

Close Procurements is the process of completing each procurement. The key benefit of this process is that it documents agreements and related documentation for future reference. The inputs, tools and techniques, and outputs of this process are depicted in Figure 12-8. Figure 12-9 depicts the data flow diagram of the process.

Inputs	Tools & Techniques	Outputs
.1 Project management plan .2 Procurement documents	.1 Procurement audits .2 Procurement negotiations .3 Records management system	.1 Closed procurements .2 Organizational process assets updates

Figure 12-8. Close Procurements: Inputs, Tools & Techniques, and Outputs

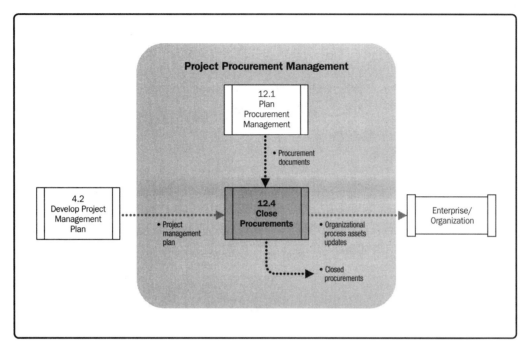

Figure 12-9. Close Procurements Data Flow Diagram

The Close Procurements process also involves administrative activities such as finalizing open claims, updating records to reflect final results, and archiving such information for future use. Close Procurements addresses each contract applicable to the project or a project phase. In multiphase projects, the term of a contract may only be applicable to a given phase of the project. In these cases, the Close Procurements process closes the procurement(s) applicable to that phase of the project. Unresolved claims may be subject to litigation after closure. The contract terms and conditions can prescribe specific procedures for agreement closure. The Close Procurements process supports the Close Project or Phase process (Section 4.6) by ensuring contractual agreements are completed or terminated.

Early termination of a contract is a special case of procurement closure that can result from a mutual agreement by both parties, from the default of one party, or for convenience of the buyer if provided for in the contract. The rights and responsibilities of the parties in the event of an early termination are contained in the terminations clause of the contract. Based upon those procurement terms and conditions, the buyer may have the right to terminate the whole contract or a portion of the contract, at any time, for cause or convenience. However, based upon those contract terms and conditions, the buyer may have to compensate the seller for seller's preparations and for any completed and accepted work related to the terminated part of the contract.

12.4.1 Close Procurements: Inputs

12.4.1.1 Project Management Plan

Described in Section 4.2.3.1. The project management plan contains the procurement management plan, which provides the details and guidelines for closing out procurements.

12.4.1.2 Procurement Documents

To close the contract, all procurement documentation is collected, indexed, and filed. Information on contract schedule, scope, quality, and cost performance along with all contract change documentation, payment records, and inspection results are cataloged. This information can be used for lessons learned information and as a basis for evaluating contractors for future contracts.

12.4.2 Close Procurements: Tools and Techniques

12.4.2.1 Procurement Audits

A procurement audit is a structured review of the procurement process originating from the Plan Procurement Management process through Control Procurements. The objective of a procurement audit is to identify successes and failures that warrant recognition in the preparation or administration of other procurement contracts on the project, or on other projects within the performing organization.

12.4.2.2 Procurement Negotiations

In all procurement relationships, the final equitable settlement of all outstanding issues, claims, and disputes by negotiation is a primary goal. Whenever settlement cannot be achieved through direct negotiation, some form of alternative dispute resolution (ADR) including mediation or arbitration may be explored. When all else fails, litigation in the courts is the least desirable option.

12.4.2.3 Records Management System

Described in Section 12.3.2.7. A records management system is used by the project manager to manage contract and procurement documentation and records. Contract documents and correspondence are archived through the records management system as part of the Close Procurements process.

12.4.3 Close Procurements: Outputs

12.4.3.1 Closed Procurements

The buyer, usually through its authorized procurement administrator, provides the seller with formal written notice that the contract has been completed. Requirements for formal procurement closure are usually defined in the terms and conditions of the contract and are included in the procurement management plan.

12.4.3.2 Organizational Process Assets Updates

Elements of the organizational process assets that may be updated include, but are not limited to:

- **Procurement file.** A complete set of indexed contract documentation, including the closed contract, is prepared for inclusion with the final project files.

- **Deliverable acceptance.** Documentation of formal acceptance of seller-provided deliverables may be required to be retained by the organization. The Close Procurement process ensures this documentation requirement is satisfied. Requirements for formal deliverable acceptance and how to address nonconforming deliverables are usually defined in the agreement.

- **Lessons learned documentation.** Lessons learned, what has been experienced, and process improvement recommendations, should be developed for the project file to improve future procurements.

12

13

PROJECT STAKEHOLDER MANAGEMENT

Project Stakeholder Management includes the processes required to identify the people, groups, or organizations that could impact or be impacted by the project, to analyze stakeholder expectations and their impact on the project, and to develop appropriate management strategies for effectively engaging stakeholders in project decisions and execution. Stakeholder management also focuses on continuous communication with stakeholders to understand their needs and expectations, addressing issues as they occur, managing conflicting interests and fostering appropriate stakeholder engagement in project decisions and activities. Stakeholder satisfaction should be managed as a key project objective.

Figure 13-1 provides an overview of the Project Stakeholder Management processes that include the following:

13.1 Identify Stakeholders—The process of identifying the people, groups, or organizations that could impact or be impacted by a decision, activity, or outcome of the project; and analyzing and documenting relevant information regarding their interests, involvement, interdependencies, influence, and potential impact on project success.

13.2 Plan Stakeholder Management—The process of developing appropriate management strategies to effectively engage stakeholders throughout the project life cycle, based on the analysis of their needs, interests, and potential impact on project success.

13.3 Manage Stakeholder Engagement—The process of communicating and working with stakeholders to meet their needs/expectations, address issues as they occur, and foster appropriate stakeholder engagement in project activities throughout the project life cycle.

13.4 Control Stakeholder Engagement—The process of monitoring overall project stakeholder relationships and adjusting strategies and plans for engaging stakeholders.

These processes interact with each other and with processes in other Knowledge Areas as described in detail in Section 3 and Annex A1.

Every project will have stakeholders who are impacted by or can impact the project in a positive or negative way. While some stakeholders may have a limited ability to influence the project, others may have significant influence on the project and its expected outcomes. The ability of the project manager to correctly identify and manage these stakeholders in an appropriate manner can mean the difference between success and failure.

13

Project Stakeholder Management Overview

13.1 Identify Stakeholders

.1 Inputs
.1 Project charter
.2 Procurement documents
.3 Enterprise environmental factors
.4 Organizational process assets

.2 Tools & Techniques
.1 Stakeholder analysis
.2 Expert judgment
.3 Meetings

.3 Outputs
.1 Stakeholder register

13.2 Plan Stakeholder Management

.1 Inputs
.1 Project management plan
.2 Stakeholder register
.3 Enterprise environmental factors
.4 Organizational process assets

.2 Tools & Techniques
.1 Expert judgment
.2 Meetings
.3 Analytical techniques

.3 Outputs
.1 Stakeholder management plan
.2 Project documents updates

13.3 Manage Stakeholder Engagement

.1 Inputs
.1 Stakeholder management plan
.2 Communications management plan
.3 Change log
.4 Organizational process assets

.2 Tools & Techniques
.1 Communication methods
.2 Interpersonal skills
.3 Management skills

.3 Outputs
.1 Issue log
.2 Change requests
.3 Project management plan updates
.4 Project documents updates
.5 Organizational process assets updates

13.4 Control Stakeholder Engagement

.1 Inputs
.1 Project management plan
.2 Issue log
.3 Work performance data
.4 Project documents

.2 Tools & Techniques
.1 Information management systems
.2 Expert judgment
.3 Meetings

.3 Outputs
.1 Work performance information
.2 Change requests
.3 Project management plan updates
.4 Project documents updates
.5 Organizational process assets updates

Figure 13-1. Project Stakeholder Management Overview

13.1 Identify Stakeholders

Identify Stakeholders is the process of identifying the people, groups, or organizations that could impact or be impacted by a decision, activity, or outcome of the project, analyzing and documenting relevant information regarding their interests, involvement, interdependencies, influence, and potential impact on project success. The key benefit of this process is that it allows the project manager to identify the appropriate focus for each stakeholder or group of stakeholders. The inputs, tools and techniques, and outputs of this process are depicted in Figure 13-2. Figure 13-3 depicts the data flow diagram of the process.

Inputs	Tools & Techniques	Outputs
.1 Project charter .2 Procurement documents .3 Enterprise environmental factors .4 Organizational process assets	.1 Stakeholder analysis .2 Expert judgment .3 Meetings	.1 Stakeholder register

Figure 13-2. Identify Stakeholders: Inputs, Tools & Techniques, and Outputs

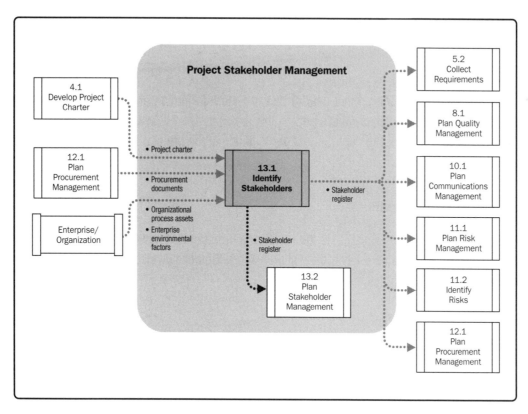

Figure 13-3. Identify Stakeholders Data Flow Diagram

Project stakeholders are individuals, groups, or organizations who may affect, be affected by, or perceive themselves to be affected by a decision, activity, or outcome of a project. They are comprised of persons and organizations such as customers, sponsors, the performing organization, and the public who are actively involved in the project, or whose interests may be positively or negatively affected by the execution or completion of the project. They may also exert influence over the project and its deliverables. Stakeholders may be at different levels within the organization and may possess different authority levels, or may be external to the performing organization for the project. Section 13.1.2.1 identifies various types of project stakeholders.

It is critical for project success to identify the stakeholders early in the project or phase and to analyze their levels of interest, their individual expectations, as well as their importance and influence. This initial assessment should be reviewed and updated regularly. Most projects will have a diverse number of stakeholders depending on their size, type, and complexity. While the project manager's time is limited and should be used as efficiently as possible, these stakeholders should be classified according to their interest, influence, and involvement in the project, taking into consideration the fact that the affect or influence of a stakeholder may not occur or become evident until later stages in the project or phase. This enables the project manager to focus on the relationships necessary to ensure the success of the project.

13.1.1 Identify Stakeholders: Inputs

13.1.1.1 Project Charter

Described in Section 4.1.3.1. The project charter can provide information about internal and external parties related with the project and affected by the result or the execution of the project, such as project sponsor(s), customers, team members, groups and departments participating in the project, and other people or organizations affected by the project.

13.1.1.2 Procurement Documents

Described in Section 12.1.3.3. If a project is the result of a procurement activity or is based on an established contract, the parties in that contract are key project stakeholders. Other relevant parties, such as suppliers, should also be considered as part of the project stakeholder list.

13.1.1.3 Enterprise Environmental Factors

Described in Section 2.1.5. The enterprise environmental factors that can influence the Identify Stakeholders process include, but are not limited to:

- Organizational culture and structure;
- Governmental or industry standards (e.g., regulations, product standards); and
- Global, regional or local trends, and practices or habits.

13.1.1.4 Organizational Process Assets

Described in Section 2.1.4. The organizational process assets that can influence the Identify Stakeholders process include, but are not limited to:

- Stakeholder register templates,
- Lessons learned from previous projects or phases, and
- Stakeholder registers from previous projects.

13.1.2 Identify Stakeholders: Tools and Techniques

13.1.2.1 Stakeholder Analysis

Stakeholder analysis is a technique of systematically gathering and analyzing quantitative and qualitative information to determine whose interests should be taken into account throughout the project. It identifies the interests, expectations, and influence of the stakeholders and relates them to the purpose of the project. It also helps to identify stakeholder relationships (with the project and with other stakeholders) that can be leveraged to build coalitions and potential partnerships to enhance the project's chance of success, along with stakeholder relationships that need to be influenced differently at different stages of the project or phase.

Stakeholder analysis generally follows the steps described below:

- Identify all potential project stakeholders and relevant information, such as their roles, departments, interests, knowledge, expectations, and influence levels. Key stakeholders are usually easy to identify. They include anyone in a decision-making or management role who is impacted by the project outcome, such as the sponsor, the project manager, and the primary customer. Identifying other stakeholders is usually done by interviewing identified stakeholders and expanding the list until all potential stakeholders are included.

- Analyze the potential impact or support each stakeholder could generate, and classify them so as to define an approach strategy. In large stakeholder communities, it is important to prioritize the stakeholders to ensure the efficient use of effort to communicate and manage their expectations.

- Assess how key stakeholders are likely to react or respond in various situations, in order to plan how to influence them to enhance their support and mitigate potential negative impacts.

There are multiple classification models used for stakeholders analysis, such as:

- *Power/interest grid*, grouping the stakeholders based on their level of authority ("power") and their level or concern ("interest") regarding the project outcomes;

- *Power/influence grid*, grouping the stakeholders based on their level of authority ("power") and their active involvement ("influence") in the project;

- *Influence/impact grid*, grouping the stakeholders based on their active involvement ("influence") in the project and their ability to effect changes to the project's planning or execution ("impact"); and

- *Salience model*, describing classes of stakeholders based on their power (ability to impose their will), urgency (need for immediate attention), and legitimacy (their involvement is appropriate).

Figure 13-4 presents an example of a power/interest grid with A-H representing the placement of generic stakeholders.

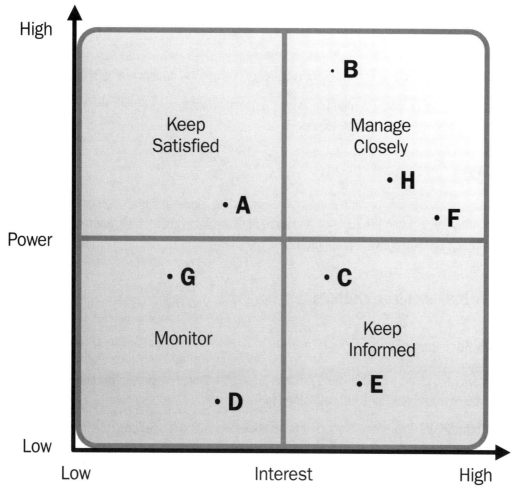

Figure 13-4. Example Power/Interest Grid with Stakeholders

13.1.2.2 Expert Judgment

To ensure comprehensive identification and listing of stakeholders, judgment and expertise should be sought from groups or individuals with specialized training or subject matter expertise, such as:

- Senior management;
- Other units within the organization;
- Identified key stakeholders;

- Project managers who have worked on projects in the same area (directly or through lessons learned);
- Subject matter experts (SMEs) in the business or project area;
- Industry groups and consultants; and
- Professional and technical associations, regulatory bodies, and nongovernmental organizations (NGOs).

Expert judgment can be obtained through individual consultations (one-on-one meetings, interviews, etc.) or through a panel format (focus groups, surveys, etc.).

13.1.2.3 Meetings

Profile analysis meetings are project meetings designed to develop an understanding of major project stakeholders, and they can be used to exchange and analyze information about roles, interests, knowledge, and the overall position of each stakeholder facing the project.

13.1.3 Identify Stakeholders: Outputs

13.1.3.1 Stakeholder Register

The main output of the Identify Stakeholders process is the stakeholder register. This contains all details related to the identified stakeholders including, but not limited to:

- **Identification information.** Name, organizational position, location, role in the project, contact information;
- **Assessment information.** Major requirements, main expectations, potential influence in the project, phase in the life cycle with the most interest; and
- **Stakeholder classification.** Internal/external, supporter/neutral/resistor, etc.

The stakeholder register should be consulted and updated on a regular basis, as stakeholders may change—or new ones identified—throughout the life cycle of the project.

13.2 Plan Stakeholder Management

Plan Stakeholder Management is the process of developing appropriate management strategies to effectively engage stakeholders throughout the project life cycle, based on the analysis of their needs, interests, and potential impact on project success. The key benefit of this process is that it provides a clear, actionable plan to interact with project stakeholders to support the project's interests. The inputs, tools and techniques, and outputs of this process are depicted in Figure 13-5. Figure 13-6 depicts the data flow diagram of the process.

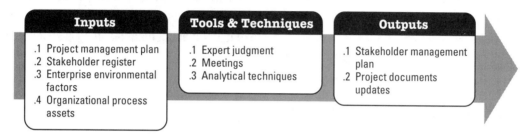

Inputs	Tools & Techniques	Outputs
.1 Project management plan .2 Stakeholder register .3 Enterprise environmental factors .4 Organizational process assets	.1 Expert judgment .2 Meetings .3 Analytical techniques	.1 Stakeholder management plan .2 Project documents updates

Figure 13-5. Plan Stakeholder Management: Inputs, Tools & Techniques, and Outputs

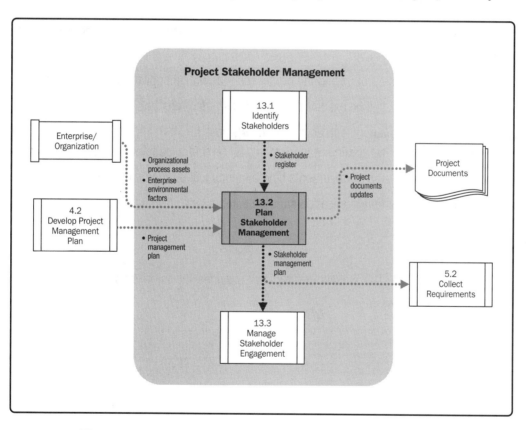

Figure 13-6. Plan Stakeholder Management Data Flow Diagram

Plan Stakeholder Management identifies how the project will affect stakeholders, which then allows the project manager to develop various ways to effectively engage stakeholders in the project, to manage their expectations, and to ultimately achieving the project objectives. Stakeholder management is more than improving communications and requires more than managing a team. Stakeholder management is about creation and maintenance of relationships between the project team and stakeholders, with the aim to satisfy their respective needs and requirements within project boundaries.

This process generates the stakeholder management plan, which contains detailed plans on how effective stakeholder management can be realized. As the project progresses, the membership of the stakeholder community and required level of engagement may change, therefore, stakeholder management planning is an iterative process that is reviewed on a regular basis by the project manager.

13.2.1 Plan Stakeholder Management: Inputs

13.2.1.1 Project Management Plan

Described in Section 4.2.3.1. The information used for the development of the stakeholder management plan includes, but is not limited to:

- Life cycle selected for the project and the processes that will be applied to each phase;
- Description of how work will be executed to accomplish the project objectives;
- Description of how human resources requirements will be met and how roles and responsibilities, reporting relationships, and staffing management will be addressed and structured for the project;
- Change management plan that documents how changes will be monitored and controlled; and
- Need and techniques for communication among stakeholders.

13.2.1.2 Stakeholder Register

Described in Section 13.1.3.1. The stakeholder register provides the information needed to plan appropriate ways to engage project stakeholders.

13.2.1.3 Enterprise Environmental Factors

Described in Section 2.1.5. All enterprise environmental factors are used as inputs to this process, because the management of stakeholders should be adapted to the project environment. Of these, organizational culture, structure, and political climate are of particular importance, because they help in determining the best options to support a better adaptive process for managing stakeholders.

13.2.1.4 Organizational Process Assets

Described in Section 2.1.4. All organizational process assets are used as inputs for the Plan Stakeholder Management process. Of these, lessons learned database and historical information are of particular importance, because they provide insights on previous stakeholder management plans and their effectiveness. These can be used to plan the stakeholder management activities for the current project.

13.2.2 Plan Stakeholder Management: Tools and Techniques

13.2.2.1 Expert Judgment

Based on the project objectives, the project manager should apply expert judgment to decide upon the level of engagement required at each stage of the project from each stakeholder. For example, at the beginning of a project, it may be necessary for senior stakeholders to be highly engaged in order to clear away any obstacles to success. Once these have been successfully removed, it may be sufficient for senior stakeholders to change their level of engagement from leading to supportive, and other stakeholders, such as end users, may become more important.

In order to create the stakeholder management plan, judgment and expertise should be sought from groups or individuals with specialized training or subject matter expertise or insight into the relationships within the organization, such as:

- Senior management;
- Project team members;
- Other units or individuals within the organization;
- Identified key stakeholders;

- Project managers who have worked on projects in the same area (directly or through lessons learned);
- Subject matter experts in business or project area;
- Industry groups and consultants; and
- Professional and technical associations, regulatory bodies, and nongovernmental organization (NGOs).

Expert judgment can be obtained through individual consultations (one-on-one meetings, interviews, etc.) or through a panel format (focus groups, surveys, etc.).

13.2.2.2 Meetings

Meetings should be held with experts and the project team to define the required engagement levels of all stakeholders. This information can be used to prepare the stakeholder management plan.

13.2.2.3 Analytical Techniques

The current engagement level of all stakeholders needs to be compared to the planned engagement levels required for successful project completion. Stakeholder engagement throughout the life cycle of the project is critical to project success.

The engagement level of the stakeholders can be classified as follows:

- **Unaware.** Unaware of project and potential impacts.
- **Resistant.** Aware of project and potential impacts and resistant to change.
- **Neutral.** Aware of project yet neither supportive nor resistant.
- **Supportive.** Aware of project and potential impacts and supportive to change.
- **Leading.** Aware of project and potential impacts and actively engaged in ensuring the project is a success.

The current engagement can be documented using Stakeholders Engagement Assessment Matrix, as shown in Figure 13-7, where C indicates the current engagement, and D indicates the desired engagement. The project team needs to identify the desired engagement level for the current phase of the project, based on available information.

The example in Figure 13-7 shows that stakeholder 3 is at the desired engagement level, while stakeholders 1 and 2 require further communications and additional actions to move them to the desired level of engagement.

Stakeholder	Unaware	Resistant	Neutral	Supportive	Leading
Stakeholder 1	C			D	
Stakeholder 2			C	D	
Stakeholder 3				D C	

Figure 13-7. Stakeholders Engagement Assessment Matrix

Through this analytical process, gaps between the current and desired engagement levels can be identified. Actions and communications required to close these gaps can be identified by the project team using expert judgment.

13.2.3 Plan Stakeholder Management: Outputs

13.2.3.1 Stakeholder Management Plan

The stakeholder management plan is a component of the project management plan (Section 4.2.3.1) and identifies the management strategies required to effectively engage stakeholders. The stakeholder management plan can be formal or informal, highly detailed or broadly framed, based on the needs of the project.

In addition to the data gathered in the stakeholder register, the stakeholder management plan often provides:

- Desired and current engagement levels of key stakeholders;
- Scope and impact of change to stakeholders;
- Identified interrelationships and potential overlap between stakeholders;
- Stakeholder communication requirements for the current project phase;
- Information to be distributed to stakeholders, including language, format, content, and level of detail;
- Reason for the distribution of that information and the expected impact to stakeholder engagement;
- Time frame and frequency for the distribution of required information to stakeholders; and
- Method for updating and refining the stakeholder management plan as the project progresses and develops.

13

Project managers should be aware of the sensitive nature of the stakeholder management plan and take appropriate precautions. For example, information on stakeholders who are resistant to the project can be potentially damaging, and due consideration should be given regarding the distribution of such information. When updating the stakeholder management plan, the validity of underlying assumptions should be reviewed to ensure continued accuracy and relevancy.

13.2.3.2 Project Documents Updates

Project documents that may be updated include, but are not limited to:

- Project schedule, and
- Stakeholder register.

13.3 Manage Stakeholder Engagement

Manage Stakeholder Engagement is the process of communicating and working with stakeholders to meet their needs/expectations, address issues as they occur, and foster appropriate stakeholder engagement in project activities throughout the project life cycle. The key benefit of this process is that it allows the project manager to increase support and minimize resistance from stakeholders, significantly increasing the chances to achieve project success. The inputs, tools and techniques, and outputs of this process are depicted in Figure 13-8. Figure 13-9 depicts the data flow diagram of the process.

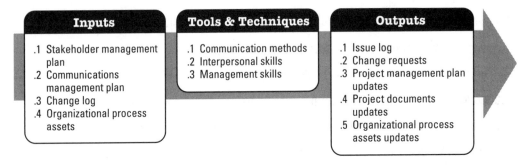

Inputs	Tools & Techniques	Outputs
.1 Stakeholder management plan .2 Communications management plan .3 Change log .4 Organizational process assets	.1 Communication methods .2 Interpersonal skills .3 Management skills	.1 Issue log .2 Change requests .3 Project management plan updates .4 Project documents updates .5 Organizational process assets updates

Figure 13-8. Manage Stakeholder Engagement: Inputs, Tools & Techniques, and Outputs

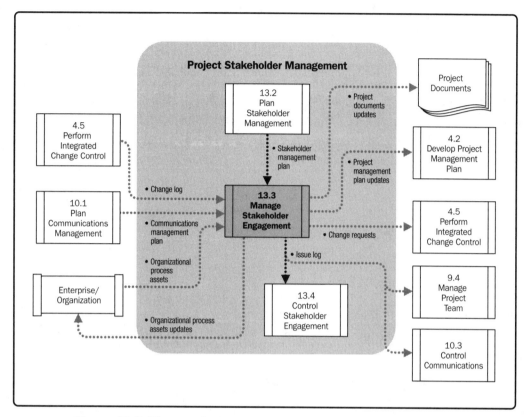

Figure 13-9. Manage Stakeholder Engagement Data Flow Diagram

Manage Stakeholder Engagement involves activities such as:

- Engaging stakeholders at appropriate project stages to obtain or confirm their continued commitment to the success of the project;

- Managing stakeholder expectations through negotiation and communication, ensuring project goals are achieved;

- Addressing potential concerns that have not yet become issues and anticipating future problems that may be raised by stakeholders. Such concerns need to be identified and discussed as soon as possible to assess associated project risks; and

- Clarifying and resolving issues that have been identified.

Managing stakeholder engagement helps to increase the probability of project success by ensuring that stakeholders clearly understand the project goals, objectives, benefits, and risks. This enables them to be active supporters of the project and to help guide activities and project decisions. By anticipating people's reactions to the project, proactive actions can be taken to win support or minimize negative impacts.

The ability of stakeholders to influence the project is typically highest during the initial stages and gets progressively lower as the project progresses. The project manager is responsible for engaging and managing the various stakeholders in a project and may call upon the project sponsor to assist as needed. Active management of stakeholder involvement decreases the risk of the project failing to meet its goals and objectives.

13.3.1 Manage Stakeholder Engagement: Inputs

13.3.1.1 Stakeholder Management Plan

Described in Section 13.2.3.1. The stakeholder management plan provides guidance on how the various stakeholders can be best involved in the project. The stakeholder management plan describes the methods and technologies used for stakeholder communication.

This plan is used to determine the level of interactions of various stakeholders and—together with other documents—helps define a strategy for identifying and managing stakeholders throughout the project life cycle.

13.3.1.2 Communications Management Plan

Described in Section 10.1.3.1. The communications management plan provides guidance and information on managing stakeholder expectations. The information used includes, but is not limited to:

- Stakeholder communications requirements;
- Information to be communicated, including language, format, content, and level of detail;
- Reason for distribution of information;
- Person or groups who will receive information; and
- Escalation process.

13.3.1.3 Change Log

Described in Section 4.5.3.2. A change log is used to document changes that occur during a project. These changes—and their impact on the project in terms of time, cost, and risk—are communicated to the appropriate stakeholders.

13.3.1.4 Organizational Process Assets

Described in Section 2.1.4. The organizational process assets that can influence the Manage Stakeholder Engagement process include, but are not limited to:

- Organizational communication requirements,
- Issue management procedures,
- Change control procedures, and
- Historical information about previous projects.

13.3.2 Manage Stakeholder Engagement: Tools and Techniques

13.3.2.1 Communication Methods

Described in Section 10.1.2.4. The methods of communication identified for each stakeholder in the communications management plan are utilized during stakeholder engagement management. Based on the stakeholders' communication requirements, the project manager decides how, when, and which of these communication methods are to be used in the project.

13.3.2.2 Interpersonal Skills

The project manager applies interpersonal skills to manage stakeholders' expectations. For example:

- Building trust,
- Resolving conflict,
- Active listening, and
- Overcoming resistance to change.

13.3.2.3 Management Skills

The project manager applies management skills to coordinate and harmonize the group toward accomplishing the project objectives. For example:

- Facilitate consensus toward project objectives,

- Influence people to support the project,

- Negotiate agreements to satisfy the project needs, and

- Modify organizational behavior to accept the project outcomes.

13.3.3 Manage Stakeholder Engagement: Outputs

13.3.3.1 Issue Log

Managing stakeholder engagement may result in the development of an issue log. This log is updated as new issues are identified and current issues are resolved.

13.3.3.2 Change Requests

Managing stakeholder engagement may result in a change request to the product or the project. It may also include corrective or preventive actions to the project itself or to the interaction with the impacted stakeholders, as appropriate.

13.3.3.3 Project Management Plan Updates

Elements of the project management plan that may be updated include, but are not limited to, the stakeholder management plan. This plan is updated when new or changed stakeholders requirements are identified. For example, some communications may no longer be necessary, an ineffective communication method may be replaced by another method, or a new communication requirement may be identified. It is also updated as a result of addressing concerns and resolving issues. For example, it may be determined that a stakeholder has additional informational needs.

13.3.3.4 Project Documents Updates

Project documents that may be updated include, but are not limited to, the stakeholder register. This is updated as information on stakeholders change, when new stakeholders are identified, or if registered stakeholders are no longer involved in or impacted by the project, or other updates for specific stakeholders are required.

13.3.3.5 Organizational Process Assets Updates

The organizational process assets that may be updated include, but are not limited to:

- **Stakeholder notifications.** Information may be provided to stakeholders about resolved issues, approved changes, and general project status.

- **Project reports.** Formal and informal project reports describe project status and include lessons learned, issue logs, project closure reports, and outputs from other Knowledge Areas (Sections 4-12).

- **Project presentations.** Information formally or informally provided by the project team to any or all project stakeholders.

- **Project records.** Project records include correspondence, memos, meeting minutes, and other documents describing the project.

- **Feedback from stakeholders.** Information received from stakeholders concerning project operations can be distributed and used to modify or improve future performance of the project.

- **Lessons learned documentation.** Documentation includes the root cause analysis of issues faced, reasoning behind the corrective action chosen, and other types of lessons learned about stakeholder management. Lessons learned are documented and distributed, and become part of the historical database for both the project and the performing organization.

13.4 Control Stakeholder Engagement

Control Stakeholder Engagement is the process of monitoring overall project stakeholder relationships and adjusting strategies and plans for engaging stakeholders. The key benefit of this process is that it will maintain or increase the efficiency and effectiveness of stakeholder engagement activities as the project evolves and its environment changes. The inputs, tools and techniques, and outputs of this process are depicted in Figure 13-10. Figure 13-11 depicts the data flow diagram of the process.

13

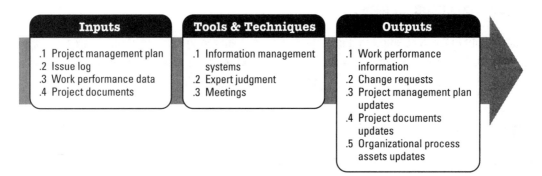

Figure 13-10. Control Stakeholder Engagement: Inputs, Tools & Techniques, and Outputs

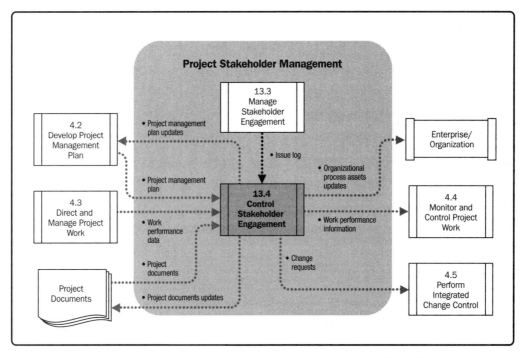

Figure 13-11. Control Stakeholder Engagement: Data Flow Diagram

Stakeholder engagement activities are included in the stakeholder management plan and are executed during the life cycle of the project. Stakeholder engagement should be continuously controlled.

13.4.1 Control Stakeholder Engagement: Inputs

13.4.1.1 Project Management Plan

Described in Section 4.2.3.1. The project management plan is used to develop the stakeholder management plan, as described in Section 13.1.3.1. The information used to Control Stakeholder Engagement includes, but is not limited to:

- The life cycle selected for the project and the processes that will be applied to each phase;
- How work will be executed to accomplish the project objectives;
- How human resources requirements will be met, how roles and responsibilities, reporting relationships, and staffing management will be addressed and structured for the project;
- A change management plan that documents how changes will be monitored and controlled; and
- Needs and techniques for communication among stakeholders.

13.4.1.2 Issue Log

Described in Section 13.3.3.1. The issue log is updated as new issues are identified and current issues are resolved.

13.4.1.3 Work Performance Data

Described in Section 4.3.3.2. The work performance data are the primary observations and measurements identified during activities being performed to carry out the project work. Various measurements on project activities and deliverables are collected during various controlling processes. Data are often viewed as the lowest level of abstraction from which information is derived by other processes.

Examples of work performance data include reported percentage of work completed, technical performance measures, start and finish dates of schedule activities, number of change requests, number of defects, actual costs, actual durations etc.

13.4.1.4 Project Documents

Multiple project documents originating from initiation, planning, execution, or control processes may be used as supporting inputs for controlling stakeholder engagement. These include, but are not limited to:

13

- Project schedule,
- Stakeholder register,
- Issue log,
- Change log, and
- Project communications.

13.4.2 Control Stakeholder Engagement: Tools and Techniques

13.4.2.1 Information Management Systems

An information management system provides a standard tool for the project manager to capture, store, and distribute information to stakeholders about the project cost, schedule progress, and performance. It also allows the project manager to consolidate reports from several systems and facilitate report distribution to the project stakeholders. Examples of distribution formats may include table reporting, spreadsheet analysis, and presentations. Graphical capabilities can be used to create visual representations of project performance information.

13.4.2.2 Expert Judgment

To ensure comprehensive identification and listing of new stakeholders, reassessment of current stakeholders can be performed. Input should be sought from groups or individuals with specialized training or subject matter expertise, such as:

- Senior management;
- Other units or individuals within the organization;
- Identified key stakeholders;
- Project managers who have worked on projects in the same area (directly or through lessons learned);
- Subject matter experts in the business or project area;
- Industry groups and consultants; and
- Professional and technical associations, regulatory bodies, and nongovernmental organizations.

Expert judgment can be obtained through individual consultations (such as one-on-one meetings or interviews) or through a panel format (such as focus groups or surveys).

13.4.2.3 Meetings

Status review meetings are used to exchange and analyze information about stakeholder engagement.

13.4.3 Control Stakeholder Engagement: Outputs

13.4.3.1 Work Performance Information

The work performance information is the performance data collected from various controlling processes, analyzed in context, and integrated based on relationships across areas. Thus work performance data have been transformed into work performance information. Data per se are not used in the decision-making process, because the meaning may be misinterpreted. Information, however, is correlated and contextualized and provides a sound foundation for project decisions.

Work performance information is circulated through communication processes. Examples of performance information are status of deliverables, implementation status for change requests, and forecasted estimates to complete.

13.4.3.2 Change Requests

Analysis of project performance and interactions with stakeholders often generates change requests. These change requests are processed through the Perform Integrated Change Control process (Section 4.5) as follows:

- Recommended corrective actions include changes that bring the expected future performance of the project in line with the project management plan; and

- Recommended preventive actions can reduce the probability of incurring future negative project performance.

13.4.3.3 Project Management Plan Updates

As stakeholders engage with the project the overall effectiveness of the stakeholder management strategy can be evaluated. As needed changes in approach or strategy are identified, affected sections of the project management plan may need to be updated to reflect these changes. Elements of the project management plan that may be updated include, but are not limited to the:

13

- Change management plan,

- Communications management plan,

- Cost management plan,

- Human resource management plan,

- Procurement management plan,

- Quality management plan,

- Requirements management plan,

- Risk management plan,

- Schedule management plan,

- Scope management plan, and

- Stakeholder management plan.

13.4.3.4 Project Documents Updates

Project documents that may be updated include, but are not limited to:

- **Stakeholder register.** This is updated as information on stakeholders change, when new stakeholders are identified, or if registered stakeholders are no longer involved in or impacted by the project, or other updates for specific stakeholders are required.

- **Issue log.** This is updated as new issues are identified and current issues are resolved.

13.4.3.5 Organizational Process Assets Updates

The organizational process assets, which may be updated include, but are not limited to:

- **Stakeholder notifications.** Information may be provided to stakeholders about resolved issues, approved changes, and general project status.

- **Project reports.** Formal and informal project reports describe project status and include lessons learned, issue logs, project closure reports, and outputs from other Knowledge Areas (Sections 4-12).

- **Project presentations.** Information formally or informally provided by the project team to any or all project stakeholders.

- **Project records.** Project records include correspondence, memos, meeting minutes, and other documents describing the project.

- **Feedback from stakeholders.** Information received from stakeholders concerning project operations can be distributed and used to modify or improve future performance of the project.

- **Lessons learned documentation.** Documentation includes the root cause analysis of issues faced, reasoning behind the corrective action chosen, and other types of lessons learned about stakeholder management. Lessons learned are documented and distributed so that they become part of the historical database for both the project and the performing organization.

13

ANNEX A1
THE STANDARD FOR PROJECT MANAGEMENT OF A PROJECT

A project is a temporary endeavor undertaken to create a unique product, service, or result. The temporary nature of projects indicates a definite beginning and end. The end is reached when the project's objectives have been achieved or when the project is terminated because its objectives will not or cannot be met, or when the need for the project no longer exists.

Project management is the application of knowledge, skills, tools, and techniques to project activities to meet project requirements. Project management is accomplished through the appropriate application and integration of logically grouped project management processes.

Managing a project typically includes:

- Identifying requirements;
- Addressing the various needs, concerns, and expectations of the stakeholders as the project is planned and carried out;
- Setting and maintaining active communication with stakeholders; and
- Balancing the competing project constraints, which include, but are not limited to:
    - Scope,
    - Quality,
    - Schedule,
    - Budget,
    - Resources, and
    - Risks.

The specific project circumstances will influence the constraints on which the project manager needs to focus and require effective application and management of appropriate project management processes.

A1.1 What is a Standard?

The International Organization for Standardization (ISO) and others define a standard as a *"Document approved by a recognized body, that provides, for common and repeated use, rules, guidelines, or characteristics for products, processes or services with which compliance are not mandatory."* (ISO 9453) [11]

In October 1998, PMI was accredited as a standards developer by the American National Standards Institute (ANSI). The processes outlined in this Annex, which are described in the *PMBOK® Guide* – Fifth Edition, provide the standard for project management of a project.

A1.2 Framework for this Standard

This standard describes the nature of project management processes in terms of the integration between the processes, their interactions, and the purposes they serve. For this standard, it is assumed that the project, the project manager and the project team are assigned to the performing organization. Project management processes are grouped into five categories known as Project Management Process Groups (or Process Groups):

- **Initiating Process Group.** Those processes performed to define a new project or a new phase of an existing project by obtaining authorization to start the project or phase.

- **Planning Process Group.** Those processes required to establish the scope of the project, refine the objectives, and define the course of action required to attain the objectives that the project was undertaken to achieve.

- **Executing Process Group.** Those processes performed to complete the work defined in the project management plan to satisfy the project specifications.

- **Monitoring and Controlling Process Group.** Those processes required to track, review, and regulate the progress and performance of the project; identify any areas in which changes to the plan are required; and initiate the corresponding changes.

- **Closing Process Group.** Those processes performed to finalize all activities across all Process Groups to formally close the project or phase.

Project Management Process Groups are linked by the outputs they produce. The Process Groups are seldom either discrete or one-time events; they are overlapping activities that occur throughout the project. The output of one process generally becomes an input to another process or is a deliverable of the project, subproject, or project phase. Deliverables at the subproject or project level may be called incremental deliverables. The Planning Process Group provides the Executing Process Group with the project management plan and project documents, and, as the project progresses, it often creates updates to the project management plan and the project documents. Figure A1-1 illustrates how the Process Groups interact and shows the level of overlap at various times. If the project is divided into phases, the Process Groups interact within each phase.

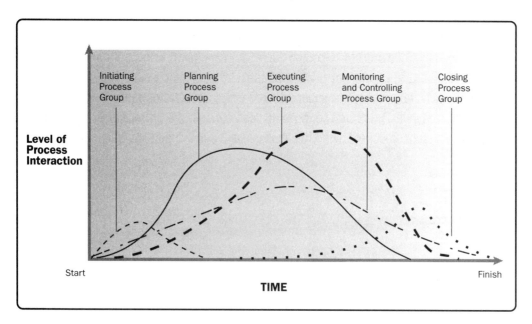

Figure A1-1. Process Group Interactions in a Project

An example of this interaction would be the exit of a design phase, which requires sponsor acceptance of the design document. Once it is available, the design document provides the product description for the Planning and Executing Process Groups in one or more subsequent phases. When a project is divided into phases, the Process Groups are carried out, as appropriate, to effectively drive the project to completion in a controlled manner. In multiphase projects, processes are repeated within each phase until the criteria for phase completion have been satisfied.

A1.3 Project Management Process Groups

The following sections identify and describe the five Project Management Process Groups required for any project. These five Process Groups have clear dependencies and are typically performed in each project and highly interact with one another. These five Process Groups are independent of application areas or industry focus. Individual Process Groups and individual processes are often iterated prior to completing the project and can have interactions within a Process Group and among Process Groups. The nature of these interactions varies from project to project and may or may not be performed in a particular order.

The process flow diagram, Figure A1-2, provides an overall summary of the basic flow and interactions among Process Groups and specific stakeholders. The project management processes are linked by inputs and outputs where the result or outcome of one process becomes the input to another process but not necessarily in the same Process Group. **The Process Groups are not project phases**. In fact, it is possible that all Process Groups could be conducted within a phase. As projects are separated into distinct phases or subcomponents, such as concept development, feasibility study, design, prototype, build, or test, etc., all of the Process Groups would normally be repeated for each phase or subcomponent along the lines explained above and illustrated in Figure A1-2.

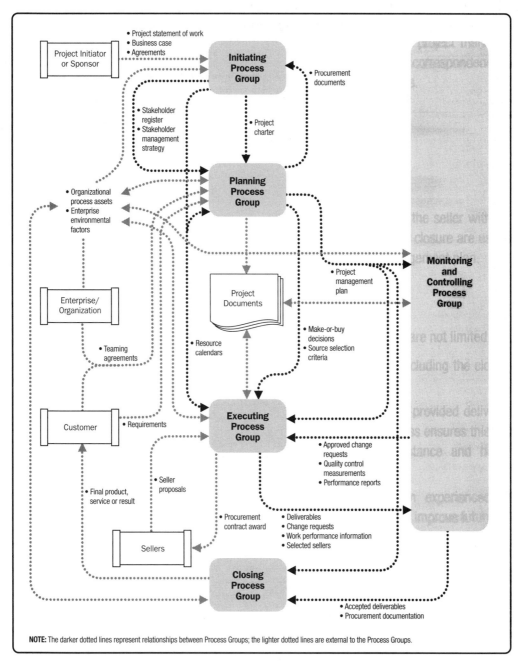

NOTE: The darker dotted lines represent relationships between Process Groups; the lighter dotted lines are external to the Process Groups.

Figure A1-2. Project Management Process Interactions

Table A1-1 reflects the mapping of the 47 project management processes into the 5 Project Management Process Groups and the 10 Project Management Knowledge Areas.

The project management processes are shown in the Process Group in which most of the activity takes place. For example, when a process that normally takes place in the Planning Process Group is updated in the Executing Process Group, it is not considered a new process. The iterative nature of project management means that processes from any group may be used throughout the project life cycle. For example, executing a risk response may trigger the Perform Quantitative Risk Analysis process to evaluate the impact.

Table A1-1. Project Management Process Group and Knowledge Area Mapping

Knowledge Areas	Project Management Process Groups				
	Initiating Process Group	Planning Process Group	Executing Process Group	Monitoring and Controlling Process Group	Closing Process Group
4. Project Integration Management	4.1 Develop Project Charter	4.2 Develop Project Management Plan	4.3 Direct and Manage Project Work	4.4 Monitor and Control Project Work 4.5 Perform Integrated Change Control	4.6 Close Project or Phase
5. Project Scope Management		5.1 Plan Scope Management 5.2 Collect Requirements 5.3 Define Scope 5.4 Create WBS		5.5 Validate Scope 5.6 Control Scope	
6. Project Time Management		6.1 Plan Schedule Management 6.2 Define Activities 6.3 Sequence Activities 6.4 Estimate Activity Resources 6.5 Estimate Activity Durations 6.6 Develop Schedule		6.7 Control Schedule	
7. Project Cost Management		7.1 Plan Cost Management 7.2 Estimate Costs 7.3 Determine Budget		7.4 Control Costs	
8. Project Quality Management		8.1 Plan Quality Management	8.2 Perform Quality Assurance	8.3 Control Quality	
9. Project Human Resource Management		9.1 Plan Human Resource Management	9.2 Acquire Project Team 9.3 Develop Project Team 9.4 Manage Project Team		
10. Project Communications Management		10.1 Plan Communications Management	10.2 Manage Communications	10.3 Control Communications	
11. Project Risk Management		11.1 Plan Risk Management 11.2 Identify Risks 11.3 Perform Qualitative Risk Analysis 11.4 Perform Quantitative Risk Analysis 11.5 Plan Risk Responses		11.6 Control Risks	
12. Project Procurement Management		12.1 Plan Procurement Management	12.2 Conduct Procurements	12.3 Control Procurements	12.4 Close Procurements
13. Project Stakeholder Management	13.1 Identify Stakeholders	13.2 Plan Stakeholder Management	13.3 Manage Stakeholder Engagement	13.4 Control Stakeholder Engagement	

A1.4 Initiating Process Group

The Initiating Process Group consists of those processes performed to define a new project or a new phase of an existing project by obtaining authorization to start the project or phase. Within the Initiating processes, the initial scope is defined and initial financial resources are committed. Internal and external stakeholders who will interact and influence the overall outcome of the project are identified. If not already assigned, the project manager will be selected. This information is captured in the project charter and stakeholder register. When the project charter is approved, the project becomes officially authorized. Although the project management team may help to write the project charter, this standard assumes that business case assessment, approval, and funding are handled external to the project boundaries (Figure A1-3). A project boundary is defined as the point in time that a project or project phase is authorized to its completion. The key purpose of this Process Group is to align the stakeholders' expectations with the project's purpose, give them visibility about the scope and objectives, and show how their participation in the project and it associated phases can ensure that their expectations are achieved. These processes help to set the vision of the project—what is needed to be accomplished.

Large complex projects should be divided into separate phases. In such projects, the Initiating processes are carried out during subsequent phases to validate the decisions made during the original Develop Project Charter and Identify Stakeholders processes. Performing the Initiating processes at the start of each phase helps to keep the project focused on the business need that the project was undertaken to address. The success criteria are verified, and the influence, drivers, and objectives of the project stakeholders are reviewed. A decision is then made as to whether the project should be continued, delayed, or discontinued.

Involving the sponsors, customers, and other stakeholders during initiation creates a shared understanding of success criteria, reduces the overhead of involvement, and generally improves deliverable acceptance, customer, and other stakeholder satisfaction.

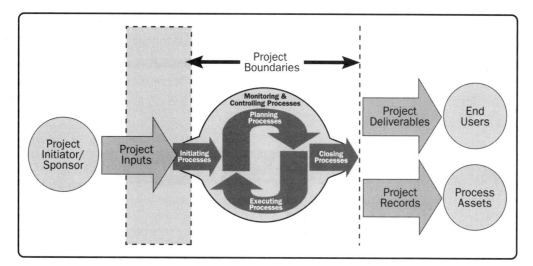

Figure A1-3. Project Boundaries

Initiating processes may be performed at the organizational, program, or portfolio level and would then be outside of the project's level of control. For example, prior to commencing a project, the need for high-level requirements may be documented as part of a larger organizational initiative. A process of evaluating alternatives may be utilized to determine the feasibility of the new undertaking. Clear descriptions of the project objectives may be developed, including the reasons why a specific project is the best alternative to satisfy the requirements. The documentation for this decision may also contain the initial project scope statement, deliverables, project duration, and a forecast of the resources for the organization's investment analysis. As part of the Initiating processes, the project manager is given the authority to apply organizational resources to the subsequent project activities.

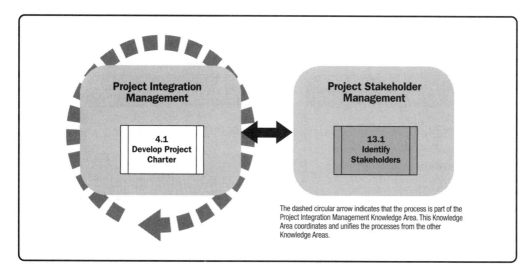

Figure A1-4. Initiating Process Group

A1.4.1 Develop Project Charter

Develop Project Charter is the process of developing a document that formally authorizes the existence of a project and provides the project manager with the authority to apply organizational resources to project activities. The key benefit of this process is a well-defined project start and project boundaries, creation of a formal record of the project, and a direct way for senior management to formally accept and commit to the project. The inputs and outputs for this process are shown in Figure A1-5.

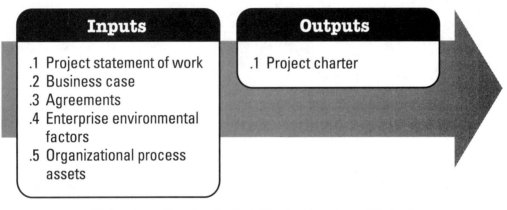

Figure A1-5. Develop Project Charter: Inputs and Outputs

A1.4.2 Identify Stakeholders

Identify Stakeholders is the process of identifying the people, groups, or organizations that could impact or be impacted by a decision, activity, or outcome of the project; and analyzing and documenting relevant information regarding their interests, involvement, interdependencies, influence, and potential impact on project success. The key benefit of this process is that it allows the project manager to identify the appropriate focus for each stakeholder or group of stakeholders. The inputs and outputs of this process are depicted in Figure A1-6.

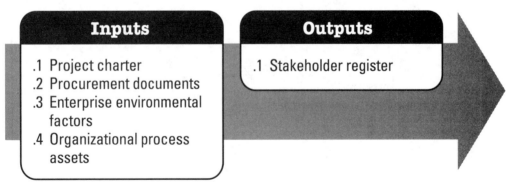

Figure A1-6. Identify Stakeholders: Inputs and Outputs

A1.5 Planning Process Group

The Planning Process Group consists of those processes performed to establish the total scope of the effort, define and refine the objectives, and develop the course of action required to attain those objectives. The Planning processes develop the project management plan and the project documents that will be used to carry out the project. The complex nature of project management may require the use of repeated feedback loops for additional analysis. As more project information or characteristics are gathered and understood, additional planning will likely be required. Significant changes occurring throughout the project life cycle trigger a need to revisit one or more of the planning processes and, possibly, some of the initiating processes. This progressive detailing of the project management plan is called progressive elaboration, indicating that planning and documentation are iterative and ongoing activities. The key benefit of this Process Group is to delineate the strategy and tactics as well as the course of action or a path to successfully complete the project or phase. When the Planning Process Group is well managed, it is much easier to get stakeholder buy-in and engagement. These processes describe how this will be done, resulting in the desired objectives.

The project management plan and project documents developed as outputs from the Planning Process Group will explore all aspects of the scope, time, costs, quality, communications, human resources, risks, procurements, and stakeholder management.

Updates arising from approved changes during the project (generally during Monitoring and Controlling processes and specifically during Direct and Manage Project Work process) may significantly impact parts of the project management plan and the project documents. Updates to these documents provide greater precision with respect to schedule, costs, and resource requirements to meet the defined project scope.

The project team seeks input and encourages involvement from all stakeholders when planning the project and developing the project management plan and project documents. Since the feedback and refinement process cannot continue indefinitely, procedures set by the organization dictate when the initial planning effort ends. These procedures will be affected by the nature of the project, the established project boundaries, appropriate monitoring and controlling activities, as well as the environment in which the project will be performed.

Other interactions among the processes within the Planning Process Group are dependent upon the nature of the project. For example, for some projects there will be little or no identifiable risks until after significant planning has been done. At that time, the team might recognize that the cost and schedule targets are overly aggressive, thus involving considerably more risk than previously understood. The results of the iterations are documented as updates to the project management plan or to various project documents.

The Planning Process Group (Figure A1-7) includes the project management processes identified in Figures A1-8 through A1-31 (see Sections A1.5.1 through A1.5.24).

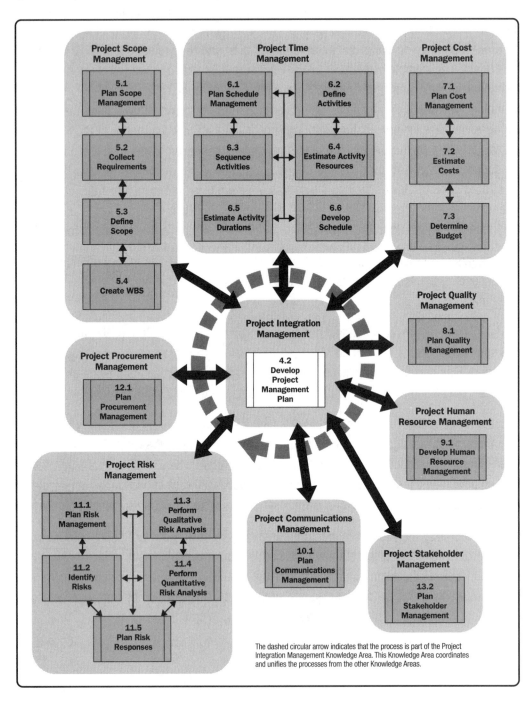

Figure A1-7. Planning Process Group

A1.5.1 Develop Project Management Plan

Develop Project Management Plan is the process of defining, preparing, and coordinating all subsidiary plans and integrating them into a comprehensive project management plan. The key benefit of this process is a central document that defines the basis of all project work. The inputs and outputs for this process are depicted in Figure A1-8.

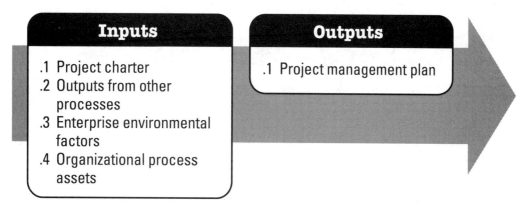

Figure A1-8. Develop Project Management Plan: Inputs and Outputs

A1.5.2 Plan Scope Management

Plan Scope Management is the process of creating a scope management plan that documents how the project scope will be defined, validated, and controlled. The key benefit of this process is that it provides guidance and direction on how scope will be managed throughout the project. The inputs and outputs of this process are depicted in Figure A1-9.

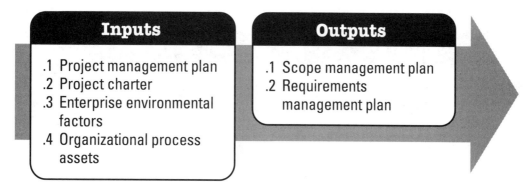

Figure A1-9. Plan Scope Management: Inputs and Outputs

A1.5.3 Collect Requirements

Collect Requirements is the process of determining, documenting, and managing stakeholder needs and requirements to meet project objectives. The key benefit of this process is that it provides the basis for defining and managing the project scope including product scope. The inputs and outputs of this process are depicted in Figure A1-10.

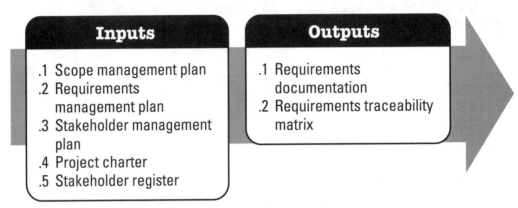

Figure A1-10. Collect Requirements: Inputs and Outputs

A1.5.4 Define Scope

Define Scope is the process of developing a detailed description of the project and product. The key benefit of this process is that it describes the project, service, or result boundaries by defining which of the requirements collected will be included in and excluded from the project scope. The inputs and outputs of this process are depicted in Figure A1-11.

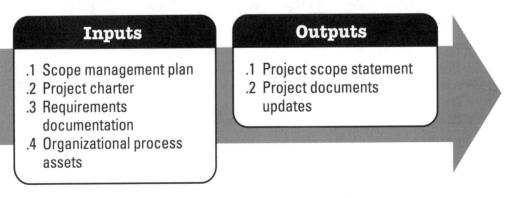

Figure A1-11. Define Scope: Inputs and Outputs

A1.5.5 Create WBS

Create WBS is the process of subdividing project deliverables and project work into smaller, more manageable components. The key benefit of this process is that it provides a structured vision of what has to be delivered. The inputs and outputs of this process are depicted in Figure A1-12.

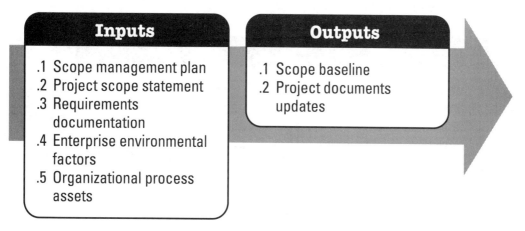

Figure A1-12. Create WBS: Inputs and Outputs

A1.5.6 Plan Schedule Management

Plan Schedule Management is the process of establishing the policies, procedures, and documentation for planning, developing, managing, executing, and controlling the project schedule. The key benefit of this process is that it provides guidance and direction on how the project schedule will be managed throughout the project. The inputs and outputs of this process are depicted in Figure A1-13.

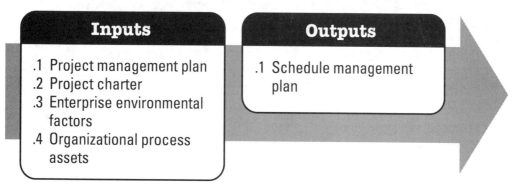

Figure A1-13. Plan Schedule Management: Inputs and Outputs

A1.5.7 Define Activities

Define Activities is the process of identifying and documenting the specific actions to be performed to produce the project deliverables. The key benefit of this process is to break down work packages into activities that provide a basis for estimating, scheduling, executing, monitoring, and controlling the project work. The inputs and outputs of this process are depicted in Figure A1-14.

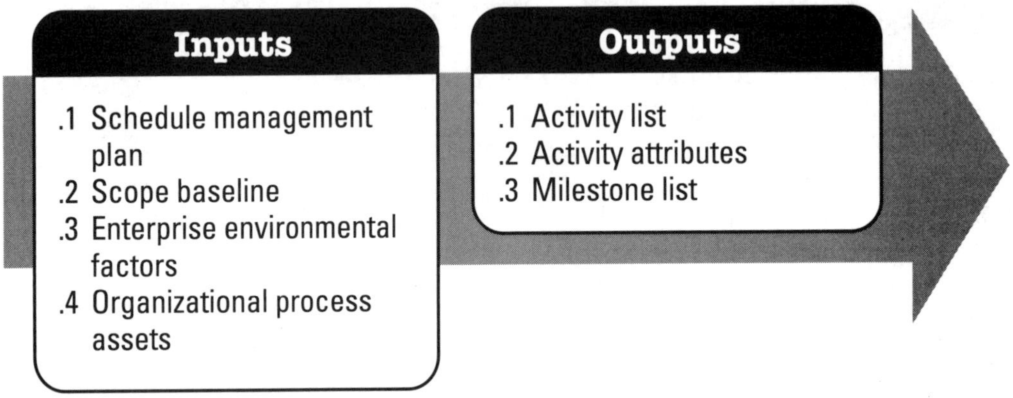

Inputs

.1 Schedule management plan
.2 Scope baseline
.3 Enterprise environmental factors
.4 Organizational process assets

Outputs

.1 Activity list
.2 Activity attributes
.3 Milestone list

Figure A1-14. Define Activities: Inputs and Outputs

A1.5.8 Sequence Activities

Sequence Activities is the process of identifying and documenting relationships among the project activities. The key benefit of this process is that it defines the logical sequence of work to obtain the greatest efficiency given all project constraints. The inputs and outputs of this process are depicted in Figure A1-15.

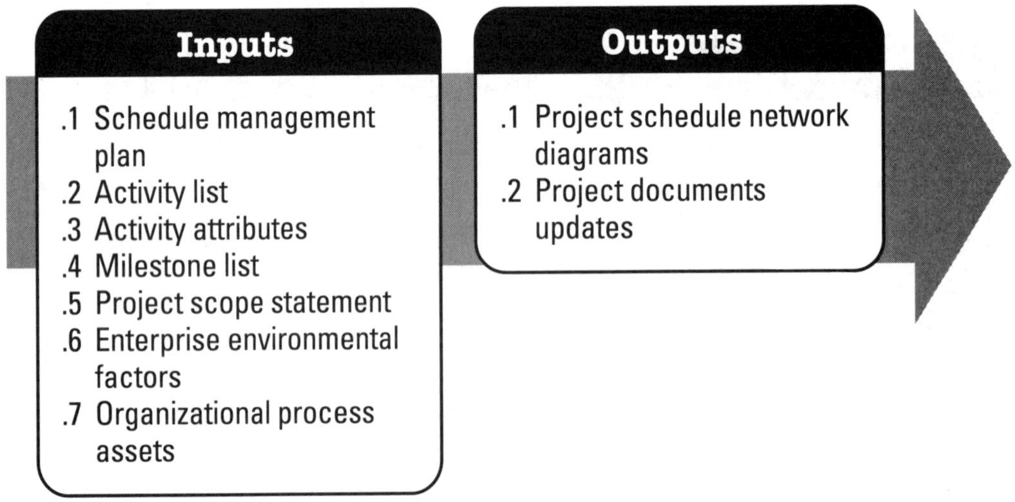

Inputs

.1 Schedule management plan
.2 Activity list
.3 Activity attributes
.4 Milestone list
.5 Project scope statement
.6 Enterprise environmental factors
.7 Organizational process assets

Outputs

.1 Project schedule network diagrams
.2 Project documents updates

Figure A1-15. Sequence Activities: Inputs and Outputs

A1.5.9 Estimate Activity Resources

Estimate Activity Resources is the process of estimating the type and quantities of material, human resources, equipment, or supplies required to perform each activity. The key benefit of this process is that it identifies the type, quantity, and characteristics of resources required to complete the activity which allows more accurate cost and duration estimates. The inputs and outputs of this process are depicted in Figure A1-16.

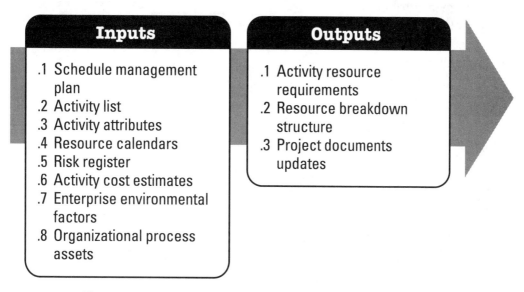

Figure A1-16. Estimate Activity Resources: Inputs and Outputs

A1.5.10 Estimate Activity Durations

Estimate Activity Durations is the process of estimating the number of work periods needed to complete individual activities with estimated resources. The key benefit of this process is that it provides the amount of time each activity will take to complete, which is a major input into the Develop Schedule process. The inputs and outputs of this process are depicted in Figure A1-17.

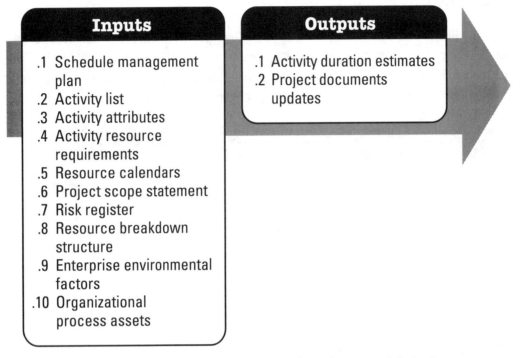

Figure A1-17. Estimate Activity Durations: Inputs and Outputs

A1.5.11 Develop Schedule

Develop Schedule is the process of analyzing activity sequences, durations, resource requirements, and schedule constraints to create the project schedule model. The key benefit of this process is that by entering schedule activities, durations, resources, resource availabilities, and logical relationships into the scheduling tool, it generates a schedule model with planned dates for completing project activities. The inputs and outputs of this process are depicted in Figure A1-18.

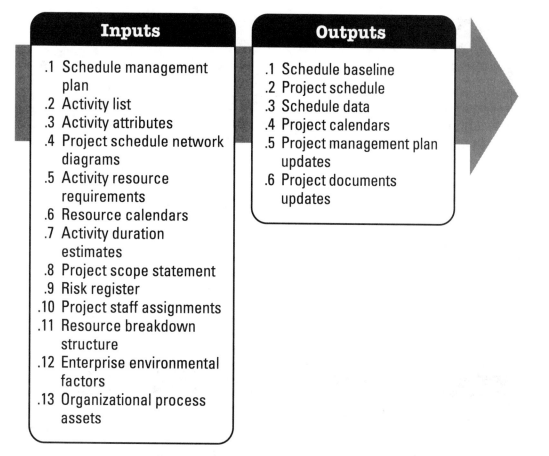

Inputs

- .1 Schedule management plan
- .2 Activity list
- .3 Activity attributes
- .4 Project schedule network diagrams
- .5 Activity resource requirements
- .6 Resource calendars
- .7 Activity duration estimates
- .8 Project scope statement
- .9 Risk register
- .10 Project staff assignments
- .11 Resource breakdown structure
- .12 Enterprise environmental factors
- .13 Organizational process assets

Outputs

- .1 Schedule baseline
- .2 Project schedule
- .3 Schedule data
- .4 Project calendars
- .5 Project management plan updates
- .6 Project documents updates

Figure A1-18. Develop Schedule: Inputs and Outputs

A1.5.12 Plan Cost Management

Plan Cost Management is the process that establishes the policies, procedures, and documentation for planning, managing, expending, and controlling project costs. The key benefit of this process is that it provides guidance and direction on how the project costs will be managed throughout the project. The inputs and outputs of this process are depicted in Figure A1-19.

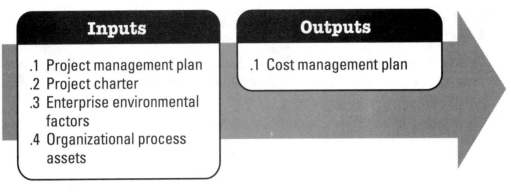

Figure A1-19. Plan Cost Management: Inputs and Outputs

A1.5.13 Estimate Costs

Estimate Costs is the process of developing an approximation of the monetary resources needed to complete project activities. The key benefit of this process is that it determines the amount of cost required to complete project work. The inputs and outputs of this process are depicted in Figure A1-20.

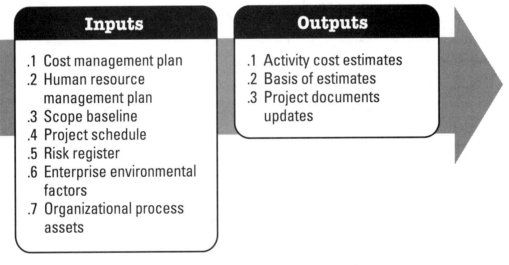

Figure A1-20. Estimate Costs: Inputs and Outputs

A1.5.14 Determine Budget

Determine Budget is the process of aggregating the estimated costs of individual activities or work packages to establish an authorized cost baseline. The key benefit of this process is that it determines the cost baseline against which project performance can be monitored and controlled. The inputs and outputs of this process are depicted in Figure A1-21.

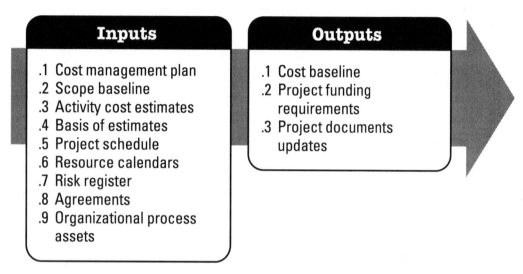

Figure A1-21. Determine Budget: Inputs and Outputs

A1.5.15 Plan Quality Management

Plan Quality Management is the process of identifying quality requirements and/or standards for the project and its deliverables, and documenting how the project will demonstrate compliance with relevant quality requirements. The key benefit of this process is that it provides guidance and direction on how quality will be managed and validated throughout the project. The input and outputs of this process are depicted in Figure A1-22.

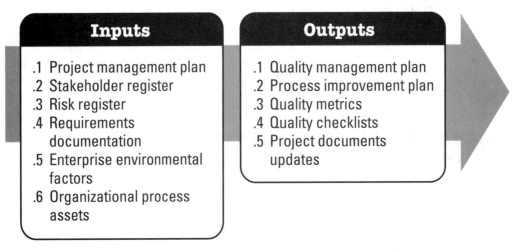

Figure A1-22. Plan Quality Management: Inputs and Outputs

A1.5.16 Plan Human Resource Management

Plan Human Resource Management is the process of identifying and documenting project roles, responsibilities, required skills, reporting relationships, and creating a staffing management plan. The key benefit of this process is that it establishes project roles and responsibilities, project organization charts, and the staffing management plan including the timetable for staff acquisition and release. The input and outputs of this process are depicted in Figure A1-23.

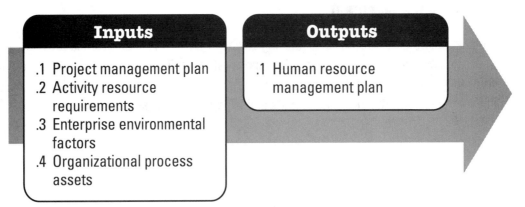

Figure A1-23. Plan Human Resource Management: Inputs and Outputs

A1.5.17 Plan Communications Management

Plan Communications Management is the process of developing an appropriate approach and plan for project communications based on stakeholder's information needs and requirements, and available organizational assets. The key benefit of this process is that it identifies and documents the approach to communicate most effectively and efficiently with stakeholders. The inputs and outputs of this process are depicted in Figure A1-24.

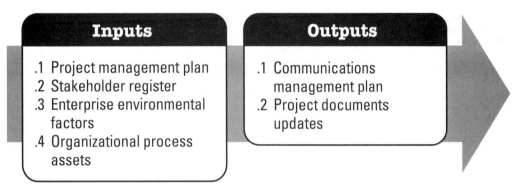

Figure A1-24. Plan Communications Management: Inputs and Outputs

A1.5.18 Plan Risk Management

Plan Risk Management is the process of defining how to conduct risk management activities for a project. The key benefit of this process is that it ensures that the degree, type, and visibility of risk management are commensurate with both the risks and the importance of the project to the organization. The input and outputs of this process are depicted in Figure A1-25.

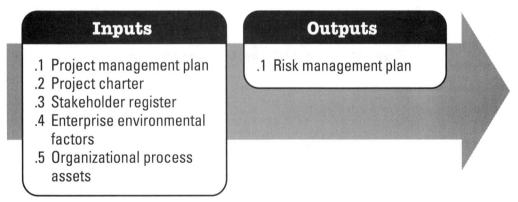

Figure A1-25. Plan Risk Management: Inputs and Outputs

A1.5.19 Identify Risks

Identify Risks is the process of determining which risks may affect the project and documenting their characteristics. The key benefit of this process is the documentation of existing risks and the knowledge and ability it provides to the project team to anticipate events. The inputs and outputs of this process are depicted in Figure A1-26.

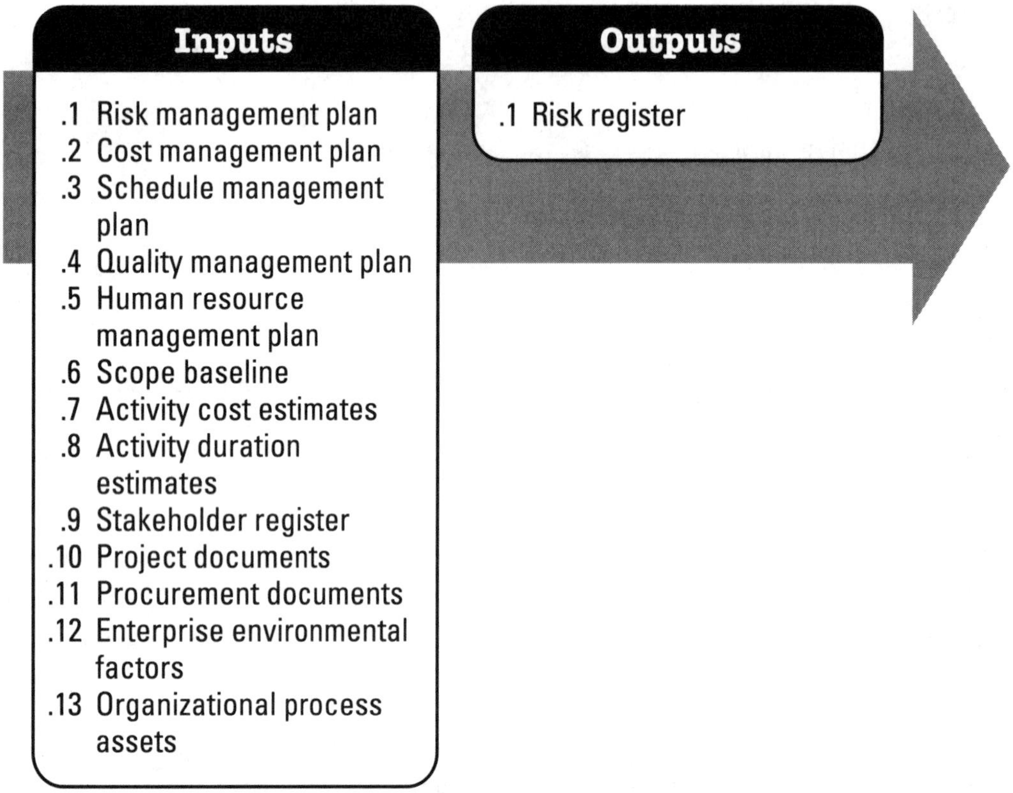

Inputs

.1 Risk management plan
.2 Cost management plan
.3 Schedule management plan
.4 Quality management plan
.5 Human resource management plan
.6 Scope baseline
.7 Activity cost estimates
.8 Activity duration estimates
.9 Stakeholder register
.10 Project documents
.11 Procurement documents
.12 Enterprise environmental factors
.13 Organizational process assets

Outputs

.1 Risk register

Figure A1-26. Identify Risks: Inputs and Outputs

A1.5.20 Perform Qualitative Risk Analysis

Perform Qualitative Risk Analysis is the process of prioritizing risks for further analysis or action by assessing and combining their probability of occurrence and impact. The key benefit of this process is that it enables project managers to reduce the level of uncertainty and to focus on high-priority risks. The inputs and outputs of this process are depicted in Figure A1-27.

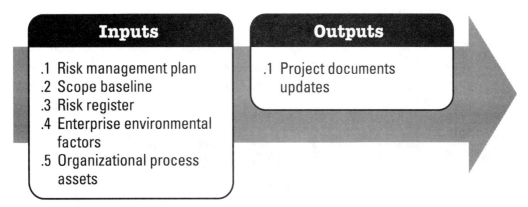

Figure A1-27. Perform Qualitative Risk Analysis: Inputs and Outputs

A1.5.21 Perform Quantitative Risk Analysis

Perform Quantitative Risk Analysis is the process of numerically analyzing the effect of identified risks on overall project objectives. The key benefit of this process is that it produces quantitative risk information to support decision making in order to reduce project uncertainty. The inputs and outputs of this process are depicted in Figure A1-28.

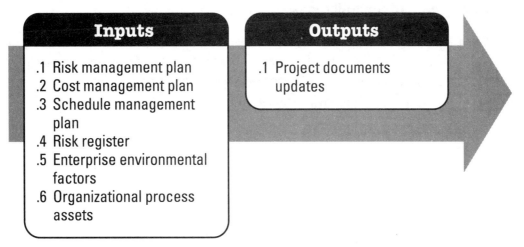

Figure A1-28. Perform Quantitative Risk Analysis: Inputs and Outputs

A1.5.22 Plan Risk Responses

Plan Risk Responses is the process of developing options and actions to enhance opportunities and to reduce threats to project objectives. The key benefit of this process is that it addresses the risks by their priority, inserting resources and activities into the budget, schedule and project management plan as needed. The inputs and outputs of this process are depicted in Figure A1-29.

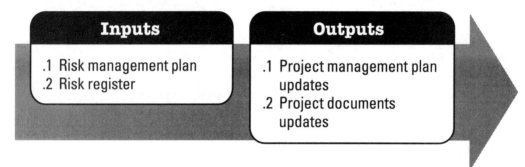

Figure A1-29. Plan Risk Responses: Inputs and Outputs

A1.5.23 Plan Procurement Management

Plan Procurement Management is the process of documenting project procurement decisions, specifying the approach, and identifying potential sellers. The key benefit of this process is that it determines whether to acquire outside support, and if so, what to acquire, how to acquire it, how much is needed, and when to acquire it. The inputs and outputs of this process are depicted in Figure A1-30.

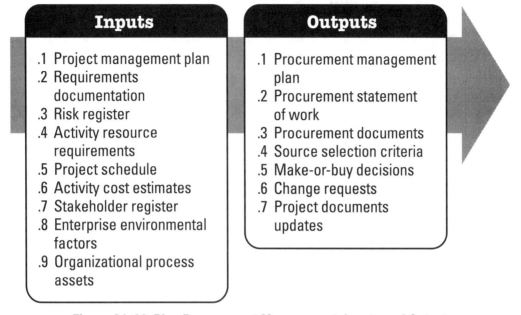

Figure A1-30. Plan Procurement Management: Inputs and Outputs

A1.5.24 Plan Stakeholder Management

Plan Stakeholder Management is the process of developing appropriate management strategies to effectively engage stakeholders throughout the project life cycle, based on the analysis of their needs, interests, and potential impact on project success. The key benefit of this process is that it provides a clear, actionable plan to interact with project stakeholders to support the project's interests. The inputs and outputs of this process are depicted in Figure A1-31.

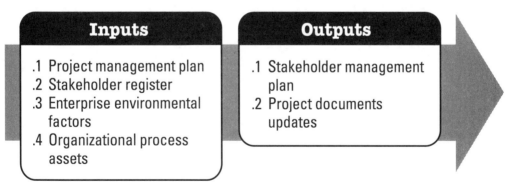

Figure A1-31. Plan Stakeholder Management: Inputs and Outputs

A1.6 Executing Process Group

The Executing Process Group consists of those processes performed to complete the work defined in the project management plan to satisfy the project specifications. This Process Group involves coordinating people and resources, managing stakeholder expectations, as well as integrating and performing the activities of the project in accordance with the project management plan (Figure A1-32).

During project execution, results may require planning updates and rebaselining. This can include changes to expected activity durations, changes in resource productivity and availability, and unanticipated risks. Such variances may affect the project management plan or project documents and may require detailed analysis and development of appropriate project management responses. The results of the analysis can trigger change requests that, if approved, may modify the project management plan or other project documents and possibly require establishing new baselines. A large portion of the project's budget will be expended in performing the Executing Process Group processes. The Executing Process Group (Figure A1-32) includes the project management processes identified in Figures A1-33 through A1-40 (see Sections A1.6.1 through A1.6.8).

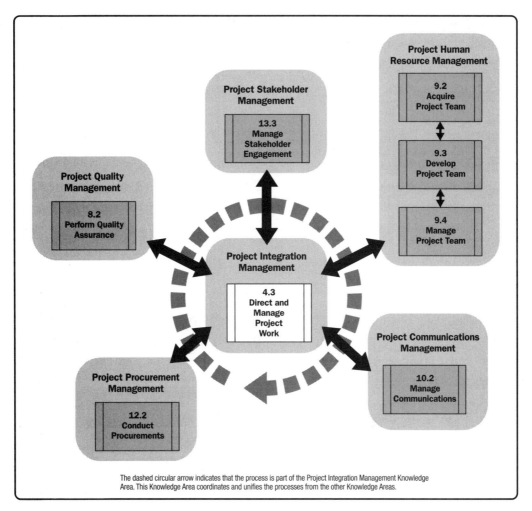

The dashed circular arrow indicates that the process is part of the Project Integration Management Knowledge Area. This Knowledge Area coordinates and unifies the processes from the other Knowledge Areas.

Figure A1-32. Executing Process Group

A1.6.1 Direct and Manage Project Work

Direct and Manage Project Work is the process of leading and performing the work defined in the project management plan and implementing approved changes to achieve the project's objectives. The key benefit of this process is that it provides overall management of the project work. The inputs and outputs of this process are depicted in Figure A1-33.

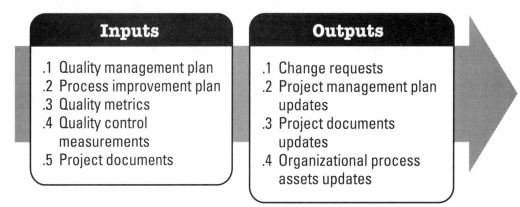

Inputs

.1 Project management plan
.2 Approved change requests
.3 Enterprise environmental factors
.4 Organizational process assets

Outputs

.1 Deliverables
.2 Work performance data
.3 Change requests
.4 Project management plan updates
.5 Project documents updates

Figure A1-33. Direct and Manage Project Work: Inputs and Outputs

A1.6.2 Perform Quality Assurance

Perform Quality Assurance is the process of auditing the quality requirements and the results from quality control measurements to ensure that appropriate quality standards and operational definitions are used. The key benefit of this process is it facilitates the improvement of quality processes. The input and outputs of this process are depicted in Figure A1-34.

Inputs

.1 Quality management plan
.2 Process improvement plan
.3 Quality metrics
.4 Quality control measurements
.5 Project documents

Outputs

.1 Change requests
.2 Project management plan updates
.3 Project documents updates
.4 Organizational process assets updates

Figure A1-34. Perform Quality Assurance: Inputs and Outputs

A1.6.3 Acquire Project Team

Acquire Project Team is the process of confirming human resource availability and obtaining the team necessary to complete project activities. The key benefit of this process consists of outlining and guiding the team selection and responsibility assignment to obtain a successful team. The inputs and outputs of this process are depicted in Figure A1-35.

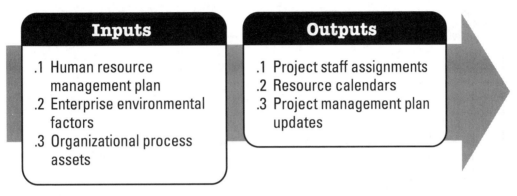

Figure A1-35. Acquire Project Team: Inputs and Outputs

A1.6.4 Develop Project Team

Develop Project Team is the process of improving competencies, team member interaction, and overall team environment to enhance project performance. The key benefit of this process is that it results in improved teamwork, enhanced people skills and competencies, motivated employees, reduced staff turnover rates, and improved overall project performance. The inputs and outputs of this process are depicted in Figure A1-36.

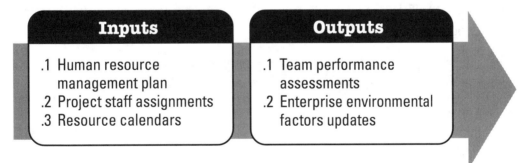

Figure A1-36. Develop Project Team: Inputs and Outputs

A1.6.5 Manage Project Team

Manage Project Team is the process of tracking team member performance, providing feedback, resolving issues, and managing team changes to optimize project performance. The key benefit of this process is that it influences team behavior, manages conflict, resolves issues, and appraises team member performance. The inputs and outputs of this process are depicted in Figure A1-37.

Inputs	Outputs
.1 Human resource management plan	.1 Change requests
.2 Project staff assignments	.2 Project management plan updates
.3 Team performance assessments	.3 Project documents updates
.4 Issue log	.4 Enterprise environmental factors updates
.5 Work performance reports	.5 Organizational process assets updates
.6 Organizational process assets	

Figure A1-37. Manage Project Team: Inputs and Outputs

A1.6.6 Manage Communications

Manage Communications is the process of creating, collecting, distributing, storing, retrieving, and the ultimate disposition of project information in accordance with the communications management plan. The key benefit of this process is that it enables an efficient and effective communications flow between project stakeholders. The inputs and outputs of this process are depicted in Figure A1-38.

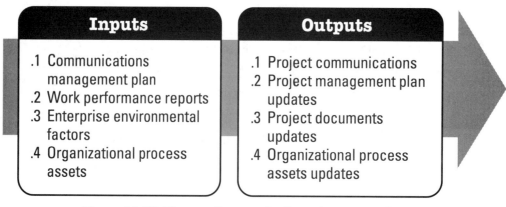

Inputs	Outputs
.1 Communications management plan	.1 Project communications
.2 Work performance reports	.2 Project management plan updates
.3 Enterprise environmental factors	.3 Project documents updates
.4 Organizational process assets	.4 Organizational process assets updates

Figure A1-38. Manage Communications: Inputs and Outputs

A1.6.7 Conduct Procurements

Conduct Procurements is the process of obtaining seller responses, selecting a seller, and awarding a contract. The key benefit of this process is that it provides alignment of internal and external stakeholder expectations through established agreements. The inputs and outputs of this process are depicted in Figure A1-39.

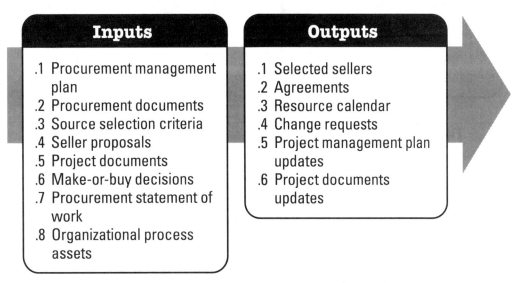

Inputs	Outputs
.1 Procurement management plan	.1 Selected sellers
.2 Procurement documents	.2 Agreements
.3 Source selection criteria	.3 Resource calendar
.4 Seller proposals	.4 Change requests
.5 Project documents	.5 Project management plan updates
.6 Make-or-buy decisions	.6 Project documents updates
.7 Procurement statement of work	
.8 Organizational process assets	

Figure A1-39. Conduct Procurements: Inputs and Outputs

A1.6.8 Manage Stakeholder Engagement

Manage Stakeholder Engagement is the process of communicating and working with stakeholders to meet their needs/expectations, address issues as they occur, and foster appropriate stakeholder engagement in project activities throughout the project life cycle. The key benefit of this process is that it allows the project manager to increase support and minimize resistance from stakeholders, significantly increasing the chances to achieve project success. The inputs and outputs of this process are depicted in Figure A1-40.

A1.7.1 Monitor and Control Project Work

Monitor and Control Project Work is the process of tracking, reviewing, and reporting the progress to meet the performance objectives defined in the project management plan. The key benefit of this process is that it allows stakeholders to understand the current state of the project; the steps taken; and budget, schedule, and scope forecasts. The inputs and outputs for this process are depicted in Figure A1-42.

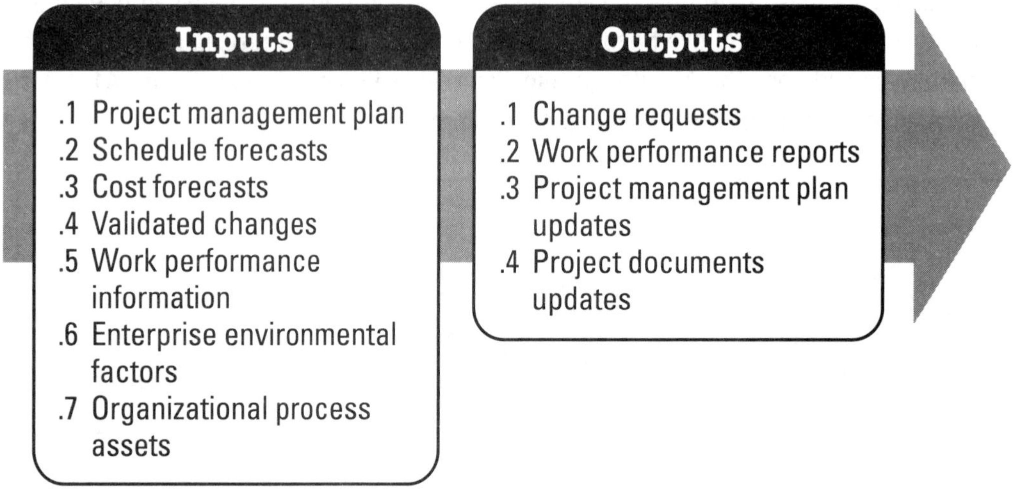

Inputs

.1 Project management plan
.2 Schedule forecasts
.3 Cost forecasts
.4 Validated changes
.5 Work performance information
.6 Enterprise environmental factors
.7 Organizational process assets

Outputs

.1 Change requests
.2 Work performance reports
.3 Project management plan updates
.4 Project documents updates

Figure A1-42. Monitor and Control Project Work: Inputs and Outputs

A1.7.2 Perform Integrated Change Control

Perform Integrated Change Control is the process of reviewing all change requests; approving changes and managing changes to deliverables, organizational process assets, project documents, and the project management plan; and communicating their disposition. It reviews all requests for changes or modifications to project documents, deliverables, baselines or the project management plan, and approves or rejects the changes. The key benefit of this process is that it allows for documented changes within the project to be considered in an integrated fashion while reducing project risk, which often arises from changes made without consideration to the overall project objectives or plans. The inputs and outputs of this process are depicted in Figure A1-43.

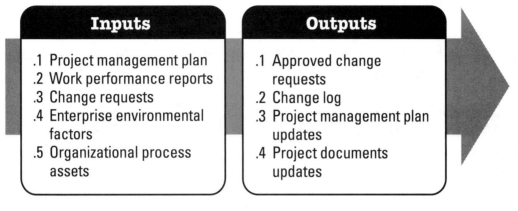

Inputs

.1 Project management plan
.2 Work performance reports
.3 Change requests
.4 Enterprise environmental factors
.5 Organizational process assets

Outputs

.1 Approved change requests
.2 Change log
.3 Project management plan updates
.4 Project documents updates

Figure A1-43. Perform Integrated Change Control: Inputs and Outputs

A1.7.3 Validate Scope

Validate Scope is the process of formalizing acceptance of the completed project deliverables. The key benefit of this process is that it brings objectivity to the acceptance process and increases the chance of final product, service, or result acceptance by validating each deliverable. The inputs and outputs of this process are depicted in Figure A1-44.

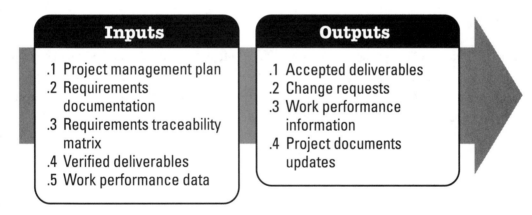

Inputs

.1 Project management plan
.2 Requirements documentation
.3 Requirements traceability matrix
.4 Verified deliverables
.5 Work performance data

Outputs

.1 Accepted deliverables
.2 Change requests
.3 Work performance information
.4 Project documents updates

Figure A1-44. Validate Scope: Inputs and Outputs

A1.7.4 Control Scope

Control Scope is the process of monitoring the status of the project and product scope and managing changes to the scope baseline. The key benefit of this process is that it allows the scope baseline to be maintained throughout the project. The inputs and outputs of this process are depicted in Figure A1-45.

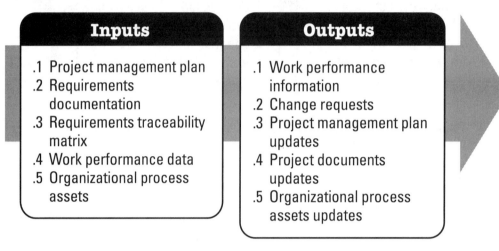

Inputs

.1 Project management plan
.2 Requirements documentation
.3 Requirements traceability matrix
.4 Work performance data
.5 Organizational process assets

Outputs

.1 Work performance information
.2 Change requests
.3 Project management plan updates
.4 Project documents updates
.5 Organizational process assets updates

Figure A1-45. Control Scope: Inputs and Outputs

A1.7.5 Control Schedule

Control Schedule is the process of monitoring the status of project activities to update project progress and manage changes to the schedule baseline to achieve the plan. The key benefit of this process is that it provides the means to recognize deviation from the plan and take corrective and preventive actions and thus minimize risk. The inputs and outputs of this process are depicted in Figure A1-46.

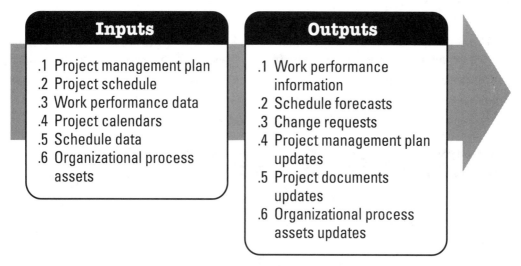

Figure A1-46. Control Schedule: Inputs and Outputs

A1.7.6 Control Costs

Control Costs is the process of monitoring the status of the project to update the project costs and managing changes to the cost baseline. The key benefit of this process is that it provides the means to recognize variance from the plan in order to take corrective action and minimize risk. The inputs and outputs of this process are depicted in Figure A1-47.

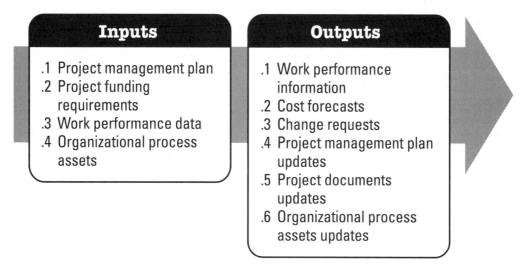

Figure A1-47. Control Costs: Inputs and Outputs

A1.7.7 Control Quality

Control Quality is the process of monitoring and recording results of executing the quality activities to assess performance and recommend necessary changes. The key benefits of this process include: (1) identifying the causes of poor process or product quality and recommending and/or taking action to eliminate them; and (2) validating that project deliverables and work meet the requirements specified by key stakeholders necessary for final acceptance. The inputs and outputs of this process are depicted in Figure A1-48.

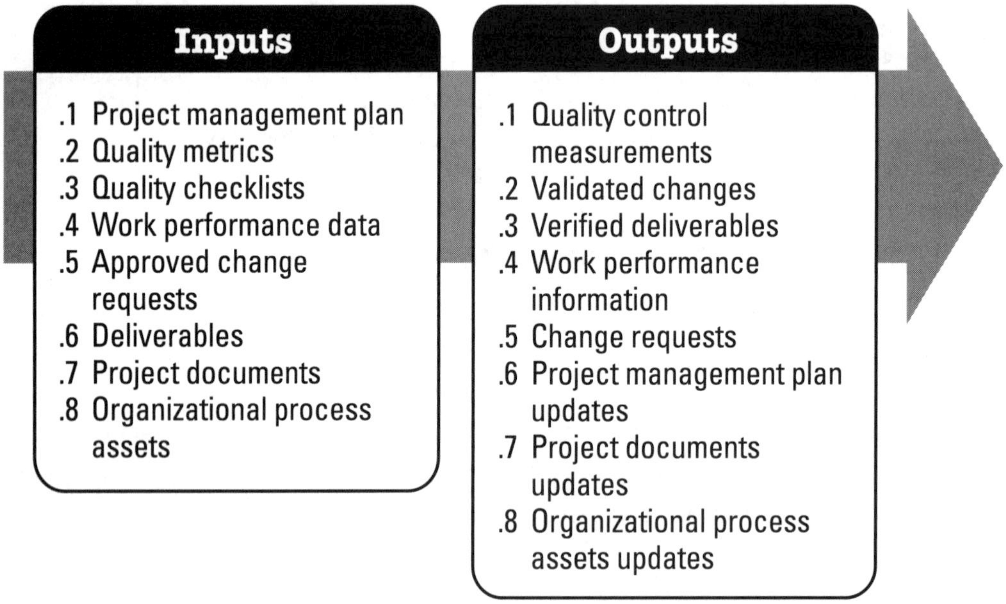

Inputs	Outputs
.1 Project management plan .2 Quality metrics .3 Quality checklists .4 Work performance data .5 Approved change requests .6 Deliverables .7 Project documents .8 Organizational process assets	.1 Quality control measurements .2 Validated changes .3 Verified deliverables .4 Work performance information .5 Change requests .6 Project management plan updates .7 Project documents updates .8 Organizational process assets updates

Figure A1-48. Control Quality: Inputs and Outputs

A1.7.8 Control Communications

Control Communications is the process of monitoring and controlling communications throughout the entire project life cycle to ensure the information needs of the project stakeholders are met. The key benefit of this process is that it ensures an optimal information flow among all communication participants at any moment in time. The inputs and outputs of this process are depicted in Figure A1-49.

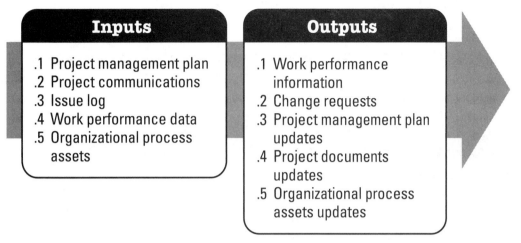

Figure A1-49. Control Communications: Inputs and Outputs

A1.7.9 Control Risks

Control Risks is the process of implementing risk response plans, tracking identified risks, monitoring residual risks, identifying new risks, and evaluating risk process effectiveness throughout the project. The key benefit of this process is that it improves efficiency of the risk approach throughout the project life cycle to continuously optimize risk responses. The inputs and outputs of this process are depicted in Figure A1-50.

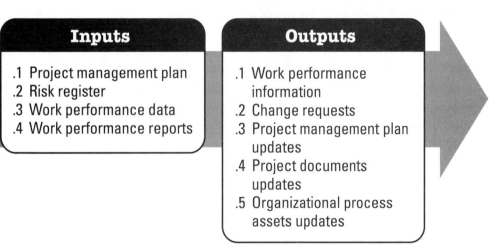

Figure A1-50. Control Risks: Inputs and Outputs

A1.7.10 Control Procurements

Control Procurements is the process of managing procurement relationships, monitoring contract performance, and making changes and corrections to contracts as appropriate. The key benefit of this process is that it ensures that both the seller's and buyer's performance meets procurement requirements according to the terms of the legal agreement. The inputs and outputs of this process are depicted in Figure A1-51.

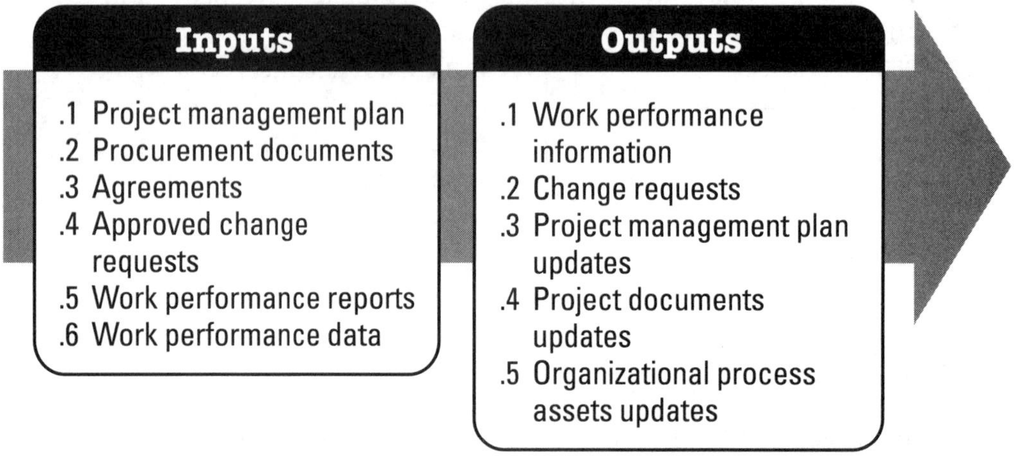

Inputs	Outputs
.1 Project management plan .2 Procurement documents .3 Agreements .4 Approved change requests .5 Work performance reports .6 Work performance data	.1 Work performance information .2 Change requests .3 Project management plan updates .4 Project documents updates .5 Organizational process assets updates

Figure A1-51. Control Procurements: Inputs and Outputs

A1.7.11 Control Stakeholder Engagement

Control Stakeholder Engagement is the process of monitoring overall project stakeholder relationships and adjusting strategies and plans for engaging stakeholders. The key benefit of this process is that it will maintain or increase the efficiency and effectiveness of stakeholder engagement activities as the project evolves and its environment changes. The inputs and outputs of this process are depicted in Figure A1-52.

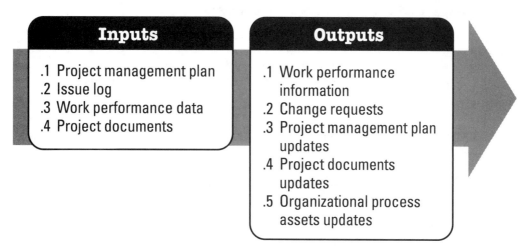

Figure A1-52. Control Stakeholder Engagement: Inputs and Outputs

A1.8 Closing Process Group

The Closing Process Group consists of those processes performed to conclude all activities across all Project Management Process Groups to formally complete the project, phase, or contractual obligations. This Process Group, when completed, verifies that the defined processes are completed within all the Process Groups to close the project or a project phase, as appropriate, and formally establishes that the project or project phase is complete.

This Process Group also formally establishes the premature closure of the project. Prematurely closed projects may include, for example: aborted projects, cancelled projects, and projects in a critical situation. In specific cases, when some contracts cannot be formally closed (e.g. claims, ending clauses etc.) or some activities are to be transferred to other organizational units, specific hand-over procedures may be arranged and finalized.

At project or phase closure, the following may occur:

- Obtain acceptance by the customer or sponsor to formally close the project or phase,
- Conduct post-project or phase-end review,
- Record impacts of tailoring to any process,
- Document lessons learned,

- Apply appropriate updates to organizational process assets,

- Archive all relevant project documents in the project management information system (PMIS) to be used as historical data,

- Close out all procurements activities ensuring termination of all relevant agreements, and

- Perform team members' assessment and release project resources.

The Closing Process Group (Figure A1-53) includes the following project management processes (See Sections A1.8.1 and A1.8.2):

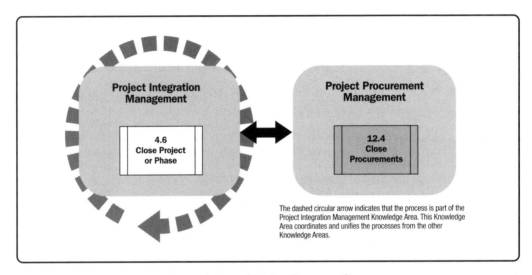

Figure A1-53. Closing Process Group

A1.8.1 Close Project or Phase

Close Project or Phase is the process of finalizing all activities across all of the Project Management Process Groups to formally complete the project or phase. The key benefit of this process is that it provides lessons learned, the formal ending of project work, and the release of organization resources to pursue new endeavors. The inputs and outputs of this process are depicted in Figure A1-54.

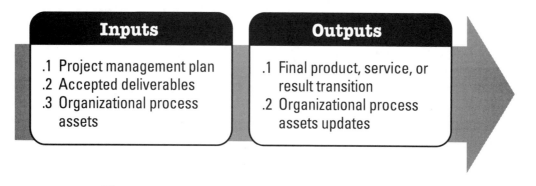

Figure A1-54. Close Project or Phase: Inputs and Outputs

A1.8.2 Close Procurements

Close Procurements is the process of completing each procurement. The key benefit of this process is that it documents agreements and related documentation for future reference. The inputs and outputs of this process are depicted in Figure A1-55.

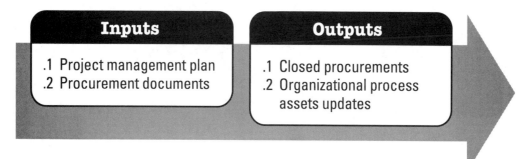

Figure A1-55. Close Procurements: Inputs and Outputs

APPENDIX X1
FIFTH EDITION CHANGES

The purpose of this appendix is to give a detailed explanation of the changes made to *A Guide to the Project Management Body of Knowledge (PMBOK® Guide)*—Fourth Edition to create the *PMBOK® Guide*—Fifth Edition.

X1.1 Scope of Update

The approved scope for the *PMBOK® Guide* – Fifth Edition explicitly states:

- Comments and feedback, both deferred during the development of the *PMBOK® Guide* – Fourth Edition and received by PMI since its development, will be reviewed and determined whether material will be included or excluded in the new edition.

- Review all text and graphics in the document to make sure the information is accurate, clear, complete and relevant, revising as necessary.

- Review, interpret, and ensure appropriate alignment with ISO 21500 [12] in the development of the standard.

- Ensure harmonization with any other relevant PMI standards.

- Consider project management role delineation study results, as appropriate.

- Reposition Section 3 (The Standard for Project Management) as a stand-alone, ANSI-approved standard included within the Fifth Edition as an Appendix or attachment.

- Standard is written for project management practitioners and other stakeholders of the project management profession.

- Standard describes the principles and processes that shape the practices that are unique to projects.

- Standard ensures that any terminology contained within the *PMI Lexicon* is represented consistently and identically in the standard.

With that directive in mind, the update team adopted an approach aimed at achieving a greater degree of consistency and clarity by refining the processes, standardizing inputs and outputs where possible, and implementing a global approach for documenting the inputs and outputs.

Along with a focus on consistency and clarity, the update team worked to complete the requirements for factoring feedback received for the *PMBOK® Guide – Fourth Edition*, and ensure alignment and harmonization with relevant PMI standards, ISO 21500, *PMI Lexicon of Project Management Terms*, and the PMI role delineation study for project managers.

X1.2 Rules for Handling Inputs, Tools and Techniques, and Outputs (ITTOs)

Business rules were established to further aid consistency in handling the order and detail of information within the ITTOs for each project management process. These rules are:

- *ITTO Fundamental Rules:*
    - Inputs are any documents that are *key* to the process.
    - Process outputs should map as an input to another project management process unless the output is a terminal output or embedded within another input such as process documents.
    - Process inputs should map as an output from another project management process unless the input comes from outside the project.

- *Project Documents Rules:*
    - On the ITTO input list, if the input is a major project document, it needs to be specifically listed out.
    - On the ITTO output list, specific project documents are put on the list the first time they are created as an output. Subsequently, these are listed as "project document updates" on the ITTO output list, and described in the section narrative.

- *Project Management Plan Rules:*
    - On the ITTO input list, if the subsidiary plans and baselines from the project management plan serve as major process inputs, then these need to be specifically listed out.
    - On the ITTO output list, subsidiary plans and baselines for the project management plan are grouped as a single output as "project management plan updates" and described in the section narrative.
    - On the ITTO input list, for those planning processes that create a subsidiary plan, the project management plan is listed as the key input.
    - For control processes, the key input is "project management plan," rather than specific subsidiary plans. And the output is "project management plan updates" rather than an update to a specific subsidiary plan.

- *EEF/OPA Referencing Rule for Process Inputs:*
  - ○ When referencing EEFs or OPAs, include the phrase "Described in Section" and state 2.1.4 for OPAs or 2.1.5 for EEFs.
- *Other Consistency Rules:*
  - ○ Rename "project document update" and "organizational process asset updates" to "project documents updates" and "organizational process assets updates."
  - ○ For consistency across the *PMBOK® Guide*, document titles are not to be capitalized in the text.
- *Sequencing Rules:*
  - ○ For inputs and outputs: plans, subsidiary plans, and baselines are listed first.
    - ○ Project management plan first, then subsidiary plans, then baselines.
    - ○ When plans are a major output, they are always listed first.
  - ○ For inputs work performance data/information/reports, these are listed immediately before the enterprise environmental factors.
  - ○ Enterprise environmental factors and organizational process assets are listed last in that order.
  - ○ Tools and techniques have meetings listed last.
  - ○ When updates are an output they are listed in the following sequence:
    - ○ Project management plan/subsidiary plan updates,
    - ○ Project documents updates,
    - ○ Enterprise environmental factors updates, and
    - ○ Organizational process assets updates.

X1.3 Established Rules for Ensuring Harmonization Between Glossary Terms and the PMI Lexicon of Project Management Terms

To ensure that terms used in the *PMBOK® Guide* align with the *PMI Lexicon of Project Management Terms* and harmonize with other PMI standards, business rules were established and adhered to in the Fifth Edition update.

- For terms found in both the *PMBOK® Guide* and the *PMI Lexicon*, the definition from the *PMI Lexicon* takes precedence.

- Where terms used in the *PMBOK® Guide* are not found in the *PMI Lexicon* but are found in other relevant PMI standards (e.g., *The Standard for Program Management, Organizational Project Management Maturity Model (OPM3®), The Standard for Portfolio Management, Practice Standard for Earned Value Management, Practice Standard for Scheduling*, etc.), the definition of the terms shall be the same. If the definitions do not align with the respective standards, the term is elevated to the PMI Lexicon team for assistance in creating an acceptable common definition.

X1.4 Project Management Plan and Its Subsidiary Plans

To improve consistency and aid clarity around the various subsidiary plans that make up the overall project management plan, the team added four planning processes: Plan Scope Management, Plan Schedule Management, Plan Cost Management, and Plan Stakeholder Management. These changes bring back the scope planning process from the Third Edition and add three new planning processes. The additions provide clearer guidance for the concept that each major Knowledge Area has a need for the project team to actively think through and plan how aspects from the related processes are planned and managed. It also reinforces the concept that each of the subsidiary plans are integrated through the overall project management plan, which becomes the major planning document for guiding further project planning and execution.

This change also ensures harmonization with other PMI standards. For example, a detailed planning process for Plan Schedule Management reinforces the need for detailed planning to address project scheduling issues such as selecting the scheduling method and tool during early planning stages as part of the overall Project Time Management processes. This concept of detailed planning for project scheduling related decisions aligns with the *Practice Standard for Scheduling* and ensures harmonization across PMI standards.

X1.5 Consistency in Handling Project Management Work Execution Data and Information Flow

To improve consistency and add clarity regarding project data and information flows during project work execution, the team redefined work performance data, work performance information, and work performance reports to align with the DIKW (Data, Information, Knowledge, Wisdom) model used in the field of Knowledge Management.

- **Work Performance Data**. The raw observations and measurements identified during activities performed to carry out the project work. Examples include reported percent of work physically completed, quality technical performance measures, start and finish dates of schedule activities, number of change requests, number of defects, actual costs, actual durations, etc.

- **Work Performance Information**. The performance data collected from various controlling processes, analyzed in context and integrated based on relationships across areas. Examples of performance information are status of deliverables, implementation status for change requests, forecasted estimates to complete.

- **Work Performance Reports.** The physical or electronic representation of work performance information compiled in project documents, intended to generate decisions, raise issues, actions, or awareness. Examples include status reports, memos, justifications, information notes, electronic dashboards, recommendations, and updates.

The redefined data model was then applied consistently to the inputs and outputs for the various controlling and executing processes as illustrated in Figure X1-1.

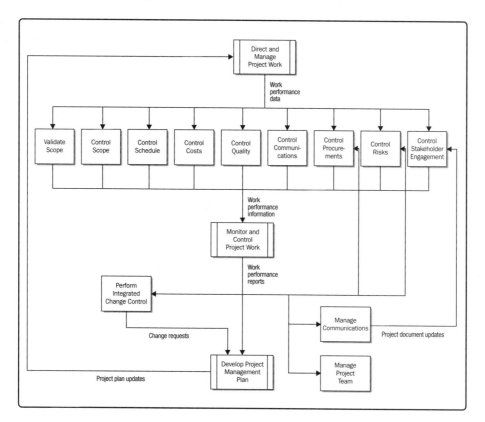

Figure X1-1. Refined Data Model

X1.6 Section 1—Introduction

Sections 1.2, 1.4, and 1.6 were realigned and harmonized with first sections in *The Standard for Program Management* – Third Edition and *The Standard for Portfolio Management* – Third Edition. This ensures the information regarding the relationship between projects, programs, and portfolios is treated consistently across all three standards. Additional text was added to Section 1.4.4 to expand the discussion on project management offices. Section 1.5 on Project Management and Operations Management was expanded to more broadly address the relationship among project management, operations management, and organizational strategy. A new section was added to address the importance of interpersonal skills of a project manager and refers the reader to Appendix X3 of the *PMBOK® Guide* for further discussion on the importance of interpersonal skills in managing projects. Section 1.8 on Enterprise Environmental Factors was moved to Section 2.

X1.7 Section 2—Project Life Cycle and Organization

The content of Section 2 was reorganized to improve content flow and understanding. The section on organizational influence on project management was moved to the beginning of the section and expanded to provide broader coverage of how organizational factors can influence the conduct of project teams. The discussion of enterprise environmental factors was moved into this section from Section 1. The section on stakeholders was expanded to better address project stakeholders and their impact on project governance. A new section was added to address the characteristics and structure of the project team. The section on project life cycle was moved to the end of the section and expanded to further explain life cycles and phases.

X1.8 Section 3 Project Management Processes for a Project

Section 3 of the *PMBOK® Guide* – Fourth Edition was moved into a new Annex in the *PMBOK® Guide* – Fifth Edition (Annex A1 – The Standard for Project Management of a Project). The introduction to this section was cleaned up and expanded to enable this annex to serve as a stand-alone document. This positions the Standard for Project Management away from the main body of the *PMBOK® Guide* material allowing the evolution of the Body of Knowledge material to be separate from the actual Standard for Project Management.

X1.9 New Section 3 for *PMBOK® Guide* – Fifth Edition

A replacement Section 3 was developed for the *PMBOK® Guide* – Fifth edition. This new section bridges the content between Sections 1 and 2 and the Knowledge Area sections. The new section introduces the project management processes and Process Groups as in the previous editions of the *PMBOK® Guide*. However, it does not list each of the processes associated with each of the Project Management Process Groups.

X1.10 Split Section 10 on Project Communications Management into Two Separate Sections

Deferred and post-publication comments on the Project Communications Knowledge Area of the *PMBOK® Guide* – Fourth Edition uncovered a need to modify this Knowledge Area as well as the processes within the Knowledge Area. In general, the comments fell into three groups:

- Eliminate confusion created between the processes of Distribute Information and Report Performance and their overlap with processes for Control Scope, Control Schedule, and Control Cost.

- Tighten the focus of Project Communications Management to planning for the communications needs of the project, collecting, storing, and disseminating project information, and monitoring overall project communications to ensure its efficiency.

- Break out and expand on stakeholder management concepts to reflect not solely upon (a) analyzing stakeholder expectations and its impact on the project, and (b) developing appropriate management strategies for effectively engaging stakeholders in project decisions and execution, but also upon continuous dialogue with stakeholders to meet their needs and expectations, address issues as they occur, and foster appropriate stakeholder engagement in project decisions and activities.

Planning for and managing the communication needs of the project as well as the stakeholders' needs are two distinct keys to project success. The concept being reinforced is that both are discrete Knowledge Areas in which stakeholder management is not simply better management of communications nor which improved communications is simply better stakeholder management. This concept drives the need to treat these two critical keys for project success as distinct areas.

Revamping this Knowledge Area by separating Project Stakeholders Management from Project Communications Management provides the following benefits:

- Focuses on not only managing the expectations of the various stakeholder groups but actively working to ensure an appropriate level of engagement of project stakeholders in the decision making and activities of the project.

- Aligns with the growing body of research showing stakeholder engagement as one of the keys to overall project success.

- Improves the alignment between the *PMBOK® Guide* and *The Standard for Program Management*.

- Aligns better with the focus on stakeholder management being put forward with the new ISO 21500 standard.

- Allows better emphasis on Project Communications Management by focusing on the main purpose of communication activities to collect, store, organize, and distribute project information.

- Enables the realignment of project communications processes, thus addressing the confusion and overlap surrounding project performance analysis and reporting.

Section 10 was separated into two distinct Knowledge Areas: Project Communications Management and Project Stakeholder Management. This change takes the communication processes currently contained in Section 10 and refocuses them to project communications planning, executing, and controlling. The two current stakeholder aligned processes within Section 10 (Identify Stakeholders and Manage Stakeholder Expectations) were moved into a new section addressing stakeholder management. Stakeholder-related text from Section 2.3 was also moved into this new section. The project management processes related to managing project stakeholders were expanded to include:

- Identify Stakeholders,

- Develop Stakeholder Management Plan,

- Manage Stakeholder Engagement, and

- Control Stakeholder Engagement.

X1.11 Process Changes

As part of the process, changes several process names were changed to improve consistency across the processes and to improve clarity. All processes that create a subsidiary plan were named using the form of Plan {XXX} Management. The Monitor and Controlling processes were named using the form Control {XXX}, since the act of controlling a process includes monitoring the process. These changes improved the consistency of how processes are named across all processes. In addition to process name changes, several other processes were added or modified as described elsewhere in this appendix. The list below summarizes the process changes.

- 4.3 Direct and Manage Project Execution—changed to Direct and Manage Project Work
- 5.1 Plan Scope Management—added
- 5.5 Verify Scope—changed to Validate Scope
- 6.1 Plan Schedule Management—added
- 7.1 Plan Cost Management—added
- 8.1 Plan Quality—changed to Plan Quality Management
- 8.3 Perform Quality Control—changed to Control Quality
- 9.1 Develop Human Resource Plan—changed to Plan Human Resource Management
- 10.2 Plan Communications—changed to Section 10.1 Plan Communications Management
- 10.3 Distribute Information—changed to Section 10.2 Manage Communications
- 10.5 Report Performance—changed to Section 10.3 Control Communications
- 11.6 Monitor and Control Risks—changed to Control Risks
- 12.1 Plan Procurements—changed to Plan Procurement Management
- 12.3 Administer Procurements—changed to Control Procurements
- 10.1 Identify Stakeholders—moved to Section 13.1 Identify Stakeholders
- 13.2 Plan Stakeholder Management—added
- 10.4 Manage Stakeholder Expectations—changed to Section 13.3 Manage Stakeholders Engagement
- 13.4 Control Stakeholders Engagement—added

X1.12 Section 4—Project Integration Management Changes

Process definitions were revised for Develop Project Charter, Develop Project Management Plan, Direct and Manage Project Work, Monitor and Control Project Work, and Perform Integrated Change Control to better align with the *PMI Lexicon* and improve clarity of the definitions. The Direct and Manage Project Execution was renamed to Direct and Manage Project Work to better align with its definition and reinforce that this process applies beyond the Executing processes. Other changes consist primarily of expanded explanations, refinements to tools and techniques for several processes, and refinements to the inputs and outputs for several processes to better tie the integration processes to other project management processes. A table was added to the discussion of the output for of the Develop Project Management Plan process to bring clarity to the differentiation between project documents and Inputs and outputs were adjusted for several processes to reflect the new model of project data and information flow during the execution of project work.

The following table summarizes the Section 4 processes:

Table X1-1. Section 4 Changes

Fourth Edition Sections	Fifth Edition Sections
4.1 Develop Project Charter	4.1 Develop Project Charter
4.2 Develop Project Management Plan	4.2 Develop Project Management Plan
4.3 Direct and Manage Project Execution	4.3 Direct and Manage Project Work
4.4 Monitor and Control Project Work	4.4 Monitor and Control Project Work
4.5 Perform Integrated Change Control	4.5 Perform Integrated Change Control
4.6 Close Project or Phase	4.6 Close Project or Phase

X1.13 Section 5—Project Scope Management Changes

In Section 5.1, the concept of a Develop Scope Management Plan process was brought back as a way to ensure consistency across all project planning processes and to reinforce that subsidiary plans are developed to plan the details for each major Knowledge Area. To support consistency in naming, the processes that create the subsidiary plans, the Develop Scope Management Plan was named Plan Scope Management. The discussion within the Collect Requirements process was expanded to make clear this process focuses on collecting all requirements necessary for project success. These requirements include the requirements for the product, service, or result to be delivered by the project, any quality requirements the project must meet, and any other project management related requirements deemed critical for project success. The Verify Scope process was renamed to Validate Scope and the text was reworked to add emphasis that this process is not solely about accepting deliverables but validating that the deliverables will deliver value to the business and confirms that the deliverables, as provided, will fulfill the project objectives, as well as their intended use to the project stakeholders. Inputs and outputs were adjusted for several processes to reflect the new model of project data and information flow during the execution of project work.

The following table summarizes the Section 5 processes:

Table X1-2. Section 5 Changes

Fourth Edition Sections	Fifth Edition Sections
	5.1 Plan Scope Management
5.1 Collect Requirements	5.2 Collect Requirements
5.2 Define Scope	5.3 Define Scope
5.3 Create WBS	5.4 Create WBS
5.4 Verify Scope	5.5 Validate Scope
5.5 Control Scope	5.6 Control Scope

X1.14 Section 6—Project Time Management Changes

Section 6 reflects changes within the industry and detailed in the *Practice Standard for Scheduling – Second Edition.*

As part of reinforcing the concept of detailed subsidiary plans being created for each major Knowledge Area and then aggregated into the overall project management plan, a new process was added for Plan Schedule Management. This process adds focus on the preliminary decisions around developing and maintaining the project's schedule model. Process definitions were revised for Define Activities, Estimate Activity Resources, Estimate Activity Durations, and Control Schedule to improve clarity of the definitions. Several processes were modified with new inputs and/or updated outputs. Agile concepts were incorporated into the Develop Schedule process. Figures and associated text were updated to clarify scheduling concepts addressed in the section. Added emphasis was placed on resource optimization techniques used in project scheduling. Some inputs and outputs were renamed for several processes to support consistency between the various project management processes. Inputs and outputs were adjusted for several processes to reflect the new model of project data and information flow during the execution of project work.

The following table summarizes the Section 6 processes:

Table X1-3. Section 6 Changes

Fourth Edition Sections	Fifth Edition Sections
	6.1 Plan Schedule Management
6.1 Define Activities	6.2 Define Activities
6.2 Sequence Activities	6.3 Sequence Activities
6.3 Estimate Activity Resources	6.4 Estimate Activity Resources
6.4 Estimate Activity Durations	6.5 Estimate Activity Durations
6.5 Develop Schedule	6.6 Develop Schedule
6.6 Control Schedule	6.7 Control Schedule

X1.15 Section 7—Project Cost Management Changes

Section 7 reflects changes coming from within the industry and detailed in the *Practice Standard for Estimating* and the *Practice Standard for Earned Value Management* – Second Edition.

As part of reinforcing the concept of detailed subsidiary plans being created for each major Knowledge Area and then aggregated into the overall project management plan, a new process was added for Plan Cost Management. This process adds focus on the preliminary decisions around developing and maintaining the project's cost estimates and budget. Added emphasis was placed on reserve analysis including contingency and management reserves with a new figure, Figure 7-8, added to illustrate the various components making up the project budget. A new table, Table 7-1 on earned value calculations summary, was added to collect in one place all of the formulas used for earned value analysis. Figures for earned value and project funding requirements were updated to reflect the added emphasis on management reserves. Some inputs and outputs were renamed for several processes to support consistency between the various project management processes. Inputs and outputs were adjusted for several processes to reflect the new model of project data and information flow during the execution of project work.

The following table summarizes the Section 7 processes:

Table X1-4. Section 7 Changes

Fourth Edition Sections	Fifth Edition Sections
	7.1 Plan Cost Management
7.1 Estimate Costs	7.2 Estimate Costs
7.2 Determine Budget	7.3 Determine Budget
7.3 Control Cost	7.4 Control Costs

X1.16 Section 8—Project Quality Management Changes

No new processes were added in the project management processes contained within this section. The Quality Planning process was renamed Plan Quality Management to support consistency in naming the processes that create the subsidiary plans. The definition for Plan Quality Management was updated to better align with the added focus on quality requirements for the project. The Perform Quality Control process was renamed Control Quality to support consistency in naming the various controlling processes. Changes consist primarily of expanding discussion on various tools and techniques within the Quality Management processes. Figure 8-2 on IPECC and PDCA Cycles in Relation to QA, QC, and COQ, was added to illustrate the fundamental relationships between quality assurance, quality control, and cost of quality to the Plan-Do-Check-Act and Initiate-Plan-Execute-Control-Close models. A new input was added for the Plan Quality Management process to better tie the requirements gathered during the Collect Requirements process to the overall quality planning for the project. More emphasis was placed on the basic quality management tools used in managing project quality. New figures were added to better summarize the seven basic quality tools and the seven quality management and control tools. Some inputs and outputs were renamed for several processes to support consistency between the various project management processes. Inputs and outputs were adjusted for several processes to reflect the new model of project data and information flow during the execution of project work.

The following table summarizes the Section 8 processes:

Table X1-5. Section 8 Changes

Fourth Edition Sections	Fifth Edition Sections
8.1 Plan Quality	8.1 Plan Quality Management
8.2 Perform Quality Assurance	8.2 Perform Quality Assurance
8.3 Perform Quality Control	8.3 Control Quality

X1.17 Section 9—Project Human Resource Management Changes

No significant changes were implemented in project management processes contained within this section. The Human Resource Planning process was renamed Plan Human Resource Management to support consistency in naming the processes that create the subsidiary plans. Changes consist primarily of some added or modified inputs, tools and techniques, and outputs, and the replacement of project management plan by human resource plan as an input of processes 9.2 Acquire Project Team, 9.3 Develop Project Team, and 9.4.Manage Project Team for consistency with processes in other Knowledge Areas. The definitions for Plan Human Resource Management, Acquire Project Team, and Develop Project Team were updated to better align with the details of these processes. Some inputs and outputs were renamed for several processes to support consistency in how information flows between the various project management processes.

The following table summarizes the Section 9 processes:

Table X1-6. Section 9 Changes

Fourth Edition Sections	Fifth Edition Sections
9.1 Develop Human Resource Plan	9.1 Plan Human Resource Management
9.2 Acquire Project Team	9.2 Acquire Project Team
9.3 Develop Project Team	9.3 Develop Project Team
9.4 Manage Project Team	9.4 Manage Project Team

X1.18 Section 10—Project Communications Management Changes

Information about stakeholder management was moved from Section 10 to a new Knowledge Area for Stakeholder Management. The Plan Communications process was renamed Plan Communications Management to support consistency in naming the processes that create the subsidiary plans. The processes for Distribute Information and Report Performance were reworked to clear up confusion between these processes and their overlap with processes for Control Scope, Control Schedule, and Control Cost. The processes were refocused toward the activity of communication as performed in projects, considering more the process of communicating rather than the intent or desired outcome of the message with emphasis on planning for the communications needs of the project, collecting, storing, and disseminating project information, and monitoring overall project communications to ensure its efficiency. The process names were changed to Manage Communications and Control Communications. The definitions for Plan Communications Management, Manage Communications, and Control Communications were updated to reflect these changes. Some inputs and outputs were renamed for several processes to support consistency between the various project management processes. Inputs and outputs were adjusted for several processes to reflect the new model of project data and information flow during the execution of project work.

The following table summarizes the Section 10 processes:

Table X1-7. Section 10 Changes

Fourth Edition Sections	Fifth Edition Sections
10.1 Identify Stakeholders	Moved to 13.1
10.2 Plan Communications	10.1 Plan Communications Management
10.3 Distribute Information	10.2 Manage Communications
10.4 Manage Stakeholder Expectations	Moved to 13.3
10.5 Report Performance	10.3 Control Communications

X1.19 Section 11—Project Risk Management Changes

No significant changes were implemented in project management processes contained within this section. The Monitor and Control Risks process was renamed Control Risks to support consistency in naming the various controlling processes. Changes were made to move the emphasis away from the term "positive risks" toward "opportunity" to better align with the feedback from the project management community. Text was added to expand upon the concepts of risk attitude, risk appetite, risk tolerance, and risk thresholds. Other changes consist primarily of cleaning up text, incorporating feedback, and aligning inputs and outputs with changes from other Knowledge Areas. Some inputs and outputs were renamed for several processes to support consistency between the various project management processes. Inputs and outputs were adjusted for several processes to reflect the new model of project data and information flow during the execution of project work.

The following table summarizes the Section 11 processes:

Table X1-8. Section 11 Changes

Fourth Edition Sections	Fifth Edition Sections
11.1 Plan Risk Management	11.1 Plan Risk Management
11.2 Identify Risks	11.2 Identify Risks
11.3 Perform Qualitative Risk Analysis	11.3 Perform Qualitative Risk Analysis
11.4 Perform Quantitative Risk Analysis	11.4 Perform Quantitative Risk Analysis
11.5 Plan Risk Responses	11.5 Plan Risk Responses
11.6 Monitor and Control Risk	11.6 Control Risks

X1.20 Section 12—Project Procurement Management Changes

The Plan Procurements process was renamed Plan Procurement Management to support consistency in naming the processes that create the subsidiary plans. The Administer Procurement process was renamed Control Procurements to support consistency in naming the various controlling processes. Other changes consist primarily of cleaning up text, incorporating feedback, and aligning inputs and outputs with changes from other Knowledge Areas. Some inputs and outputs were renamed for several processes to support consistency between the various project management processes. Inputs and outputs were adjusted for several processes to reflect the new model of project data and information flow during the execution of project work.

The following table summarizes the Section 12 processes:

Table X1-9. Section 12 Changes

Fourth Edition Sections	Fifth Edition Sections
12.1 Plan Procurements	12.1 Plan Procurement Management
12.2 Conduct Procurements	12.2 Conduct Procurements
12.3 Administer Procurements	12.3 Control Procurements
12.4 Close Procurements	12.4 Close Procurements

X1.21 Section 13—Project Stakeholder Management Changes

In keeping with the evolution of thinking regarding stakeholder management within projects, a new Knowledge Area was added addressing Project Stakeholder Management. Information on stakeholder identification and managing stakeholder expectations was moved from Section 10 on Project Communications Management to this new Knowledge Area to expand upon and increase the focus on the importance of appropriately engaging project stakeholders in the key decisions and activities associated with the project. New processes were added for Plan Stakeholders Management and Control Stakeholders Engagement. Some inputs and outputs were renamed for several processes to support consistency between the various project management processes. Inputs and outputs were adjusted for several processes to reflect the new model of project data and information flow during the execution of project work.

The following table summarizes the Section 13 processes:

Table X1-10. Section 13 Changes

Fourth Edition Sections	Fifth Edition Sections
10.1 Identify Stakeholders	13.1 Identify Stakeholders
	13.2 Plan Stakeholder Management
10.4 Manage Stakeholders Expectations	13.3 Manage Stakeholder Engagement
	13.4 Control Stakeholder Engagement

X1.22 Glossary

The glossary of the *PMBOK® Guide* – Fifth Edition has been expanded and updated to include those terms within the *PMBOK® Guide* that need to be defined to support an understanding of the document's contents:

- Clarify meaning and improve the quality and accuracy of any translations;
- Eliminate terms not used within the *PMBOK® Guide* – Fifth Edition; and
- Ensure terms align and harmonize with the terms in the *PMI Lexicon* and other key PMI standards.

X1.23 Data Flow Diagrams

The data flow diagrams for all project management processes were cleaned up and updated to remove inconsistencies and ensure each diagram accurately reflects the inputs and outputs associated with a given process.

APPENDIX X2
CONTRIBUTORS AND REVIEWERS OF
THE *PMBOK® GUIDE*—FIFTH EDITION:

PMI volunteers first attempted to codify the Project Management Body of Knowledge in the *Special Report on Ethics, Standards, and Accreditation*, published in 1983. Since that time, other volunteers have come forward to update and improve that original document and contribute to this globally recognized standard for project management, PMI's *A Guide to the Project Management Body of Knowledge* (*PMBOK® Guide*). This appendix lists, alphabetically within groupings, those individuals who have contributed to the development and production of the *PMBOK® Guide* – Fifth Edition. No simple list or even multiple lists can adequately portray all the contributions of those who have volunteered to develop the *PMBOK® Guide* – Fifth Edition.

The Project Management Institute is grateful to all of these individuals for their support and acknowledges their contributions to the project management profession.

X2.1 *PMBOK® Guide—Fifth Edition* Core Committee

The following individuals served as members, were contributors of text or concepts, and served as leaders within the Project Core Committee:

The following individuals served as members, were contributors of text or concepts, and served as leaders within the Project Core Committee:

Dave Violette, MPM, PMP, Chair
Joseph W. Kestel, PMP, Vice Chair
Nick Clemens, PMP (Sections 3 and 4 Lead)
Dan Deakin, PMP (Sections 11 and 12 Lead)
Theofanis C. Giotis, PMP, PMI-ACP (Sections 1 and 2 Lead)
Marie A. Gunnerson, (Sections 6 and 7 Lead)
Vanina Mangano, PMP, PMI-RMP (Integrated Content and Change Control Lead)
Mercedes Martinez Sanz, PMP (Sections 5 and 8 Lead)
Carolina Gabriela Spindola, PMP, SSBB (Quality Control Lead)
Kristin L. Vitello, CAPM, Standards Project Specialist

X2.2 *PMBOK® Guide—Fifth Edition* Subcommittee

The following individuals served as contributors of text or concepts and as leaders of the Project Subcommittee:

Matthew B. Anderson, PMP, PMI-ACP (Section 4 Leader)
Gilbert B. Asher, MBA, PMP (Data Flow Working Group Leader)
Brad Bigelow, PMP, MSP (Section 2 Leader)
Cecilia Boggi, PMP (Section 9 Leader)
Bernardo O. Bustamante, PE, PMP (Section 1 Leader)
Akshata Karanth, PMP (Section 6 Leader)
David L. Keeney, PMP, CTT+ (Section 8 Leader)
David Kramer (Section 12 Leader)
Karthikeyan Kumaraguru MS, PMP (Section 11 Leader)
Mary-Elizabeth Larson, PMP, CBAP (Section 5 Leader)
Charles J. Lesko, Jr., Ph.D., PMP (Section 10 Leader)
Claudia Alex Morris, MBA, PMP (Editorial Leader)
John M. Nevison (Section 7 Leader)
M.K.Ramesh, BE, PMP (Section 3 Leader through 6/2011)
Krupakar Reddy, PMP, PRINCE2 Practitioner (Section 3 Leader)
Yad Senapathy (Section 4 Leader through 6/2011)
Anca E. Slușanschi, MSc, PMP (Section 13 Leader)

X2.3 Significant Contributors

In addition to the members of the Project Core Committee and Subcommittee, the following individuals provided significant input or concepts:

George F. Burton MBA, PMP
Tammy Clark
Joel R. Erickson, MAcc, PMP
Stanisław Gasik, PhD
Ashok Jain, PMP, CSM
Andrea Pantano, PMP
Federico Roman Demo, PMP, ITIL
Anthony Tsui, MIT, PMP
Jennifer L. Walker, PMP

Glen R. Palmer
Jon Palmquist
Nick Palumbo, PMP
David Parker
Jerry L. Partridge, PMP
George Pasieka, PMP
Eric Patel
Anil Peer, PEng, PMP
Francisco Perez-Polo
Paul W. Phister, Jr., PhD, PE
Crispin (Kik) Piney, BSc, PMP
Natasha Pollard
Sreenivasa Rao Potti, MCA, PMP
Manohar Powar, PMP
Ravindranath P S
Patrick J. Quairoli
Ge Qun
Vara Prasad Raju Kunada
Gurdev Randhawa
Prem Ranganath, PMP
Raju Rao, PMP
Ulka Rathi
Carol Rauh, PhD, PMP
Tony Raymond
Vijay Sai Reddy, PMP, CSQA
J. Logan C. Rice
Steven Ricks, PMP
Steven F. Ritter, PMP
Thad B. Ring, PMP
Dee Rizor
Susan Rizzi
Michael C. Roach
Alexandre G. Rodrigues, PhD

Cheryl N. Rogers, PMP
Asbjorn Rolstadas, PhD
Hans (Ron) Ronhovde, PMP
Scott A. Rose, PMP
Ed Rosenstein, PMP
David W. Ross, PMP
Samuel S. Roth, PMP
Joseph A. Roushdi
Gurdev Roy, PMP
Paul S. Royer, PMP
James J. Rutushni, PMP
Robbi Ryan
Frank Ryle, PMP
Anjali Sabharwal, PMP
Srinivasa R. Sajja, PMP
Brian Salk, MA Ed, PMP
Nashaat A. Salman, PMP
Kyoichi Sato
Markus Scheibel, PMP, Dipl-Ing
Suzanne Lee Schmidt, PMP
John Schmitt, PMP
Amy Schneider, PMP
Michael J. Schollmeyer, PMP
Randa Schollmeyer, PMP
Richard E. Schwartz
Andrea R. Scott
Benjamin R. Sellers, PMP, CPCM
Tufan Sevim, PMP
Sanjay Shah, PMP
Mundaje S. Shetty, PMP
Kazuo Shimizu, PMP
Rali Shital
Ganga Siebertz

Larry Sieck
Melvin Silverman, PhD, PE
Fernando Demattio de O.
    Simoes, PMP
Richard L. Sinatra, PhD, PMP
Raghavendra Singh
John E. Singley, PhD, PMP
Edward Smith
Patricia Smith
Cynthia Snyder, MBA, PMP
Antonio Soares
Paul Solomon, PMP
Richard Spector, PMP
Allison St. Jean
Michael Stefanovic, PEng, PMP
Geree Streun, PMP
Juergen Sturany
Donglin Su
Sambasivam S., PMP, CSQA
George Sukumar, MSChe, OE
Karen Z. Sullivan, PMP
Karen Tate, MBA, PMP
David E. Taylor, PMP
James E. Teer, Jr.
Sai K. Thallam, MBA, PMP
John A. Thoren, Jr., PhD, PMP
Surendra Tipparaju, ME
Massimo Torre, PhD, PMP
Luis Eduardo Torres Calzada,
    MBA, PMP
Rogerio Carlos Traballi
Lee Towe, MBA, PMP
Rufis A. Turpin, CQA, CSQE

Marion J. Tyler, PMP
M. Raj Ullagaraj, PhD
Bobbye Underwood, PMP
Eric Uyttewaal, PMP
Dalton L. Valeriano-Alves, ME
JR Vanden Eynde, PMP
Gary Van Eck
Judy Van Meter
J.R. Vanden Eynde, PMP
Gerrit van Otterdijk, BSc
Thomas G. Van Scoyoc, PMP
Paula X. Varas, PMP
Ricardo Vargas
Ricardo Viana Vargas, MSc, PMP
Aloysio Vianna, Jr.
Mark M. Vertin, PE, PMP

Craig Veteto, PMP, CPIM
Roberto Viale, PMP
Eduardo Newton Vieira, PMP
Dave Violette, MPM, PMP
Desmond Joseph Vize, PMP
Cornelius (Kees) Vonk, PMP
J. Wendell Wagner, PMP
Barbara Walsh
Thomas M. Walsh, PMP
William W. Wassel, PE, PMP
Patrick Weaver, PMP, FAICD
Kevin R. Wegryn, PMP, CPM
Timothy E. Welker, PMP
Linda Westfall, PE, CSQE
Gwen Whitman, PMP
Tammo T. Wilkens, PE, PMP

Alan K. Williams, Sr., PMP
Charles M. Williamson,
  MBA, PMP
Stephen D. Wise
Allan Wong
Robert Wood
Kristin L. Wright
Thomas Wuttke, PMP, CPM
Uma S. Yalamanchili, PMP
Clement C.L. Yeung, PMP
Angela F. Young, PMP
John Zachar, BSc, APMP
Kathy Zandbergen
Cristine Zerpa
Paul Zilmer
Eire E. Zimmermann, PMP

X2.11 The *PMBOK® Guide*—2000 Edition

Cynthia A. Berg, PMP
Judith A. Doll, PMP
Daniel Dudek, PMP
Quentin Fleming
Greg Githens, PMP
Earl Glenwright
David T. Hulett, PhD
Gregory J. Skulmoski

X2.11.1 Other Contributors:

Muhamed Abdomerovic, PMP, D. Eng.
John R. Adams
Yassir Afaneh
Frank Allen, PMP
Jon D. Allen, PMP
MaryGrace Allenchey, PMP
Robert A. Andrejko, PMP
Ichizo Aoki
Paul C. Aspinwall
Ronald Auffrédou, PMP
Edward Averill, PMP
Frederick L. Ayer, PMP
William W. Bahnmaier, PMP
A. C. "Fred" Baker, PMP
Carole J. Bass, PMP
George Belev
Berndt Bellman
Sally Bernstein, PMP
Nigel Blampied, PE, PMP
John Blatta
Patrick Brown, PMP
Alfredo del Caño
Chris Cartwright, PMP
Bruce C. Chadbourne, PMP
Michael T. Clark, PMP
Raymond C. Clark, PE
Elizabeth Clarke
David Coates, PMP
Kim Colenso, PMP

Edmund H. Conrow, PMP
Kenneth G. Cooper
Sergio Coronado Arrechedera
John Cornman, PMP
Richard F. Cowan, PMP
Kevin Daly, PMP
Mario Damiani, PMP
Thomas Diethelm, PMP
David M. Drevinsky, PMP
William R. Duncan
Frank D. Einhorn, PMP
Steven L. Fahrenkrog
Edward Fern, PMP
Lisa Fisher
Christian Frankenberg, PMP
Scott D. Freauf, PMP
Jean-Luc Frere, PMP
Ichiro Fujita, PMP
Chikako Futamura, PMP
Serge Garon, PEng, PMP
Brian L. Garrison, PMP
Lewis M. Gedansky
Linda V. Gillman
Eric Glover
Eva T. Goldman
Peter Bryan Goldsbury
Michael Goodman, PMP
Jean Gouix, PMP
Paul Grace
Alexander Grassi Sr., PMP

Roger Graves
Franz X. Hake
Peter Heffron
Chris Herbert, PMP
Dr. David Hillson, PMP, FAPM
J. Brian Hobbs, PMP
Marion Diane Holbrook
Robin Hornby
David Hotchkiss, PMP
Bill Hubbard
Charles L. Hunt
Thomas P. Hurley, PMP
George Jackelen
Angyan P. Jagathnarayanan
Sandy Jenkins
Elden F. Jones II, PMP, CMII
Sada Joshi, PMP
Lewis Kana, PMP
Subramaniam Kandaswamy, PhD, PMP
Ronald L. Kempf, PMP
Robert Dohn Kissinger, PhD, PMP
Kurt V. Kloecker
Toni D. Knott
Jan Kristrom
Blase Kwok, PMP
Sam Lane
Lawrence P. Leach
Philip A. Lindeman

Gábor Lipi
Lyle W. Lockwood, PMP
J. W. Lowthian, PMP
Arif Mahmood, PMP
James Martin (on behalf
    of INCOSE)
Stephen S. Mattingly
Glen Maxfield
Peter McCarthy
Rob McCormack, PMP
John McHugh
Krik D. McManus
Dewey L. Messer
David Michaud
Mary F. Miekoski, PMP
Oscar A. Mignone
Gordon R. Miller, PMP
Roy E. Morgan, PMP
Jim Morris, PMP
Bert Mosterd, PMP
William A. Moylan, PMP
John D. Nelson, PMP
Wolfgang Obermeier
Cathy Oest, PMP
Masato Ohori, PMP
Kazuhiko Okubo, PE, PMP
Edward Oliver
Michelle Triggs Owen
Mark S. Parker
Shirley B. Parker
Matthew H. Parry

Jerry Partridge, PMP
Francisco Perez-Polo, PMP
James M. Phillips, PMP
Crispin (Kik) Piney, PMP
George Pitagorsky, PMP
David L. Prater, PMP
Janice Preston
Bradford S. Price, PMP
Samuel L. Raisch, PMP
Naga Rajan
G. Ramachandran, PMP
Stephen Reed
Bill Righter, PMP
Bernice L. Rocque, PMP
Wolfgang Theodore Roesch
Fernando Romero Peñailillo
Jon Rude
Linda Rust, PMP
Fabian Sagristani, PMP
James N. Salapatas, PMP
Seymour Samuels
Bradford N. Scales
H. Peter Schiller
John R. Schuyler, PMP
Maria Scott, PMP
Shoukat Sheikh, MBA, PMP
Larry Sieck
Kazuo Shimizu, PMP
David Shuster
Melvin Silverman, PhD, PE
Loren J. Simer Jr.

Keith Skilling, PE, PMP
Ed Smith
Kenneth F. Smith, PMP
Barry Smythe, PMP
Paul J. Solomon
Joe Soto Sr., PMP
Christopher Wessley Sours, PMP
Charlene Spoede, PMP
Joyce Statz, PMP
Emmett Stine, PMP
Alan Stretton
Thangavel Subbu
Jim Szpakowski
Ahmet N. Taspinar, PMP
John A. Thoren Jr., PMP
Iesha D. Turner-Brown
Alan D. Uren, PMP
Juan Luis Valero, PMP
S. Rao Vallabhaneni
William Simon Vaughan
    Robinson
Ana Isabel Vazquez Urbina
Ricardo Viana Vargas, PMP
Mike Wakshull
Stephen E. Wall, PMP
William W. Wassel, PMP
R. Max Wideman
Tammo T. Wilkens, PE, PMP
Robert Williford, PMP
Robert Youker

X2.12 The *PMBOK® Guide*—1996 Edition

William R. Duncan
Frederick Ayer
Cynthia Berg
Mark Burgess
Helen Cooke
Judy Doll
Drew Fetters
Brian Fletcher
Earl Glenwright
Eric Jenett
Deborah O'Bray
Diane Quinn
Anthony Rizzotto
Alan Stretton
Douglas E. Tryloff

X2.12.1 Other Contributors:

John Adams	Jeannette M. Cabanis	Maureen Dougherty
Edward L. Averill	Louis J. Cabano	John J. Downing
C. "Fred" Baker	Kim Colenso	Daniel D. Dudek
F. J. "Bud" Baker	Samuel K. Collier	Lawrence East
Tom Belanger	Karen Condos-Alfonsi	Quentin W. Fleming
John A. Bing	E. J. Coyle	Rick Fletcher
Brian Bock	Darlene Crane	Linda V. Gillman
Paul Bosakowski	David Curling	Greg Githens
Keely Brunner	Russ Darnall	Douglas Gordon
Dorothy J. Burton	Misty N. Dillard	Leo Giulianeti

Martha D. Hammonds
Abdulrazak Hajibrahim
G. Alan Hellawell
Bobby R. Hensley
Jonathan Hicks
Paul Hinkley
Wayne L. Hinthorn
Mark E. Hodson
David T. Hulett
Edward Ionata
Lew Ireland
Elvin Isgrig
Murray Janzen
Frank Jenes
Sandy Jenkins
Walter Karpowski
William F. Kerrigan
Harold Kerzner
Robert L. Kimmons
Richard King
J. D. "Kaay" Koch
Lauri Koskela
Richard E. Little
Lyle W. Lockwood
Lawrence Mack
Christopher Madigan
Michael L. McCauley
Hugh McLaughlin
Frank McNeely
Pierre Menard
Dewey L. Messer

Rick Michaels
Raymond Miller
Alan Minson
Colin Morris
R. Bruce Morris
Danell Moses
David J. Mueller
Gary Nelson
John M. Nevison
John P. Nolan
Louise C. Novakowski
James O'Brien
JoAnn C. Osmer
Jon V. Palmquist
Mark S. Parker
Shirley B. Parker
Matthew Parry
John G. Phippen
Hans E. Picard
Melissa Pendergast
James S. Pennypacker
Serge Y. Piotte
PMI Houston Chapter
PMI Manitoba Chapter
PMI New Zealand Chapter
Charles J. Pospisil
Janice Y. Preston
Mark T. Price
Christopher Quaife
Peter E. Quinn
Hadley Reynolds

Steven F. Ritter
William S. Ruggles
Ralph B. Sackman
Agnes Salvo
Alice Sapienza
W. Stephen Sawle
Darryl M. Selleck
Melvin Silverman
Roy Smith
Leonard Stolba
Craig T. Stone
Hiroshi Tanaka
Ahmet Taspinar
Robert Templeton
Dick Thiel
Saul Thomashow
J. Tidhar
Janet Toepfer
Michelle Triggs
Vijay K. Verma
Alex Walton
Jack Way
Francis M. Webster Jr.
R. Max Wideman
Rebecca Winston
Hugh M. Woodward
Lisa Woodring
Robert Youker
Shakir H. Zuberi
Dirk Zwart

APPENDIX X3
INTERPERSONAL SKILLS

Project managers accomplish work through the project team and other stakeholders. Effective project managers acquire a balance of technical, interpersonal, and conceptual skills that help them analyze situations and interact appropriately. This appendix describes important interpersonal skills, such as:

- Leadership
- Team building
- Motivation
- Communication
- Influencing
- Decision making
- Political and cultural awareness
- Negotiation
- Trust building
- Conflict management
- Coaching

While there are additional interpersonal skills that project managers use, the appropriate use of these skills assists the project manager in effectively managing the project.

X3.1 Leadership

Leadership involves focusing the efforts of a group of people toward a common goal and enabling them to work as a team. In general terms, leadership is the ability to get things done through others. Respect and trust, rather than fear and submission, are the key elements of effective leadership. Although important throughout all project phases, effective leadership is critical during the beginning phases of a project when the emphasis is on communicating the vision and motivating and inspiring project participants to achieve high performance.

Throughout the project, the project team leaders are responsible for establishing and maintaining the vision, strategy, and communications; fostering trust and team building; influencing, mentoring, and monitoring; and evaluating the performance of the team and the project.

X3.2 Team Building

Team building is the process of helping a group of individuals, bound by a common purpose, to work with each other, the leader, external stakeholders, and the organization. The result of good leadership and good team building is teamwork.

Team-building activities consist of tasks (establish goals, define, and negotiate roles, responsibilities, and procedures) and processes (interpersonal behavior with emphasis on communication, conflict management, motivation, and leadership). Developing a team environment involves handling project team problems and discussing these as team issues without placing blame on individuals. Team building can be further enhanced by obtaining top management support; encouraging team member commitment; introducing appropriate rewards, recognition, and ethics; creating a team identity; managing conflicts effectively; promoting trust and open communication among team members; and providing leadership.

While team building is essential during the front end of a project, it is an ongoing process. Changes in a project environment are inevitable. To manage these changes effectively, a continued or renewed team-building effort is required. Outcomes of team building include mutual trust, high quality of information exchange, better decision making, and effective project management.

X3.3 Motivation

Project teams are comprised of team members with diverse backgrounds, expectations, and individual objectives. The overall success of the project depends upon the project team's commitment, which is directly related to their level of motivation.

Motivating in a project environment involves creating an environment to meet project objectives while providing maximum satisfaction related to what people value most. These values may include job satisfaction, challenging work, a sense of accomplishment, achievement and growth, sufficient financial compensation, and other rewards and recognition the individual considers necessary and important.

X3.4 Communication

Communication has been identified as one of the single biggest reasons for project success or failure. Effective communication within the project team and between the project manager, team members, and all external stakeholders is essential. Openness in communication is a gateway to teamwork and high performance. It improves relationships among project team members and creates mutual trust.

To communicate effectively, the project manager should be aware of the communication styles of other parties, cultural nuances/norms, relationships, personalities, and the overall context of the situation. Awareness of these factors leads to mutual understanding and thus to effective communication. Project managers should identify various communication channels, understand what information they need to provide, what information they need to receive, and which interpersonal skills will help them communicate effectively with various project stakeholders. Carrying out team-building activities to determine team member communications styles (e.g., directive, collaborative, logical, explorer, etc.), allows managers to plan their communications with appropriate sensitivity to relationships and cultural differences.

Listening is an important part of communication. Listening techniques, both active and passive give the user insight to problem areas, negotiation and conflict management strategies, decision making, and problem resolution.

X3.5 Influencing

Influencing is a strategy of sharing power and relying on interpersonal skills to get others to cooperate towards common goals. Using the following guidelines can influence team members:

- Lead by example, and follow through with commitments.
- Clarify how a decision will be made.
- Use a flexible interpersonal style and adjust the style to the audience.

Apply your power skillfully and cautiously. Think of long-term collaboration.

X3.6 Decision Making

There are four basic decision styles normally used by project managers: command, consultation, consensus, and coin flip (random). There are four major factors that affect the decision style: time constraints, trust, quality, and acceptance. Project managers may make decisions individually, or they may involve the project team in the decision-making process.

Project managers and project teams use a decision-making model or process such as the six-phase model shown below.

- **Problem Definition.** Fully explore, clarify, and define the problem.
- **Problem Solution Generation.** Prolong the new idea-generating process by brainstorming multiple solutions and discouraging premature decisions.
- **Ideas to Action.** Define evaluation criteria, rate pros and cons of alternatives, select best solution.
- **Solution Action Planning.** Involve key participants to gain acceptance and commitment to making the solution work.
- **Solution Evaluation Planning.** Perform post-implementation analysis, evaluation, and lessons learned.
- **Evaluation of the Outcome and Process.** Evaluate how well the problem was solved or project goals were achieved (extension of previous phase).

X3.7 Political and Cultural Awareness

Organizational politics are inevitable in project environments due to the diversity in norms, backgrounds, and expectations of the people involved with a project. The skillful use of politics and power helps the project manager to be successful. Conversely, ignoring or avoiding project politics and inappropriate use of power can lead to difficulty in managing projects.

Today project managers operate in a global environment, and many projects exist in an environment of cultural diversity. By understanding and capitalizing on cultural differences, the project management team is more likely to create an environment of mutual trust and a win-win atmosphere. Cultural differences can be both individual and corporate in nature and may involve both internal and external stakeholders. An effective way to manage this cultural diversity is through getting to know the various team members and the use of good communication planning as part of the overall project plan.

Culture at a behavioral level includes those behaviors and expectations that occur independently of geography, ethnic heritage, or common and disparate languages. Culture can impact the speed of working, the decision-making process, and the impulse to act without appropriate planning. This may lead to conflict and stress in some organizations, thereby affecting the performance of project managers and project teams.

X3.8 Negotiation

Negotiation is a strategy of conferring with parties of shared or opposed interests with a view toward compromise or reaching an agreement. Negotiation is an integral part of project management and done well, increases the probability of project success.

The following skills and behaviors are useful in negotiating successfully:

- Analyze the situation.
- Differentiate between wants and needs, both theirs and yours.
- Focus on interests and issues rather than on positions.
- Ask high and offer low, but be realistic.
- When you make a concession, act as if you are yielding something of value, don't just give in.
- Both parties should feel as if they have won. This win-win negotiating style is preferred but not always achievable. If possible, don't let the other party leave feeling as though he or she has been taken advantage of.
- Listen attentively and communicate articulately.

X3.9 Trust Building

The ability to build trust across the project team and other key stakeholders is a critical component in effective team leadership. Trust is associated with cooperation, information sharing, and effective problem resolution. Without trust it is difficult to establish the positive relationships necessary between the various stakeholders engaged in the project. When trust is compromised, relationships deteriorate, people disengage, and collaboration becomes more difficult, if not impossible.

Some actions project managers can take to help build trust:

- Engage in open and direct communications to resolve problems.

- Keep all stakeholders informed, especially when fulfilling commitments is at risk.

- Spend time directly engaged with the team asking nonassumptive questions to gain a better understanding of the situations affecting the team.

- Be direct and explicit about what you need or expect.

- Do not withhold information out of a fear of being wrong but be willing to share information even if you may be wrong.

- Be receptive to innovation and address any issues or concerns in a forthright manner.

- Look beyond your own interests.

- Demonstrate a true concern for others and avoid engaging in pursuits that could be viewed as being detrimental to the interest of others.

X3.10 Conflict Management

Conflict is inevitable in a project environment. Incongruent requirements, competition for resources, breakdowns in communications, and many other factors could become sources of conflict. Within a project's environment, conflict may yield dysfunctional outcomes. However, if actively managed, conflicts can actually help the team arrive at a better solution. The project manager must be able to identify the causes for conflict and then actively manage the conflict thus minimizing potential negative impacts. The project team is then able to deliver better solutions and increase the probability of project success.

Project managers must develop the skills and experience necessary to effectively adapt their personal conflict management style to the situation. Managing conflict in a project environment involves building the trust necessary for all involved parties to be open and honest, and to engage in seeking a positive resolution to the situation creating the conflict. Project managers strive to establish a collaborative approach among the team members involved in order to fully resolve the problems. In situations where a collaborative approach is not possible, the project manager must then revert to other active management styles for handling the conflict; e.g., assertiveness, accommodation, avoidance, or compromise.

Managing conflict is one of the biggest challenges a project manager faces. It draws upon all of the other interpersonal skills of a project manager in order to lead the team to a successful resolution of the situation in conflict.

X3.11 Coaching

Coaching is a means of developing the project team to higher levels of competency and performance. Coaching is about helping people recognize their potential through empowerment and development. Coaching is used to aid team members in developing or enhancing their skills or to build new skills required to enable project success. Coaching can take many forms and approaches. In some instances, formal or informal training may be developed to increase technical skills or assist team-building efforts and facilitate consistent interpersonal interactions.

Coaching is also used to address poor performance and to help team members overcome deficiencies in their skill sets. Coaching is distinct from counseling. Counseling focuses on addressing situations where team members "won't do" something rather than "can't do." If the situation is one where the team member is not performing or meeting expectations due to a lack of skill, knowledge, or experience, coaching can be employed to help the team member to develop this skill and thus turn a "can't do" situation into one of "can do."

Coaching can be a powerful motivator for teams. As teams develop their skills, abilities, and confidence, their willingness to take on challenging or demanding tasks is increased. This can lead to more effective and productive teams.

X3.12 References

Covey, S. R. "Seven Habits of Highly Effective People," A Fireside Book, Simon and Schuster, New York, NY.

Dinsmore, P.C. "Human Factors in Project Management (Revised Edition)," American Management Association: New York, NY.

Levin, G. and Flannes, S. "Essential People Skills for Project Managers," Management Concepts Inc., Vienna, VA.

Verma, V. K. "Organizing Projects for Success," PMI, Newtown Square, PA.

Verma, V. K. "Human Resource Skills for the Project Manager," PMI, Newtown Square, PA.

Verma, V. K. "Managing the Project Team," PMI, Newtown Square, PA.

REFERENCES

[1] Project Management Institute. 2012. *PMI Lexicon of Project Management Terms.* Available from http://www.pmi.org/lexiconterms

[2] Project Management Institute. *PMI Code of Ethics and Professional Conduct.* Available from http://www.pmi.org/codeofethicsPDF

[3] Project Management Institute. 2013. *The Standard for Program Management* – Third Edition. Newtown Square, PA: PMI.

[4] Project Management Institute. 2013. *The Standard for Portfolio Management* – Third Edition. Newtown Square, PA: PMI.

[5] Project Management Institute. 2013. *Organizational Project Management Maturity Model* (OPM3®) – Third Edition. Newtown Square, PA: PMI.

[6] International Standards Organization. 2008. ISO/IEC 15288:2008. *Systems and Software Engineering – System Life Cycle Processes.* Geneva, Switzerland: ISO.

[7] Project Management Institute. 2006. *Practice Standard for Work Breakdown Structures (WBS)* – Second Edition (Reaffirmed). Newtown Square, PA: PMI.

[8] Project Management Institute. 2011. *Practice Standard for Scheduling* – Second Edition. Newtown Square, PA: PMI.

[9] Project Management Institute. 2011. *Practice Standard for Earned Value Management* – Second Edition. Newtown Square, PA: PMI.

[10] International Standards Organization. 2008. ISO 9000:2008. *Quality Management Systems – Fundamentals and Vocabulary.* Geneva, Switzerland: ISO.

[11] International Standards Organization. 2004. ISO/IEC 2:2004. *Standardization and Related Activities– General Vocabulary.* Geneva, Switzerland: ISO.

[12] International Standards Organization. 2012. ISO 21500:2012 *Guidance on Project Management.* Geneva, Switzerland: ISO.

GLOSSARY

1. Inclusions and Exclusions

This glossary includes terms that are:

- Unique or nearly unique to project management (e.g., project scope statement, work package, work breakdown structure, critical path method).

- Not unique to project management, but used differently or with a narrower meaning in project management than in general everyday usage (e.g., early start date,).

This glossary generally does not include:

- Application area-specific terms.

- Terms used in project management which do not differ in any material way from everyday use (e.g., calendar day, delay).

- Compound terms whose meaning is clear from the combined meanings of the component parts.

- Variants when the meaning of the variant is clear from the base term.

As a result of the above inclusions and exclusions, this glossary includes:

- A preponderance of terms related to Project Scope Management, Project Time Management, and Project Risk Management, since many of the terms used in these Knowledge Areas are unique or nearly unique to project management.

- Many terms from Project Quality Management, since these terms are used more narrowly than in their everyday usage.

- Relatively few terms related to Project Human Resource Management, Project Communications Management, and Project Stakeholder Management, since most of the terms used in these Knowledge Areas do not differ significantly from everyday usage.

- Relatively few terms related to Project Cost Management, Project Integration Management, and Project Procurement Management, since many of the terms used in these Knowledge Areas have narrow meanings that are unique to a particular application area.

2. Common Acronyms

AC	actual cost
ACWP	actual cost of work performed
BAC	budget at completion
CCB	change control board
COQ	cost of quality
CPAF	cost plus award fee
CPFF	cost plus fixed fee
CPI	cost performance index
CPIF	cost plus incentive fee
CPM	critical path methodology
CV	cost variance
EAC	estimate at completion
EF	early finish date
EMV	expected monetary value
ES	early start date
ETC	estimate to complete
EV	earned value
EVM	earned value management
FF	finish-to-finish
FFP	firm fixed price contract
FMEA	failure mode and effect analysis
FP-EPA	fixed price with economic price adjustment
FPIF	fixed price incentive fee
FS	finish to start

IFB	invitation for bid
LF	late finish date
LOE	level of effort
LS	late start date
OBS	organizational breakdown structure
PDM	precedence diagramming method
PMBOK	Project Management Body of Knowledge
PV	planned value
QFD	quality function deployment
RACI	responsible, accountable, consult, and inform
RAM	responsibility assignment matrix
RBS	risk breakdown structure
RFI	request for information
RFP	request for proposal
RFQ	request for quotation
SF	start-to-finish
SOW	statement of work
SPI	schedule performance index
SS	start-to-start
SV	schedule variance
SWOT	strengths, weaknesses, opportunities, and threats
T&M	time and material contract
WBS	work breakdown structure

3. Definitions

Many of the words defined here have broader, and in some cases different, dictionary definitions.

The definitions use the following conventions:

- In some cases, a single glossary term consists of multiple words (e.g., risk urgency assessment).
- When synonyms are included, no definition is given and the reader is directed to the preferred term (i.e., see preferred term).
- Related terms that are not synonyms are cross-referenced at the end of the definition (i.e., see also related term).

Acceptance Criteria. A set of conditions that is required to be met before deliverables are accepted.

Accepted Deliverables. Products, results, or capabilities produced by a project and validated by the project customer or sponsors as meeting their specified acceptance criteria.

Accuracy. Within the quality management system, *accuracy* is an assessment of correctness.

Acquire Project Team. The process of confirming human resource availability and obtaining the team necessary to complete project activities.

Acquisition. Obtaining human and material resources necessary to perform project activities. Acquisition implies a cost of resources, and is not necessarily financial.

Activity. A distinct, scheduled portion of work performed during the course of a project.

Activity Attributes. Multiple attributes associated with each schedule activity that can be included within the activity list. Activity attributes include activity codes, predecessor activities, successor activities, logical relationships, leads and lags, resource requirements, imposed dates, constraints, and assumptions.

Activity Code. One or more numerical or text values that identify characteristics of the work or in some way categorize the schedule activity that allows filtering and ordering of activities within reports.

Activity Cost Estimates. The projected cost of the schedule activity that includes the cost for all resources required to perform and complete the activity, including all cost types and cost components.

Activity Duration. The time in calendar units between the start and finish of a schedule activity. See also *duration*.

Activity Duration Estimate. A quantitative assessment of the likely amount or outcome for the duration of an activity.

Activity Identifier. A short, unique numeric or text identification assigned to each schedule activity to differentiate that project activity from other activities. Typically unique within any one project schedule network diagram.

Activity List. A documented tabulation of schedule activities that shows the activity description, activity identifier, and a sufficiently detailed scope of work description so project team members understand what work is to be performed.

Activity Network Diagrams. See *project schedule network diagram.*

Activity-on-Node (AON). See *precedence diagramming method (PDM).*

Activity Resource Requirements. The types and quantities of resources required for each activity in a work package.

Actual Cost (AC). The realized cost incurred for the work performed on an activity during a specific time period.

Actual Duration. The time in calendar units between the actual start date of the schedule activity and either the data date of the project schedule if the schedule activity is in progress or the actual finish date if the schedule activity is complete.

Adaptive Life Cycle. A project life cycle, also known as change-driven or agile methods, that is intended to facilitate change and require a high degree of ongoing stakeholder involvement. Adaptive life cycles are also iterative and incremental, but differ in that iterations are very rapid (usually 2–4 weeks in length) and are fixed in time and resources.

Additional Quality Planning Tools. A set of tools used to define the quality requirements and to plan effective quality management activities. They include, but are not limited to: brainstorming, force field analysis, nominal group techniques and quality management and control tools.

Adjusting Leads and Lags. A technique used to find ways to bring project activities that are behind into alignment with plan during project execution.

Advertising. The process of calling public attention to a project or effort.

Affinity Diagram. A group creativity technique that allows large numbers of ideas to be classified into groups for review and analysis.

Agreements. Any document or communication that defines the initial intentions of a project. This can take the form of a contract, memorandum of understanding (MOU), letters of agreement, verbal agreements, email, etc.

Alternative Analysis. A technique used to evaluate identified options in order to select which options or approaches to use to execute and perform the work of the project.

Alternatives Generation. A technique used to develop as many potential options as possible in order to identify different approaches to execute and perform the work of the project.

Analogous Estimating. A technique for estimating the duration or cost of an activity or a project using historical data from a similar activity or project.

Analytical Techniques. Various techniques used to evaluate, analyze, or forecast potential outcomes based on possible variations of project or environmental variables and their relationships with other variables.

Application Area. A category of projects that have common components significant in such projects, but are not needed or present in all projects. Application areas are usually defined in terms of either the product (i.e., by similar technologies or production methods) or the type of customer (i.e., internal versus external, government versus commercial) or industry sector (i.e., utilities, automotive, aerospace, information technologies, etc.). Application areas can overlap.

Applying Leads and Lags. A technique that is used to adjust the amount of time between predecessor and successor activities.

Apportioned Effort. An activity where effort is allotted proportionately across certain discrete efforts and not divisible into discrete efforts. [Note: Apportioned effort is one of three earned value management (EVM) types of activities used to measure work performance.]

Approved Change Request. A change request that has been processed through the integrated change control process and approved.

Approved Change Requests Review. A review of the change requests to verify that these were implemented as approved.

Assumption. A factor in the planning process that is considered to be true, real, or certain, without proof or demonstration.

Assumptions Analysis. A technique that explores the accuracy of assumptions and identifies risks to the project from inaccuracy, inconsistency, or incompleteness of assumptions.

Attribute Sampling. Method of measuring quality that consists of noting the presence (or absence) of some characteristic (attribute) in each of the units under consideration. After each unit is inspected, the decision is made to accept a lot, reject it, or inspect another unit.

Authority. The right to apply project resources, expend funds, make decisions, or give approvals.

Backlog. A listing of product requirements and deliverables to be completed, written as stories, and prioritized by the business to manage and organize the project's work.

Backward Pass. A critical path method technique for calculating the late start and late finish dates by working backward through the schedule model from the project end date.

Bar Chart. A graphic display of schedule-related information. In the typical bar chart, schedule activities or work breakdown structure components are listed down the left side of the chart, dates are shown across the top, and activity durations are shown as date-placed horizontal bars. See also *Gantt chart*.

Baseline. The approved version of a work product that can be changed only through formal change control procedures and is used as a basis for comparison.

Basis of Estimates. Supporting documentation outlining the details used in establishing project estimates such as assumptions, constraints, level of detail, ranges, and confidence levels.

Benchmarking. Benchmarking is the comparison of actual or planned practices, such as processes and operations, to those of comparable organizations to identify best practices, generate ideas for improvement, and provide a basis for measuring performance.

Bidder Conference. The meetings with prospective sellers prior to the preparation of a bid or proposal to ensure all prospective vendors have a clear and common understanding of the procurement. Also known as contractor conferences, vendor conferences, or pre-bid conferences.

Bottom-Up Estimating. A method of estimating project duration or cost by aggregating the estimates of the lower-level components of the work breakdown structure (WBS).

Brainstorming. A general data gathering and creativity technique that can be used to identify risks, ideas, or solutions to issues by using a group of team members or subject matter experts.

Budget. The approved estimate for the project or any work breakdown structure component or any schedule activity.

Budget at Completion (BAC). The sum of all budgets established for the work to be performed.

Buffer. See *reserve*.

Business Case. A documented economic feasibility study used to establish validity of the benefits of a selected component lacking sufficient definition and that is used as a basis for the authorization of further project management activities.

Business Value. A concept that is unique to each organization and includes tangible and intangible elements. Through the effective use of project, program, and portfolio management disciplines, organizations will possess the ability to employ reliable, established processes to meet enterprise objectives and obtain greater business value from their investments.

Buyer. The acquirer of products, services, or results for an organization.

Cause and Effect Diagram. A decomposition technique that helps trace an undesirable effect back to its root cause.

Central Tendency. A property of the central limit theorem predicting that the data observations in a distribution will tend to group around a central location. The three typical measures of central tendency are the mean, median, and mode.

Change Control. A process whereby modifications to documents, deliverables, or baselines associated with the project are identified, documented, approved, or rejected.

Change Control Board (CCB). A formally chartered group responsible for reviewing, evaluating, approving, delaying, or rejecting changes to the project, and for recording and communicating such decisions.

Change Control System. A set of procedures that describes how modifications to the project deliverables and documentation are managed and controlled.

Change Control Tools. Manual or automated tools to assist with change and/or configuration management. At a minimum, the tools should support the activities of the CCB.

Change Log. A comprehensive list of changes made during the project. This typically includes dates of the change and impacts in terms of time, cost, and risk.

Change Request. A formal proposal to modify any document, deliverable, or baseline.

Charter. See *project charter.*

Checklist Analysis. A technique for systematically reviewing materials using a list for accuracy and completeness.

Checksheets. A tally sheet that can be used as a checklist when gathering data.

Claim. A request, demand, or assertion of rights by a seller against a buyer, or vice versa, for consideration, compensation, or payment under the terms of a legally binding contract, such as for a disputed change.

Claims Administration. The process of processing, adjudicating, and communicating contract claims.

Close Procurements. The process of completing each project procurement.

Close Project or Phase. The process of finalizing all activities across all of the Project Management Process Groups to formally complete a project or phase.

Closed Procurements. Project contracts or other procurement agreements that have been formally acknowledged by the proper authorizing agent as being finalized and signed off.

Closing Process Group. Those processes performed to finalize all activities across all Process Groups to formally close a project or phase.

Code of Accounts. A numbering system used to uniquely identify each component of the work breakdown structure (WBS).

Collect Requirements. The process of determining, documenting, and managing stakeholder needs and requirements to meet project objectives.

Colocation. An organizational placement strategy where the project team members are physically located close to one another in order to improve communication, working relationships, and productivity.

Communication Constraints. Restrictions on the content, timing, audience, or individual who will deliver a communication usually stemming from specific legislation or regulation, technology, or organizational policies.

Communication Methods. A systematic procedure, technique, or process used to transfer information among project stakeholders.

Communication Models. A description, analogy or schematic used to represent how the communication process will be performed for the project.

Communication Requirements Analysis. An analytical technique to determine the information needs of the project stakeholders through interviews, workshops, study of lessons learned from previous projects, etc.

Communication Technology. Specific tools, systems, computer programs, etc., used to transfer information among project stakeholders.

Communications Management Plan. A component of the project, program, or portfolio management plan that describes how, when, and by whom information about the project will be administered and disseminated.

Compliance. A general concept of conforming to a rule, standard, law, or requirement such that the assessment of compliance results in a binomial result stated as "compliant" or "noncompliant."

Conduct Procurements. The process of obtaining seller responses, selecting a seller, and awarding a contract.

Configuration Management System. A subsystem of the overall project management system. It is a collection of formal documented procedures used to apply technical and administrative direction and surveillance to: identify and document the functional and physical characteristics of a product, result, service, or component; control any changes to such characteristics; record and report each change and its implementation status; and support the audit of the products, results, or components to verify conformance to requirements. It includes the documentation, tracking systems, and defined approval levels necessary for authorizing and controlling changes.

Conflict Management. Handling, controlling, and guiding a conflictual situation to achieve a resolution.

Conformance. Within the quality management system, conformance is a general concept of delivering results that fall within the limits that define acceptable variation for a quality requirement.

Conformance Work. In the cost of quality framework, conformance work is done to compensate for imperfections that prevent organizations from completing planned activities correctly as essential first-time work. Conformance work consists of actions that are related to prevention and inspection.

Constraint. A limiting factor that affects the execution of a project, program, portfolio, or process.

Context Diagrams. A visual depiction of the product scope showing a business system (process, equipment, computer system, etc.), and how people and other systems (actors) interact with it.

Contingency. An event or occurrence that could affect the execution of the project that may be accounted for with a reserve.

Contingency Allowance. See *reserve*.

Contingency Reserve. Budget within the cost baseline or performance measurement baseline that is allocated for identified risks that are accepted and for which contingent or mitigating responses are developed.

Contingent Response Strategies. Responses provided which may be used in the event that a specific trigger occurs.

Contract. A contract is a mutually binding agreement that obligates the seller to provide the specified product or service or result and obligates the buyer to pay for it.

Contract Change Control System. The system used to collect, track, adjudicate, and communicate changes to a contract.

Control. Comparing actual performance with planned performance, analyzing variances, assessing trends to effect process improvements, evaluating possible alternatives, and recommending appropriate corrective action as needed.

Control Account. A management control point where scope, budget, actual cost, and schedule are integrated and compared to earned value for performance measurement.

Control Chart. A graphic display of process data over time and against established control limits, which has a centerline that assists in detecting a trend of plotted values toward either control limit.

Control Communications. The process of monitoring and controlling communications throughout the entire project life cycle to ensure the information needs of the project stakeholders are met.

Control Costs. The process of monitoring the status of the project to update the project costs and managing changes to the cost baseline.

Control Limits. The area composed of three standard deviations on either side of the centerline or mean of a normal distribution of data plotted on a control chart, which reflects the expected variation in the data. See also *specification limits*.

Control Procurements. The process of managing procurement relationships, monitoring contract performance, and making changes and corrections as appropriate.

Control Quality. The process of monitoring and recording results of executing the quality activities to assess performance and recommend necessary changes.

Control Risks. The process of implementing risk response plans, tracking identified risks, monitoring residual risks, identifying new risks, and evaluating risk process effectiveness throughout the project.

Control Schedule. The process of monitoring the status of project activities to update project progress and manage changes to the schedule baseline to achieve the plan.

Control Scope. The process of monitoring the status of the project and product scope and managing changes to the scope baseline.

Control Stakeholder Engagement. The process of monitoring overall project stakeholder relationships and adjusting strategies and plans for engaging stakeholders.

Corrective Action. An intentional activity that realigns the performance of the project work with the project management plan.

Cost Aggregation. Summing the lower-level cost estimates associated with the various work packages for a given level within the project's WBS or for a given cost control account.

Cost Baseline. The approved version of the time-phased project budget, excluding any management reserves, which can be changed only through formal change control procedures and is used as a basis for comparison to actual results.

Cost Management Plan. A component of a project or program management plan that describes how costs will be planned, structured, and controlled.

Cost of Quality. A method of determining the costs incurred to ensure quality. Prevention and appraisal costs (cost of conformance) include costs for quality planning, quality control (QC), and quality assurance to ensure compliance to requirements (i.e., training, QC systems, etc.). Failure costs (cost of nonconformance) include costs to rework products, components, or processes that are non-compliant, costs of warranty work and waste, and loss of reputation.

Cost Performance Index (CPI). A measure of the cost efficiency of budgeted resources expressed as the ratio of earned value to actual cost.

Cost Plus Award Fee Contracts (CPAF). A category of contract that involves payments to the seller for all legitimate actual costs incurred for completed work, plus an award fee representing seller profit.

Cost Plus Fixed Fee Contract (CPFF). A type of cost-reimbursable contract where the buyer reimburses the seller for the seller's allowable costs (allowable costs are defined by the contract) plus a fixed amount of profit (fee).

Cost Plus Incentive Fee Contract (CPIF). A type of cost-reimbursable contract where the buyer reimburses the seller for the seller's allowable costs (allowable costs are defined by the contract), and the seller earns its profit if it meets defined performance criteria.

Cost Variance (CV). The amount of budget deficit or surplus at a given point in time, expressed as the difference between the earned value and the actual cost.

Cost-Benefit Analysis. A financial analysis tool used to determine the benefits provided by a project against its costs.

Cost-Reimbursable Contract. A type of contract involving payment to the seller for the seller's actual costs, plus a fee typically representing seller's profit. Cost-reimbursable contracts often include incentive clauses where, if the seller meets or exceeds selected project objectives, such as schedule targets or total cost, then the seller receives from the buyer an incentive or bonus payment.

Crashing. A technique used to shorten the schedule duration for the least incremental cost by adding resources.

Create WBS. The process of subdividing project deliverables and project work into smaller, more manageable components.

Criteria. Standards, rules, or tests on which a judgment or decision can be based or by which a product, service, result, or process can be evaluated.

Critical Chain Method. A schedule method that allows the project team to place buffers on any project schedule path to account for limited resources and project uncertainties.

Critical Path. The sequence of activities that represents the longest path through a project, which determines the shortest possible duration.

Critical Path Activity. Any activity on the critical path in a project schedule.

Critical Path Method. A method used to estimate the minimum project duration and determine the amount of scheduling flexibility on the logical network paths within the schedule model.

Customer. Customer is the person(s) or organization(s) that will pay for the project's product, service, or result. Customers can be internal or external to the performing organization.

Customer Satisfaction. Within the quality management system, a state of fulfillment in which the needs of a customer are met or exceeded for the customer's expected experiences as assessed by the customer at the moment of evaluation.

Data Date. A point in time when the status of the project is recorded.

Data Gathering and Representation Techniques. Techniques used to collect, organize, and present data and information.

Decision Tree Analysis. A diagramming and calculation technique for evaluating the implications of a chain of multiple options in the presence of uncertainty.

Decomposition. A technique used for dividing and subdividing the project scope and project deliverables into smaller, more manageable parts.

Defect. An imperfection or deficiency in a project component where that component does not meet its requirements or specifications and needs to be either repaired or replaced.

Defect Repair. An intentional activity to modify a nonconforming product or product component.

Define Activities. The process of identifying and documenting the specific actions to be performed to produce the project deliverables.

Define Scope. The process of developing a detailed description of the project and product.

Deliverable. Any unique and verifiable product, result, or capability to perform a service that is required to be produced to complete a process, phase, or project.

Delphi Technique. An information gathering technique used as a way to reach a consensus of experts on a subject. Experts on the subject participate in this technique anonymously. A facilitator uses a questionnaire to solicit ideas about the important project points related to the subject. The responses are summarized and are then recirculated to the experts for further comment. Consensus may be reached in a few rounds of this process. The Delphi technique helps reduce bias in the data and keeps any one person from having undue influence on the outcome.

Dependency. See *logical relationship*.

Dependency Determination. A technique used to identify the type of dependency that is used to create the logical relationships between predecessor and successor activities.

Design of Experiments. A statistical method for identifying which factors may influence specific variables of a product or process under development or in production.

Determine Budget. The process of aggregating the estimated costs of individual activities or work packages to establish an authorized cost baseline.

Develop Project Charter. The process of developing a document that formally authorizes the existence of a project and provides the project manager with the authority to apply organizational resources to project activities.

Develop Project Management Plan. The process of defining, preparing, and coordinating all subsidiary plans and integrating them into a comprehensive project management plan.

Develop Project Team. The process of improving competencies, team member interaction, and overall team environment to enhance project performance.

Develop Schedule. The process of analyzing activity sequences, durations, resource requirements, and schedule constraints to create the project schedule model.

Diagramming Techniques. Approaches to presenting information with logical linkages that aid in understanding.

Dictatorship. A group decision-making technique in which one individual makes the decision for the group.

Direct and Manage Project Work. The process of leading and performing the work defined in the project management plan and implementing approved changes to achieve the project's objectives.

Discrete Effort. An activity that can be planned and measured and that yields a specific output. [Note: Discrete effort is one of three earned value management (EVM) types of activities used to measure work performance.]

Discretionary Dependency. A relationship that is established based on knowledge of best practices within a particular application area or an aspect of the project where a specific sequence is desired.

Document Analysis. An elicitation technique that analyzes existing documentation and identifies information relevant to the requirements.

Documentation Reviews. The process of gathering a corpus of information and reviewing it to determine accuracy and completeness.

Duration (DU or DUR). The total number of work periods (not including holidays or other nonworking periods) required to complete a schedule activity or work breakdown structure component. Usually expressed as workdays or workweeks. Sometimes incorrectly equated with elapsed time. Contrast with *effort*.

Early Finish Date (EF). In the critical path method, the earliest possible point in time when the uncompleted portions of a schedule activity can finish based on the schedule network logic, the data date, and any schedule constraints.

Early Start Date (ES). In the critical path method, the earliest possible point in time when the uncompleted portions of a schedule activity can start based on the schedule network logic, the data date, and any schedule constraints.

Earned Value (EV). The measure of work performed expressed in terms of the budget authorized for that work.

Earned Value Management. A methodology that combines scope, schedule, and resource measurements to assess project performance and progress.

Effort. The number of labor units required to complete a schedule activity or work breakdown structure component, often expressed in hours, days, or weeks.

Emotional Intelligence. The capability to identify, assess, and manage the personal emotions of oneself and other people, as well as the collective emotions of groups of people.

Enterprise Environmental Factors. Conditions, not under the immediate control of the team, that influence, constrain, or direct the project, program, or portfolio.

Estimate. A quantitative assessment of the likely amount or outcome. Usually applied to project costs, resources, effort, and durations and is usually preceded by a modifier (i.e., preliminary, conceptual, feasibility, order-of-magnitude, definitive). It should always include some indication of accuracy (e.g., ± x percent). See also *budget* and *cost*.

Estimate Activity Durations. The process of estimating the number of work periods needed to complete individual activities with estimated resources.

Estimate Activity Resources. The process of estimating the type and quantities of material, human resources, equipment, or supplies required to perform each activity.

Estimate at Completion (EAC). The expected total cost of completing all work expressed as the sum of the actual cost to date and the estimate to complete.

Estimate Costs. The process of developing an approximation of the monetary resources needed to complete project activities.

Estimate to Complete (ETC). The expected cost to finish all the remaining project work.

Execute. Directing, managing, performing, and accomplishing the project work; providing the deliverables; and providing work performance information.

Executing Process Group. Those processes performed to complete the work defined in the project management plan to satisfy the project specifications.

Expected Monetary Value (EMV) Analysis. A statistical technique that calculates the average outcome when the future includes scenarios that may or may not happen. A common use of this technique is within decision tree analysis.

Expert Judgment. Judgment provided based upon expertise in an application area, knowledge area, discipline, industry, etc., as appropriate for the activity being performed. Such expertise may be provided by any group or person with specialized education, knowledge, skill, experience, or training.

External Dependency. A relationship between project activities and non-project activities.

Facilitated Workshops. An elicitation technique using focused sessions that bring key cross-functional stakeholders together to define product requirements.

Failure Mode and Effect Analysis (FMEA). An analytical procedure in which each potential failure mode in every component of a product is analyzed to determine its effect on the reliability of that component and, by itself or in combination with other possible failure modes, on the reliability of the product or system and on the required function of the component; or the examination of a product (at the system and/or lower levels) for all ways that a failure may occur. For each potential failure, an estimate is made of its effect on the total system and of its impact. In addition, a review is undertaken of the action planned to minimize the probability of failure and to minimize its effects.

Fallback Plan. Fallback plans include an alternative set of actions and tasks available in the event that the primary plan needs to be abandoned because of issues, risks, or other causes.

Fast Tracking. A schedule compression technique in which activities or phases normally done in sequence are performed in parallel for at least a portion of their duration.

Fee. Represents profit as a component of compensation to a seller.

Finish Date. A point in time associated with a schedule activity's completion. Usually qualified by one of the following: actual, planned, estimated, scheduled, early, late, baseline, target, or current.

Finish-to-Finish (FF). A logical relationship in which a successor activity cannot finish until a predecessor activity has finished.

Finish-to-Start (FS). A logical relationship in which a successor activity cannot start until a predecessor activity has finished.

Firm-Fixed-Price Contract (FFP). A type of fixed price contract where the buyer pays the seller a set amount (as defined by the contract), regardless of the seller's costs.

Fishbone diagram. See *Cause and Effect Diagram*.

Fixed Formula Method. An earned value method for assigning a specified percentage of budget value for a work package to the start milestone of the work package with the remaining budget value percentage assigned when the work package is complete.

Fixed Price Incentive Fee Contract (FPIF). A type of contract where the buyer pays the seller a set amount (as defined by the contract), and the seller can earn an additional amount if the seller meets defined performance criteria.

Fixed Price with Economic Price Adjustment Contracts (FP-EPA). A fixed-price contract, but with a special provision allowing for predefined final adjustments to the contract price due to changed conditions, such as inflation changes, or cost increases (or decreases) for specific commodities.

Fixed-Price Contracts. An agreement that sets the fee that will be paid for a defined scope of work regardless of the cost or effort to deliver it.

Float. Also called slack. See *total float* and *free float*.

Flowchart. The depiction in a diagram format of the inputs, process actions, and outputs of one or more processes within a system.

Focus Groups. An elicitation technique that brings together prequalified stakeholders and subject matter experts to learn about their expectations and attitudes about a proposed product, service, or result.

Forecast. An estimate or prediction of conditions and events in the project's future based on information and knowledge available at the time of the forecast. The information is based on the project's past performance and expected future performance, and includes information that could impact the project in the future, such as estimate at completion and estimate to complete.

Forward Pass. A critical path method technique for calculating the early start and early finish dates by working forward through the schedule model from the project start date or a given point in time.

Free Float. The amount of time that a schedule activity can be delayed without delaying the early start date of any successor or violating a schedule constraint.

Functional Manager. Someone with management authority over an organizational unit within a functional organization. The manager of any group that actually makes a product or performs a service. Sometimes called a line manager.

Functional Organization. A hierarchical organization where each employee has one clear superior, and staff are grouped by areas of specialization and managed by a person with expertise in that area.

Funding Limit Reconciliation. The process of comparing the planned expenditure of project funds against any limits on the commitment of funds for the project to identify any variances between the funding limits and the planned expenditures.

Gantt Chart. A bar chart of schedule information where activities are listed on the vertical axis, dates are shown on the horizontal axis, and activity durations are shown as horizontal bars placed according to start and finish dates.

Grade. A category or rank used to distinguish items that have the same functional use (e.g., "hammer") but do not share the same requirements for quality (e.g., different hammers may need to withstand different amounts of force).

Ground Rules. Expectations regarding acceptable behavior by project team members.

Group Creativity Techniques. Techniques that are used to generate ideas within a group of stakeholders.

Group Decision-Making Techniques. Techniques to assess multiple alternatives that will be used to generate, classify, and prioritize product requirements.

Guideline. An official recommendation or advice that indicates policies, standards, or procedures for how something should be accomplished.

Hammock Activity. See *summary activity*.

Hard Logic. See *mandatory dependency*.

Histogram. A special form of bar chart used to describe the central tendency, dispersion, and shape of a statistical distribution.

Historical Information. Documents and data on prior projects including project files, records, correspondence, closed contracts, and closed projects.

Human Resource Management Plan. A component of the project management plan that describes how the roles and responsibilities, reporting relationships, and staff management will be addressed and structured.

Idea/Mind Mapping. Technique used to consolidate ideas created through individual brainstorming sessions into a single map to reflect commonality and differences in understanding and to generate new ideas.

Identify Risks. The process of determining which risks may affect the project and documenting their characteristics.

Identify Stakeholders. The process of identifying the people, groups, or organizations that could impact or be impacted by a decision, activity, or outcome of the project; and analyzing and documenting relevant information regarding their interests, involvement, interdependencies, influence, and potential impact on project success.

Imposed Date. A fixed date imposed on a schedule activity or schedule milestone, usually in the form of a "start no earlier than" and "finish no later than" date.

Incentive Fee. A set of financial incentives related to cost, schedule, or technical performance of the seller.

Incremental Life Cycle. A project life cycle where the project scope is generally determined early in the project life cycle, but time and cost estimates are routinely modified as the project team's understanding of the product increases. Iterations develop the product through a series of repeated cycles, while increments successively add to the functionality of the product.

Independent Estimates. A process of using a third party to obtain and analyze information to support prediction of cost, schedule, or other items.

Influence Diagram. A graphical representation of situations showing causal influences, time ordering of events, and other relationships among variables and outcomes.

Information Gathering Techniques. Repeatable processes used to assemble and organize data across a spectrum of sources.

Information Management Systems. Facilities, processes, and procedures used to collect, store, and distribute information between producers and consumers of information in physical or electronic format.

Initiating Process Group. Those processes performed to define a new project or a new phase of an existing project by obtaining authorization to start the project or phase.

Input. Any item, whether internal or external to the project that is required by a process before that process proceeds. May be an output from a predecessor process.

Inspection. Examining or measuring to verify whether an activity, component, product, result, or service conforms to specified requirements.

Inspections and Audits. A process to observe performance of contracted work or a promised product against agreed-upon requirements.

Interpersonal Skills. Ability to establish and maintain relationships with other people.

Interrelationship Digraphs. A quality management planning tool, the interrelationship digraphs provide a process for creative problem-solving in moderately complex scenarios that possess intertwined logical relationships.

Interviews. A formal or informal approach to elicit information from stakeholders by talking to them directly.

Invitation for Bid (IFB). Generally, this term is equivalent to request for proposal. However, in some application areas, it may have a narrower or more specific meaning.

Issue. A point or matter in question or in dispute, or a point or matter that is not settled and is under discussion or over which there are opposing views or disagreements.

Issue Log. A project document used to document and monitor elements under discussion or in dispute between project stakeholders.

Iterative Life Cycle. A project life cycle where the project scope is generally determined early in the project life cycle, but time and cost estimates are routinely modified as the project team's understanding of the product increases. Iterations develop the product through a series of repeated cycles, while increments successively add to the functionality of the product.

Lag. The amount of time whereby a successor activity is required to be delayed with respect to a predecessor activity.

Late Finish Date (LF). In the critical path method, the latest possible point in time when the uncompleted portions of a schedule activity can finish based on the schedule network logic, the project completion date, and any schedule constraints.

Late Start Date (LS). In the critical path method, the latest possible point in time when the uncompleted portions of a schedule activity can start based on the schedule network logic, the project completion date, and any schedule constraints.

Lead. The amount of time whereby a successor activity can be advanced with respect to a predecessor activity.

Lessons Learned. The knowledge gained during a project which shows how project events were addressed or should be addressed in the future with the purpose of improving future performance.

Lessons Learned Knowledge Base. A store of historical information and lessons learned about both the outcomes of previous project selection decisions and previous project performance.

Level of Effort (LOE). An activity that does not produce definitive end products and is measured by the passage of time. [Note: Level of effort is one of three earned valued management (EVM) types of activities used to measure work performance.]

Leveling. See *resource leveling*.

Life Cycle. *See project life cycle*.

Log. A document used to record and describe or denote selected items identified during execution of a process or activity. Usually used with a modifier, such as issue, quality control, action, or defect.

Logical Relationship. A dependency between two activities, or between an activity and a milestone.

Majority. Support from more than 50 percent of the members of the group.

Make-or-Buy Analysis. The process of gathering and organizing data about product requirements and analyzing them against available alternatives including the purchase or internal manufacture of the product.

Make-or-Buy Decisions. Decisions made regarding the external purchase or internal manufacture of a product.

Manage Communications. The process of creating, collecting, distributing, storing, retrieving, and the ultimate disposition of project information in accordance with the communications management plan.

Manage Project Team. The process of tracking team member performance, providing feedback, resolving issues, and managing team changes to optimize project performance.

Manage Stakeholder Engagement. The process of communicating and working with stakeholders to meet their needs/expectations, address issues as they occur, and foster appropriate stakeholder engagement in project activities throughout the project life cycle.

Management Reserve. An amount of the project budget withheld for management control purposes. These are budgets reserved for unforeseen work that is within scope of the project. The management reserve is not included in the performance measurement baseline (PMB).

Management Skills. The ability to plan, organize, direct, and control individuals or groups of people to achieve specific goals.

Mandatory Dependency. A relationship that is contractually required or inherent in the nature of the work.

Market Research. The process of gathering information at conferences, online reviews, and a variety of sources to identify market capabilities.

Master Schedule. A summary-level project schedule that identifies the major deliverables and work breakdown structure components and key schedule milestones. See also *milestone schedule*.

Material. The aggregate of things used by an organization in any undertaking, such as equipment, apparatus, tools, machinery, gear, material, and supplies.

Matrix Diagrams. A quality management and control tool used to perform data analysis within the organizational structure created in the matrix. The matrix diagram seeks to show the strength of relationships between factors, causes, and objectives that exist between the rows and columns that form the matrix.

Matrix Organization. Any organizational structure in which the project manager shares responsibility with the functional managers for assigning priorities and for directing the work of persons assigned to the project.

Methodology. A system of practices, techniques, procedures, and rules used by those who work in a discipline.

Milestone. A significant point or event in a project, program, or portfolio.

Milestone List. A list identifying all project milestones and normally indicates whether the milestone is mandatory or optional.

Milestone Schedule. A summary-level schedule that identifies the major schedule milestones. See also *master schedule*.

Monitor. Collect project performance data with respect to a plan, produce performance measures, and report and disseminate performance information.

Monitor and Control Project Work. The process of tracking, reviewing, and reporting the progress to meet the performance objectives defined in the project management plan.

Monitoring and Controlling Process Group. Those processes required to track, review, and regulate the progress and performance of the project; identify any areas in which changes to the plan are required; and initiate the corresponding changes.

Monte Carlo Simulation. A process which generates hundreds or thousands of probable performance outcomes based on probability distributions for cost and schedule on individual tasks. The outcomes are then used to generate a probability distribution for the project as a whole.

Most Likely Duration. An estimate of the most probable activity duration that takes into account all of the known variables that could affect performance.

Multi-Criteria Decision Analysis. This technique utilizes a decision matrix to provide a systematic analytical approach for establishing criteria, such as risk levels, uncertainty, and valuation, to evaluate and rank many ideas.

Near-Critical Activity. A schedule activity that has low total float. The concept of near-critical is equally applicable to a schedule activity or schedule network path. The limit below which total float is considered near critical is subject to expert judgment and varies from project to project.

Negotiated Settlements. The process of reaching final equitable settlement of all outstanding issues, claims, and disputes through negotiation.

Negotiation. The process and activities to resolving disputes through consultations between involved parties.

Network. See *project schedule network diagram*.

Network Analysis. See *schedule network analysis*.

Network Logic. The collection of schedule activity dependencies that makes up a project schedule network diagram.

Network Path. Any continuous series of schedule activities connected with logical relationships in a project schedule network diagram.

Networking. Establishing connections and relationships with other people from the same or other organizations.

Node. One of the defining points of a schedule network; a junction point joined to some or all of the other dependency lines.

Nominal Group Technique. A technique that enhances brainstorming with a voting process used to rank the most useful ideas for further brainstorming or for prioritization.

Nonconformance Work. In the cost of quality framework, nonconformance work is done to deal with the consequences of errors and failures in doing activities correctly on the first attempt. In efficient quality management systems, the amount of nonconformance work will approach zero.

Objective. Something toward which work is to be directed, a strategic position to be attained, a purpose to be achieved, a result to be obtained, a product to be produced, or a service to be performed.

Observations. A technique that provides a direct way of viewing individuals in their environment performing their jobs or tasks and carrying out processes.

Opportunity. A risk that would have a positive effect on one or more project objectives.

Optimistic Duration. An estimate of the shortest activity duration that takes into account all of the known variables that could affect performance.

Organizational Breakdown Structure (OBS). A hierarchical representation of the project organization that illustrates the relationship between project activities and the organizational units that will perform those activities.

Organizational Process Assets. Plans, processes, policies, procedures, and knowledge bases that are specific to and used by the performing organization.

Organizational Project Management Maturity. The level of an organization's ability to deliver the desired strategic outcomes in a predictable, controllable, and reliable manner.

Output. A product, result, or service generated by a process. May be an input to a successor process.

Parametric Estimating. An estimating technique in which an algorithm is used to calculate cost or duration based on historical data and project parameters.

Pareto Diagram. A histogram, ordered by frequency of occurrence, that shows how many results were generated by each identified cause.

Path Convergence. A relationship in which a schedule activity has more than one predecessor.

Path Divergence. A relationship in which a schedule activity has more than one successor.

Payment Systems. The system used to provide and track supplier's invoices and payments for services and products.

Percent Complete. An estimate expressed as a percent of the amount of work that has been completed on an activity or a work breakdown structure component.

Perform Integrated Change Control. The process of reviewing all change requests; approving changes and managing changes to deliverables, organizational process assets, project documents, and the project management plan; and communicating their disposition.

Perform Qualitative Risk Analysis. The process of prioritizing risks for further analysis or action by assessing and combining their probability of occurrence and impact.

Perform Quality Assurance. The process of auditing the quality requirements and the results from quality control measurements to ensure that appropriate quality standards and operational definitions are used.

Perform Quantitative Risk Analysis. The process of numerically analyzing the effect of identified risks on overall project objectives.

Performance Measurement Baseline. An approved, integrated scope-schedule-cost plan for the project work against which project execution is compared to measure and manage performance. The PMB includes contingency reserve, but excludes management reserve.

Performance Reporting. See *work performance reports*.

Performance Reports. See *work performance reports*.

Performance Reviews. A technique that is used to measure, compare, and analyze actual performance of work in progress on the project against the baseline.

Performing Organization. An enterprise whose personnel are most directly involved in doing the work of the project or program.

Pessimistic Duration. Estimate of the longest activity duration that takes into account all of the known variables that could affect performance.

Phase. See *project phase*.

Phase Gate. A review at the end of a phase in which a decision is made to continue to the next phase, to continue with modification, or to end a project or program.

Plan Communications Management. The process of developing an appropriate approach and plan for project communications based on stakeholder's information needs and requirements and available organizational assets.

Plan Cost Management. The process that establishes the policies, procedures, and documentation for planning, managing, expending, and controlling project costs.

Plan Human Resource Management. The process of identifying and documenting project roles, responsibilities, required skills, reporting relationships, and creating a staffing management plan.

Plan Procurement Management. The process of documenting project procurement decisions, specifying the approach, and identifying potential sellers.

Plan Quality Management. The process of identifying quality requirements and/or standards for the project and its deliverables, and documenting how the project will demonstrate compliance with quality requirements.

Plan Risk Management. The process of defining how to conduct risk management activities for a project.

Plan Risk Responses. The process of developing options and actions to enhance opportunities and to reduce threats to project objectives.

Plan Schedule Management. The process of establishing the policies, procedures, and documentation for planning, developing, managing, executing, and controlling the project schedule.

Plan Scope Management. The process of creating a scope management plan that documents how the project scope will be defined, validated, and controlled.

Plan Stakeholder Management. The process of developing appropriate management strategies to effectively engage stakeholders throughout the project life cycle, based on the analysis of their needs, interests, and potential impact on project success.

Planned Value (PV). The authorized budget assigned to scheduled work.

Planning Package. A work breakdown structure component below the control account with known work content but without detailed schedule activities. See also *control account*.

Planning Process Group. Those processes required to establish the scope of the project, refine the objectives, and define the course of action required to attain the objectives that the project was undertaken to achieve.

Plurality. Decisions made by the largest block in a group, even if a majority is not achieved.

Policy. A structured pattern of actions adopted by an organization such that the organization's policy can be explained as a set of basic principles that govern the organization's conduct.

Portfolio. Projects, programs, subportfolios, and operations managed as a group to achieve strategic objectives.

Portfolio Management. The centralized management of one or more portfolios to achieve strategic objectives.

Practice. A specific type of professional or management activity that contributes to the execution of a process and that may employ one or more techniques and tools.

Precedence Diagramming Method (PDM). A technique used for constructing a schedule model in which activities are represented by nodes and are graphically linked by one or more logical relationships to show the sequence in which the activities are to be performed.

Precedence Relationship. The term used in the precedence diagramming method for a logical relationship. In current usage, however, precedence relationship, logical relationship, and dependency are widely used interchangeably, regardless of the diagramming method used. See also *logical relationship*.

Precision. Within the quality management system, *precision* is a measure of exactness.

Predecessor Activity. An activity that logically comes before a dependent activity in a schedule.

Predictive Life Cycle. A form of project life cycle in which the project scope, and the time and cost required to deliver that scope, are determined as early in the life cycle as possible.

Preferential Logic. See *discretionary dependency*.

Preferred Logic. See *discretionary dependency*.

Preventive Action. An intentional activity that ensures the future performance of the project work is aligned with the project management plan.

Prioritization Matrices. A quality management planning tool used to identify key issues and evaluate suitable alternatives to define a set of implementation priorities.

Probability and Impact Matrix. A grid for mapping the probability of each risk occurrence and its impact on project objectives if that risk occurs.

Procedure. An established method of accomplishing a consistent performance or result, a procedure typically can be described as the sequence of steps that will be used to execute a process.

Process. A systematic series of activities directed towards causing an end result such that one or more inputs will be acted upon to create one or more outputs.

Process Analysis. A process analysis follows the steps outlined in the process improvement plan to identify needed improvements.

Process Decision Program Charts (PDPC). The PDPC is used to understand a goal in relation to the steps for getting to the goal.

Process Improvement Plan. A subsidiary plan of the project management plan. It details the steps for analyzing processes to identify activities that enhance their value.

Procurement Audits. The review of contracts and contracting processes for completeness, accuracy, and effectiveness.

Procurement Documents. The documents utilized in bid and proposal activities, which include the buyer's Invitation for Bid, Invitation for Negotiations, Request for Information, Request for Quotation, Request for Proposal, and seller's responses.

Procurement Management Plan. A component of the project or program management plan that describes how a project team will acquire goods and services from outside the performing organization.

Procurement Performance Reviews. A structured review of the seller's progress to deliver project scope and quality, within cost and on schedule, as compared to the contract.

Procurement Statement of Work. Describes the procurement item in sufficient detail to allow prospective sellers to determine if they are capable of providing the products, services, or results.

Product. An artifact that is produced, is quantifiable, and can be either an end item in itself or a component item. Additional words for products are material and goods. Contrast with *result.* See also *deliverable.*

Product Analysis. For projects that have a product as a deliverable, it is a tool to define scope that generally means asking questions about a product and forming answers to describe the use, characteristics, and other the relevant aspects of what is going to be manufactured.

Product Life Cycle. The series of phases that represent the evolution of a product, from concept through delivery, growth, maturity, and to retirement.

Product Scope. The features and functions that characterize a product, service, or result.

Product Scope Description. The documented narrative description of the product scope.

Program. A group of related projects, subprograms, and program activities managed in a coordinated way to obtain benefits not available from managing them individually.

Program Evaluation and Review Technique (PERT). A technique for estimating that applies a weighted average of optimistic, pessimistic, and most likely estimates when there is uncertainty with the individual activity estimates.

Program Management. The application of knowledge, skills, tools, and techniques to a program to meet the program requirements and to obtain benefits and control not available by managing projects individually.

Progressive Elaboration. The iterative process of increasing the level of detail in a project management plan as greater amounts of information and more accurate estimates become available.

Project. A temporary endeavor undertaken to create a unique product, service, or result.

Project-Based Organizations (PBOs). A variety of organizational forms that involve the creation of temporary systems for the performance of projects. PBOs conduct the majority of their activities as projects and/or provide project over functional approaches.

Project Calendar. A calendar that identifies working days and shifts that are available for scheduled activities.

Project Charter. A document issued by the project initiator or sponsor that formally authorizes the existence of a project and provides the project manager with the authority to apply organizational resources to project activities.

Project Communications Management. Project Communications Management includes the processes that are required to ensure timely and appropriate planning, collection, creation, distribution, storage, retrieval, management, control, monitoring, and the ultimate disposition of project information.

Project Cost Management. Project Cost Management includes the processes involved in planning, estimating, budgeting, financing, funding, managing, and controlling costs so that the project can be completed within the approved budget.

Project Funding Requirements. Forecast project costs to be paid that are derived from the cost baseline for total or periodic requirements, including projected expenditures plus anticipated liabilities.

Project Governance. The alignment of project objectives with the strategy of the larger organization by the project sponsor and project team. A project's governance is defined by and is required to fit within the larger context of the program or organization sponsoring it, but is separate from organizational governance.

Project Human Resource Management. Project Human Resource Management includes the processes that organize, manage, and lead the project team.

Project Initiation. Launching a process that can result in the authorization of a new project.

Project Integration Management. Project Integration Management includes the processes and activities needed to identify, define, combine, unify, and coordinate the various processes and project management activities within the Project Management Process Groups.

Project Life Cycle. The series of phases that a project passes through from its initiation to its closure.

Project Management. The application of knowledge, skills, tools, and techniques to project activities to meet the project requirements.

Project Management Body of Knowledge. An inclusive term that describes the sum of knowledge within the profession of project management. As with other professions, such as law, medicine, and accounting, the body of knowledge rests with the practitioners and academics that apply and advance it. The complete project management body of knowledge includes proven traditional practices that are widely applied and innovative practices that are emerging in the profession. The body of knowledge includes both published and unpublished materials. This body of knowledge is constantly evolving. PMI's *PMBOK®* Guide identifies a subset of the project management body of knowledge that is generally recognized as good practice.

Project Management Information System. An information system consisting of the tools and techniques used to gather, integrate, and disseminate the outputs of project management processes. It is used to support all aspects of the project from initiating through closing, and can include both manual and automated systems.

Project Management Knowledge Area. An identified area of project management defined by its knowledge requirements and described in terms of its component processes, practices, inputs, outputs, tools, and techniques.

Project Management Office (PMO). An organizational structure that standardizes the project-related governance processes and facilitates the sharing of resources, methodologies, tools, and techniques.

Project Management Plan. The document that describes how the project will be executed monitored, and controlled.

Project Management Process Group. A logical grouping of project management inputs, tools and techniques, and outputs. The Project Management Process Groups include initiating processes, planning processes, executing processes, monitoring and controlling processes, and closing processes. Project Management Process Groups are not project phases.

Project Management Staff. The members of the project team who perform project management activities such as schedule, communications, risk management, etc.

Project Management System. The aggregation of the processes, tools, techniques, methodologies, resources, and procedures to manage a project.

Project Management Team. The members of the project team who are directly involved in project management activities. On some smaller projects, the project management team may include virtually all of the project team members.

Project Manager (PM). The person assigned by the performing organization to lead the team that is responsible for achieving the project objectives.

Project Organization Chart. A document that graphically depicts the project team members and their interrelationships for a specific project.

Project Phase. A collection of logically related project activities that culminates in the completion of one or more deliverables.

Project Procurement Management. Project Procurement Management includes the processes necessary to purchase or acquire products, services, or results needed from outside the project team.

Project Quality Management. Project Quality Management includes the processes and activities of the performing organization that determine quality policies, objectives, and responsibilities so that the project will satisfy the needs for which it was undertaken.

Project Risk Management. Project Risk Management includes the processes of conducting risk management planning, identification, analysis, response planning, and controlling risk on a project.

Project Schedule. An output of a schedule model that presents linked activities with planned dates, durations, milestones, and resources.

Project Schedule Network Diagram. A graphical representation of the logical relationships among the project schedule activities.

Project Scope. The work performed to deliver a product, service, or result with the specified features and functions.

Project Scope Management. Project Scope Management includes the processes required to ensure that the project includes all the work required, and only the work required, to complete the project successfully.

Project Scope Statement. The description of the project scope, major deliverables, assumptions, and constraints.

Project Stakeholder Management. Project Stakeholder Management includes the processes required to identify all people or organizations impacted by the project, analyzing stakeholder expectations and impact on the project, and developing appropriate management strategies for effectively engaging stakeholders in project decisions and execution.

Project Statement of Work. See *statement of work*.

Project Team. A set of individuals who support the project manager in performing the work of the project to achieve its objectives.

Project Team Directory. A documented list of project team members, their project roles, and communication information.

Project Time Management. Project Time Management includes the processes required to manage the timely completion of the project.

Projectized Organization. Any organizational structure in which the project manager has full authority to assign priorities, apply resources, and direct the work of persons assigned to the project.

Proposal Evaluation Techniques. The process of reviewing proposals provided by suppliers to support contract award decisions.

Prototypes. A method of obtaining early feedback on requirements by providing a working model of the expected product before actually building it.

Quality. The degree to which a set of inherent characteristics fulfills requirements.

Quality Audits. A quality audit is a structured, independent process to determine if project activities comply with organizational and project policies, processes, and procedures.

Quality Checklists. A structured tool used to verify that a set of required steps has been performed.

Quality Control Measurements. The documented results of control quality activities.

Quality Function Deployment (QFD). A facilitated workshop technique that helps to determine critical characteristics for new product development.

Quality Management and Control Tools. They are a type of quality planning tools used to link and sequence the activities identified.

Quality Management Plan. A component of the project or program management plan that describes how an organization's quality policies will be implemented.

Quality Management System. The organizational framework whose structure provides the policies, processes, procedures, and resources required to implement the quality management plan. The typical project quality management plan should be compatible to the organization's quality management system.

Quality Metrics. A description of a project or product attribute and how to measure it.

Quality Policy. A policy specific to the Project Quality Management Knowledge Area, it establishes the basic principles that should govern the organization's actions as it implements its system for quality management.

Quality Requirement. A condition or capability that will be used to assess conformance by validating the acceptability of an attribute for the quality of a result.

Quantitative Risk Analysis and Modeling Techniques. Commonly used techniques for both event-oriented and project-oriented analysis approaches.

Questionnaires and Surveys. Written sets of questions designed to quickly accumulate information from a large number of respondents.

RACI. A common type of responsibility assignment matrix that uses responsible, accountable, consult, and inform statuses to define the involvement of stakeholders in project activities.

Records Management System. A specific set of processes, related control functions, and tools that are consolidated and combined to record and retain information about the project.

Regression Analysis. An analytic technique where a series of input variables are examined in relation to their corresponding output results in order to develop a mathematical or statistical relationship.

Regulation. Requirements imposed by a governmental body. These requirements can establish product, process, or service characteristics, including applicable administrative provisions that have government-mandated compliance.

Reporting Systems. Facilities, processes, and procedures used to generate or consolidate reports from one or more information management systems and facilitate report distribution to the project stakeholders.

Request for Information (RFI). A type of procurement document whereby the buyer requests a potential seller to provide various pieces of information related to a product or service or seller capability.

Request for Proposal (RFP). A type of procurement document used to request proposals from prospective sellers of products or services. In some application areas, it may have a narrower or more specific meaning.

Request for Quotation (RFQ). A type of procurement document used to request price quotations from prospective sellers of common or standard products or services. Sometimes used in place of request for proposal and, in some application areas, it may have a narrower or more specific meaning.

Requested Change. A formally documented change request that is submitted for approval to the integrated change control process.

Requirement. A condition or capability that is required to be present in a product, service, or result to satisfy a contract or other formally imposed specification.

Requirements Documentation. A description of how individual requirements meet the business need for the project.

Requirements Management Plan. A component of the project or program management plan that describes how requirements will be analyzed, documented, and managed.

Requirements Traceability Matrix. A grid that links product requirements from their origin to the deliverables that satisfy them.

Reserve. A provision in the project management plan to mitigate cost and/or schedule risk. Often used with a modifier (e.g., management reserve, contingency reserve) to provide further detail on what types of risk are meant to be mitigated.

Reserve Analysis. An analytical technique to determine the essential features and relationships of components in the project management plan to establish a reserve for the schedule duration, budget, estimated cost, or funds for a project.

Residual Risk. A risk that remains after risk responses have been implemented.

Resource. Skilled human resources (specific disciplines either individually or in crews or teams), equipment, services, supplies, commodities, material, budgets, or funds.

Resource Breakdown Structure. A hierarchical representation of resources by category and type.

Resource Calendar. A calendar that identifies the working days and shifts on which each specific resource is available.

©2013 Project Management Institute. *A Guide to the Project Management Body of Knowledge (PMBOK® Guide) – Fifth Edition*

Resource Histogram. A bar chart showing the amount of time that a resource is scheduled to work over a series of time periods. Resource availability may be depicted as a line for comparison purposes. Contrasting bars may show actual amounts of resources used as the project progresses.

Resource Leveling. A technique in which start and finish dates are adjusted based on resource constraints with the goal of balancing demand for resources with the available supply.

Resource Optimization Techniques. A technique that is used to adjust the start and finish dates of activities that adjust planned resource use to be equal to or less than resource availability.

Resource Smoothing. A technique which adjusts the activities of a schedule model such that the requirement for resources on the project do not exceed certain predefined resource limits.

Responsibility. An assignment that can be delegated within a project management plan such that the assigned resource incurs a duty to perform the requirements of the assignment.

Responsibility Assignment Matrix (RAM). A grid that shows the project resources assigned to each work package.

Result. An output from performing project management processes and activities. Results include outcomes (e.g., integrated systems, revised process, restructured organization, tests, trained personnel, etc.) and documents (e.g., policies, plans, studies, procedures, specifications, reports, etc.). Contrast with *product*. See also *deliverable*.

Rework. Action taken to bring a defective or nonconforming component into compliance with requirements or specifications.

Risk. An uncertain event or condition that, if it occurs, has a positive or negative effect on one or more project objectives.

Risk Acceptance. A risk response strategy whereby the project team decides to acknowledge the risk and not take any action unless the risk occurs.

Risk Appetite. The degree of uncertainty an entity is willing to take on, in anticipation of a reward.

Risk Audits. Examination and documentation of the effectiveness of risk responses in dealing with identified risks and their root causes, as well as the effectiveness of the risk management process.

Risk Avoidance. A risk response strategy whereby the project team acts to eliminate the threat or protect the project from its impact.

Risk Breakdown Structure (RBS). A hierarchical representation of risks according to their risk categories.

Risk Categorization. Organization by sources of risk (e.g., using the RBS), the area of the project affected (e.g., using the WBS), or other useful category (e.g., project phase) to determine the areas of the project most exposed to the effects of uncertainty.

Risk Category. A group of potential causes of risk.

Risk Data Quality Assessment. Technique to evaluate the degree to which the data about risks is useful for risk management.

Risk Management Plan. A component of the project, program, or portfolio management plan that describes how risk management activities will be structured and performed.

Risk Mitigation. A risk response strategy whereby the project team acts to reduce the probability of occurrence or impact of a risk.

Risk Reassessment. Risk reassessment is the identification of new risks, reassessment of current risks, and the closing of risks that are outdated.

Risk Register. A document in which the results of risk analysis and risk response planning are recorded.

Risk Threshold. Measure of the level of uncertainty or the level of impact at which a stakeholder may have a specific interest. Below that risk threshold, the organization will accept the risk. Above that risk threshold, the organization will not tolerate the risk.

Risk Tolerance. The degree, amount, or volume of risk that an organization or individual will withstand.

Risk Transference. A risk response strategy whereby the project team shifts the impact of a threat to a third party, together with ownership of the response.

Risk Urgency Assessment. Review and determination of the timing of actions that may need to occur sooner than other risk items.

Role. A defined function to be performed by a project team member, such as testing, filing, inspecting, or coding.

Rolling Wave Planning. An iterative planning technique in which the work to be accomplished in the near term is planned in detail, while the work in the future is planned at a higher level.

Root Cause Analysis. An analytical technique used to determine the basic underlying reason that causes a variance or a defect or a risk. A root cause may underlie more than one variance or defect or risk.

Scatter Diagram. A correlation chart that uses a regression line to explain or to predict how the change in an independent variable will change a dependent variable.

Schedule. See *project schedule* and see also *schedule model*.

Schedule Baseline. The approved version of a schedule model that can be changed only through formal change control procedures and is used as a basis for comparison to actual results.

Schedule Compression. Techniques used to shorten the schedule duration without reducing the project scope.

Schedule Data. The collection of information for describing and controlling the schedule.

Schedule Forecasts. Estimates or predictions of conditions and events in the project's future based on information and knowledge available at the time the schedule is calculated.

Schedule Management Plan. A component of the project management plan that establishes the criteria and the activities for developing, monitoring, and controlling the schedule.

Schedule Model. A representation of the plan for executing the project's activities including durations, dependencies, and other planning information, used to produce a project schedule along with other scheduling artifacts.

Schedule Network Analysis. The technique of identifying early and late start dates, as well as early and late finish dates, for the uncompleted portions of project schedule activities. See also *backward pass, critical path method, critical chain method,* and *resource leveling*.

Schedule Network Templates. A set of activities and relationships that have been established that can be used repeatedly for a particular application area or an aspect of the project where a prescribed sequence is desired.

Schedule Performance Index (SPI). A measure of schedule efficiency expressed as the ratio of earned value to planned value.

Schedule Variance (SV). A measure of schedule performance expressed as the difference between the earned value and the planned value.

Scheduling Tool. A tool that provides schedule component names, definitions, structural relationships, and formats that support the application of a scheduling method.

Scope. The sum of the products, services, and results to be provided as a project. See also *project scope* and *product scope.*

Scope Baseline. The approved version of a scope statement, work breakdown structure (WBS), and its associated WBS dictionary, that can be changed only through formal change control procedures and is used as a basis for comparison.

Scope Change. Any change to the project scope. A scope change almost always requires an adjustment to the project cost or schedule.

Scope Creep. The uncontrolled expansion to product or project scope without adjustments to time, cost, and resources.

Scope Management Plan. A component of the project or program management plan that describes how the scope will be defined, developed, monitored, controlled, and verified.

Secondary Risk. A risk that arises as a direct result of implementing a risk response.

Selected Sellers. The sellers which have been selected to provide a contracted set of services or products.

Seller. A provider or supplier of products, services, or results to an organization.

Seller Proposals. Formal responses from sellers to a request for proposal or other procurement document specifying the price, commercial terms of sale, and technical specifications or capabilities the seller will do for the requesting organization that, if accepted, would bind the seller to perform the resulting agreement.

Sensitivity Analysis. A quantitative risk analysis and modeling technique used to help determine which risks have the most potential impact on the project. It examines the extent to which the uncertainty of each project element affects the objective being examined when all other uncertain elements are held at their baseline values. The typical display of results is in the form of a tornado diagram.

Sequence Activities. The process of identifying and documenting relationships among the project activities.

Seven Basic Quality Tools. A standard toolkit used by quality management professionals who are responsible for planning, monitoring, and controlling the issues related to quality in an organization.

Simulation. A simulation uses a project model that translates the uncertainties specified at a detailed level into their potential impact on objectives that are expressed at the level of the total project. Project simulations use computer models and estimates of risk, usually expressed as a probability distribution of possible costs or durations at a detailed work level, and are typically performed using Monte Carlo analysis.

Soft Logic. See *discretionary dependency*.

Source Selection Criteria. A set of attributes desired by the buyer which a seller is required to meet or exceed to be selected for a contract.

Specification. A document that specifies, in a complete, precise, verifiable manner, the requirements, design, behavior, or other characteristics of a system, component, product, result, or service and the procedures for determining whether these provisions have been satisfied. Examples are: requirement specification, design specification, product specification, and test specification.

Specification Limits. The area, on either side of the centerline, or mean, of data plotted on a control chart that meets the customer's requirements for a product or service. This area may be greater than or less than the area defined by the control limits. See also *control limits*.

Sponsor. A person or group who provides resources and support for the project, program, or portfolio and is accountable for enabling success.

Sponsoring Organization. The entity responsible for providing the project's sponsor and a conduit for project funding or other project resources.

Staffing Management Plan. A component of the human resource plan that describes when and how project team members will be acquired and how long they will be needed.

Stakeholder. An individual, group, or organization who may affect, be affected by, or perceive itself to be affected by a decision, activity, or outcome of a project.

Stakeholder Analysis. A technique of systematically gathering and analyzing quantitative and qualitative information to determine whose interests should be taken into account throughout the project.

Stakeholder Management Plan. The stakeholder management plan is a subsidiary plan of the project management plan that defines the processes, procedures, tools, and techniques to effectively engage stakeholders in project decisions and execution based on the analysis of their needs, interests, and potential impact.

Stakeholder Register. A project document including the identification, assessment, and classification of project stakeholders.

Standard. A document that provides, for common and repeated use, rules, guidelines, or characteristics for activities or their results, aimed at the achievement of the optimum degree of order in a given context.

Start Date. A point in time associated with a schedule activity's start, usually qualified by one of the following: actual, planned, estimated, scheduled, early, late, target, baseline, or current.

Start-to-Finish (SF). A logical relationship in which a successor activity cannot finish until a predecessor activity has started.

Start-to-Start (SS). A logical relationship in which a successor activity cannot start until a predecessor activity has started.

Statement of Work (SOW). A narrative description of products, services, or results to be delivered by the project.

Statistical Sampling. Choosing part of a population of interest for inspection.

Subnetwork. A subdivision (fragment) of a project schedule network diagram, usually representing a subproject or a work package. Often used to illustrate or study some potential or proposed schedule condition, such as changes in preferential schedule logic or project scope.

Subproject. A smaller portion of the overall project created when a project is subdivided into more manageable components or pieces.

Successor Activity. A dependent activity that logically comes after another activity in a schedule.

Summary Activity. A group of related schedule activities aggregated and displayed as a single activity.

SWOT Analysis. Analysis of strengths, weaknesses, opportunities, and threats of an organization, project, or option.

Tailor. The act of carefully selecting process and related inputs and outputs contained within the *PMBOK® Guide* to determine a subset of specific processes that will be included within a project's overall management approach.

Team Members. See *project team members*.

Technique. A defined systematic procedure employed by a human resource to perform an activity to produce a product or result or deliver a service, and that may employ one or more tools.

Templates. A partially complete document in a predefined format that provides a defined structure for collecting, organizing, and presenting information and data.

Threat. A risk that would have a negative effect on one or more project objectives.

Three-Point Estimate. A technique used to estimate cost or duration by applying an average of optimistic, pessimistic, and most likely estimates when there is uncertainty with the individual activity estimates.

Threshold. A cost, time, quality, technical, or resource value used as a parameter, and which may be included in product specifications. Crossing the threshold should trigger some action, such as generating an exception report.

Time and Material Contract (T&M). A type of contract that is a hybrid contractual arrangement containing aspects of both cost-reimbursable and fixed-price contracts. Time and material contracts resemble cost-reimbursable type arrangements in that they have no definitive end, because the full value of the arrangement is not defined at the time of the award. Thus, time and material contracts can grow in contract value as if they were cost-reimbursable-type arrangements. Conversely, time and material arrangements can also resemble fixed-price arrangements. For example, the unit rates are preset by the buyer and seller, when both parties agree on the rates for the category of senior engineers.

Time-Scaled Schedule Network Diagram. Any project schedule network diagram drawn in such a way that the positioning and length of the schedule activity represents its duration. Essentially, it is a bar chart that includes schedule network logic.

To-Complete Performance Index (TCPI). A measure of the cost performance that is required to be achieved with the remaining resources in order to meet a specified management goal, expressed as the ratio of the cost to finish the outstanding work to the remaining budget.

Tolerance. The quantified description of acceptable variation for a quality requirement.

Tornado Diagram. A special type of bar chart used in sensitivity analysis for comparing the relative importance of the variables.

Tool. Something tangible, such as a template or software program, used in performing an activity to produce a product or result.

Total Float. The amount of time that a schedule activity can be delayed or extended from its early start date without delaying the project finish date or violating a schedule constraint.

Tree Diagram. A systematic diagram of a decomposition hierarchy used to visualize as parent-to-child relationships a systematic set of rules.

Trend Analysis. An analytical technique that uses mathematical models to forecast future outcomes based on historical results. It is a method of determining the variance from a baseline of a budget, cost, schedule, or scope parameter by using prior progress reporting periods' data and projecting how much that parameter's variance from baseline might be at some future point in the project if no changes are made in executing the project.

Trigger Condition. An event or situation that indicates that a risk is about to occur.

Unanimity. Agreement by everyone in the group on a single course of action.

Validate Scope. The process of formalizing acceptance of the completed project deliverables.

Validated Deliverables. Deliverables that are result of executing quality control process to determine correctness.

Validation. The assurance that a product, service, or system meets the needs of the customer and other identified stakeholders. It often involves acceptance and suitability with external customers. Contrast with *verification*.

Value Engineering. An approach used to optimize project life cycle costs, save time, increase profits, improve quality, expand market share, solve problems, and/or use resources more effectively.

Variance. A quantifiable deviation, departure, or divergence away from a known baseline or expected value.

Variance Analysis. A technique for determining the cause and degree of difference between the baseline and actual performance.

Variance at Completion (VAC). A projection of the amount of budget deficit or surplus, expressed as the difference between the budget at completion and the estimate at completion.

Variation. An actual condition that is different from the expected condition that is contained in the baseline plan.

Velocity. A measure of a team's productivity rate at which the deliverables are produced, validated, and accepted within a predefined interval. Velocity is a capacity planning approach frequently used to forecast future project work.

Verification. The evaluation of whether or not a product, service, or system complies with a regulation, requirement, specification, or imposed condition. It is often an internal process. Contrast with *validation*.

Voice of the Customer. A planning technique used to provide products, services, and results that truly reflect customer requirements by translating those customer requirements into the appropriate technical requirements for each phase of project product development.

WBS Dictionary. A document that provides detailed deliverable, activity, and scheduling information about each component in the work breakdown structure.

Weighted Milestone Method. An earned value method that divides a work package into measurable segments, each ending with an observable milestone, and then assigns a weighted value to the achievement of each milestone.

What-If Scenario Analysis. The process of evaluating scenarios in order to predict their effect on project objectives.

Work Authorization. A permission and direction, typically written, to begin work on a specific schedule activity or work package or control account. It is a method for sanctioning project work to ensure that the work is done by the identified organization, at the right time, and in the proper sequence.

Work Authorization System. A subsystem of the overall project management system. It is a collection of formal documented procedures that defines how project work will be authorized (committed) to ensure that the work is done by the identified organization, at the right time, and in the proper sequence. It includes the steps, documents, tracking system, and defined approval levels needed to issue work authorizations.

Work Breakdown Structure (WBS). A hierarchical decomposition of the total scope of work to be carried out by the project team to accomplish the project objectives and create the required deliverables.

Work Breakdown Structure Component. An entry in the work breakdown structure that can be at any level.

Work Package. The work defined at the lowest level of the work breakdown structure for which cost and duration can be estimated and managed.

Work Performance Data. The raw observations and measurements identified during activities being performed to carry out the project work.

Work Performance Information. The performance data collected from various controlling processes, analyzed in context and integrated based on relationships across areas.

Work Performance Reports. The physical or electronic representation of work performance information compiled in project documents, intended to generate decisions, actions, or awareness

Workaround. A response to a threat that has occurred, for which a prior response had not been planned or was not effective.